Nobody Walks in America

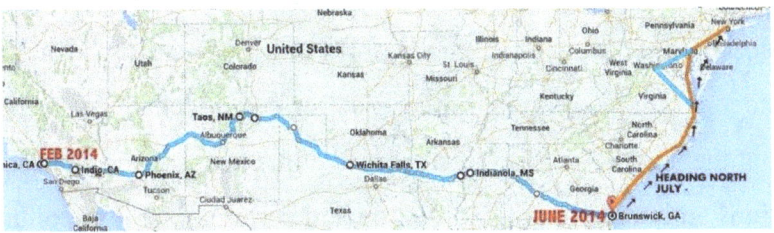

Naz Yacoob

Copyright © 2024

All rights reserved.

All rights reserved. No part of this publication may be reproduced, distributed, or transmitted in any form or by any means, including photocopying, recording, or other electronic or mechanical methods, without the author's prior written permission, except in the case of brief quotations embodied in critical reviews and certain other non-commercial uses permitted by copyright law. For permission requests, please get in touch with the author.

Contents

Dedication i
Acknowledgments ii
About the Author iii
Foreword 1
Chapter 1: Desert Trail 12
Chapter 2: On The Road 59
Chapter 3: Time In Phoenix 78
Chapter 4: Towards Payson (In the Rockies) 102
Chapter 5: You ain't gon' believe this Shit. 116
Chapter 6: On The High Plateau 135
Chapter 7: Making Tracks in The Wilderness 162
Chapter 8: Lupton, New Mexico 177
Chapter 9: A Little Off-Course 196
Chapter 10: Stride on to Texas! 207
Chapter 11: Paris, Texas 269
Chapter 12: A Little Meditation 290
Chapter 13: Mississippi 299
Chapter 14: Graceland 330
Chapter 15: Mississippi Blues 337
Chapter 16: Au Revoir Mississippi 353
Chapter 17: Trail in the Southern States 364
Chapter 18: On the Road Again 377
Chapter 19: Georgia 382

Part Two 405
Chapter 20: Jekyll Island 406
Chapter 21: Making Connections 411
Chapter 22: Towards South Carolina and Beyond 428
Chapter 23: Wilmington North Carolina....................................... 459
Chapter 24: A Change of Direction... 485
Chapter 25: The Appalachians 503
Chapter 26: On To New York.. 512
Chapter 27: Moving on up to Maine 527
Chapter 28: Manhattan and on to London 537
Epilogue: The Enigma of Homecoming 544

Dedication

To Nova Bennett, Francoise Kay, and Jim O'Keeffe.

Acknowledgments

Thanks to Jonathan Barnes, who guided, edited, and encouraged me through this long process. Thanks also to the creative writing class at City Lit and Southampton University.

Kudos to Elizabeth Glendenning for reading and her encouragement throughout the three years of writing these books.

Without Dorothy Dudek and Yvonne Overton, this trek would never have gotten off the ground. Yvonne created the blog and relayed all my messages to family and friends across the globe, but especially to the Findhorn Circle. She was the cog of projection in London. She suggested the 'nazacrossamerica' caption.

Dorothy Dudek received me in Los Angeles and helped me prepare for the journey. She took me to the shops to buy all the equipment and supplies for the journey. She also introduced me to her 'neck of the woods.' She repeatedly told me that 'I can do this' when I felt downhearted after flying over the ocean bed of sand through New Mexico, Arizona, and California.

About the Author

Naz Yacoob was born in Mauritius. He came to England in 1961. He studied two university courses, History and Engineering. He has written three books, Nobody Walks in America (Part One and Two) and a novel - Unveiling a Past Imperfect (pending publication).

Foreword

Ines, my best friend's wife, died. It was a devastating blow to all the families and friends. She was fifty, attractive, intelligent, and quick-witted. My friend Manzu understandably became depressed.

Nagging at me for thirty years ever since I saw John Cleese in a documentary about the Camino De Santiago De Compostela in 1982, year after year in passing whims, it came back to haunt me.

I spoke to my friend about doing the 780km walk from the French border of Saint Jean Pied de Port to Santiago on the west coast of Spain.

Spontaneously, barely three weeks after Ines's death, we were on the Camino. That was the most exhilarating experience we could have had. Eventually, we went to Finisterra (Lands' End), touching the Atlantic Ocean. Still, on a high, it was there that I decided that I wanted to walk across the Globe, the whole twenty-four thousand miles. This was how I discovered my impassioned love for walking.

On my return to London, life became complicated. I was back down to earth. That was June 2012. Three years later, on 4th February 2015, I started to walk from Los Angeles towards New Jersey across America.

All this took place a year before Donald Trump came to power and exposed the soft white underbelly of American society.

Some individuals are passionate about challenges like climbing Everest Mountain or man-hauling their equipment/food supplies to the South Pole. Others go silently walking for twenty-seven years around the USA and Canada. They remain out of the public imagination. And there are others like Sarah Marquis. She walked ten thousand miles in three years alone. Trekking to places like Siberia, Mongolia, China, and Australia. These adventurers do not do it because they want to be regarded as heroes or seek glory. The thought of danger is there, but it never deters them. They do it because there is a calling like the will to go to Mars, fraught with dangers. It is that inexplicable essence where one idea leads to another. It is driven by an inner cry with a passion for going and doing it, sometimes alone. During that time, I was on a quest to find the edge of my existence.

Individuals will always seek a path to find their liberation. I knew the dangers when I decided to walk across America. I understood the psychology of being alone.

I decided on this trek across America from West to East without proper planning. I needed an adequate Atlas map to guide me. The roads I chose were calculated haphazardly. My knowledge of the landscape and weather conditions could have been better.

After trekking a thousand miles and climbing 8,500 feet into the Rockies, I was frozen in my tent one night. I was in the middle of nowhere without any means to be rescued. The temperature was 12° Celsius below zero. My mobile phone was in a 'black hole,' and I couldn't get reception.

I was losing my mind, too cold to think clearly. I had every item of clothes on me tucked into my sleeping bag. I wanted to leave a note if someone happened upon me frozen and stiff. But my hands were cold without dexterity. I couldn't even hold a pen. I was afraid of falling asleep. Hypothermia might have set in, and not woken up. But sleep came on and off.

Many times, but especially that night, I regretted taking on this journey and wanted to pack it all in every day. There were demons to exorcise. Conflicts with opposing internal voices. The urge to break away from the repetitive routine of living in a big city like London. The notion of being thrust into the unknown was compelling. The territories I wanted to explore were not simply external but decidedly internal – the fear factor, the limits of my endurance, and the thought of relying on only myself—the idea of being alone in a meditative state in the vast terrain for countless days.

Sometimes, great luck and spontaneity are important to anyone's destiny. What inspired me in life came late. By trekking the Camino de Santiago de Compostela, I discovered that I love to walk. Not just for a weekend's rambling but to walk until my body was full of endorphins, serotonin, dopamine, and other chemicals that were naturally induced. Every hour, day and night, to be constantly on a high.

During the months leading up to my departure, I trained hard for my fitness. I was friendly with my General Practitioner. I mentioned my idea of walking across America to him. He gave me a look with a squinted eye with one eyebrow raised. The big doubt expression, thinking perhaps, "That's no trek for an old man." I never felt or saw myself as an old man, despite the new fashion that nature imposed on me, grey hair and beard.

"What kind of training have you been doing?" He asked.

"I have been doing four miles an hour, fifteen miles per day, and six days a week for the past two months."

"How many miles do you propose to do on this trek?"

"On paper, around three thousand miles. Perhaps more, across the USA, from the west coast to the east."

He hummed, more raised eyebrow from him. He checked my record on the computer. He knew I was a Type 2 diabetic, but my sugar level was practically average as I was on medication. He checked my age, and from the look on his face, I knew he wanted to discourage me. I believe in frightening me; he gave me an endurance test of walking a straight seventy miles without stopping.

"I want you to do this and do a blood test afterwards," he handed me a form.

I didn't feel daunted by it. I attempted his set goal and completed forty-three miles. Blisters forced me to stop. I felt capable of completing fifty-five miles at least before cramping up. I felt no tiredness even after the blisters. I did the blood test straight after the walk. The results came five days later. It showed no stress, and every part of my body was tip-top. Without hesitation, he gave me the green light.

"You must rest after two thousand miles to avoid muscle or ligament breakdown. Even top athletes would have to rest after two thousand miles. You'll need two weeks' rest before you continue your journey. A piece of advice: You'll be crossing desert terrain. Don't waste your water. Wash with sand. Make sure it's fine with no sharp or rough stones. Get immediate help if you get into trouble."

Why the USA? I'd never wanted to go to America. But there was a contradiction in my thoughts. Because of its global influence, we have all been imbued with a degree of Americanism - its culture. I fell in love with its rugged landscape and frontier life that I saw in all those Western films. The magnetic pull was there. That historical factor of people always being on the move fascinated me.

In the past, I'd felt reluctant to go there because of violence and prejudice that I would be stepping out of my comfort zone, putting myself at a disadvantage. I knew I'd have to travel through those Southern States. Their history had caused a civil war that led to a segregationist de facto society until the 1960s. Even in this new millennium, Bill Bryson's A Walk in The Woods said if a two-thousand-mile trek was drawn across any place in America, you were sure to encounter a dozen or more murder victims, not to mention muggings and injuries caused by bodily harm.

It is difficult to take on a challenge and place oneself in an uncertain situation at the frontier of many unknown factors. It's okay to city-hop by aeroplane or by car. But walking puts the trekker into a different exposure. Friends and family were fearful of the venture. They also thought I was mad, for they had read Bryson's book. They accused me of being selfish: "We will have to pick up the pieces afterwards."

I was due to leave in the middle of winter at the end of January. I chose to start from Los Angeles to the Atlantic Ocean because of favourable climate conditions. I knew it would be mild in the west and cold in the east. I didn't want to trek through the Mojave Desert in the middle of summer. I felt sure there would be several routes across the US, and there would be no difficulty with language.

At the beginning of the trek, leaving London airport.

As it was a long trek, I decided it was a good idea to raise some funds for Diabetes UK, for Sunndach, a respite home for disabled children in Scotland where my granddaughter spends her weekdays, and for a charity Disability and Development Partners (DDP) that works with local partners in South Asia and Africa and is run by a good friend, Kamala Achu. This then gave me a firm footing for my venture.

Dorothy Dudek met me at the Los Angeles airport. She kept her vitality and liveliness as I last saw her in Santiago, Spain. Her hair was longer, blonder in the Californian sun, and her sharpness of wit still amusing. "How was the trip in the tin can? Didn't the food make you want to puke?"

Dorothy Dudek (DD)

My first words to her were: "I don't think I can do this." Deep anxiety overcame me on the plane as the landscape unfolded. Hour after hour, the landmass and the desert spread like an ocean bed of sand. It occurred then that even the meagre planning of this trek was a foolish dream.

"Nonsense, you can do anything you wanna do." I got encouragement from that.

Dorothy and I met on the Camino de Santiago in 2012. As we got to know each other, I called her DD, which she liked. She had yet to do noteworthy walking or trekking before doing the 780km of the Way of Saint James.

Like many, the Camino had a profound change on her. She realised she couldn't return to being how she was before the pilgrimage. We kept in touch, not as a parting promise but as a genuine friendship connection.

She offered to help me set it up in Los Angeles. She invited me to stay at her place until I was ready to take the road. She even offered me her bed while she took to her large sofa. We worked out the route, all the roads out of California, and how to cross the Mojave Desert and get to Phoenix, Arizona. As part of my preparation, I emailed Dorothy a list of items I needed to save transporting them from England. We did all the shopping together, like buying a sleeping bag, different gadgets, and supplies. We bought the food provisions on the last day.

I arrived on Friday 31st January. She suggested I leave on Tuesday, 4th February, so we only had three full days to prepare, and she wanted to show me around "through my neck of the woods." She drove up and down California to treat me to her backyard.

We went to Santa Barbara, her favourite place, and rode through the hills and the promenade on the seafront. I needed to dip my feet into the Pacific Ocean before departing on my trek. We walked on the sandy beach I had seen in many films with a strange sensation of déjà vu. She touched on the subject that was still raw inside me.

"How is Marie Josephe?" (Mijo as she is known.)

What she meant was how I was coping. My relationship with Mijo had broken down after three years.

"I was hurt badly, DD."

"Are you still in touch with her?"

"She writes and phones sometimes. It's a sore point."

"This journey has come at a good time for you. It will help to heal you."

"I hope so, or kill me."

"You are a Leo, like me. Nothing can kill us. We are too stubborn to die and still have much to live for. We can't settle down like everyone else. Boredom would kill us. We smell death daily unless we've got our teeth into something."

Walking by the sea, our footsteps eroded as the waves washed on the beach. The sea was biting like the Atlantic on the European coast. It was not what I had expected, with a chill in the air.

It's a strange sensation being jet-lagged. Everything becomes hazy. The day before I was to leave, we worked out an appropriate place where I could start. She will drop me off early on Tuesday, 4th February. We had the orange, three-wheeled bicycle children's trailer reinforced to take the weight of all my baggage, supplies, and water. I needed to carry three gallons due to the long distances and availability of provisions. The trailer could now haul fifty-five kilos instead of thirty-five. In my mind, we had done all the preparation, but with particular know-how, something would have been forgotten.

Planning for this journey would have been difficult without the help of both Dorothy and Yvonne Overton. Yvonne helped me organise and set up my blog in London. She was my London contact to relay all my messages to family and friends and update and edit my blog.

Yvonne Overton

Although physically, I felt fine. The jet lag was akin to a bad brew. On the last evening, I prepared a meal to celebrate our reconnection, the venture, and our good luck. We cracked open a bottle of wine to help the fatigue fade into the evening.

Hendry's beach, Santa Barbara CA.

Chapter 1: Desert Trail

It was early, and Dorothy didn't want to catch the morning traffic. We began the journey beyond the paved footings of Los Angeles (LA). On studying the maps, Colton was our designated point on the outskirts of LA. We decided I would commence my walk from there.

I like cities and was raised in one of the biggest and best cities in the world – London. Leaving LA, the conglomeration and sprawling suburbs seemed an endless stretch of concrete sameness. In the early morning, I saw a vast empty town, not the familiarity of cities I was used to in Europe. If I had started from Dorothy's house in Woodland Hills, it would have taken me two days of walking to get to the green patch on the outskirts of Colton. And there wouldn't have been a place to pitch my tent.

As we drove, Dorothy asked, "How are you feeling?"

"Hazy, it must have been the wine last night. I'm scared of what's ahead. A little excited too about what's to come."

"You'll be all right."

I wanted to be optimistic. It was, after all, a big undertaking, and I needed to grab it, succeed, and enjoy every moment. We reached an appropriate point and unloaded my trailer. We hugged, and she wished me luck.

She took photos and said, "You can do this. I have faith in you."

First Day on the outskirts of L.A.

It happened to be a glorious morning of sunshine. The air smelt fresh, and the temperature was ideal for walking with my trailer ahead of me with a placard on either side with the caption: "Nazacrossamerica, walking from ocean to ocean, crossing ten states for charities," which Yvonne had made for me. The title was also her idea. The roads were empty of traffic.

As I walked ahead and looked behind, Dorothy shouted, "If you decide to go through the Southern States, be careful. They don't like different."

I understood her meaning about the Southern States and their past around slavery and segregation. I didn't want the thought to affect me. I remained open-minded about everything. I let the comment pass and waved back to her.

A couple of hours passed, and two Hell's Angels roared by with no helmets. They had beards and long hair, seemingly without a care. We were in a canyon surrounded by green hills, almost like being in Wales, except with a broader vista, not a building in sight. Within five minutes, they were back at reduced speed and checking me over as they went. Moments later, they pulled up behind me. I stopped and greeted them. They didn't smile or return my gesture. I shifted my emotion into neutral as Hell's Angels had a good and bad reputation in films. Looking like Marlon Brando, one had a small cross tattoo right between his brows. He asked me where I was going. I told him and pointed to my caption. Stern-faced, he read it and then smiled at me.

"Man, that's going to be a hell of a walk. Are you serious? Good luck to you, man."

"I need all the luck I can get. What are you guys doing?"

"Travellin' man, meetin' a bunch of other guys," said a Peter Fonda lookalike.

Then Brando again said, "Anyone trippin' out with you?"

"I'll be on my tod."

"This guy Todd is joinin' you from where?" asked Brando.

"On my tod means on my own. It's cockney slang."

"You mean it's a cocky way of sayin' on your own?"

I never thought of it that way. "In the east part of London, they speak cockney, like your own Hillbilly."

"You mean somethin' like this – ah might-could go down the woods with my go-devil."

Peter Fonda chuckled and said, "Don't go sigogglin against dem trees now."

"It sounds English, but I have no idea what any of it means," I said.

As they laughed freely, Peter Fonda's dog tattooed on his left cheek with its tongue hanging out laughed, too.

"Cockney has rhyming slang, like apple and pears, meaning stairs. This word tod is from an American Jockey called Tod Sloan, rhyming with 'on your own. It's been shortened to Tod."

Marlon Brando blurted out: "I'll be dawg gone, them Rebs get to go everywhere."

The mood had changed quickly from uncertainty to something relaxed and jovial. Soon, four more bikers pulled up and greeted us. Two were women with helmets. All the men had pioneer beards and long hair. The women were dyed blondes, dressed like "The Girl on a Motorcycle," the whole leather outfit, the young Marianne Faithfull type, naked under shiny skins. They were curious to know where I was from, and Brando told them London. They took to me and said they liked my "British" accent. It's funny how Americans think the British have a uniform tone.

I said mine "is a mixture of English and a touch of French–Franglais."

They all asked questions at the same time.

"How long will it take to finish?"

"Maybe eight months, I'm not too sure. This is my first day."

"That's awesome, man, never heard someone walkin' the States."

The voice came from the back. I could make out who he was - a double of Jack Elam, who played bit parts as a killer, sidekick, or a drunk with a humorist "mug" in so many Western movies. There was excitement on their faces. Their smiles and laughter shifted the mood of the ensemble as though they were part of the adventure, going on a long trek. I must have seemed like an exotic figure to them, maybe an eccentric. Someone pushing an orange trailer with my UK flag posted on a rod, trekking across the country. Six more bikers pulled up, and it became a gathering place. I stood out without a Harley Davidson, propelling a three-wheeler with a handlebar. They were all in black leather outfits decorated with badges. One had 666, and another, his fingers full of rings, and a third with a tattoo on his neck and forehead, above his brows. A couple of them wore bandannas with Native Indian colours.

They looked like a cross between South Sea Islanders, Native Americans, and Europeans, a modern-day tribe roaming the countryside. The new arrivals didn't get off their bikes, kept their engines running, greeted, and said, "What's up"? The motorcycles, noisy, faint whiff of the exhaust around, talked among themselves. It was no longer conducive to having conversations, so I bid them all goodbye and pushed on. The shouts of "good luck" echoed in the air. They all pressed on their horns as they sped off in the opposite direction in posse fashion.

Walking along the winding canyon road, I sensed that luck was on my side. When I initially met the Hell's Angels, I'd changed my emotions into alertness. It was my first actual meeting with strangers. I was open; whatever prejudices might have been hidden in my mind, I didn't want this to influence my judgments. Nor did I want to feel paranoid or frightened. If I were to succeed on this long journey, I would have to face whatever lay ahead without anxiety.

This thought came to mind as I made my way through the first day. My pace picked up. I planned to do an average of twenty miles per day and if need be, thirty miles at the most. My readjusted trailer could now carry one hundred and twenty pounds; it was on the limit. The three gallons of water weighed heavily. The extra precaution with supplies and pieces of equipment made it difficult on the uphill gradient of the roads. I would have to adjust and lighten my load as I get used to the journey.

In the late afternoon, the thing that preoccupied me was a place to pitch my tent and to stay less evident to passers-by. I had seen no one on foot or on a bicycle, but I didn't want to be visible to the oncoming headlamps after dark. Towards the end of the day, I saw a patch of empty, unfenced ground on the San Timoteo Canyon Road where I could camp. On the other side of a ditch and behind some tall shrubs was an area of flat ground. There were railway tracks about a hundred meters across the road. I found an entrance to the shallow part of the trench and hid my trailer behind the shrubs. I waited until twilight to set up my tent. Later that night, looking at the time, it was well past seven; I set the alarm for six in the morning. A few cars passed by intermittently with their headlights shining on my tent through the bushes. I began to reflect on the day's events. I probably did seventeen miles, a little less than what I expected.

Still, I hadn't walked for over a week, and the day's trek seemed easy: T-shirt weather and mild sunshine. The Atlas maps I bought were insufficient. Dorothy and I used Google for a more detailed walking route, which we printed out. It wasn't like the Camino de Santiago, where pilgrims would gather in the village bar after a long walk. And after a shower in the Auberge (Hostel), gather for a glass of wine or a beer and a pilgrim's menu. We would tell each other stories and make friends.

After this first day alone in my tent, I understood this journey was different. No one would share the day's events, crack a joke, laugh, or dine with. There would be no one to celebrate my fatigue whilst bonding over a drink. It would be a strictly solitary affair. I read up on this part of California. It was once the land of the Serrano people, who had lived here for a thousand years. Tribes I never knew existed. I wondered if they ever slept on the ground I was sleeping on. Soon, I went into a blank sleep without a single dream to recollect. Once a train passed, it took some time to do so and woke me. For a time, I didn't know where I was.

I decamped early in bare daylight. It was cold; I wanted a good head start and reach Banning by the afternoon. After my shave and breakfast (oats, bananas, and nuts mixed with coconut water), I heard someone singing from afar while loading my trailer. I saw a hobo figure in rags with a long grey beard and matted hair approaching me. I sensed that he might hang on and slow me down. It might be difficult to get rid of him. I decided to set my trailer on the road and push on without looking behind amidst shouts I couldn't make out. A while later, when I looked back, he turned into a dirt track road, still as vocal as Pavarotti.

The morning chill surprised me, and I had to put on my fleece despite the bright sunlight. By eleven, everything came off except for my T-shirt. I reached Banning when it was almost two o'clock, and the sun was blinding. As I turned into North Hathaway Street, I couldn't see the road that I meant to turn off into. The whole panoramic view was desert, surrounded in the distance by rocky hills and what seemed like snow-covered mountains. I was at the end of town; I searched for signs for the name of the road and saw none. After consulting my Google instructions, I carried on northward. Then, the tarmac road ended, and an unsurfaced roadway began. Big trucks were driving to and fro carrying materials from a quarry. Half a mile later, a truck driver said it was too dangerous for me to travel that road, and it only led to a quarry. My wheels pounded the dirt rocky road. The load was too heavy; I was sure something would give way. He advised me to go back and look for another direction.

I offloaded some of my provisions and unnecessary items and dumped them in a trash can. I emptied a whole gallon of water. It eased the pressure on my trailer. Back on the asphalt road, sitting on the sidewalk studying my map, a truck driver pulled up and asked if I needed help. Together, we found the route; it cut through the Morongo Reservation opposite. The Reservation was across the road through a checkpoint, which I had assumed was private property. I told the guard on duty that my directions pointed to the Reservation. Would he allow me through the gate?

He said, "I don't have the authority to do that."

I showed him the footnote on the map, which said Morongo Road "was partially a restricted usage road" and was often open to use.

"I need to get to the other side of the Reservation," I pleaded.

"I'm afraid somethin' gonna happen to you if the young Braves got tanked up."

"You mean with alcohol?"

"Ye, and other kinds of narcotics."

I thought he was palming me off. Was he giving me a stereotypical view of a cowboy image of what Native Americans were like, and was it true? Were they locked up on the Reservation and never allowed to go out into the big world? Why put security guards at the gates? Who are the Morongo people? I hadn't heard of this tribe and only knew those by names portrayed in Western films or those barely touched on in history books. His reaction stunned me because, as he pointed out, I would have to take a ten-mile detour to reconnect to my route. My anxiety level rose.

He said, "Highway 10 is a block down the bottom of the road; you should try to get on it." He pointed to a tower block in the very far distance, "This is where your map will take you."

I said, "I'm not allowed to go on the highway."

At that moment, I understood that I was an embarrassment to him. Someone pulled up in a car by the gate, and he left me. The multi-story building in the east seemed far. I headed toward the highway, and it would have been suicide to attempt to get on it. The traffic was heavy and fast, with large trucks and cars driving way more than the speed limit. I went back to the road I came from and phoned Dorothy.

She said, "I'll ring you back in fifteen minutes with an alternative route."

I had come to a dead-end and wasted a precious hour or more. Unless I could reach my destination, I would unlikely find a spot to rest for the night. While waiting for her call by a wall of someone's front garden, I noticed five spent cartridges on the ground. It increased my uneasiness, and I moved on. Soon Dorothy gave me the new route. I was to take the bridge across the highway. Then, cross the railway tracks and turn the first left parallel to the tracks until I reach a tunnel crossing. Easy, I muttered, and a sense of relief came over me. On my way, minutes later, I spotted a motel before crossing the bridge over the highway. I made inquiries as an option, as it was getting late, and I had been on the road for nine hours. I found the cuisine at the reception overpowering. They wanted $50 per night, and the aroma came free. Sleeping on a spicy aroma's pillowcase did not appeal, and my option slipped straight into the afternoon sky.

Much later, after a few bleak miles, the road by the side of the railway track came to a cul-de-sac. Google had directed Dorothy to send me on a promising promenade. Two workers in one of the storehouses nearby assured me that the road did go all the way. They were also wrong. Making my way back, I could feel my tension rising again with the setting sun. I phoned Dorothy, and this time, she told me to take the road before the railway tracks.

It wasn't a road, just a service track made of ballast, which they put on railway tracks to hold the wooden or concrete cross ties/sleepers' firmly and the rails in place. It was very bumpy and caused so much friction to my trailer, which was still overloaded. The sun reached orange, pre-twilight brightness. The service road pounded my trailer; I expected it to break at any moment, and that would have been the end. A median of tall trees and some shrubs with a metal fence lay between the highway and the railway tracks. The traffic noise level resonated above any acceptable decibel. The chip-stone track led to a 'tarmac' lane; perhaps it should change to Potholes Avenue. I skirted the grassy edges to avoid erosion, making progress impossible. In the ever-increasing dusk, what looked like grass were common weeds and tumbleweeds with thorns. The trailer felt heavier than usual, and the back wheels were punctured flat when I checked the tyres. The front wheel was solid and made of hard rubber. I pushed on as it wouldn't have been possible to camp anywhere.

Out of complete darkness for a time then came a gas station, the Circle K. I spoke to the manager and asked him if I could pitch my tent for the night on the grounds behind some date's palms. His features were Hispanic. He was in his 50s, with an American accent. He sported a moustache, which made him look a little like Groucho Marx, with the same eyes, eyebrows, and nose.

He seemed uneasy, went out to check my trailer, and said, "Move it to the back. It'll scare the customers."

I was baffled as to why clients would be frightened by my trailer. It looked innocent enough, nothing like Godzilla. I was in no position to argue. I had placed a burden on him, and he didn't appear as someone who could make snap decisions. While drinking my coffee, I waited for an answer. He was agitated. His facial expression was of someone terrified of creepy crawlies. It gave that stunned look like he was about to run straight out of his skin. I placed him in the spider's phobia category. With my continued presence, I must have resembled a giant tarantula. He transferred his anxieties to me, where nightmares were already playing havoc. If he refused, where could I go? Outside the halo of neon lights of the gas station was only blackness.

Finally, he said, "I can't let you stay. If the sheriff found you here, it could mean trouble for me."

He knew I was desperate, exhausted, and stressed. His mood caught between wanting to help and being afraid to do so. He walked up and down behind his counter, pretending to keep busy. I read his every thought. And no doubt he read mine. I stood sipping a coffee, waiting for something to happen.

Then he said, "If the sheriff gives you the okay, it'd be fine with me."

His face became somewhat relaxed; he found an antidote. He pointed me toward the sheriff's office, "one block away." I didn't know if it was a few hundred meters or a quarter of a mile on a black night. Dragging my trailer with flat tyres, relying on my instinct to get there. At the Sheriff's station, only the security lights were on. Everyone had gone home. I felt lost, and the chill in the air was discomforting. I saw a small patch of lawn, part of the Office's Garden, flat, trimmed, and tidy. I thought about pitching my tent there and waking up early, long before anyone arrived at work. It would be easy to set up camp with lights on. I touched the grass; my pegs would easily sink in.

In my contemplation, a Sheriff arrived with his headlights blinding me. I relayed the message to him about what the gas station manager said. He looked in his early thirties with a wedding ring on his finger, which glittered in the bright beam.

He politely said, "I have no problem with it if it's all right with the station manager."

Later, the gas station manager said, "Go ahead, put your tent where no one will see you," and offered me coffee.

In my state of tension, I hadn't asked him his name, and he didn't ask mine. It took a while to pitch my tent as the ground was rock hard. I found a concealed spot near the far end of the petrol station, close to a gas cylinder, behind some shrubs. Once in the tent, the stress of the day overwhelmed me. Drained and off the map, I lost my appetite. I had two punctured tyres, and it was hot during the day. The night brought the cold with the wind flapping at my tent. The pegs secured the flysheet tent as best they could on the hard ground. With the increasing wind, I became fearful my tent might take off. The traffic on the highway was continuous and loud, and my tiredness was overwhelming. My emotions got the better of me.

Placed between the railway tracks and the highway, each time a train passed by, it blew its horn. The trains were so long that they took ten minutes to pass, and one went by every twenty minutes. On the highway, the honking was continuous by the juggernaut trucks driving fast, competing with the faster vehicles. I went to bed at nine and was still awake at one in the morning, but the wind had died. Every time I drifted off to sleep, the carnival of noise tormented me.

The traffic to and from the gas station early the next day broke my sleep. I decamped; it wasn't seven. The sun was already bright, but it was still goosebumps cold. It's desert country; the mountains ahead looked camel-like in shape and shade. In the distance, the vegetation covered in dust seemed small. The fine desert sand engulfed every shrub and tree on the station grounds. The palms lining the entrance looked thirsty, thin, tall, and exhausted. The station seemed like an invasion of the landscape with its bright blue paint of the service area and the geometric design of the main building. Perversely, it represented disorder in this rugged view.

With the new morning, I wanted to leave behind the thoughts of the day before and look forward. The sun brought calmness to me. Everything seemed clearer. First, I needed coffee and then to repair my punctured wheels. The night manager had finished his shift and left. A new manager had taken over. Francisco was married with two children, a boy and a girl. He had always lived in California. Striking with a full head of hair, he was in his late thirties and of Hispanic descent. He said he'd noticed my tent when he arrived at six. I told him I was from England, trekking across America.

He said, "It's an old ambition of mine to visit Europe someday when the kids have grown up. I've been to Arizona, but that was as far as I've travelled. Life is hard."

His sentiments were sincere, as though he was speaking about life and the harshness of the environment itself. He was curious about my trek, which allowed me to mention my punctured wheels.

"I need a bucket of water to check for punctures," I said.

He offered to help me repair the wheels.

He pointed out: "See these thorns?" and made me feel inside the tyre with my fingers. "They came from tumbleweeds." They were needle-sharp and hard.

"There must be half a dozen in each wheel, making the punctures. It's easy to fix. I'll show you."

The area manager came in, and he had to see her. A while later, three young men arrived and had seen my trailer with the caption 'Naz across America' and wanted to know who was doing the trek. Francisco introduced me to them. They were regular customers and were taken by the idea.

One said, "Get the camera outta' the truck."

With great morning enthusiasm, I posed for half a dozen photos with them. Then Francisco wanted to have his photo taken with me.

"I'm gonna show my wife this great guy I met today."

As people walked in, they wanted to know what the commotions were about. In turn, they wanted to shake my hand and wish me good luck, and "awesome" became the dominant word time and again. My tyres were still flat, but my head had got slightly bigger by then.

Francisco showed me how to fix the tyres. I knew how but hadn't done so for forty years. I watched how he did it with his expertise.

By nine, I was ready to be on my way and thanked Francisco for all his help and kindness.

"Good luck, man. I'll follow you on your blog."

I felt full of energy again. Within two hundred meters, I realised that the place I had planned to make camp the day before was precisely on the other side of the station, a stone's throw away. It gave me such a boost to know that I found my route.

Four hours later, I was in White Water, having gone through dusty pothole roads and desert tracks where I was once lost, and Google led me in a labyrinth to nowhere. A helicopter hovered over me for a long time while I sat in the desert, ate a sandwich, and thought about what to do. I had been feeling stressed from the beginning of my journey, looking at the landscape above on the aeroplane. I had hidden my feelings, but they had resurfaced the day before and at night. Now, once more, tension gripped me at a crossroads. The directions were clear, but it led to another winding dirt road up a hill that was more like a mountain. I stood for a time and pondered.

At the crossroads, two women chatted and waited for a school bus. It seemed like a dream. I couldn't see a village in sight. I asked them to point me in the right way. They asked me why I was pushing this trailer, so I pointed to my caption.

They said, "Oh my god, but you've got a long way to go."

"Right now, I just want to get to Desert Hot Springs," I said.

They pointed at the highway miles away across the desert, where miniature vehicles looked like a chain of moving ants. I said I needed an alternative route, but they didn't know one. I sought to verify with someone else if my direction was correct, as there were no road sign markings. Google surely wouldn't have sent me up these big hills. I spent thirty minutes studying and pondering and waiting for somebody to happen by. Ultimately, I felt the direction was up those hills on the dirt track road surrounded by hundreds of wind turbines. I had no maps, just instructions downloaded from Google (In all the shops in LA, I couldn't find a detailed map for walkers).

More than an hour later, I was exhausted and on top of the hills. According to the directions, I needed to turn on the first road to the right once on the hills. It was a sandy track with a gate with a padlock. The wind-propelled turbines created an ecosystem of a desert storm. It all seemed like a place barren except for the tumbleweeds. The turbines were huge. They were perhaps four hundred feet tall with blades nearly one hundred and fifty feet wide. Their tonnage is beyond three hundred tons, maybe like a jumbo jet. It suggested being on an alien planet, walking among the remnants of a dead civilisation, surrounded by hundreds of those mechanical giants.

Dragging my trailer to the top left me sapped. In the middle of a "storm," unable to pass through my route, I looked for an area to camp out. There were none, with no hiding place. I sat down, sheltered from the wind behind my trailer, drank some water, ate some dates, and time became irrelevant, not knowing where to go. It seems foolish to think I should have embarked on such a crazy escapade alone. I may as well have chosen the North Pole without a compass or drifted on an ocean wave in a dinghy.

An old ambition came back to haunt me: riding into the desert, disappearing over the distance into the unknown with all my possessions in the panniers of my Harley Davidson. Perhaps this ought to have been my true goal, without exhaustion or sand in every crevice of my body and with little anxiety. Was this my middle-age crisis and my test to running life's gauntlet? I have been on an easy street for a long time, and now it looks like the payback was overdue. Has time caught up with me? Perhaps mine was to an end in the desert and be buried among the dunes. Then, to be discovered two thousand years later by archaeologists. With the fossilised remains mistakenly identified as Morongo Indians with an obscure DNA.

It's strange how the desert is deceptive. It had been rough sand and small rocks underfoot all day long. Now, in this moment of rest, among broken ochre and hard sandy rocks, sharp, chiseled-like, and smashed to create the rough service road to build and service those turbines. Nothing seemed impossible to grow out of this desert, but every crevice, rock surface, and flat land acreage dwarf shrubs clung hard and flourished. They looked dried as though the meagre rainfall had long been overdue. Then, it occurred to me that my tent was wet with moisture during the morning, as though light rain had fallen after dark. So, plant life strived in this desert by collecting moisture from the cold night air. The line of tall white turbine structures cast long shadows in the afternoon. From a distance, the look suggested that a parallel of black turbines was lined up behind them.

The roar of an engine was approaching. I waved down the truck, and two young turbine engineers greeted me. They both sported long beards that seemed in fashion. They said the road I wanted was out-of-bounds. They would take me to the intersection road if I waited ten minutes. I waited for thirty. It was getting cold; my fingers were frozen.

Eventually, they came: "We've been called on an emergency, can't give you the lift. But if you carry on up the hill until you get to a black pylon, turn right into the dirt road; it'll lead you to where you need to go."

I climbed some more before reaching the black pylon. It stood like a crucifix atop the hill. Then, I turned into the road with the sand so thick I had trouble pushing my trailer. Heavy service trucks' constant road usage had trampled the sand into fine dust. The wind blew sand onto the track, making hauling my trailer difficult. What was a mile seemed like three. A while later, a tarmac road appeared, and the name of the road I was looking for faced me in bold letters. I felt relieved for the first time since I had left Circle K that morning.

Further along, I saw a man pulled up to his front garden in a desert settlement of about a dozen prefab houses. I wanted to check on the distance to Desert Hot Springs.

We chatted, and he said with a chuckle: "So you're walkin' across America; it's easier by car."

He was middle-aged, bearded, and carried a little weight but still seemed fit and introduced himself as John.

"Where are you from?" I told him, England. His face lit up.

"I've always wanted to go there. My sister is married to a guy from Kent. They moved there some fifteen years back. Not seen much of 'em since. Near a place called the garden ..."

Scratching the back of his ears, he seemed to be searching for a place name – "The Garden of England?" I spoke.

"That's it. The damn name is difficult to remember in all this desert dust. It gets to the brain. Know what I'm saying?"

Hesitantly, I said, "I'm beginning to."

"Does it still get foggy there?"

It was a strange question; I told him I hadn't seen thick fog since 1963 in London in any way from my recollections. His image of England must have come from old movies.

He came back to me: "I walked across America twice when I was young."

Once would have been enough, judging by what I was going through. It surprised me. He read the reaction on my face and chuckled with a wide grin.

"I'm just kiddin'. Don't get any walkers around these parts, just sidewinders."

I must have been an odd distraction for him, and I wasn't sure whether he meant real snakes or the venomous human type. Either one would be horrible.

I wanted to move on. I asked: "Could you tell me how far it is to Desert Hot Springs?"

He rubbed his ears, causing his spectacles to move up and down slightly. He said, "If you keep on that road for two miles, turn right at the end. Cross the main road and take the opposite road. Ten miles that should get you there."

He'd helped pluck up my courage as it was approaching late afternoon. It would be a three-hour trek down into Desert Hot Springs, flanked on either side by the mountains in the distance. Within a mile of either side of the road leading to the town, desert shrubland parcelled off for future development. Already here and there, a few houses had been built and trees planted, giving an image of a half-fertile desert. Nearing the town, grassland fields to one side of the road were manicured with date palms, and pines lined the streets in the distance. On the other side of the road, walled housing developments, uniformly constructed, contrasted with the rugged vista of the panorama. The median was lined with date palms; gaps between the housing projects revealed undeveloped shrubland.

I reached the outskirts of the town at twilight. I always aimed to arrive at my destination well before dark; it was the safest thing to do. I still had an hour of daylight, and pain pierced through every part of my body. All I could think of was a shower and a bed to collapse into. The aching affected my stride. It felt as though I was floating and intoxicated as dusk descended and the dim streetlights glowed. A few specks shimmered in the distant night sky, and the moonlight reflected an outline of the mountains.

It was that time of the evening when I shouldn't have been on the road pushing a trailer to nowhere like a madman. Everyone I asked didn't know where to find a hotel. It wasn't as if it was a big town. The tourist office was shut. I asked a young man wearing his cap in the dandy style if he knew of a hotel.

He said, "If you walk three blocks and ask someone for Miguel Diaz, he has rooms to rent."

It seemed like a leap into the unknown at that moment, and I didn't want to pursue that option. I made an inquiry in a grocery store. The proprietor pointed me up a hill on Palm Drive and said, "Two blocks away on the right-hand side of the road, there is a white hotel."

I felt drained and relieved as I entered the entrance of the hotel. The manager asked where I was from; I said England. I asked him where he was from, and he said South Korea. I enquired about a room and told him I had a trailer outside. He wanted to see it.

Afterwards, with a straight face, he said, "I have room for you but not for the trailer."

With my tiredness, I protested and must have looked haggard, "Are you kidding me?"

He laughed and said, "Just joking."

I brought my trailer inside and said I needed a ground-floor room.

"No room on the ground floor, upstairs, 4th floor, no elevator."

"You must be joking. I can't go four flights of stairs with all this gear."

Looking serious, faced down, he slowly looked up at me and said, "Yes, only joking," then more laughs from him.

"You crazy man walking in America; everybody drives, you walk, why?"

"I'm still trying to find that out."

"You want to save money?"

I gave him a dirty stare for his cheap joke.

Further laughs from him. He gave me the key, and as I went to my room, he said, "Passaport."

With a deadpan face, I said, "No passport. It was stolen by a jackal last night." It was my turn to play a joke on him.

"No passport, no room."

"I'm only joking. But you didn't laugh; why?"

"You're funny, man, very crazy," and grinned.

After he handed me back my passport, he said, "Wait, trailer too big to enter the room, door small."

"Are you having me on?"

"Yes, only joking."

He wanted to have the last laugh, but he wasn't joking. I had to remove the back wheels and empty the load to enable my trailer to go through the door sideways. He gave me a double room with a king-size bed and comfortable surroundings.

The shower came as a great comfort. In the mirror, I noticed that I had lost considerable weight and that my face was almost unrecognisable. I looked gaunt and worn out, my eyes deep in their sockets. The last three days had been gruelling with so much going against me, and now, having settled in, the stress overwhelmed me. A panic attack started, and I decided to Skype Yvonne in London to calm down.

"You've changed. I've never seen you like this before. Are you in a hotel? You can relax for a bit. You don't have to go on if you think you can't continue."

As she tried to calm me down, my body kept on shaking.

"You don't have to push yourself anymore. It would be fine. The charities won't feel let down. Just come home. Maybe you ought to see a doctor."

I felt relief from hearing her words, but the tears wouldn't stop. Afterwards, when we ended, my body shook again, and my teeth chattered. I went into overdrive, a kind of hyperventilation. I tried to relax and lay on the bed to stop the trembling, but it was useless. It carried on through the night. In the morning, with bright sunlight on the balcony, I was still shuddering, the chilly winter sun making it worse. The last thing that came to mind was, if this doesn't stop, I should send for a doctor. I must have fainted. I woke up after eight in the evening. The shaking had stopped, and I felt hungry. I had eaten nothing since the afternoon of the day before.

Jeff, our jovial manager, suggested the Mexican restaurant a hundred metres down the road. He also said that I should use the hot spring pool. Only then did I discover that the hot water in the pool came below ground. This was due to the San Andreas Fault bisecting the Basin where one side had hot water and the other side cold. The next morning, I entered the pool early. The hot mineral water was soothing, and I stayed in for two hours. I needed to get all the tiredness and stress out of my body.

When in Los Angeles, I wanted to go to San Diego to visit the Museum of Contemporary Art to check on James Turrell's sculptures, but it never happened. Jeff recommended I go to the Pueblo Museum created by Cabot Yerxa. The five-mile distance seemed too far to walk, and I needed the rest. I began to think I was missing out on my bucket list. It wasn't just the physical break I needed; I was wiped out mentally and emotionally. I needed the extra day's rest to think of where I was heading: back to England, California, or push ahead.

That morning, somebody at the breakfast table mentioned that Clark Gable and Carole Lombard used to get away from Hollywood and use Desert Hot Springs as their hideaway. In the late 1930s and early 1940s, it was a desert country, an oasis in the middle of a basin region with just a few hundred inhabitants. Then, someone else said it was a hideaway place for Al Capone. It was a good resort to rest and hide, but to stay undercover there would have been difficult. With a small community of people, any trivial rumour could spread like a tumbleweed on a windy day. The paparazzi would have left a trail of dust on the one road to the retreat. It seemed far-fetched for Al Capone to have come from Chicago to hide here. But in effect, people use the town as a winter escape from the harsh northern climate. Jeff had told me they lodge many Russian tourists, too, which had surprised me. "They come for hot mineral water". The town is bigger now than ever, supporting a population of nearly forty thousand.

Desert Hot Springs is a sprawling town, and every effort was being made to turn the desert green. During the afternoon, for my second stint in the pool surrounded by palm trees, it came to me that Palm Springs was where Gable and Lombard fled for seclusion some twenty miles southwest on the old roadway. In the water, sandwiched between the blue February sky and its reflection, immersed in the mineral spring water, I felt the fading of my tiredness.

In the evening, after dinner at the Mexican restaurant for the second time, Jeff asked me what my plans were. I said I wasn't sure but might head towards Indio in the morning. He looked affected by my leaving. I had been his "straight man" in our comedy act. He was always play-acting with me and not with any other clients. I was a distraction for him, a "crazy man" who didn't quite fit into the landscape or the normal way of being. He told me he left Korea ten years before and hadn't been back. He came with his wife to start a new life. He could not have been more than thirty-five. He was managing this hotel, and it was hard work, but he didn't mind the undertaking. In his stride, he took the challenge of learning another language, fitting into a different culture, and finding employment. He was prepared to take on the daily hustle relating to his profession, acclimatising to his new surroundings and not thinking of ever returning.

"I'm an American citizen," he said.

The gleam which showed on his face was full of pride and confidence. He has a six-year-old boy named Dan.

Does he plan to have any more children?

"Maybe my wife doesn't want," then the impish grin came back to him, the one he has on when he says, "Just joking."

We shook hands, and he wished me good luck. As I turned my back on him to go to my room, he said, "Be careful of snakes in the desert."

"What snakes?"

He laughed out loud, and his eyes shut into the crescents of two moons.

Sleep came quickly into the secrets of the night. By morning, my body had recovered from the physical pains. While still in bed, my thinking played on the negative, and I wondered whether I was emotionally recovered. Can I cross the Mojave Desert? It's not a good idea to think when lying down. The worst scenarios come to the fore. I decided to push on. I was ready, all loaded up, and on the road just after eight. Jeff was nowhere in sight as I left the hotel. I stopped by the Mexican restaurant to refund the $10 they had overpaid me the night before, but no one was there.

Google suggested I go to Indio via Varner Road, but I didn't want to walk in parallel, hugging the highway and breathing in excess carbon dioxide. I chose the longer route instead. The walk from the hotel to the Dillon Road crossing seemed more than four miles long. The sun was shining when I left, and the air was chilly. I took Dillon Road in Riverside County, which hugged the mountain range west of the Joshua Tree National Park. The grid system on the road in the USA makes navigation straightforward—no winding road or sudden contours that lead to a meandering path into a cul-de-sac. Nevertheless, Google had led me onto a few Indian trails off the tarmac into the desert, where I meditated on the maps.

Upon turning into Dillon Road, my direction deflated me; before me were miles that led up to the sky. I pulled off the road, sat on a rock, gazed at what was before me, and felt self-pity. Everything I relayed to Dorothy after landing came back to me – "I can't do this." I kept repeating the sentence.

A Hispanic fellow passing by saw me in distress and asked: "Are you all right? You look in bad shape, my friend. Do you need help?"

"No, there is nothing you can do to help."

He wanted to stay, but I told him I needed to be alone. All the vulnerability lurking below surfaced, and the shakings and the doubts began again. I made my mind up to quit. I'll abandon this folly, take a bus to Los Angeles, and spend a few months holidaying in the USA. Dorothy had suggested this if I couldn't carry on.

"Just come back and spend the rest of your time in Woodland Hills."

We could do whatever we pleased in her backyard, and exploring places up and down California would be a treat. It was madness to have reached this far with hundreds of miles of the desert still ahead. Phoenix was a city in another country, and the journey was unplanned. It was foolish, an epic undertaking from some children's adventure book, reckless, headstrong childishness that got out of control. Perhaps in all men, a child is harbouring.

Thousands of images can flash through the brain at incredible speed in shock. The next stage would be severe nervous tension. The body and the mind get to such a high-stress level that a panic attack becomes a release valve that gives a sense that a heart attack is imminent. I stood up and breathed forty, fifty times, exhaling rapidly until a sense of composure returned.

In the return of calmness, I knew that I needed determination and luck to pull me through. Even at an early age, the thought of giving up was not part of my spirit. In essence, I didn't want to give up and accept defeat. The last few days have drained me. In my hour of weakness, I placed the burden of the entire three-thousand-mile trek in my thoughts. In every moment of difficulty, I felt weighed down.

In a flash of clarity, I came upon a new strategy; everything needed to be done calmly. I decided I wouldn't look at the elevation of the road. I would put one foot forward and then the other and focus on only five metres ahead, to concentrate only on the day's journey. Learn not to project anything into the day after or a week in advance. This would allow me to narrow my target to the hour's events. It liberated me and helped me to concentrate on these moments that mattered. All our yesterdays were the past, and tomorrow did not exist. Today was the only day that was real. My world in England will only happen on my return. Now, my life fitted in a cocoon-like existence, and all my possessions were in the trailer before me.

As the walk began, the sun was warm, the sky blue, and the desert and dust in my midst. Time became irrelevant. I sang out loud. I would hear an occasional toot of encouragement as the car went by. There was hardly a sound except for the intermittent echoes of crows squawking. I stopped when it was necessary and kept my eyes on the ground. Two and a half hours later, I reached the summit. I turned around and saw Dillon Road leading down to the distant foothills of the far-off mountains where I had been a few days earlier. I screamed: "Made it, Ma! Top of the world!" After the climb, the euphoria gave me renewed vigour. I'll give up on mountain climbing after this trek, I thought.

Naz – 'Top of the world'

***

Soon after, there was an urgent pace to my stride. My shoes felt comfortable and light. These were the same pair that trekked the Camino de Santiago and the ones I wore to train for this journey. They had already hiked nearly a thousand miles yet looked almost new. I dared to bargain for them in a well-known sports travel shop in London. The manager offered me a large discount. It was the best pair of marching shoes I have ever owned.

The road was flat and straight after the ascend as far as my eyes could see. Dead shrubs scattered among the desert, which winged both sides of the road. No human traces were apparent anywhere behind or ahead. In the far distance, bordered on either side, low, jagged, burnt sienna mountain ranges bottle-necked. Thin clouds quilled the wide blue sky. In the Californian outback at noon in February, temperatures can soar into the 80s Fahrenheit (F). In the morning, it was 48° F. It was T-shirt weather as I trekked along the route while the power pylons paraded across the desert.

Camping in the outback.

A designated route across the USA didn't appeal to me. This was due to the wintry months of the year if I had taken a northern course from East to West. But I also wanted to blaze my path into "unknown" small villages and towns and plan as I crossed each state. Some three hours passed, and I was cheerfully singing, only to find a road sign that gave a different name to the one I was walking on. Panic set in. Have I taken a wrong turn at one of the crossroads? I recalled seeing two on the way. At that moment, I arrived near a small oasis. Perhaps a dozen prefab houses formed a small village settlement. I stopped under the shade of a tree at the lane entrance leading to the hamlet. I looked at my map and pondered on how I could have lost concentration. Juggling my thoughts, I could have veered into a tarmac road I passed before without noticing. Have I gone ten miles off my course? I cursed myself for not paying attention, being focused, and drifting into daydreams.

Then suddenly, a woman appeared out of the house nearest to the road. I asked her if I was on Dillon Road. She reassured me I hadn't lost my way.

"Don't you have a map?"

"I do, but it isn't detailed enough. I hadn't found one in LA."

She got into her car, gave me a local map of the area, and introduced herself as Connie. She spoke with a soft voice. Her skin was smooth, pastel white, and she was gentle.

"Why aren't you wearing any shades?"

"I accidentally snapped those hours ago," I said.

She took out of her glove compartment and brought back a pair, "You can have my spare ones. Would you like some food and water?"

"My trailer is full of supplies. Thanks all the same."

"Why are you on this venture, walking?"

"It's something I meant to do for a long time, and I'm doing it for three charities in Britain."

She assumed I was living in America and only realised I came directly from London.

"I wondered about your accent and was trying to figure out which country you came from. I thought Brazil."

"You were close, only five thousand miles out."

She smiled, her eyes lit up, and a dimple showed on her left cheek. I became curious about why she lived in such a remote place in the desert.

"I don't find it remote. This village is between two towns, Indio and Desert Hot Springs. The distance between the two is an hour away by car."

I suggested it was very quiet.

"I like it quiet," she said.

"Have you always lived in the desert?"

"I lived a good part of my life in Los Angeles. I was a teacher. I also cared for my mother."

"Does she still live with you?"

"She passed away. I decided to move out of the city."

"Do you have a family in LA?"

For a moment, she looked shy, tilting her head slightly as though my question was too direct. She smiled again, and her pupils enlarged in her bright green eyes.

"Things haven't worked out that way."

Then, she took the initiative and asked me questions.

"Does your family live in England?"

"I have two grown-up daughters. They are both married to Scottish guys. They live in Scotland."

"But you and your wife live in England?"

"Things haven't worked out that way."

She laughed, and her mood changed, and she looked relaxed. I asked her if she was still teaching.

"The teaching profession wore me out. After my mother's death, I needed a change. I searched for somewhere peaceful. This was the reason I came here. Later, I found a job at a lawyer's office. I have been lucky."

We stood for a while studying the map, and she showed me the best way to get to Indio.

She asked, "Have you had anything to eat? I haven't eaten yet. We can share lunch and talk some more."

I wanted to take up her offer. It would have been interesting to compare our experiences, but being on the road is about momentum and keeping a rhythm. To stop would have put me back an hour or three. It was already mid-afternoon, and I wanted to set up camp by five o'clock at the latest. I thanked her and wished it had happened earlier in the day. I wanted to hug her but touched her shoulder instead as a goodbye gesture. I looked at her for the last time; her green eyes held a sad stillness.

Later, I turned around, and she was still there, staring into the distance of my trail. I waved to her as I sank into the dip in the road as she disappeared. The expression on her face affected me. I should have accepted her offer for lunch. There was an urge to return, but my feet kept going robotically. The heightened anxiety over the past few days and the fainting spell in the hotel played on my decision-making. Our short encounter was warm in friendship, yet we were strangers. Now, I hurtled through space in the opposite direction, never to speak again or exchange thoughts. As I walked in the glare of the afternoon sunshine, a shiver of a penumbra came over me. I saw no one else after, and in the aloneness, it felt like I was the only person on the planet.

I set up camp behind a shrub a good length away from the road on the flat part of the sandy desert. While lying down and reflecting on the day's events, Connie came to mind. I missed the intimacy of contact since I left Los Angeles. It was an early lesson in how not to be reserved. This journey was about walking, making connections, learning, and understanding the ways of the people I met. I was scarred emotionally the last few days. I was not myself; severe stress made me vulnerable. I was hazy and too slow to react.

Amid my reflection, a vehicle passing by stopped. Footsteps approached, and a torch shone on my tent. My solar light had attracted their notice.

Someone with a deep voice shouted, "Are you all right in there?"

I knew in an instant it was the Police Patrol.

I said, "Yes, just camping for the night. I'm here on a long walking journey."

Perhaps he saw the caption on my trailer and said, "Okay," then left.

If he spotted me, then others could also see me. It was too dark to move to a more concealed site. In my scant reading on lone travellers, the advice given on survival was to camp in a hidden area. The less attention I draw to myself, the easier sleep will be. It was sound, but I never conceded to nor was swayed by any fear. This trek was going to take months. If fright had been allowed to be a factor, I might not have gotten started. However, I feared stepping on snakes, finding scorpions creeping into my tent, or hiding in my shoes.

During the night, I heard dry twigs crackling, animals foraging and trying to get inside, making haunting, unfamiliar sounds echoing in the distance. I felt unprotected, a trespasser, someone who had invaded a boundary, which perturbed the hunting territory of some animals. In the night, I could be the hunted. I yelled and banged my goblet and breakfast bowl together to frighten them. It worked, but my sleep broke a couple of times by howling cries and more scratching on the ground nearby. I didn't dare to go out into the darkness to see what kind of nocturnal creatures they were, just in case I stepped on a rattlesnake or something. Judging by their steps, they must have been big, and I didn't want their claws tearing into my canvas either. My utensils' percussions made them skedaddled once again.

Except for some articles on survival, I hadn't read up on anything before this venture. I wanted this journey to be like the original Indians who travelled without knowing the terrain when they first settled here. Likewise, modern settlers from Europe once had to caravan through this unknown wilderness. Nothing was familiar, not the landscape or the creatures that inhabit this part of the country. The only advice I received from the camping shop was to carry bear spray to fend off such large beasts as mountain lions, bears, and wild boars. I hadn't thought of encounters with such animals. Closeted inside, listening for the next approach, sleep got the better of me.

When I woke, it was already daylight and cold, perhaps only 43° F. Outside, I saw no traces of foraging or footprints. Maybe they were further off than I had imagined, twelve feet away, near some prickly shrubs? Best, I thought to leave sleeping animals alone.

I planned to set out as early as I could. After decamping, I shaved and breakfasted; I was on the march again. The hard shoulder was a rough surface of gravel and sand. As cars approached, I pushed my trailer on the road and darted on and off the verge. A vehicle blew its horn as it passed me and slowed down into a lay-by a hundred meters away. As I got a short distance from the car, the door opened, and a figure stepped out. It was Connie. I called her name. Her face lit up in the morning sun.

"Where are you going?" I shouted.

She reached out to me to greet me. Her lips felt warm on my cheek.

"I'm going to work."

"But whereabouts do you work?"

"In Palm Springs, didn't I mention it yesterday?"

"Oh, are you late?"

"No, I've time. Get in the car. We can talk. It's cold out."

In the car, I said, "Look, I made a mistake yesterday. I should have stayed for lunch and talked. I thought about that last night. I shouldn't have gone so suddenly."

"I wondered why you did that. I was looking at you while you were walking away. You cut a lonely figure. I was worried about you."

"Why do you say that?"

"People can be strange and hurt you. Nobody walks in America. Anything can happen. Aren't you afraid?"

"I've blocked that. I've put up a shield around me."

"Oh, so you've become a knight in shining armour?"

"Well, maybe, but no one is calling me Sir."

"Can I ask you a personal question?"

"Go ahead."

"What animal sign are you?"

"You mean zodiac?"

"How do you see yourself?"

"Not as a cockroach."

I said that to change the mood, but she didn't respond.

"Well, I'm a lion, born in August."

"Is that how you see yourself?"

"I've never seen myself as an animal. I never read these things."

"I saw you like a dog."

"Do I smell like a dog?"

"You've never owned a dog, have you? I saw you as a wounded dog."

For a moment, the wounded dog sounded like a Native Indian tribal name.

"Do I look like a dog?"

"It's not the look. It's the aura," she said calmly.

"You're right; I've never owned a dog. But what's with the wounded?"

She looked at me with her eyes unblinking. Like a magic woman, she touched her heart and rested her hand on her left breast. In that moment of impasse, Mijo hurtled through space and entered my thoughts. The corners of my eyes burned and stung, and I tried to hold back my emotions.

"Just let it all go," she said soothingly.

She held me for a while, and her warmth comforted me.

Then she whispered, "I've got to get going."

She squeezed my hand. I left the car in silence. She drove away when I reached my trailer, and I felt left behind. It puzzled me how she saw through me. Why my aura was that of a dog?

The road dipped on the tarmac runway that led to the mountain range at the skyline. Later in the day, in the far distance, a fertile area appeared with thin, tall palm trees. The green density that one expects of palms was absent. Instead, the trees were dusty and thirsty but not unhealthy. They could tap water from somewhere near a fault line. Among them were date palms, and a dozen manufactured houses lay hidden between the trees and desert shrubs. The extent of the green patch must have only been a few hundred square metres.

A man in an army-like outfit, almost camouflaged amid the foliage, came out to greet me. He introduced himself as Eddie. His reaction was very complimentary when he learned I was from England and about what I was doing. He looked in his mid-forties and needed the last notch in his belt. He wasn't handsome, but he held a soft smile which made him agreeable.

When asked, he said, "I'm from New York. But got tired of the winter and was outta work. A friend said to come over. He had a job for me. So, I got on the next plane and moved to the Californian desert twenty years ago. And I ain't been back since."

He said he had an Italian, Irish, and Dutch lineage. How did he find the change from east to west?

"It wasn't easy leavin' family and friends behind; I wanted to 'test' the ground. But the job suited me, and I did well, made friends, and later got married."

I asked him what his profession was.

"I'm a manager in a real estate business."

Has he returned to New York since he left?

"Getting married was kissin' New York goodbye, man."

He scratched the back of his head and creased his forehead.

"Havin' a family kinda keeps you broke." There was a grin on his face. "The cost of living, holding down a job and time, man, time ain't on your side. If I can afford it, I want to go back one day, so I need to make up time."

He mentioned time three times, and I didn't understand his concept.

He explained, "If you wanna holiday, you need to work for it. It ain't a given. You build up your days; maybe you get two weeks' pay-check holidays. That is the custom where I work and in many other workplaces. But not all workplaces have the same rules." He laughed, "New York is a long way, man. This is a big country."

This idea of the big country hadn't sunk into my understanding. I saw the USA as a country with efficient internal transport facilities and assumed that getting from one place to another was relatively cheap and easy. Only when flying over did I begin to grasp its vastness. Plane journeys are costly. By road was cheaper, but starting from Dillon Road to New York would be like travelling from London to Moscow overland.

Had he toured much since he came to California?

"Been to Dallas once visitin' my brother Steve and been to Vegas and often visit my other brother down in Mecca."

"What Mecca, Saudi Arabia?"

He laughed, knowing he had pulled a fast one on me.

"No Mecca thirty miles up the road."

I have heard of Paris, Texas, and now Mecca in California.

"Have your whole family moved out of New York?"

"They're all still there except for my two brothers and a nephew who lives in LA. You gotta go where the job is these days. After the Stock Market crash (2008), my nephew Joe came to California. He is doing fine now."

Soon, it was time to go; he walked with me for a few hundred yards and said slowly:

"One day, all this is gonna be real-estate development," pointing to the vast land all around.

We bid goodbye, and he hugged me and wished me luck on my trip. Our time together was less than thirty minutes. Eddie had been open as I was. He was genuine with his warmth. At first, I didn't see him as good-looking. After spending time with him, his personality changed from how I saw him, a kind of visage that slowly grew on me.

I picked up the pace and felt enclosed by the vastness of the landscape. I liked the ruggedness, the chaos of it all. The shrubs adapted to thrive and gather moisture from the night air or survive by sending their roots deep into the ground. It's a free-for-all for those that can adapt, be it flora or fauna. To the naked eye, the desert seems like a place blighted that does not tolerate carelessness. A false move, one is liable to be left for dead. The wind could swirl into a storm. The sun pierced through the blue sky and may reach 104° Fahrenheit in the summer. Yet, in winter, at night, the temperatures often fall to zero. In places, the sand is as hard as rocks, and the rocks are as soft as crumbling sand. The air is pure, and everything is motionless; no sound usually stands out. The wide-open space casts an illusionary view; mountains that appear nearby are far away. The desert is teeming with life night and day. In a way, it is as deceptive as a mirage. It would be a tragedy if we were to encroach on it with our concept of the human jungle.

Something is enthralling about the desert plain. A straight road was carved through, stretching in both directions, not a soul or vehicle, not a fleeting passing of a gentle breeze. It is as if one is staring at a panoramic painting of a great piece of art on a universal scale in an outdoor gallery. I am beginning to understand why some artists paint huge canvases in a solid tone and call it art. Under the glaring sunlight, I am engrossed in an abstruse mood in this desert, and unfamiliar perceptions invade my senses. I can find comfort in solitude instead of fear and loneliness in the middle of a bleak reality. Hearing becomes acute, as though the planet has no sound. A great natural order exists in what is invariably seen as barren land in a perpetual state of denudation. Not chaos as I saw it initially, but a place where everything fits together in a harmonious entanglement. The desert profoundly sharpens one's sensory awareness and enables us to reach great depths of feeling. In this indefatigable mood, looking at a blank canvas and trying to understand an artist's conception brings clarity. The road cuts through the desert with its geometric precision like a blade of vandalism on a painted tableau.

Chapter 2: On the Road

As the trailer rolled before me on the flat asphalt road, I felt excited about what lay beyond. What pot of gold was at my rainbow's end? I gathered pace as the sun beat down. My mood, momentum, and fitness level excited me, and soon Indio came into view. I made for a campsite four miles away from downtown, which turned out to be a private resort. I learned later to always look for a KOA sign that shows a public campsite. Although I felt annoyed about going the extra mile, I didn't let it affect my upbeat spirit. The best part of the day was still to come. I bought a coffee and a sandwich in a nearby petrol station not far from downtown. It tasted bland, and then studied the inadequate Atlas maps of the difficulties ahead.

While doing so, an elderly gentleman pulled up in his car. His wife remained seated and passed me by. Then, he stopped and looked at my NazacrossAmerica captions and enquired about the purpose of my journey.

I said, "It's for charities, diabetes, and disabled children. I'm attempting to cross ten states to reach the Atlantic Ocean."

He raised an eyebrow, sighed, "hum," and went to the gas station shop. When he came out, he dropped me some loose change – pennies which amounted to less than thirty cents. I guess he didn't want them rattling in his pocket.

He then asked, "How old are you?"

So, I told him with a smile, "Young."

He said, "I am twelve years older," smiled back, and left.

I was still scrutinising the map when, thirty minutes later, he returned.

"I have brought these for you," and gave me two Mormon bibles to read. They were heavy and of high quality.

"These will help you on your travels."

I was born a Catholic, and I have become a humanist over time.

I said, "My trailer is already overloaded."

"Listen, my friend, you will need these. Take them; they will comfort you in your tent at night. Have these, too."

He handed me a plastic carrier bag full of apples, pears, and energy bars. Then he put a $50 note in my hand and said, "Just a little cash to help you along the way."

I couldn't accept funds as the American Embassy had clarified that in London. For the second time, I said, "Please, I cannot accept that. It's illegal for me to do so."

He insisted that I should keep the cash, "No one will begrudge you money for food. You will need to maintain your strength. You have a long way to go, brother."

At that moment, I pondered why this person who knew nothing about me made this grand gesture. I was a stranger and a misfit pushing a trailer.

Both Dorothy and Connie mentioned that nobody walks in America. I had seen no one walking since arriving here. His kindness kicked in a sudden deep feeling and overwhelmed me.

He held me tight and said: "It will be fine, brother. This happens to all of us."

He asked: "Where are you from?"

"London. I'm Naz," and we shook hands.

"I'm John, a mixture of Welsh, Scottish, English, and Irish - a mongrel, a true Brit."

I giggled. "Aren't we all?" I said, "A good mix, don't you think?"

He said, "Something was on my mind this morning. I had a premonition that I would meet someone like you. The Good Lord sent you. May God bless you."

The books were bound in leather. I left the Bibles in a place for someone else to find. All the energy bars contained sugar in them. I donated them to people coming out of the shop. Even though my beard was grey and not white, maybe they thought Christmas had come early.

I spent nearly two hours at the gas station looking and studying my route's maps and Google printouts. It would be one hundred miles of desert and dirt mountain tracks before I could get food and water supplies. Perhaps six days on the mountain roads. It was already hot, and my need for up to a gallon of water a day meant I would have to carry at least six gallons. Fifty-four pounds plus my other luggage would total one hundred and forty pounds. That would be way above the maximum limit. My tyres became a concern: would I have enough spares if punctured? I would be stranded and need more time to prepare and buy a repair kit for the trailer.

While studying the map, I discovered that part of my designated route was a militarised zone for dive bombing practice. I would have been killed or arrested if I had taken that route. Google directions for walkers were sending me into the most dangerous part of that corner of the country. I decided to stay one day in Indio and booked into a motel. It was fifty dollars for the night, plus another three dollars for the Internet. I felt duped.

Early in the afternoon, I inquired about a bicycle shop for spare tubes for my wheels, but there were none in Indio. I browsed the net; the nearest was in Palm Springs, which was twenty miles away. It meant a forty-mile return trek plus the cost of a two-day stay in a motel. Already, Google directions were giving me anxiety about my route. I treble-checked, and it looked dire. The dirt tracks not only led into a high mountainous area, but no defined route was specific. Some of these tracks came to a dead-end or led into a path where five different routes diverged in various directions. Using Google for walking was madness. I needed topographical maps for the areas of my trek. There had been none in Los Angeles and none in Indio either. I searched for an alternative route and thought I could go to Yuma further south and later to Phoenix. But that meant going via Route 111 and on Highway 8 to Yuma. The legality of walking on that Highway was unknown. It was against the law to walk on Highway 10 and Highway 40 further north.

Even if Highway 8 were legal, it would add another hundred and fifty miles to my journey. I would need a further day to plan and work out my provisions to ensure my safety. I could buy my spare parts in Yuma. But that meant going the extra mile south without backup until I arrived. What if I broke down? What about the mountains east of Yuma near Fortuna Hills?

I had a restless night. Every dream and each waking thought focused on failure. I woke up with pains in my belly with a wave of vomiting and nausea. A little later, I went out and stood in the morning sunlight. It felt chilly even with the tepid sun on my face. I knew that the end was here. I had reached a blind alley and became overwhelmed by a feeling of resignation.

At the motel reception, I asked if there was a bus service, and the receptionist said, "Yes, one is going to Phoenix today, just three blocks down the road."

Phoenix, Arizona, had not been in my mind. I thought of returning to Los Angeles and giving up on this trek. Back in my room, I toyed with getting to the Arizona metropolis. Rupa, the sister of my good friend, had offered to put me up if I happened to go her way. I could make up for the lost miles by walking around the city. It would give me time to prepare well for the rest of my trek. After many attempts, I managed to reach her.

"Come, you are welcome. We have a room for you. You can stay as long as you like. We can pick you up at the Bus Station. Let us know the time when you will arrive."

I loaded up and rushed to the terminal, and booked a ticket. The bus was not due to leave until 3:30 that afternoon. I had five hours to sit and kill. I felt relieved of the stress that weighed on me the past twenty-four hours.

The woman at the ticket office said I needed to dismantle my trailer and tape it like a flat pack. Otherwise, the bus driver would not take my luggage. Only two pieces of baggage are allowed per person. Any more would cost $25 each. I didn't want to pay the extra cost and couldn't reduce the quantity either. With hours to spare, I ventured outside. The Bus Terminal was in the main square and consisted of two large rectangular mobile home structures. Mature palm trees and beds of desert flowers and shrubs made up the boulevard's garden. It had a tranquil atmosphere. A patch of green vegetation in the city, despite the fly-over which traversed nearby. The whole area looked clean, neat, and well-kept.

It was where I met Nick, the gardener and cleaner of the station. He was approaching his mid-fifties, slim with a moustache, but looked and acted older than his years.

I asked if he knew of a café that catered for vegetarian food. He said that there was one and could take me there near noontime. I hadn't eaten breakfast, and the rumble in my belly demanded attention.

It felt too hot for mid-morning in the February winter. I went back inside and pressed for a coffee from the machine. A man was having a tantrum about the scheduled time of departure.

"I can't believe this. Why can't you have a bus leaving at noon?"

The woman at the ticket counter said, "The schedule is 8.35 in the morning and one at 3.35 in the afternoon."

The man seemed in a hurry to get to his destination. He was a driver of oversized vehicles. He wore a suit like a white-collar worker, greying at the temples. He looked in his mid-forties, a bright, florid man and self-obsessed. Everything he said was summed into dollars, trying to converse with another man sitting in the corner.

He said: "I make $10K per month on average. All the costs are paid for by whoever hires me. Last month, I picked up just over eleven thousand bucks."

He advertised how much his house, car, and dog cost him. He was impetuous, and nothing in his eyes revealed a self-conscious notion. His exaggerated sense of importance created an oppressive atmosphere that encroached on the confined space in the waiting area. The man in the corner, who looked bored by it all, was only interested in focusing on his laptop. I asked the woman at the ticket counter if there was a lavatory; she pointed outside to the left.

As I exited, the man with the laptop glanced at me as if to say, "Lucky bugger, now I have to suffer this son of a jackal alone." In the restroom, within a minute, the laptop man joined me and sighed "man" with an American drawl, "He fucking sucked all the oxygen outta the room."

I had time and didn't want to go back inside to get my ears bombarded with his palaver. I searched for a place in the shade, but the palm leaves fanned their shadows where sunlight easily penetrated through. Nick recognised my agitation, said, "Let's take an early lunch," and notified the office.

I said: "It's on me," and he smiled.

We ended up in a Mexican restaurant under the fly-over a short distance away. They had a good vegetarian section on the menu, and the air conditioning in the conservatory extension made it pleasant. The aroma of chilli beans and corn tortillas increased my appetite.

He said: "Drinking, drugs, cigarettes, and women have been my downfall."

When I looked at him, he retracted the last part of that sentence with a sardonic grin. Underneath his weathered features, there was an attractiveness that had faded. Had he ever been married?

"I was a long time ago. We fought a lot. She wanted children; I didn't want any. She got tired of me chasing women. One day, when I came home from work, I found the house empty."

There was a melancholic look on his face as he reminisced. He lived alone with his dog, Pedro. It took time to find peace, and his voice was sincere as he spoke about his religion.

"I have a one-to-one relationship with God, not of any religion, just with the Almighty."

Had California always been his home?

"I have lived in California all my life, and my grandfather was born here."

The food came; there was a lot, and he had a beef wrap.

"I'm gonna save some of this for my dog. He likes to wait for me to see what I have for him. He can smell the food on me. When I sit at the table to open the wraps, he will come and sit at my feet. He knows when I've something good for him."

I kept to the vegetarian option and had beans, rice, vegetables wrapped in a corn tortilla, salad, and hot salsa.

Later, before the bus arrived, Nick said: "Tape your tent and the sleeping bag to the flat pack. That'll make it two lots. I'll load it on; I know the driver."

I did as he suggested, but what was flat before became bulky. When we were about to load, the driver looked displeased, but before he could say anything, Nick took my entire luggage, went to the other side, and loaded it. We said goodbye, and Nick hugged me as the driver hurried me on. It was hard leaving him; we had bonded like brothers in just a few hours. I sat down on the crowded bus and waved as he signalled back with a face of sudden loss. The bus sped away.

The $10K per month man found a seat at the rear of the bus. The other traveller sat two seats ahead of me. The last available place was in the middle of the bus, and Josh, a young man from Kentucky, was my seating companion. We introduced ourselves but didn't speak for a while. Sleep came in and out of my drowsiness. The murmuring of young children shook me from my stupor. When I came to, we were well out of town and in the middle of the desert.

Highway 10 cuts through this vast uninhabited land with a four-lane carriageway. Two going in the opposite direction with the voluminous traffic of heavy trucks. In the imagination, a desert is a desolate place. Once, while driving through the Namibian desert searching for the Welwitschia plant, which can live for over a thousand years, the desert seemed utterly lifeless—standing on the edge of a vast crater, perhaps five miles in diameter. Not a single blade of grass or weed could be seen. It had been a spectacular Mars scape—the scenery of subtle shades of pink, ochre, and sienna. The remoteness of it was frightening. We finally found the Welwitschia deep inland, defying all the possibilities in the art of plant life survival.

Like humans, every desert has its face and its uniqueness. As the bus drove, I could see how difficult it would have been to walk across this boundless space unprepared. It would have been a practical attempt at suicide. Too dry even for the tumbleweeds whose thorns caused me so much trouble. The weeds uproot when dry and get scattered by the wind. They go tumbling along, spreading their thorns with each somersault covering new parts of the land, waiting for an eventual downpour. In contrast, a dead-looking shrub could still be green and alive. The Rocky Mountains are partly caked with sand - solid yet easy to crumble. Maybe rain hadn't fallen for a hundred years. Perhaps the people who once lived here knew the gods of this desolation, made peace, and then fell out with them again.

The light was fading, and the blue sky was deepening. Beyond the mountains, to the west, the setting sun painted the sky orange. Then, tinted it scarlet and turned the faded blue of the sky to indigo. The world beyond seemed as if it were on fire. In the blueness, a few specks of light were glittering. As the bus swallowed up the miles, the gradation of light changed into twilight, dusk, and then darkness. A shade that brings with it the shadowy cold of a winter's night.

My initial shyness when boarding the crowded bus evaporated, and I became an extroverted spirit. The big lunch and the gentle vibration of the bus had made me groggy, and in no time, sleep had come. Now in contemplation and awake, Josh offered me some crisps. In return, I offered him an organic carrot. He studied it as though it was a strange offering. He was in his twenties, with dark hair; Gregory Peck looked about him with a smiling face even when he was serious. I asked him where he was going, and he said home.

"I'm from Kentucky and moved to California three years ago lookin' for work. The situation at home was bad. I couldn't find work for over a year and moved out west."

He gained employment in the construction trade and worked for two years, but everything had dried up. He hadn't been able to find work for eight months save for a week here and there doing stints in fast food restaurants.

"I was feelin' down and didn't see the point stayin' any longer. In Kentucky, I've got my family and my friends. I would have a roof over my head and food on the table. California is dry; I miss the green of Kentucky."

He said he has a gun, and Kentucky is a very fertile country where he will hunt and bring home wild game.

"Was that legal?"

"Everybody has guns back home, and people like to go huntin'."

He said he had nine rifles and two handguns in the house.

"Why own so many guns?" I asked.

"It's the American way."

I became puzzled by the answer.

I said, "If my neighbour had five cars, that doesn't mean I have to follow what he does. I can walk or ride a bicycle or own just one car."

"Don't you have a gun in England?"

"Having guns in Britain is illegal, and a special license is required."

I told him about the spent cartridges on the road in Banning a few days before and how it had brought goosebumps.

"This is how people settle their scores, gangs mostly, and if you keep a gun in the house, people will think twice before deciding to rob or kill you. How do you defend your home in England?"

"We don't have a gun culture in Britain. People don't feel threatened by having to protect their homes with a weapon. The citizens are defiant when thieves break into their houses or terrorists try to brutalise society. Don't you think the excessive number of guns is why people go on a rampage here?"

"Most folks respect the gun; it's our way of life. Of course, there are a few mad sons of bitches on the loose."

I was finding this hard to digest, this central sentiment of the need for a gun. It doesn't resonate in modern society. There was no thought behind the phrase "The American Way" and its consequences of weapons on the streets. It seemed like a throwback. An appendix, like someone using a

Hamish buggy with a horse going to work in rush hour in Los Angeles today. There was something stubborn, backward, and out of step with our technological world. The more we advance civilisation, the more we carry backwardness in conflict with our self-interest and preservation. It's as though no thought and consequences were given to the phrase "The American Way," just a folklore mantra.

Blythe, a town on the frontier of Arizona, came into view, and the bus driver made it clear that we would make a stop for precisely thirty minutes. It was a relief; I wanted to get off the topic with Josh. The subject didn't sit well with me. Everyone longed to stretch their legs and use the lavatory.

It has a strange effect on the perception of the arrival time after dark. Through miles of desert, Blythe appeared like a town in the Middle East or North Africa amid dunes. It was a medium-sized flat without a high-rise building in view, perhaps with fifteen thousand plus inhabitants. The tallest objects were lampposts and advertisement totem poles for fast food, cafes, and motels, and tall palms lined the avenues. The streetlights were bright and gave a picture of a bustling township. The temperature dropped, reminding us that we were still in winter.

***

The driver signalled that it was time for us to return to the bus. Blythe did not show itself despite the bright lights on the intersected road. The town was flanked to the east by the Colorado River and, on the other side, the Arizona frontier. People of the Native American Mohave and Quechan

(Yuma) tribes lived on this river before Europeans came to settle here. They grew crops of maise, grass seeds, and vegetables and fished, hunted, and traded. John, who had given me the Mormon Bibles, told me that if I walked through Blythe, I should check out the Geoglyphs Intaglios north of the town (I wrote the words down). The Geoglyphs depict human figures incised into the earth by people living in the region some two thousand years ago. Drawing gigantic shapes, they removed a thin rock and soil top layer. I had seen a documentary by Alan Whicker where people had done the same thing in Peru. The chance to visit the site slipped by in the night. Even the river crossing into Arizona went unnoticed.

The road ahead was flat, and only the reflected lights of the vehicles pierced through in the far distance. Josh wanted to talk, and I didn't want to return to guns. We talked about the politics of Tony Blair and George Bush. They became despised figures by a large section of the ordinary British public for having caused the war in Iraq. The demonstration against the war in Britain was the biggest in its history. The British people viewed Bush and Blair as the lackeys of the vested interests of people interested in the arms, oil, and subsidiary industries. Saddam Hussein became the archetypal bogeyman, and we, the people, as the patsy. In Britain, ordinary people could see the power politics of scarce resources. They felt Blair and Bush were ready to sacrifice people on both sides of the divide to secure those resources.

Josh said: "We went to war because Saddam had weapons of mass destruction. We all know how they found nothing. A few people were sayin' Saddam didn't have anything. But the politicians, the press, the news and talks on TV fed us with bullshit. If people heard you talkin' that way two years ago, you would've got beaten up."

"What is the attitude of the public today?"

"Many people still siding with Bush even if he is no longer President. But many others feel they've been fed moonshine."

How does he see it now?

After a pause, he said: "I like to think that we were defendin' our country against terrorism; we all thought that. It was our reason for goin' to Afghanistan. We wanted to show support to our fighting men. I've got a brother in the army. But things have been coming out that don't look good. It doesn't look pretty."

I intended to give him a view of how a significant part of the public in Britain and Europe felt. An angle from the non-apologist's papers about the war. Subjectively, it was not my opinion, but he took it as though I represented that view. I glanced around and noticed that some people were listening to our conversation even though we spoke in a low voice. I offered him a banana to change the subject. He said he still had the carrot I gave him.

After chewing on a bite, he said: "I could dig this raw rabbit food."

I said: "What's up Doc?" and he laughed.

Josh was not married but said he would someday like to get married and have children. He revealed that when he first saw me, he thought I was from Brazil, not the first one to do so. I asked him where his ancestry had come from.

"We have Scots, Irish, German, and maybe some Natives, and my father's father came from Cuba."

Then he asked: "Are you married?"

"No wife or partner would have allowed me to do this mad trek."

He laughed and said: "I kinda guess they would have."

He was curious about the route I was to take. I wanted to give him a rough idea, but I needed help connecting to the internet. He said he would try and manage to connect my tablet.

"How did you do that?"

"Ah, but you have to know how to."

I showed him the map of a provisional route, a straight line from West to East. Initially, I intended to go trekking through Tennessee, but not Kentucky.

He said: "If you ever change your mind, you are welcome to stay at my home."

I thanked him and said it was unlikely I would head his way. He did it out of courtesy, and I understood that. He would have welcomed me even if I thought of turning up at his doorstep. We didn't exchange phone numbers, but I mentioned my blog if he wished to follow it and gave him the address. He said he would.

Approaching the metropolis of Phoenix for the first time, I felt as apprehensive as entering any big city at night. As the bus drove at speed, the neon and streetlights dazzled and played on the discomfort of its strangeness. As travellers, we search for the familiar, cosiness that would invite our isolation, our strangeness to its heart. But found only what would appear in the night as a series of block units that walled the city as though it were a Gothic conglomeration in a post-modern world. No one was walking, no thoroughfares or hubbub as other cities would have revealed. Just intermittent blocks or lined walls with low buildings, some light from the inside, some with outside security lights. The streets were as wide as aeroplane runways. The structures were low in stature except for a group of tower blocks far away. The artificial lights clung to the ground in the dark distance as though the city stretched to the end of the earth, only to fall off its edge. Everyone on the bus stayed silent, mesmerised by the city's glitter as an animal would freeze by a car's headlights at night. As the bus turned into the terminal, Josh shook my hand.

He said: "It's been a good journey. The ride wasn't boring. I've some way to go and must change buses. I'll not be home for another twenty-four hours."

For a fleeting moment, I could feel the tiredness he would have to go through before getting to his destination. But he was up for it. The return home had created excitement in him, meeting his family and friends he hadn't seen for over two-and-a-half years. To reconnect again with his homeland, where everything returns to familiarity. As if the time he spent away from home was his rite of passage. He had lived in different surroundings and felt the displacement. He had adjusted to the rhythm of being an Outlander, where life must have seemed American and yet foreign. He mentioned "Southern hospitality" on several occasions. And it is this sense of cordiality that went missing for him during his stay in California. He was forced to seek employment from afar, only to return equipped with the knowledge that he knew the grass was greener in Kentucky.

During the bus journey, I felt physically restricted and redundant. I couldn't wait to get back on the road again. Rupa and Craig were waiting inside the terminal, and their welcome came as a relief.

Chapter 3: Time in Phoenix

Settling in Phoenix was easy due to Rupa's generous nature. The whole family welcomed me like a brother and gave me a key to the house. I felt so grateful for this when I needed it most. It was my great luck to have the company of good people – Rupa, Craig, Tutu (17 years old), Nitu (13), and Jumana (10). She also has a son, Na'im, who was studying medicine in Bangladesh. The girls didn't have an ounce of teenage angst amongst them. They were studious, organised, and relaxed in the way they carried on in their daily practice. Both Rupa and Craig are dynamic people and professionals. They lead very busy lives, yet they appear unconcerned as they do their day-to-day duty. Rupa was petite with an affable face with hooded eyelids. We had met on a couple of occasions in London when she was in her late teens and again in her early twenties before she moved to the USA. The sincerity she had then seemed reinforced by her maturity. While Craig was calm, gentle, and looked like a man thinking deeply about a subject.

Rupa's girls. Left, Jumana, Tutu & Nitu

Even though the temperature could shoot up to 79° Fahrenheit during the day, the water remained cold in the swimming pool. The February mornings held the chill night air until past nine o'clock. It suited me to use the time to plan for the day while everyone got ready for work or school. I kept out of their routine. From the outset, preparing myself for the long journey ahead was important. Each day, I completed a task from the list of priorities I set forth. I also calculated the mileage I missed by taking the bus across the latter part of the desert. I assessed that I was short by two hundred and fifty miles and allowed myself two weeks to complete it. Rupa reassured me that I could stay for as long as I wished. In our location in Chandler, only two hundred yards down the road, there was a small shopping mall. My fluke continued as they had a bicycle shop with a maintenance section at the rear. I prioritised getting my trailer in tip-top condition with all the spare parts.

I met John Martin, who sported a well-kept beard. He ran the repair part of the shop. I explained my venture to him and why I needed to know about the trailer in case of mechanical difficulties. He took everything apart, reassembled them, and added an extra layer of solid rubber around the inner side of the tyres while I watched.

"You'll have no problems with Tumbleweed thorns after this."

He explained as he went along why he did it this way instead of that way and so on. After an hour with me, he asked, "Why are you making this trip?"

I gave him a picture of my aims and my reasons for doing them. Two other customers were waiting, but he took his time and was thorough. The two people became fascinated and listened to our conversation.

One client, a balding man, became interested in our talk and said, "I have heard of people walking the Californian west coast but never across America. You're going to need all the strength you can muster. You've got some tough country ahead of you."

"I haven't looked at what's ahead. I don't want to scare myself to death."

"In that case, I'd better keep quiet," said the man with a grin.

"Okay, now you've frightened me," I said.

Earlier at the counter, they informed me that John charges ten dollars for a simple service. So, I took out my wallet to pay him.

He said, "It's free."

"Please don't do that. It's your living."

"Let's call it my pitch to your venture. I wish I were on the road with you. For a long time, I dreamed of doing something like that. Now I am a family man."

He was polite, courteous, and efficient at his job, friendly to talk to, giving out great vibes that drifted into our conversation. The two bikers waiting behind me wished me luck; they said they felt inspired and might make their own journey.

Each day, I embarked on a routine to complete my daily tasks and set off on a twenty-mile walk. After the first couple of days, I completed thirty-two miles. Phoenix is big and sprawling. The city's design based on a grid system made it easy to follow and not get lost. It's just huge squares on the map, and each one was a square mile. Here in the USA, they are called blocks. So, if you walk six blocks, it means you've walked six miles in Phoenix. Regrettably, on the fourth day, I overdid it. I searched for a map shop, the biggest one in Phoenix. It was ten and a half miles from Rupa's house in Chandler. A return trip would be perfect training and reduce the mileage I calculated on doing. The walk turned out to be twenty-eight miles instead of twenty-one. My feet were aching when I reached home at eight in the evening. I had lost my way on the canal walk, which had taken me further away from my destination.

The shop was the largest I had ever seen. It did not cater to walkers. So far, they don't have cartographers in California and Arizona to provide maps for ramblers or long-distance trekkers. Nor did they have good maps for cyclists, except for a radius of a hundred miles around Phoenix.

When I questioned the man in the shop, he said, "The US is a big country," with a proud smile.

It was a lazy answer. I said, "Europe is a big place, too, and there are topographical or Ordnance survey maps for every corner of it."

He looked blank as if he hadn't heard what I said. He seemed like a man who only understood his immediate functions and nothing beyond that. I spent the next two days working on a route from Phoenix to Albuquerque. Google was not wholly trustworthy and didn't entirely match my general Atlas. I was wary of negotiating several mountains en route and was looking to bypass as many as possible.

The daily walk was more than just to make up for the lost mileage. It was a way of getting to know Phoenix block by block, preparing well for the journey ahead, and waiting for my friend. Manzu is Rupa's brother and a good friend who lives in England. He had promised that he would join me for a week's walk. We planned to visit the Grand Canyon.

The walks around Phoenix were exhilarating, for it was a garden in the desert. Everywhere, these gardens were well organised and presented. It incorporated the local vegetation into a 'harsh' landscape. The Cactus, Palms, Palo Verde, Acacias, Olives, Oranges, Lemons, and Jacaranda emerged from the brownstone gravel. The stone gravel is brushed and groomed similarly to the classical Japanese garden. The visual effect was that of order and cleanliness. In contrast, the green density in the dry landscape was like the sprouting of hundreds of little lush patches. It was surprising to see the amount of birdlife, especially sparrows, which were in decline in London.

Phoenix was not designed for a person to get from A to B by walking. All amenities were far from one another. There were no corner shops, a local greengrocer, newsagents, or a fish and chip shop. It was so unlike Europe, where a stroll in any city or town, a corner shop could be found. Here a car is necessary. I got looks walking along the pavements because it was simply not done. I encountered three people on the road, two jogging, and one hooded teenager walking. The city is flat with low-lying buildings except for a cluster near Downtown. Almost all the houses had swimming pools.

At night, I dreamed of being a ghost in the Phoenix Gardens, returning as a reincarnated Apache and speaking their language. I later learned that the name Apache was from the Zuni language (another Indian tribe), meaning "our enemies." It's strange that they got stuck with it. Yet they call themselves Ndee or Inday or Dine'é, meaning "The People."

The next morning, I woke up with a sore throat and felt feverish. No doubt the twenty-eight miles and arriving in the evening chill the day before had contributed to it.

Rupa commented, "It's just as well you are in the house. You'd have shivered in your tent in the mountains without pain relief."

For two days I couldn't do my usual walk. The fever came and went, and just when I thought it had gone, it took hold again. It reminded me of the fever I used to have as a child when everything tasted bitter in my mouth. Orange juice was the only food that seemed palatable. My grandmother would come in and say: "Ill again, I see; it serves you right for playing in the sun."

Perhaps it was sunstroke that made me ill. Often, it brought on hallucinations. Being unwell reminded me of those sunny days, as in

Phoenix, from morning till dusk. There is no chance of my vitamin D going down. It made such a difference to my mood waking up with the sun daily. My 'spirit' would be uplifted, and I would walk with a jovial smile. Later that morning, still in bed with a pen and paper, I retraced the dream or hallucination about this ghost in the gardens of Phoenix. It unfolded like this –

Geronimo's ghost

In dreams sleep-walking

The cold morning air

Refreshes my aching limbs

With the rising sun

Falling as warm shadow

Walking on Natas Boulevard

In the sound of silence

Except for the humming drone

Of robots on four wheels

With faceless figures

Behind tinted windows

Stiff as dressed manikins

One robot after another

Images of packages

On conveyor belts

Controlled by other robots

With red helmets

Walking with no sound

Of children playing

Or birds squawking

For there were no echoes

The carrion hover

As once did the Phoenix

High above the green desert

No tumbleweed

The wind no longer rustles the leaves

As the heat rises

The branches droop with exhaustion

The trees release their fruits

lessening their load

In the far distance

A man sweeping the pathways

And the gardens of the Boulevard

I asked him, "Where is everybody?"

He shrugged his shoulders

I noticed he was not cleaning the sidewalk

Or the Boulevard gardens

But raking the granite gravel

Into perfect ornamental winding contours

I asked him, "Why are you doing that?"

"To stop snakes climbing the apple trees."

There aren't any apple trees.

"Oranges, lemons, apples

What is the difference?

The fruits tempt them."

I asked him who the man was

They named the Boulevard after

"Natas was a rich man

He spent time in the Inns of Spirits.

Loved by all

Learned, a match for everyone

He allowed his intelligence

Usurped by his cleverness."

A fruit fell on my back

I bent down to pick it up

Turned around again

The Boulevard gardener was gone

I couldn't see where he had disappeared

The sun became hot

The flowers of the Lantana

Stared at me with bright, colourful eyes

As I walked among many

Casting shadows of the fan palms

It occurred to me that I had no shadow.

Only a pale penumbra.

***

Feeling unwell in a place of comfort anchors you somewhat. Lost in thought, impressions raced in and out like a mirage. Trekking out and about never ceases to surprise me. Every day is new, different, and full of wonder. Walking is a spur to get up at the last dark before dawn. To be awake in the freshness of the morning. Seeing the fragmented sky above as the sun emerges and sets the heavens on fire with a burnt orange-red texture as it gives birth to daybreak. The feeling that it is "great to be alive" comes to the fore. In the act of walking, something new emerges, that invigorating feeling and encounters made. You feel fitter and healthier, as if you have been given wings. You float as you trek mile after mile. You also find a release for all the mishmash of a lifetime, the accumulated debris of unimportant things. You are in stride and at ease with yourself and with others.

Being out after sunup sets you through a cleansing process. The fresh air filters through your hair and massages your scalp. Your ears ring with the chorus sounds of early birds. With each step, the stiffness of your body evaporates. The rhythm and pace of every stride bring on a swagger and fine-tune the flow of energy. This flow of energy triggers endorphins and makes you happy. And when you are happy, you feel as if you could walk on this earth forever and feel connected to everything around you. We are linked to all things; somehow, we've been made to feel disconnected. You walk with a smile, and sometimes you catch yourself laughing. You laugh because you've found yourself in a state of enchantment. Your good humour becomes infectious, and people want to relate to you. As you walk, you learn to look not at your latest device but at the beauty in the details of our breathtaking planet.

"I hadn't the faintest idea that walking long distances wouldn't tire me. The opposite is true. I feel fitter after just three days," a friend wrote after a ten-day trek in Italy. Another friend said after the Camino, "My life has changed. What was important before is no longer important." She gave up her job as a solicitor. Perhaps it isn't a fluke that trekking takes you into an altered state, into a time out of time. When you go on a walkabout, it isn't only a physical uplift you feel but something inside that stirs. A current, unfelt before, happens with solitude. With acute self-awareness, you tap into your instinct, which balances your thoughts, and you feel personal growth emerging. Slowly, there is a new prism that transforms the way you see everything and your place in it. You have been instilled with a drug and can never return to how you were. You begin to realise and understand that you are part of what is around you and feel the longing to disturb the dust of the great outdoors forever. The openness of space seems as essential as food or water and shelter to the part of us that is 'spiritual.'

After the Camino, I found what I wanted to do: walk the earth and get out of a life of routine for fear of being redundant. I wanted to stay fit and not resign myself to being lethargic with the increasing years. The thought of an adventure around the planet at a snail's pace grew inside me. To stay out of the 'limelight' and the hyped-up frenzy of what life should be, away from living in a cocoon of existence and doing only what is expected of us.

Outdoor life is not entirely free. I may be deluding myself, or absolute freedom is not attainable. The space to meet my day-to-day challenges is there – walking through extreme heat, cold, and rain, bitten by bugs, chased by mad dogs, illness even; that of the unknown and the unexpected. They are challenging at times. Being on the road is a journey of immense discovery. It is as near as anyone can get to be unassailable. It would have been good to travel with a companion. The human instinct is to opt for a shared experience, but life could be more complex as conflict and irritation are always possible. Things being what they are, you do the best you can.

Adventures are very enticing. I've all too often wandered into the dreamland of my imagination to paint a picture of wonder. I toyed with being in that other place, intended it, but did nothing about it. This idea of travelling on that fantasy road has occurred to us all. Our secret conversation with ourselves felt trapped between belief and doubt in the ability to take on a challenge. To then do anything at variance or monumental alone. Having been taken in by seduction, the hunger for true adventure remains unfulfilled. Our desire spins as though on the edge of a coin. It could fall into the reality of fantasy, where everything is simpler and makes more sense. Or into the unknown, which may or may not undermine our perception of who we are. Ultimately, how the coin falls will depend on our faith, intuition, and volition. Then, one day, I woke up and turned my fantasy into a reality.

***

Rupa and Craig suggested going to the South Mountain on a Saturday. The climb was steep, and I hadn't entirely gained full fitness. The view was rugged and magnificent, with many plants I did not know. I knew the Saguaro cactus, most prominent near Tucson, AZ, but the mountains were lit here with them. Although the cactus has long, sharp, downwards-facing, prickly thorns, this does not deter birds from burrowing their trunk to create nests. Hundreds, if not thousands, use this method on the Saguaros.

Rupa, Craig, my hosts here on the South Mountain, Pheonix, AZ

Craig said, "The Gila woodpecker and the white wing dove were two of the birds hard at work," pointing his finger at them to show me.

He explained their survival strategy of mutual dependency or dispersive mutualism.

"The cacti provide a home and food, and the birds disperse the seeds and fertilise them in different places. It's a safe place to nest away from predators such as snakes. As you can see, they can burrow between the channels of thorns high up."

The Palo Verde grew everywhere in Arizona, a tree where even the trunk was green. Craig pointed out a shrub I saw along the trek but could not put a name to, "It's the Chuparosa. Isn't it beautiful?" The orange/red tint of the shrub blended with the rocky desert landscape. There were also petroglyphs on the rocks left by an ancient Indian tribe a thousand years ago, "numbering half a million at one time," said Craig.

The morning grew hotter than the usual climate for that time of the year, 82° Fahrenheit (F), whereas the maximum was usually 72° F. It was oppressive even when we went higher up the mountain, hoping for a little breeze. Further up, we could see the basin in which Phoenix metropolis sat, as though it was once a great lake enclosed by the surrounding mountains.

Driving on the long straight road high up on a ridge - once, passing by the Kalahari Desert in Botswana - reminded me of a similar landscape. The desert, flat, semi-fertile with sandy soil, and animals suggested it was once a vast lake but now drained off for some mysterious reason. Heading back to base, Craig said, "The South Mountain area is one of the biggest parks in the world."

Somehow, we all anticipated it would be an adventurous weekend. On Sunday, after lunch, Craig drove us to Sedona. The girls (Tutu, Nitu, and Jumana) came with us this time.

Jumana said, "The last time we travelled on this road, we went to Prescott to see our friends."

Rupa once mentioned that she lived in the town during a time of upheaval.

"We used to live in Prescott, where my husband ran his renal clinic. We settled well and made good friends. Then, unexpectedly, he died, and I was left with four young children. I had the support of friends to help me get through the spell after his death. It was the most difficult period of my life. I was in a state of shock. I don't know how I pulled through."

"How old were the children?"

"They were under ten; I put the grieving aside and got on with our lives. I sold our assets and moved to Phoenix. It wasn't as if you were selling a business with stocks and the potential of a market, just bricks and mortar, and some medical equipment."

"What made you move to Phoenix since you knew people in Prescott?"

"I had close friends in the city. I needed people around me for support and as a family. Also, thinking ahead made it easier for me to find work. My background is in business and finance. But after a while, I started a business in real estate, and it slowly paid off. I was able to stand on my own two feet. The children and the business kept me busy. I had no time to think about depression."

"It must have been a difficult time. How did you cope with the grieving?"

"I don't know how I managed it. I am sure I must have looked distraught. Once I tucked the children into bed at night, I cried myself to sleep. I felt exhausted at the end of each day, so sleep came quickly, thank God. It takes a while to discover who you are, being on your own as a single parent."

"You mean rediscovering your individuality?"

"Well, yes, I rediscovered myself and learned to be a mother, father, and teacher to the children. Somehow, I found the strength, and one day; it seemed like years, I woke up and realised something had changed; this new person emerged."

"So, you've managed to put the past behind you?"

"I can't forget; the memory will never die, but I sense a wellness."

It was a two-hour journey up north, about one hundred miles. The views changed as we journeyed higher up, and it became cooler, around 68° Fahrenheit. There was more grassland, and the local pines, Pinyon, Arizona Cypress, and Ponderosa, dominated the landscape. Gradually, the backdrop changed again to a red earth tincture. Sedona is a small town of about ten thousand people, although it is estimated to receive an average of three million tourists annually. The architecture is all low geometric buildings that are exquisitely built. The colours blend in, and the plants hide many of the buildings' contours as though dressing them.

The town caters to tourists who come to this part of the country for spiritual healing purposes. There are many places to eat in town, and snakes are on the menu too. Whatever animal that can hurt man, man can devour. The mountains which surround this town are fabulous, red, and made up of sandstone. The elements have sculpted them and transformed them into monumental 'castles.' Each stand-alone, side by side, is unique in its form. Many paths are marked out for trekking, with the distance varying from two to fifteen miles. The trek is like a meditation ground. It places the visitor in a mood of repose. This red semi-desert landscape with its hypnotic mountains puts passersby into an alternate mindset. People talk of their ethereal affiliation with being in this place. The spiritual association would create huge interest for those searching for intangible healing.

This journey has taught me how to stay grounded on this earth, on this planet. Through exertion with my feet firmly aground, the energy emanates from beneath my feet and wraps me with its swirling turbulence. The more energy my body took in, the more garbage it threw out. The garbage gained through conditioning by culture and community, claptrap ideas, food, and pollution all swallowed over a lifetime. It's what walking the long haul does when alone in the desert. The Sedona panorama, packaged well, makes it a special site. It would be easy to feel the benefit of doing a relaxed walk of, say, seven miles, sitting in a nice, secluded spot around these elevations, and having a picnic. The body and the mind are revitalised by sheer beauty and tranquillity. Being sedated and euphoric simultaneously would amount to being on morphine by the body's induced chemicals.

It is an experience I have often had. Certain places can suck you in and hold on to you, so the normal state becomes altered. It happened once in Kashmir, India, voyaging on a bus on the edge of a gorge. It wouldn't have mattered if the bus had gone over the cliff's edge. In my state of equanimity, I almost wanted it to happen.

A place like Sedona can take anyone into a trance-like state. There may be a willingness to be seduced by the beauty of this area. Perhaps the psyche gets affected by its wonder and quietude. Kashmir was like that. The first men on the moon must have entered a similar emotional vortex when they touched down. Certain human circumstances may be profound, and the magic of it lies in this magnetic earth and its impact on our mental state. In those moments, these morsels of exalted experience emerge. It is sad when people who go through such experiences narrow their field of vision and place the occurrence into the laps of some extra-terrestrial order. Humans are capable as conscious animals of reaching an incredible depth of feelings as the 'gods' would have us believe in their myths. That we may never be at home within ourselves does not mean we should look outside of ourselves. Conceivably, that is how it should be, not feeling wholly at home, leading to deeper understanding. Because if we observe life around us more closely, then we should see that nothing ever fits into this world. Everything and everyone are interdependent yet collide with something or one another. That is the way of the elements and our existence. We exist in a perpetual state of flux.

***

In Phoenix, it is with churches as with pubs in London. To see so many churches at every turn and corner is astounding. It is as though they are there in enormous numbers to ward off deep fears that have arisen to infest the city. From our fears and teachings, we look out of ourselves and reach for the sky. We yearn for this other place, always pointing beyond ourselves and our existence. Almost everyone I spoke to has the desire to live in two universes—one of the Earth and the other in the dreams of the afterlife. We should investigate the cosmic solitude in our deep interior to experience something true of ourselves, our essence. There indeed lies our kingdom, in our trepidation, among the unknowing and the silence. Our obsessive search for the 'man/spirit' in the sky seems a delusional appendix, an un-evolved part of our psyche. Fear is the most significant boundary we must cross. Beyond that lies the true 'god' we've been looking for, the universe from within.

The daily walks were quite stimulating towards the end of my stay in Phoenix. And I got to learn about the different plants that adorn the streets. In the median, oleanders in bloom separate the opposite lanes of traffic. The dense foliage of trees and shrubs lined both sides of the road. Sandwiched between those plants are the sidewalks. The trees vary from eucalyptus to olive, orange, and lemon, willows, pines, acacia, Palo Verde, palms, and other trees unknown to me. Desert shrubs intermingled with a variety of flowers. There were many species of cacti, some wild rosemary and bougainvillaea in red, white, orange, damson, and mauve. Walking in the city is like strolling in an immaculate, unending garden, a little paradise in the Arizona desert.

Arizona desert

There is traffic, but it's not heavy or constant. I never felt congested with fumes or anything of the sort. There is a long canal; walking along its bank was often a pleasant experience. Many types of fish swam close to the surface. On one occasion, I asked someone fishing what type he was trying to catch.

He said, "I caught a big catfish this morning and a twenty-seven-pound carp."

The water has other kinds of fish stock, such as chub and tilapia. Golf courses, parks, and sports venues flank both sides of the banks. Nearer to the subsidiary outlet, approaching Chandler, there is a large water plant to supply the metropolis. Thirty meters wide, the canal cuts right through the heart of the city. As I walked, I received looks and friendly remarks from people. A slim, fit, grey-haired man speeding five miles an hour in his sleeveless t-shirt is a strange sight in these parts. I got a fantastic smile from a young woman parked at the stoplight two days earlier. I smiled back and waved at her, and did a little swagger. She shook her head from side to side, laughed, and waved back. I held her gaze, and my pace did not slow. It is these little incidents that add to my momentum. Within two days, the plan was to leave Phoenix and enter the high Apache country.

It rained the night before after months without a drop. As I was doing my last stretch of the walk, I noticed how green, fresh, and healthy all the trees were along the roads. Their branches expanded, pointing upward. They looked like they were about to take off like a glider, reaching the sky yet solid in the ground. I tried to find an image to fit this ready for the take-off they projected, but I was not inspired. They reminded me of the floppy ears of a hound dog lying down, feeling bored, suddenly alert, with ears pricked up. After the rain had fallen, an absurd idea came to mind: the dog-eared effect on plants. Dogwood?

My time in Phoenix with Rupa's family ended, and being with them had been a pleasure. On the eve of my departure, Rupa and Craig said, "We would like you to celebrate with us. We want you to be the first to know we've decided to get married in July."

I didn't know where I would be, possibly on the east coast. It was too far in the distance to make any projection. "I'll do my best to make the event happy."

Craig and Rupa met on an extra-curricular course and had slowly become close.

"We found we had a lot in common, and our temperament suited each other," Rupa said.

It took nearly a decade for her to be healed and be with someone who would give her happiness.

"I think if you stay optimistic despite hardship, the results are almost all at once delightful."

They were lovely people who accepted me as part of the family. They chaperoned me to places; we ate and laughed together. They invited me to restaurants for treats, and the girls introduced me to Bollywood musical movies. I was grateful for their hospitality and kindness. Our meeting was cordial and too brief; there is always sadness in parting. Rupa dropped me outside the city. I looked away, wiping the back of my hand across my face.

"Save those; you must keep as much liquid as possible. It's going to be a hot day," she said.

It was her telling me there would be time for reflection. I had become attached quickly to everyone. She invited her friends, such as Nasim Amanatullah, Lubna, and others, to meet me. They had put me at ease as though I had been a long-lost brother. They followed my blog and wrote encouraging remarks whenever I was in difficulty.

I watched as her car drove off opposite my trail. Suddenly, I was all on my own again. I wanted to feel all the momentum behind me and hoped what lay ahead would be wonderful and full of surprises. A pulse of adrenaline kicked in.

Much later, Nasim remarked, "Keep your head high; the finish line is down the horizon. Enjoy nature at your core. Your bravery leaves me in awe." And Rupa wrote, "We all miss you here in Phoenix since you left… we often talk about you and wonder how you are on the road. You are an inspiration to us all."

Chapter 4: Towards Payson (In the Rockies)

Despite the adrenaline, I felt tired even before my trailer wheels turned. The last few days have been frustrating, hours spent on the computer figuring out a route to Santa Fe, New Mexico. Google was the only solution because there wasn't an adequate map to cover a state for walkers. A Global Positioning System (GPS) was no good as it would not have given details to shortcuts for trekkers. For obvious reasons, walkers weren't allowed on Highways (as on Motorways in Europe). The state of Arizona provides no alternative route for Ramblers. Google is good for cars but not for people on foot. Occasionally, it has led me to dirt tracks in the outback in the desert, with crossroads pointing in five directions.

The general atlas is okay for guidance, but the distances are enormous even though they look small on the map. A scale of a detour could add an extra hundred and fifty miles. Other essential factors to consider were, for instance, the distance between food/water supplies. What could I carry at any time; how many mountains were ahead, and how high were they? All these were considerations that needed working out. In such moments, an Indian Scout would have come in handy. I telephoned the Highway Patrol in Holbrook, AZ, a town on my route plan, and spoke to an officer.

She said, "Come up and see me on your way. We will talk about your problem of using the Highway."

She gave me a sixty-percent chance when I pressed her for a figure. It was better than an even chance, but it still left me apprehensive about what would come. What if they refused once I got to Holbrook?

Perhaps I should have taken a day's complete rest before leaving. The thought hadn't occurred to me. The final day's walk to make up the lost mileage was only twelve hours before, exactly a month since I began my trek. I had done three hundred and fifty-seven miles since, not a steady average. The sunstroke had put me out of action for a few days. There was time for reflection and planning, though, as my wheels turned on the hard shoulder on Route 87. My steps gathered pace; a sense of anxiety surfaced. Yet I felt excited knowing I was in the middle of an experience. An adventure of a lifetime. Before me lay the Navajo and Apache country. I was sure there would be encounters with these First Nation people.

It was difficult from the start. My trailer was heavier than usual. The three gallons of water, the food, and all the other equipment in my bag weighed 110 lbs. I had intended to keep my total to less than 80 lbs., but that was impossible. I needed provisions for five days as there was no food store or anything between Phoenix and Payson.

I started late, well after ten, as so many things needed my attention. It was colder than normal. The morning chill warmed up by eleven; the sun was hot and making it sweaty. The road was steep and elevated as the miles got left behind. The whole day was just one big climb. My fitness level was at a peak. Yet I was puffing and had to deflect away negative thoughts.

Fourteen miles of non-stop climbing, the time was past five in the afternoon. I found a spot in the middle of those Saguaro cacti beside a leafy shrub a good distance from the road. It had been a desert country since leaving Phoenix. In my sheer ignorance, I didn't know what the Rockies meant.

The day's tally, though, was less than my planned mileage. The Atlas gave me no trace of the rising landscape. On Google, the zoomed-in roads looked flat on the screen, with only a few low mountains in the far distance.

The flat area at the back of the bush needed a clearing of pebbles and rocks for a space for my tent. Grasshoppers and crickets kept on jumping on me. The rain had turned the desert green. In just three days since the downpour, the desert looked luscious. So quickly, it transformed the land as if the earth had acquired a new layer of skin. It made it vibrant, healthier, and dense with foliage. It bloomed with spring flowers, yellow, some red, and purple too, their names unknown. There was recognition in a couple, only six inches tall. One, dwarf lupines in lilac, and the other, hollyhocks in vivid bright orange.

By six-thirty, twilight was approaching, and gunshots echoed from afar with intermittent rapid firing. I figured it must have been clay pigeon shooting practice. No villages were depicted on the map, and doubt came over me. In my diary, I wrote, "Jackrabbit getting shot, I hope the stray bullets don't pierce my tent." After a while, the gunfire stopped, and darkness and the crickets' chorus sent me into a haze. I heard barking and howling, not dogs but wild and similar. The temperature cooled; wrapped up in my thermals, sleep came undisturbed.

The birds woke me, and the sun shone through the gap at the bottom of the tent's flysheet. Waking up among the cacti was an exhilarating experience for a city dweller. The scenery was overwhelming. These saguaros have taken over the desert and mountains. They stand tall like totems or sculptured statues erected like giant phalli and prickly. Others have four or five arms resembling a huge hand planted in the ground with the middle finger pointing to the sky. Craig mentioned that these cacti were fertilised by cross-pollination. They produce sweet nectar, which lays at the base of the tube of the flowers. They attract birds and insects that pollinate the flowers while feeding. I thought how magnificent it was to have breakfast at the best café, looking at one of the most glorious views in the world. I discovered that coconut water was delicious with my oats. But this new type of concealed corn syrup was in the small print. Despite the label saying no added sugar or sweetener, just natural. No wonder my energy levels kept yo-yo-ing.

I took my time to decamp and was on the way by nine. The going was tough, mountain after mountain with no respite. The sun was hot, and I drank more than my water quota. Sometime later, a man and an elderly woman stopped their car on the hard shoulder and were waiting for me out of curiosity. He introduced himself as Travis Stanton and his mother as May.

We talked, and he asked me why I was walking. I put him into the picture, and all he could say was, "Awesome, awesome."

He said he was a photographer and then asked: "Can I do a video of you? I have got a copter camera that'll do the trick."

I have never seen one in live-action before; he took it out of his car boot. He said, "We'll do a little rehearsal. Go back fifty yards with your trailer and slowly come towards me."

I did as he asked and then action 'take one.' The camera was attached to a four-propeller frame and managed by remote control. It hovered and flew and did whatever he wanted it to do with precision. It was an incredible piece of technology and silent, too. We were standing near a mini gorge with those Saguaros carpeting the backdrop to the hills a distance away. He sent the copter-camera way up into the gorge and kept it still without movement like a hummingbird. Then, he asked me to walk towards him, pushing my trailer as he tilted the camera angle to suit my pace. We did it twice to make sure he captured everything. He then had the camera hovering above us motionless about five feet away. We had an interview as to why I was crossing America on foot. I gave him my email address, and he said he would send me the recording. We hugged goodbye, and I offered him one of my cards.

His mother, May, wanted to shake my hand and said, "May Jesus be with you."

While on my way, I was glad he had come along. The thirty minutes we chatted was the first time in a day and a half since I opened my mouth to utter a sentence. I felt the need to be in contact with another person. My jaw ached from not speaking.

A big mountain lay ahead a mile later, and the road headed straight into the clouds. I sat, ate, drank as much as possible, and went up. I was dripping with sweat, and every step pushing my trailer was like pushing a broken-down car uphill. Three hours passed, and I was at the top. The road veered into a sudden contour only to lead into another upper tier. It was at this point that it occurred that I was in a series of Rocky Mountains. How could I not have detected that on the map or Google? How much of it was there? I was walking into the unknown.

A quarter of a mile later, I noticed that it could have been a giant meteorite that created this part of the mountain range. The 'crater' was maybe three miles in diameter. The ripple effect of the impact of the explosion formed waves of mountains and hills surrounding the area I had climbed all day. Going downhill into the depression brought relief after two days of ascending.

Then this 'Ape' in my head, the discouraging voice that always talks back at you, said, "if you go down, you know you have to go back up again."

I descended with a deflated mood; my pedometer read thirteen miles for the day. Later, I reached a point on the mountaintop where I couldn't go one step more. By sheer good fortune, I arrived at a small, flat, grassy area hidden behind some shrubs on the other side of the route. I pitched up my tent in the secluded spot under a white sycamore. I wiped myself with a 'cold' wet sponge and felt refreshed. Chance had saved me, but that luck would run out in the morning.

I slept for twelve hours. I woke up exhausted. It felt like I hadn't had any rest at all. It was demoralising to face a mountain at first sight. I was on the road at 8 a.m. I hadn't stopped climbing since Phoenix. My mind and body were spent, yet I had days ahead. After a mere part of a mile, I understood there would be no let-up. Every fifty metres, I took a break. It went on like that for five miles. I hoped a flat stretch would be around the corner each time there was a bend. But there were none. It was just another climb. When tired, the negative play mischief. I fought against that almost every hundred metres and slapped my face many times. I took my flagpole, a metal rod, and hit my thighs hard until it hurt. I was angry and needed to shake out the gloomy thoughts.

The 'Ape' in my head kept saying: "Give up; you've had it, pal."

In times like this, it's so painful to be alone. I needed a companion, and it's one of the vipers of tiredness that comes to bite. Only then does the realisation come of how comforting, safe, and protected it is at home. It was not a cry of homesickness but a need for occasional relief.

My phone rang, and I thought it was Dorothy or Yvonne, wondering about my whereabouts since I had contacted no one. It was Mijo from

France, and when I explained my state of exhaustion to her, seeking comfort, she became mean and unsympathetic.

"You wanted to do this trek, didn't you?" raising her voice down the phone and in a moment of utter weakness, I broke down, and my voice cracked, and she put the 'boot in': "Why don't you give up if you are so tired? Tu es têtu. You deserve everything you are feeling."

While she continued to shout down the phone, a sense of lightness entered me, and my grief for missing her no longer weighed down on me as it had done.

I said: "Thank you, Mijo, you've been a great help," and hung up.

It was on the Camino that I met her, three years since. She had a sweet face with large, sad, light brown eyes and brown hair. She sashayed along in her movement, and her voice attracted me. It seemed effortless; we were drawn to each other. I was her cure. Her marriage had broken down after her husband admitted to numerous affairs. She was distraught and remained disoriented for over a year after her divorce. Her sister Marie-France had suggested the Camino.

We met intermittently throughout the trek and became closer as the journey ended. A month after the Camino, we were to meet at her place in St. Nazaire, west of France. But she broke her leg on a randonnée after returning to France and had metal plates and screws inserted at the base of her shin. I flew over, and her friend Nicole met me at the airport. She was out of the hospital in a wheelchair with one leg up in the air. She looked gloriously beautiful. A tsunami of love engulfed us. I became her healer. We were inseparable. I stayed for a month and cared for her – cleaned and cooked. We shopped together and went a mere stroll away on the promenade by the seafront. She loved being pushed along as I bent over and kissed her neck from behind.

I would fly over from London for three weeks a month. I did this for a year. (I was able to do this, as I have said, for great luck was on my side. I was made redundant as a laser engineer, and a compensation package was offered. I decided to invest the whole sum, which was considerable, and within three months, I quadrupled my investment. This good fortune, plus my pension and some savings, gave me the space and security to have a moderately adventurous life.) Then her leg healed, and she walked as before; we would go on long walks in the west part of France in the Loire Valley to places such as La Baule, Le Croisic, and Pornic, and I showed her London in return.

She used to say, "I love the way you speak French; it is so cute." A couple of years later, she found faults in how I spoke and dressed and my bushy, long hairstyle. She once said, "You look like a clochard - a down and out."

On our third year together, on the day of my mother's death, who had been ill for some time, she rang and said the relationship was over. It was unexpected. A shock travelled through me. A feeling of strangeness overwhelmed me. I put the phone down. My flat became claustrophobic, and breathlessness gripped me. I became depressed but put aside everything until after my mother's funeral. Later, the rawness of it all surfaced. I was a child again, innocent, lost, wounded as though my skin had been ripped off and my insides exposed, gutted. I hated the image in the mirror every morning. I knew an easy way out of my depression. I needed to grab it, but I needed a goal. Walking to exhaustion was the key. Striding around the planet was an old ambition; the twenty-five thousand miles of it.

Her bitter outpouring stayed with me, tapping into its emotion. The difficulties of the climb shifted into the unconscious. For the first time, I saw that I hadn't been important to her, perhaps for a while. I kept up hope despite the months of separation and was willing to give her the space she had asked for. My intuition was right all along. Something had changed; she had begun to pick fault in me.

There was fickleness about the whole thing, maybe even dishonesty. You either trust someone, or what was the point? If there were betrayal, then I would be blind to it. We were open in the beginning, but something altered, and I sensed it nearing the time of my mother's death. Whatever was left of my feelings now dwindled with the morning mists in these mountains.

I lost count of the days of climbing. The day was cooler. I became dehydrated, and my urine turned bright yellow. I took some rehydration powder and kept my eyes open if it changed to red. If it did, I would have to pack up and go home. This vegan diet on the road was fine, but I got tired of chewing nuts.

A police patrol officer stopped me. He said: "Truck drivers have been phoning the station all morning, saying a crazy man is walking the mountains, pushing a trailer."

I said: "I haven't seen anyone?"

He smiled and said: "Wise guy, eh." Then he asked, "Are you all right?" showing concern.

"Tired and a little crazy; any flat roads ahead?"

I knew it was a stupid question to ask. He asked, "Where are you going, and how many miles are you going daily?"

"I'm going to Payson then Holbrook, maybe thirteen miles per day, if that."

"Well, you've some ways to go. It's up till you get to Holbrook. I reckon you've got three days more to get to Payson. And let's see, ten more after that to Holbrook. You think you can make it?"

I kept to my strategy and said, "I'll take a day at a time, officer, and see what happens."

"Have you got some warm clothes? It gets mighty cold up in these mountains. There might even be snow on the ground."

I hadn't counted on snow. I had some warm clothes but not a lot. It was considerate of the police patrol to keep a check on me. In an emergency, I might have to call on them.

The view changed the higher the climb, with the mountains full of pine forests. Looking at the high peaks, I shouted at the top of my voice, "I could do with a lift now." No one heard me.

Another day went by, and in the middle of the night, I had the urge to sprinkle the alpine garden. I checked my watch; it was just after one in the morning. The sky was littered with stars, so many and huge. We look at the sky with our human eye and are warped by its illusion. We say we've seen tens of thousands lighting the night, but our observation has no truth. It's only a perception. The human eye can only make out a little over four and a half thousand stars at any time. By chance, scanning the Milky Way to its beginning in the south-easterly direction, I caught sight of our nearest galaxy, Andromeda. I read it could only be seen in the Andes and New Zealand. Here in the Rockies, it looked like a giant Ferris wheel. On Earth, though, I listened to the night insects' symphony. The vocal sounds of crickets, frogs, and other nocturnal animals, as many as stars in the inky night.

Then, it was a new day, and I wanted the dawn fresh in my thoughts. And leave the tiredness behind even though there were other mountains to climb. It was cooler. Higher up, everything became more familiar with an alpine view and the thick forest. Though I felt weak, at least the cloud was low and dark. It motivated me to walk fast to keep warm. Despite the cold, within a short distance, I was puffing, and my forehead expelled droplets of perspiration. Then, it was one hundred metres at a time before I paused for a rest. Later, down to fifty, then up to five hundred, a thousand before I took a break. In no time, I was back down to fifty.

"It never ends. It will never end." The 'Ape' was back.

The trailer's load steadily decreased by eating and drinking my supplies, but the dead weight seemed heavier than ever. My energy dropped; I was walking on empty. My face looked scrawny in the tiny vanity mirror. I often wanted to stop, rest, and camp for a few days. The thought of overconsumption of water played on my mind. What if I ran out? I could wave someone down and ask them for some. But it is known here that vehicles are afraid to stop if anyone thumbs for a lift. They are frightened of being hurt or robbed. They would drive past as if you were invisible. This idea of dehydration kept me moving and gave me no respite. Maybe my body weight dropped to 135 pounds, tipping the scale in my boxing days when I was eighteen. Before starting this trek, I weighed 157 pounds.

How did all these people make it across uncharted terrains? Driving their caravans and horses with little water and low food rations, except for the wild animals they hunted. How did the Conquistadors make it one hundred years before the settlers moved in on the Indians? How did the Indians themselves come to adjust to this harsh terrain? Maybe the new arrivals used Indian scouts and trails, small dirt tracks. They must have been savvied to find water in these parts. Everything is a big undertaking. When looking up at the road, it looks endlessly high, but there's always a contour and another ascent, and then the road ahead looks almost gradual. Nevertheless, pushing the trailer is very arduous. Only when you look back, once you've stopped, does the elevation become clear. The huge cascading descent made me feel like a conqueror - King Kong at the top of the Empire State Building. Then, as I turned around again, I was back to being small. Insignificant as all humans, with another peak ahead.

Chapter 5: You ain't gon' believe this Shit.

(It's a Southern colloquial way of saying Once Upon a Time)

Being on the road is not simply being in the outer landscape. It places you in a constant meditative mood, with no one to contact except your inner self for long periods. It is only fleetingly as though in a dream, even when meeting people. On one occasion, something confounding and extraordinary happened. It's difficult to convey as recollections are so elusive. At that moment, I was conscious and in control of all my faculties, without a doubt.

I arrived at a point where I parked my trailer on a verge behind a shrub near a rock face with a concave depression. I needed a snack break. I reached into my food bag, and when I stood up, the incurved rock face had changed into a luminous cave. It now had a chiselled surface. The walls were untouched by organic matter, earth, or dirt. It wasn't smooth but chipped away like an unfinished piece of sculpture. The mica where the rock recently hacked glittered and returned strange richness. An unfathomable number of shades bounced off each other. As if the millions of rays reflected off angled positioned mirrors, spinning into geometric-like graphics. A small entrance became a long tunnel that drew me in. It radiated an incredible array of intense pinpoints of light, the colours shifting and constantly changing.

The urge to go in deeper overwhelmed me. There was a noise, like trampling on something, crackling like dry leaves and twigs underfoot. Perhaps not under my feet, but all around. Then, another sound resonated. An electromagnetic hum, like the end of a chant in a Buddhist monastery. The tailing off in the wind of a fading gong. I understood it as part of me, inside and out, inseparable.

At one point, the passageway opened into a huge chamber so big that I pinched myself hard. I bit my tongue to ensure it wasn't a dream or hallucination. It was painful. After, I no longer felt my body, for the chamber made me weightless. In this great hollow of calm, nothing frightened me. Instead, entranced by the array of these bright reflections, I tried to hold on to their pigment, but it seemed impossible. These shades were unknown, like nothing I had ever seen. They came in waves at every angle. I wasn't sure whether the myriad tincture was moving, the great cave itself, or even me. Maybe it all happened at the same time.

These images appeared with abstract faces like conceptual paintings, distorted and Picasso-esque, except they were as real as me. They dressed in flamboyant "gowns," and the fittings seemed part of them like flapping skins, hermaphrodite in appearance. They looked harmless and inviting, saying: "Are we going to dance?" They repeated the exact words over and over. It wasn't what they said at all. It was what I interpreted, for they spoke in a language I hesitate to say, "Extra-terrestrial." They used pronunciations unutterable to my ears. Made-up alphabets that sounded nonsensical but with enunciation and great sophistication, which I intuitively understood. They invited me to a platform and wanted me to ride a carousel. I sat down, and everything spun. They did something that resembled laughing. We stood on this graviton-like spinning surface, and I fell on my back. There was a void above as though we were trapped in a sublime vortex. The complexity became elongated and twisted, spiralling in a vertical corkscrew tunnel. I was being pulled into this swirling space.

My instinct was always to comprehend and understand my circumstances. But there I became this being without instinct, as though I was no longer a separate entity, just part of everything around me. My thought process didn't alter as it would be of a drug substance or alcohol. I remained conscious on an average level. While I lay crouching, these figures performed magic tricks, producing what appeared fruit-like. These strange fruits had their own lives, for they, too, could talk. One of these figures kept flashing at me. Each time I looked at it, it pretended to dance and returned to its original posture. I suspected it was being mischievous. When it lifted the thin veil of skin, instead of its sex, it was an animal in the guise of a mongoose-like creature that went in and out of a hole as a cuckoo clock.

When the graviton stopped, a magnetic pull drew me back into the tunnel in slow motion. These figures waved at me and, by my understanding, called out, "Come back again, come back again" until they were out of sight. I didn't want to leave. But suddenly, I was sucked out of the cave into the open. The sunlight was bright; I couldn't open my eyes. All the exhaustion I felt before the experience came back. I couldn't recall how long I was in the chamber, perhaps thirty minutes, an hour, or maybe just one minute. There was no concept of time.

I tried to trace back what I had eaten the night before that may have caused such an effect, but I had eaten nothing. I had purged myself and had nuts, raisins, and oats for breakfast, nothing unusual. I knew my body at that stage contained endorphins and BDNF (Brain-Derived Neurotrophic Factor), but beyond that, I lived in a state of bliss. I looked ahead, and the road seemed to be heading straight into the blue. I remained in shock for some time and pondered whether I was going insane. Perhaps being in silence these past few days was influencing me. I had seen articles that said silence can drive people insane. That was done under laboratory conditions in an anechoic chamber. I was engaged in a powerful and profoundly beguiling experience. As I began to walk, the effort faded away from my thoughts of insanity.

***

Sometimes, at a low point, things happen. That is how it was for me - a sign saying to drive in low gear for the next five miles. I thought I was having one of those days when unusual things occurred. I knew it was decent, but five miles of it. It took me an hour and ten minutes to do those miles, which showed how acute the descent was. I was practically running, an unbelievable sensation, holding on to the handlebar and leaning backwards to stop the trailer from careering out of control. For the second time in two days, when I was almost at the bottom, a police patrol officer pulled me over.

He said, "The police station took a lot of calls all morning. Truck drivers and people in cars phoned saying there is a madman with a cart on the highway."

He looked calm with light blue eyes and a smiling face with his helmet on. He towered over me.

"I haven't seen him, officer, and I have been on this road all day."

He stared at me, scanning up and down, then said, "A moose on the loose, eh."

Back in California, I was a dog, now a moose; if I managed to finish this journey, I would be named after every animal in Noah's Ark.

"You are the second officer called out to look for me in the last two days. Doesn't your office coordinate any messages?"

"We need to check every incident."

"Sorry officer, I didn't mean to…." Before I could finish –

"I went lookin' for you over an hour ago and couldn't find you."

"If I told you the truth, you wouldn't believe me."

"Try me," he said.

"Well, look, officer, I don't want you to take this the wrong way. This is going to sound strange. But some aliens abducted me."

He paused for a while, and I could feel what he was thinking with his mild, almost sarcastic smile, which said, 'He must have escaped from somewhere.'

Then he said, "I see; you're a real down-to-earth kinda guy. Where are you from?"

"London, England, officer."

"I knew it the minute I set eyes on you. You're all a bunch of comedians over there."

"Yes, officer, a lot of us are, especially that lot in our Parliament."

He didn't respond. Instead, he asked: "Where are you headin'?"

"Hopefully, to the Atlantic Ocean, officer."

He looked at me as though in deep thought again, swaying his head from side to side ever so slightly.

He said, "So you're the mad clown on the loose, right?"

"Does that mean I'm in trouble, officer?"

"Well, I can't arrest you for being on the road. I can't arrest you for having a screw loose, either. It's not a law in Arizona yet. But I must ask you to be careful."

"I appreciate that, officer."

"What's your next stop?"

"I plan to stop for a rest in Payson."

In a firm way: "Are you sure you are all right?"

"I'm fine with food and water, but the going is heavy."

"Well, you've been through most of the mountains if you came from Phoenix. Wrap up well at night; it gets cold in these parts. Just a few more peaks, and then it's flat into Payson. In two or three days, you should be in town."

He wanted to shake my hand. As we did so, he wished me good luck.

"You got a long way to go to the ocean. Be careful of these big trucks. They take the shoulder on the sharp curve."

He was right; I had a few near misses when those trucks blasted their horns, causing my heart to jump ten beats and force a fart. I envied him on his Kawasaki 1400cc black motorcycle. As he drove away, he was tall, 6'3", maybe, like a knight in black shining armour.

At the bottom of the descent was a resting place large enough to take a dozen cars. There was a dirt track with a stream running at the end and a forest of stunted pine on the other side of the brook. It was mid-afternoon. I met up with three elderly people touring in a camper. No one else was there. They initially felt a little suspicious of me, but they were polite.

Someone speaking in an unfamiliar accent and pushing a trailer in the middle of the Rockies must have seemed strange. There were two women and a man, possibly in their mid-seventies.

To be chatty, I asked: "Where have you been travelling from?"

There was no response, and the silence made everyone awkward. When I was just about to go, assessing perhaps I was intruding, a voice spoke.

"We came from Denver," said the more extrovert of the two women.

She had an appealing smile and grey eyes that were alert.

"That's a long way to come."

"We wanted to get away from the cold."

"Who does the driving?"

"I do," said the man with a grumpy old face as though he was suffering from a stomach upset or constipation.

"I drove some of the ways," said the Introvert with the long, thick grey hair.

"So, you did. I plumb forgot," said the man.

His face changed with slight embarrassment.

"He likes to take over the wheel," said the Introvert.

The old man chuckled.

"Are you on a grand tour?"

"We are heading' to Willow Springs Canyon. There's a lake there," said the Extrovert.

"I had no idea there would be a lake in these mountains. I didn't see it on the map."

"Oh yes, it's a fair size, due south," said the Extrovert.

"After a while, we might head south," said the old man.

"We haven't decided yet," said the Introvert sternly, looking at the old man.

"Are you all related, if you don't mind me asking?"

After an awkward, long pause, I felt my tiredness and this mountain air must have affected me to prompt such a question.

The Extrovert said, "Yes, this is my sister Arlene and her husband Bob. I'm Debbie."

"So, you do this every year in winter?"

"It beats sitting' in front of the TV watching a load of ads and crap," said Bob.

"We like to travel while we still can. Last year, we travelled to New Mexico", said Arlene, and she was searching for a place name.

Debbie butted in and said, "Los Ojos by the lake."

"How long will you be on the road for?"

Bob, looking at Arlene for reassurance, said, "We'll be heading' back for Easter, we reckon."

I saw that Debbie had a wedding ring on her finger. Her husband had probably died or was in a home. It seemed too private to ask. Her eyes still had a sparkle.

After a chat about my adventure, Bob said, "We need to get going. It'll be getting dark in a couple of hours."

In a short time, they left. I looked for a flat, concealed area to pitch my tent, walked to the stream, and had a wash. The water was ice-cold, but I braved it and felt cleansed for the first time in days. Not a soul in sight. At a glimpse, when I saw the road for the morning journey, it depressed me. I was racing into the next day once again. Going against my motto of a day at a time. That only now helped me relax, and in the tent, I wrote in my diary, "Today was a stupendous day."

Just then, the 'Ape' came back at me: "Did you see that hill waiting for you in the morning, all five miles of it?"

"Damn, go and climb a tree or something."

I woke up, and my clock said it was too early; dawn peeked through the air vent. I decamped anyway. I had never been so cold. My hands were frozen by the time my wheels rolled onto the tarmac. I leaned my right shoulder against the handlebar and pushed and puffed until I was at the top of the mound, what was surely a mountain. I made good headway, and the steep incline became gradual. Three hours later, I stopped for breakfast at a lay-by. In view were a huge descent and an enormous climb once more. By noon, I was done for the day. The lactic build-up rendered me legless, and Payson was still some distance away beyond other mountains. I needed to rest, and another lay-by was ahead. Suddenly, a car pulled up and entered the space I was about to park. A man came out of his car and said, "You were wavering. You look like you are struggling."

"Yes, I am. I think this is my sixth day climbing these mountains."

"Where are you heading'?"

"Towards the Atlantic Ocean."

"My, oh my, that's a long way. I'm afraid I can't take you there. I don't have enough gas. Back there, you looked like Moses crossing the desert."

"Well, I've been in these mountains a while but haven't had any proclamation yet."

"You ain't likely to get any, but you can have a lift to town."

"Are you offering me one?"

"I can if you want it."

But his car was small, a Mini Cooper 1.6. He was over six feet four inches; I had never caught on to why tall men like small cars. I understood the implication of small men in big cars, but big men liking small cars is still beyond me.

I said, "The trailer won't fit in."

"It might; let's give it a try. I'll collapse the back seats."

Once I had removed the wheels and lowered the handlebar, it went in easily with some room to spare. I needed that stroke of luck. It was roomy inside, and John didn't seem too tall for the car; I thought it was deceptive. He had introduced himself as John while we were loading up. Since he saw me as Moses, I called him John the Baptist. He had performed a miracle – saved me from my exhaustion. As we drove, it felt strange travelling at speed, and everything passed by so rapidly. I was aware of the grand vista but none of its details, and then they were quickly forgotten. Only the larger picture remained that we were going to a town in the middle of a large forest high in the mountains. Whilst loading, I mentioned that I had walked from Phoenix, and whilst driving, John talked.

He said, "I couldn't live in Phoenix. My mother lives there. It's not my type of place.

He gave no reason. "I prefer it here in this small town. I live alone, a simple life."

He was a diabetic; I said, "I am too."

That surprised him. He was sixty-five and wasn't doing well with his diabetes; although he tried to walk daily, his diet wasn't so good.

I said, "Try to be more disciplined, eat whole foods, and increase your daily walk. A little in the morning and some in the evening. A couple of hours after you've eaten is the best time."

"How long have you been a diabetic?" he asked.

"Just over ten years."

"Me twelve; how much medication do you take?"

"I've taken none these last three months. If I walk ten miles daily, I don't need medication. I am cured. My sugar level stays normal."

"I can't walk that distance. Most days, I find it hard to get out of bed."

He was tall and weighed nearly two hundred and thirty pounds, perhaps more. At his age with diabetes, he needed to be around two hundred, even less.

I said, "It's a matter of incentive. You must force yourself in the beginning. After ten days you will feel better. Do a quarter of a mile a day. Start small. Then do half a mile, and in ten days, you may do two miles: one in the morning and one in the evening. In a month, you might do three. In two years, you will be running a marathon."

With a chuckle, "That'll never happen."

I mentioned the story of an eighty-seven-year-old man I met in the gym before starting the trek. He had smoked twenty cigarettes a day since the age of fifteen. He became a diabetic. The doctor's prognosis had frightened him when he was sixty-four. He had taken up jogging ever since.

"So, there is hope," said John.

"There is proof, John, for all of us. What do we want with the rest of this life? All we need to do is to get motivated, and the body will take care of itself."

"Was he still on medication?" asked John.

"I didn't ask him. Maybe he's on a low dosage. He had a firm body and looked lean."

"I'm on eight tablets a day, and that's just for my diabetes. I take pills for high blood pressure and cholesterol. The Doc said I might've to go on insulin."

"How do you feel about that?"

"Never did like needles at the dentist."

"There is your motivation. If you try hard, you could reduce your medication by three-quarters in a couple of years. Set your goal and tell yourself you will do this one thing today. Don't think about tomorrow."

"What gave you the motivation to do this walk?"

"I love walking. I tend to leap in. I don't think beyond that. I'm stubborn. Once my mind is set, I must go all the way."

"That's the problem with me. I can get going, but a while later, my heart's not in it."

"But this is not about something abstract or a dream we are talking about. Not something like what I'm doing. This is about your health and your life."

We both went silent for a while. John said the drive was only five miles to the town when he picked me up. While driving, we passed two huge mounts that could have taken us into the "laps of the gods." It would have taken four hours to do the five miles. The car took less than ten minutes. I might not have made it.

Breaking the silence. He said, "You should go to the local paper and speak to them about what you're doing. They'd be interested in doing a feature on your venture. There is not much news in these parts, just a small community of people here. This would make a good read."

He dropped me off at a motel in the centre of town.

He said, "When I first came to this town some twenty years ago, I stayed in this motel. It was good, then. The price was reasonable. I stayed for a month until I found a place to rent. It should still be good. If you don't want to stay longer, you can change if you don't like it. There're three other motels on this stretch of road."

We bade each other goodbye, and he wished me luck. I thanked him and was sorry to see him go. He looked frail for a moment. He was single and had the responsibility of an aged mother. His diabetes was out of control. He was a big man looking as though he was approaching seventy-five. His eyes showed sadness, yet there was kindness in them.

It was a nice motel run by a jovial Chinese man named Allen, perhaps in his mid-thirties. He was helpful from the start. He gave me the largest room in the motel and charged me for a single.

He said, "It will be better for your trailer."

The next day, I saw the editor of the local paper. Within twenty minutes, she'd interviewed me, taken my photograph, and said to check their online edition at the end of the week. It wasn't a good interview. I was still in a daze, and I felt she hadn't posed me any proper questions. I wasn't sharp or coordinated enough to make suggestions to her.

Before leaving the premises, an English woman greeted me. Her name was Pia, and she was attractive, charming, and easy to converse with.

"I originally came from a small English village in Buckinghamshire. I have lived here in Payson for a long time."

When asked if she had gone back since, with her English accent slightly altered, she said, "I haven't been able to afford the trip."

She married an American. I wanted to invite her and her husband for an evening meal to chat about their experience living in such a town. It was inconvenient at the time. When I tried to see her the next day, she was not in her office.

Payson was like a big village in the English countryside. It was unlike any town I had seen so far. People walked, and all the shops and boutiques were like any in Europe. Except they were detached, and the American style of architecture gave an impression of walking into a Western movie set.

Early in the morning, I bumped into Allen with a fishing rod. I asked: "Where are you going with that fishing rod?"

"I went fishing at five o'clock this morning in the lake. I go every morning."

That was how I found out about the lake. Payson has three small lakes made up of recycled water. You can't swim in them, but they had over thirty fish species. However, people can fish and take their catch home, only two per person. They have ten types of bream and eight kinds of trout. The Apache trout is a local species, and it's the most beautiful bright yellow freshwater fish I have ever seen. The rainbow trout did not get a mention. It was early spring, and the trees' tender leaves had a lime green tint, giving them a metallic look under the bright morning sunlight. The lakes with the mountains in the far ground with patches of snow near the summit. Everything seemed still except for flocks of birds lined up like silhouettes across the sky.

While walking in Payson, I saw a magnificent bloomed tree with big white flowers in a doctor's surgery garden. I stood on the street for a while and asked four passers-by if they knew the name of the tree. None could tell me its name. I went into the surgeon's office and asked the secretary if she knew the tree's name outside her window.

With a receptionist smile, she said, "I hadn't noticed a tree there."

The doctor came out of his office. He looked in his late thirties with receding hair.

He said, "How can I help you?"

I asked if he knew the name of the tree.

He shook his head and said, "I can't tell you."

I couldn't help but think I was in paradise lost. I found it strange that none of the people I asked knew the name of this magnificent tree. I never found out.

There was a local Apache antique shop for Indian artefacts. I wanted to buy a souvenir, but it was shut. Big Bear ran it. I caught a glimpse of him coming out of the shop the previous evening. He was big but didn't look like a bear.

It says on the door that the opening hours are thus;

"Open most days about 9 or 10 a.m, occasionally as early as 7 a.m.

But on some days, as late as 12 or 1 p.m.

Closed about 5.30 or 6 p.m.

Occasionally, about 4 or 5 p.m.

But sometimes as late as 11 or 12 p.m.

Some days in the afternoon, we are not here at all, and lately, I've been here just about all the time except when I am someplace else, but I should be here then, too."

Big Bear's laid-back attitude said it all; maybe I should have adopted Walking Bear as my name linked to the Chinese proverb "Man who walks on the mountain, him not level." Not being level-headed was more my mood at that point.

I hadn't eaten cooked food for a while, and the Mexican menu suited me, especially the rice and hot chillies. They did a good version of the vegetarian recipe, while most restaurants stuck to fast food. I stayed off alcohol as I was still dehydrated. My stomach had shrunk, and I could only eat a portion of the servings and felt stoned after the meal. I needed a soft bed.

I wrote in my diary: 'It seemed unbelievable that I should have made it so far.' For two days, I remained in a state of feebleness. I came to understand the limits of my endurance. For once, I was fearful of what was to come.

Chapter 6: On the High Plateau

There was a need to test my resilience. I decided on a ten-mile walk carrying nothing except a small bottle of water to check on the difficulties of the road. It was my third day in Payson. I walked toward Show Low on Route 260 instead of the longer route to Holbrook, AZ. I had intended to carry on with Route 87 to Winslow. John told me it was more mountainous than I had already trekked on: "Winslow is a dump. The road to Show Low is a little flatter."

After four miles, I felt feeble and feverish. But the weakness left me as I pushed on and got into a rhythm. My pedometer read five miles. The road had no hard shoulder, just enough space to walk on its edge. Still, cars tooted me for being on the road, especially those pulling big caravans, which took a wider berth. It's the law in the US to always travel in the same direction as moving vehicles. The traffic, therefore, came from behind, which made it more dangerous for the walker. Industrial pine forests flanked the road. In the late winter, there was snow on the ground. And beneath the trees, pools of water saturated the terrain where the ice had melted.

It was sunny, and the temperature was around 57° F. At night, it would drop to sub-zero. The first five miles were not mountainous but undulating with a steep climb. Back in Payson, I realised I wasn't ready to go back on the road, certainly not to sleep on the wet, cold ground with low temperatures. John said that going towards Show Low was still hilly, with just two or three monster climbs. I know from experience that a car's gauging of hills is deceptive. On foot, you feel even the slightest rise. My tired mind mulled over that trek. I might have to stay two more days in Payson before I was fit enough for the road. The lack of a hard shoulder worried me, as did the mountains, hills, wet, snowy surface, and cold nights ahead. In the evening, I found a bus going to Show Low and another to Holbrook. My mind was made up. Besides, by taking that route to Albuquerque, I would have added one hundred and fifty miles of the trek across America. So, I didn't feel troubled by taking the bus; it came as a relief, and all the pain and pressure lifted from me.

As the bus sped along, I saw large patches of snow still on the ground in the forest. In parts, the melted snow turned into miniature lakes that flooded the forest floor. The road was rugged, steep, and mountainous. A large section of the forest had caught fire the previous year - as many as 1.3 million acres (2000 square miles) - and some people were killed in the blaze. The land beside the road looked like the aftermath of a bombed area. Show Low was ninety miles away from Payson. The nature of the road and the condition I was in meant that it would have taken me seven days, probably eight, to get to Show Low. There was one place available for supplies. Most likely, I would have needed rescuing.

It was a minibus with a maximum of fourteen passengers and a luggage trailer behind. The bus was half full, and most people went to sleep right away. I sat next to a young man with a red-haired and freckled face. Zak lived in Phoenix, and he was eighteen years old. He was going to stay with his grandfather for a few weeks. His grandfather had built a cabin in the pine forest just outside Show Low. The photos of the log cabin looked like an ideal way to escape city life, at least for a while. He wanted to train at altitude in the mountains, in the woods.

"I'm preparing for a marathon in Phoenix in April. The temperature will be 90° Fahrenheit."

"So, it'll be a half-marathon then?" I was taking the heat into account.

"It's thirty-one miles; the first fifteen will be uphill."

It surprised me that it was beyond the normal twenty-six miles and under the hot sun.

He continued, "The cut-off point will be ten hours. Anyone finishing outside ten hours would be disqualified."

He seemed well-informed on how he would handle the race.

"I'll be here in the mountains for a month. High altitude training will help me gain an advantage."

"In what way will it help you?"

"High altitude training allows my body to produce more red blood cells. My body will give me an edge over the others when I go down to a lower level. When I get back, I'll do eight days of pre-race training in the Phoenix heat. I'll be ready then."

After a pause, he asked: "Have you heard of the Leadville Marathon?"

"No, I haven't heard of it."

"I wanna do that next year. The marathon is a hundred miles long and must be completed in two days."

"That's fifty miles a day. Will your body stand up to that?"

"Many people have done it. I'll be training hard in the coming winter. It's all to do with pace. You've got to know how to pace yourself. I'll do 6.2 mph on the first day. Get a good sleep, then increase my speed to 7.5 mph on the second day. I wanna go faster on the hills. That's where they all struggle."

"Won't it be hot?"

"Ye, it'll be in hundred degrees heat. I aim to finish. Anybody who finishes is a winner."

"That'll be some achievement."

A smile came to his face as though he had been duly rewarded. He asked me what brought me here, and I told him of my venture. He became interested, and his eyebrows rose. It gave him some possibilities, he said later. I mentioned the Camino de Santiago to him; it would be a good starting point for understanding the spirit of walking. He wanted to know more about it. His facial expression changed to a glow as I gave him a sense of the pilgrimage. He said he would be graduating from high school in a few months.

Was he going to take up a university course?

"I haven't thought about it. Maybe something in sports. I wanna do it, but I want to make some money first. I can't decide. What advice would you give?"

The question threw me a little. I saw Zak as a confident young man; now, there was uncertainty.

"You need to talk to your parents and teachers about it?"

"My parents have left it up to me, and my teachers suggested sports science. I love sports, but I'm not sure if I wanna career in it."

"What about your career counsellor? I can't give you advice on something like that. You are young and have plenty of time ahead of you to decide. You don't need to rush."

"I finish high school in a few months. I must decide what I wanna do. How did you decide what to do?"

"I had no idea at your age. I knew that I wanted to carry on with my education. But that was cut short, and I started work. It was different in those days. You did what you had to do. The only advice I can give you would be to focus hard on what gives you the most enthusiasm. Go with your instinct, not by what others tell you to do. Remember, changing your mind later is not against the law."

When we finally arrived, his grandfather was waiting for him at the bus station in Show Low. He introduced me after we shook hands and wished each other luck.

The driver said, "You got a choice of two motels. You choose." He pointed me in the right direction.

I booked into Budget Inn. The room was awful and dark; the shower was damp, with tiny black flies flying around. From the start, it didn't appeal. It was already getting late to check into the other. The couple managing the motel was curious about my background and asked if I was Indian. I said partly.

"Which tribe, Apache?"

And before I could answer, in unison, they both said they were part Cherokee and started to tell me their life story. I was hungry and needed a way out. I asked for a restaurant they could recommend. They suggested the Branding Iron Steakhouse. But with the thought of facing all that sinew, I opted for trout, French fries, and a great salad bowl.

Hanna, who waited on me, understood I wasn't a local, wanted to talk, and became curious about my venture.

She said, "You'll have no trouble from here onwards. From Holbrook to Albuquerque is all flat."

That bit of news gave me a real lift. She was young, twenty maybe, pretty, and her plumpness suited her tall frame. I asked her if she was a local girl.

"I live ten miles away."

It seemed a fair distance, and I asked her how she could make it worth her while. "Oh, it's only a fifteen-minute drive from here."

I calculated the cost of petrol at British rates while in the USA it was sixty-five per cent cheaper than in Britain. Did she have a day job?

"I'm studying as a junior schoolteacher but work here to supplement my studies."

She had a shy smile, affable and polite. Later, the manager came and spoke about my trek. Hanna must have said something to her. She was also curious and wanted to know if I had found it difficult on the way up.

"I almost didn't make it here. Too many mountains."

"Yes, you are six thousand three hundred feet above sea level on top of the Rockies. What you are doing is a generous thing for the children."

It sounded like I was on top of the world receiving all the gratitude. The service was excellent, and the attention was cordial.

When asked for the bill, Hanna said, "The manager said it was on the house."

I gave Hanna a good tip and went to see the manager. I put my hand out to say thank you and goodbye.

She said, "I want to hug you and wish you all the luck."

As I was leaving, two other staff members and Hanna did likewise. I hadn't expected such generosity, kindness, and warmth. Getting back to the motel was depressing. It was dark and dingy with a musty smell. The old furniture crowded the room, and I was unsure if they had changed the sheets. I tucked into my sleeping bag silk liners given to me by Dorothy and couldn't sleep. The thought of arriving in this strange place disorientated me.

John came to mind, and something he said about being unable to adjust to life in Phoenix rubbed off on me. There was an inkling of what he meant that played on my mind. Almost all the westerns I remember portrayed communities of people moving west in search of new pastures or settling in townships or villages. Central to these communities was how strong relationships and shared interests bound them. Yet, on the streets of Los Angeles and Phoenix, I experienced loneliness like nowhere else. People were in their cars alone (almost all the cars had a sole driver), and no one walked the streets. There was no face-to-face contact. No exchanges of glances or human traces. There is no one to speak to in open spaces except in shopping malls. Perhaps people were controlled at home by robots like TVs, phones, and endless modern gadgets.

These cities are designed in a deliberate way to avoid human contact. For John, moving to Phoenix was too much of a frontier to cross. He wanted to keep what he already had: his humanity. He preferred to live in a small village in the mountains where he could greet people in the streets. He preferred to keep the sense of human tenderness and connectedness and walk or hang about in the square. Kept in touch with his inner rhythm as others did in the old West and his village. As people still do in many places all over the world.

Feeling disorientated in my motel room, I drifted into a deep sleep and woke up early. Ghostly dreams of unknown faces peopled my imaginings in the night. Upon waking, I couldn't trace any of them.

I was still weak, and the bus to Holbrook was not due until late morning. I wanted to escape that motel room as quickly as possible. After my oats, I went to a little café near the other motel three minutes away. There, I met Mel. Seeing me sitting alone, he asked me to join a few others. People like the local reverend and other regulars who made this café their morning meeting room over a cup of coffee and chats. There were others like me, travellers passing through. The café was managed efficiently by a woman called Ann. It was cosy, not too small, and comfortable, and there was a lively atmosphere. Later, Mel introduced me to Patricia and other members of the entourage. The conversation flowed, but I remained on the fringe, for

I knew no one and had no reference to what they talked about. A while later, just three of us, Patricia, Mel, and me.

The talk created a harmonious feeling between us. I discovered Mel was retired and had worked in films for a long time. He showed us a lot of fascinating behind-the-scenes photos taken on location. It gave us some great insider information about many actors and stuntmen, always focusing on the pleasant side of their personalities.

He said, "I met Linda and Paul McCartney when they were living in Tucson, Arizona. She was the perfect partner for him."

Mel had a calm aura, silvery hair, and an ageing calmness.

He said, "I've had some trouble with one eye. It's bothersome and caused me to stop work."

I asked him if he had missed the work routine.

"There comes the point when you know it's time to stop working. I'd been thinking about it for two or three years. I had a good time on the scene while it lasted. I met many great people like Linda Crystal, Bob Mitchum, Angie Dickinson, and Paul Newman."

The names rolled off his tongue.

"What do you do with your time now that you've retired?"

"I'm taking care of my wife, Sandy. She broke her ankle recently and can't walk. I do what I can around the house. But you know, with my eye the way it is, I can't read or watch TV for long periods. It's a strain."

Patricia said, "Haven't you got anyone to help until your wife gets better?"

"We have a few people looking after us, but we do all right. Tell Naz a bit about your island."

Patricia was from western Canada and lived on a tiny island with her son. The island belongs to her.

"It's just Jake and me who live there. You are free to come any time. You'll be welcome to do some work and stay awhile," she laughed.

I believe she meant it. She had already been to the places I was heading to in Arizona.

She said, "You must visit the Painted Desert and the Petrified Forest when you go past there. They are magical places."

"In what way did you feel inspired?"

"I don't want to take away the surprise."

"I don't think you can do that. It's not as if you are giving the plot away."

"I suppose not, but I don't want to give away the visual effect. Let's say it has all the colours of the rainbow and all the different shapes you could imagine. There are remnants of ancient buildings of the people who lived in the area. It's a sacred land, and it has more to do with the impact you feel when you first see it."

"You mean spiritually?"

"I mean, you lose your sense of being and become possessed. If you can imagine being in the biggest cathedral the world has ever seen, and inside it is an art gallery that only this earth could create, you'll understand what it's like. You can sit for hours without being hungry in the great silence. When you are ready to leave, you find you can't. You've found something new implanted in yourself and feel awed by it."

She became silent for a moment, and Mel and I stayed in the lull of the stillness.

I broke the silence by asking, "Have you travelled much?"

"I have a son, Jake; he is sixteen and still depends on me. I can't travel as much as I would like. I have visited Europe and South America."

Openly, she said, "I have been through a lot, two marriages, in and out of the limelight, and I have been ill. My illness helped me gain a different perspective on life."

"In what way did it change you?"

"I was doing too much. I got caught up in the big world of success and chased shadows. When the shock of an illness comes, you realise how disconnected you've become. Initially, you know you have hit rock bottom. You have been in shock for a long time."

"Were you on your own at the time?"

"Yes and no. My relationship was breaking up, and he soon left when he found out I was ill. I had my son with me."

Her eyes moistened, and she went silent for a while. Then she continued.

"The fear that death could be sudden, and you are not ready to leave this life. You try everything to hold on to it. Not now, you say to yourself over and over. I'm not ready. In all our sufferings, this earth is not enough. You try every kind of therapy to get better."

She wiped her tears with the serviette.

"In the end, I went under the knife. Recovery is slow and painful, and you are never sure you'll wake up the next day. When the tears stop, you think you've been given a second chance, but for how long? Then you know what you need to do."

Despite the tears at our table, she recovered from her past trauma. She didn't say what her illness was. But by the paleness of her face, she looked as if she had been through chemotherapy. Her hair, though long, was not thick and lacked the natural gloss. Still, a dynamic energy exuded from her in the effortless way she spoke.

She connected with people expecting nothing in return and refined her spirituality to fit her new perspective. She blended her maturity with her charisma, which made her quite magnetic. Mel and I enjoyed being around her. She brought warmth and made us laugh at the table. Neither Mel nor I wanted our conversation to end. We all felt at ease with one another. Perhaps that was her newfound secret. To mingle with people, lift their spirits, hold their interest, transfer her energy to others and get some back in return.

It was getting late, and I needed to get ready to catch my bus. Patricia egged Mel to give me a lift to Holbrook. But it wasn't a problem to catch a bus. We all hugged farewell. There was a reluctance to let go of each other.

I arrived near the bus station, and Sheila Malone, a pleasant woman working in an office building nearby, showed me the way to the bus stop. There, I met a man waiting, alone. He looked strange at first, middle-aged yet old-looking. His features were rugged, with a big, chiselled nose, wide cascading wrinkles on his cheeks, and an upward-pointed chin. He had oily shoulder-length hair with strands of grey. He lacked elegance, but his firm, distinctive face made up for it. He introduced himself as Nathan. I noticed his eyes, glassy and jaundiced looking. I asked him if he was ill.

"I've had problems with alcohol. I haven't touched a drop for six months."

He looked like a man suffering every second of the day from withdrawal symptoms. I asked him if he was a local.

He stared hard and said, "For a thousand years. This is where I live. I'm Ndee."

I have always wanted to meet an Apache, and there I was talking to one. I asked if he had a wife and children.

He gave a loud bourbon-and-cigar laugh and said, "I was married long ago. She was a Navajo woman."

"Does that often happen, inter-tribal marriages?"

"It happens; she left me after a year. I drank too much and brought everything down. I was bad like a hungry wolf."

After a pause, "I wanted her back. She came, and then she left again. She said I was too stuck in my ways. I went to see her at her family's house. Her brothers told me to leave her alone. She doesn't want me back."

"So, you loved her?"

He looked at me with a blank face. After another long pause, he said, "She was a hard woman. I liked her body at night, in the cold winter. She had soft skin."

He seemed old when I first saw him, but now I understood that he could be in his early forties, even younger. It was difficult to tell. I asked him what his Apache name was.

"Nathan was my given name."

"How do you feel to be called by a name, not of your heritage?"

He answered with a hand signal, suggesting that a name had no profound meaning.

Then he said, "Why do you ask so many questions?"

I didn't want to pursue things any further. Perhaps he had an Apache name but didn't want to use it. Maybe I had been too demanding. He asked me what I was doing in Show Low and wanted to know why I was trekking and what England was like. I gave him my version of the venture and an idea of England. He gave me a mischievous stare and blurted out.

"You are crazy."

I nodded my head in agreement.

He said, "I live in a mission in Holbrook for alcoholics."

I said, "I'm going to stay at a campsite there."

"The campsite is five hundred yards from the mission. You must come and visit and eat with us. You are welcome. You can talk about your walk to the others."

The bus soon arrived. They wouldn't let me on due to safety precautions as they didn't have a luggage provision for my trailer. The driver double-checked with the head office on the phone, and they gave a definite no.

Nathan and I shook hands, and he said, "Do you want an Apache name?"

Surprised, I hesitated, "Sure."

"You are Passing Cloud, don't lose it. See you in Holbrook."

The bus drove away, and he waved at me through the window. I signalled back, and others on the bus waved, too. For a while, I felt transported to Carlos Castaneda's book with the old Yaqui Indian, Don Juan. The thrusting of the name Passing Cloud so suddenly upon me felt like an invisible blanket wrapped around me. In that instant, it fitted as though it had always been my given name.

My mood had changed when I strode back to Sheila Malone's office to tell her of my plight. Sheila couldn't make any suggestions. Heading back to Budget Inn, an awful shiver engulfed me. The manager said she would ask her husband to taxi me to Holbrook. I sat at the reception for a long time. An hour passed, and then he came down looking sheepish and said he couldn't.

I went back to the café in the hope of finding Mel. Ann, who runs it, said, "Mel went out searching for you earlier. He wanted to take you to Holbrook and couldn't find you."

"He must have gone to the old bus station, which had since been closed," I said.

The motel attached to the cafe looked deserted; everyone had left. There weren't any cars parked. It was a sunny early afternoon, but it was too late for me to head north to Holbrook. Everyone had gone their way. A pang sensation gripped me that I used to get as a child watching ships sail away from Port Louis harbour, Mauritius. I watched hundreds of passengers going somewhere, and I was left behind sitting on a bollard until the ship's lights disappeared over the dark distance. Each time, a sense of emptiness and abdominal pain filled me like I was marooned on the island.

A sickness came over me. I took a room at the motel behind the café and closed the door, and it felt like my whole insides punched out. I showered, and the absence inside was no better. I tried to get on the net. The reception was terrible, on and off every five minutes. I phoned Dorothy in LA for a chat and relayed my day's events to her. She said the universe would find an answer.

It was late afternoon. Lying on the bed, I picked up my book of poems by Ai and chose a page at random. The poem was "Passage," dedicated to Allen Ginsberg. In it, she is on a dual journey, on a train and to her end. Each line spoke of her wish to remain, to stay alive. She knew she was on a journey of no return, "only to go on and on and then just go." Ai died a few months after writing that poem. Yet her words removed my sadness and made me realise that my world was privileged. All my good luck so far has held out beyond belief. In that time of reflection, sleep came as a relief.

I was up at sunrise; my trailer packed and ate breakfast in my room. It was the usual oats with dried fruits and a banana. I was determined to make headway and walk twenty miles, maybe. The thought of being left had almost evaporated. I felt wretched and was wary of my weakness. I wanted to pound the road, walk away from the stagnant energy, and tear all the strands of 'being left behind' out of me. First, I needed a hot coffee, then disappeared into the bright sunrise strip on Route 77.

As I walked into the café to my surprise, Mel was there with a cup in hand. I had assumed he was also a traveller living in Tucson, where he worked before retiring. He, too, was surprised to see me.

"How come you're still here?"

"I couldn't get on the bus; they wouldn't allow me. The trailer broke safety regulations".

"Sit down, and we'll talk," he said.

"Did Patricia get off okay?"

"She is still here."

"She didn't go?"

"She said she couldn't go."

"But why?"

"She didn't think the time was right."

Minutes later, she walked in. Her eyes lit up as she saw us; she hugged us. In our triangular embrace, the feelings and connections were complete. Racing through my mind were the moments, the life stories, the philosophies, the sufferings, the expectations, and being in the now together.

Soon, we would each be going our own way. I told them of my desperation yesterday afternoon.

When it was time to leave, Mel said he would take me to Holbrook. It was then that it occurred to me that he lived just outside Show Low. Patricia took photos as we loaded up; we hugged for the last time as a threesome, and she gave me a good luck offering.

"As a rule, I dislike making people feel awkward. Take these as a gift for luck."

She chose two small brown pebbles she picked up from Painted Desert from a tiny cloth pouch and handed them to me. She was leaving that day and heading towards Flagstaff, Northwest of Arizona. I had nothing to offer her in return except the memory of our encounter.

"That's more than enough," she said.

In the car, I stayed silent except for the occasional prompting. Mel guided me as we passed landscapes and villages along the way.

"Most people are Mormons in those small village communities - farmers of cattle and pigs."

We passed three villages along the way in that fifty-mile stretch. The land on either side of the road was flat. There was very little in the way of trees, stunted cedars here and there. They were dotted sparsely in the open with bent branches blown by the harsh wind. It is semi-fertile, hardy grassland in clumps instead of uniformly spread. At this time of the year, in the late winter, the soil is sandy and dark like henna. A few white-faced cattle in herds foraged along the way, with water holes specially built for these animals.

We arrived at a point on the road when the way ahead was straight and empty, with no hard shoulders that reached beyond the distant land. Had I not had a lift from Mel, it would have been three testing nights out in the open under the howling wind and sub-zero temperature. The farms, fenced in with barbed wire, left no space for camping. There was something unusual and beautiful about the vastness of the view. Yet it was flat, exposed, and penetrating in its desolation. You cannot tame that harsh environment; it makes overwhelming demands. Driving at speed in the car, the pale cobalt sky gave an illusion that it was a giant blue planet and that we were travelling on one of its moons.

"This is what Montana looks like. In the past, many Indians got drunk at night and then tried to make their way back to the reservation. They died of hypothermia. It was the reason a mission was built not far from the campsite. It's where they can stay and have three meals a day and a bed."

I didn't want to feel pity or see them as victims when I heard the story of the mission back at the bus stop from Nathan in Show Low. I had no room to put that burden on them or me.

Driving through Holbrook to the campsite, Mel said, "We damaged these people; we made them the way they are."

After we unloaded my trailer, we hugged and said goodbye for the last time. Patricia going her way, the silent drive, the fierce meditative landscape, and our genuine connection all helped to put us in a sensitive mood. It saddened me when Mel burst into tears, for I had hoped our parting would be cheerful. It was a rare moment to meet a true gentleman like him. There have been a few good encounters in California and Arizona. My luck was still holding out.

***

I was the only one with a tent at the Holbrook Petrified Forest campsite. Everyone had a mobile caravan, and the reception gave me an exposed spot. The ground was rock-hard, and I had trouble driving in my pegs. Afterwards, I went towards the Mission and stayed on the road. I lacked the courage to see Nathan and the other lodges. I felt like an intruder trespassing over their privacy. Talking to them and asking questions would have been like invading their hospitality. I walked away and went in the wrong direction and was lost. I found myself on the highway to nowhere. I was jaywalking and needed to get off before the police patrol got hold of me. I climbed over a high metal fence. On the other side, three young men rode their motorcycles on dirt tracks of vacant land. I approached them, and they seemed friendly. They noticed my accent and asked where I was from. England, I said.

They asked me the often-asked questions, and I answered routinely. I could have predicted their answers, "Awesome man, awesome". They wanted us to take photos together, and we did, and immediately, they stuck them on Facebook. They pointed me to the police station.

It was a long half-mile walk away. The female police officer said I had come to the wrong station and needed the Patrol Police's permission to walk on the highway. She said it was not far from my campsite but the best time to see them would be in the morning. It occurred to me that I would need to stay another day in Holbrook. By late afternoon, the temperature dropped considerably. It had been pleasant during the day, 59° Fahrenheit, and now it was approaching 50° F. My evening meal was synthetic with plenty of salt, pepper, and sauce, and I had to get the food down fast. I thought, was that why it was called fast food?

The campsite was near the old Route 66, which was dark when I returned. Apart from my thermal wear, I put on an extra layer of clothes. Under the solar light, I reflected on the day in my diary. Mel and Patricia came to mind. Mel's wife Sandy had rung him while we drove along to Holbrook. He told me she was housebound after breaking her ankle. He turned on the loudspeaker so I could hear her voice and talk with her. It hadn't seemed strange making conversation despite not having met her. The vibration in her voice was welcoming, polite, and well-spoken. Mel had already told her about me, and she wished me a farewell journey. A fleeting thought came to mind. Perhaps the instant connections between Mel, Patricia, Nathan, Sandy, and me went beyond our moods despite the moment and the circumstances.

In the night's thin air, it came to me that, some sixty-five thousand years ago, it is said, two prominent tribes left Africa and began a series of journeys across the globe. Perhaps we all originated from the same tribe, the same immediate family. And we have been globetrotting to the far corners of this earth, in time and lineage, to meet here in this remote place in Show Low. Finally, to make an ancestral reconnection as if to say that this was as far away a place could be to pause and have a "picnic" and meet destiny.

It was a restless night, cold, and the juggernaut trucks on the highway were noisy. As soon as it was daylight, I decamped in sub-zero temperatures. I needed a hot breakfast and coffee, and at that moment, I had only one choice of junk food: French fries, two eggs, and coffee. It filled a hole in my stomach, as best to describe it. I killed time until it was late enough to check into a motel. The manager, a Navajo, allowed me early into my room, which was good of him. I couldn't have spent another night in my tent.

The Super 6 was clean and reasonably priced, and the manager and his assistant were courteous. The shower refreshed me and gave me the impetus to do what I had to do. At the Patrol Police office, I met the officer I had spoken with back in Phoenix. She said she did all the necessary checking, and I was okay using the highway. The news came as a relief.

"It was a highly unusual request," she said. "And since we understood the nature of your trek, we decided to make an exception."

But I needed to be careful of the heavy traffic "and exploding tyres with loose nuts and bolts and bits of metals that flew like bullets." She seemed concerned that it was a hazardous journey. I had no other route except Route 66, now renamed Route 40 to Albuquerque. With the rest of the day in my hands, I became a tourist.

Holbrook is divided by Route 66; upper Holbrook is the new part with motels, restaurants, and the airport—a bleak functional place. Lower Holbrook is an old town with a few motels, restaurants, and more of the residential sector. The road that connects the two sections is Navajo Boulevard. The Navajo Nation makes up about a quarter of the town's population, about five thousand. The town has a feel of the turn of the twentieth century. It was cheaply built except for the old County Courthouse, now a nineteenth-century museum. It has many artefacts that would set any visitor into a bygone period. Spending one whole day there would not be enough.

Further on searching for a supermarket, I stumbled onto the Wigwam Motel on West Hopi Drive. It is a motel where you can lodge in a wigwam. I was unsure whether you would have to use the shower and washroom in the central part of the building. The grid system of the town made it difficult to get lost. I drifted along the back streets, and the prefabricated houses were cheaply built. It was like stepping into a third-world environment. The sidewalks were nonexistent or made of dirt or cracked slabs. Some of the roads needed resurfacing. The electric cable overhead and the signpost and neon lights were like graffiti vandalism on the landscape, yet a twenty-first-century necessity.

Maybe it would have been a pristine landscape a hundred and thirty years ago. The elderly woman at the museum suggested I visit a street named 'Bucket of Blood Street' and told me a little story behind the name. In the late nineteenth century, the population would have been only two hundred and fifty, and Holbrook became notorious for being too harsh for 'women and churches.' It was cowboy country and right smack in Navajo territory. As though in a Hollywood story, there were feuds. Big ranch owners, motivated by greed, wheeled power. The big ranches became muddled with cattle rustling, the railroad, and drunken fights in the harsh winter weather that could touch 29° below zero. Men could become bored working on this vast vista punching cows. It transformed their character to match that of the landscape. That is hard, raw, demanding, wild and uncompromising. It was the Wild West, and gunfights were a frequent occurrence. As the story goes, in one year, there were twenty-six deaths by shooting. Those deaths would have touched everyone. Perhaps it was inevitable that vigilantism would have been the result, as the law exists only for those with the power of the gun.

A fight had ensued in the Central saloon on Central Street after an accusation of cattle stealing by rival gang ranch members. It resulted in many being killed and wounded, making the gunfight at the OK Corral look like shooting ducks at a Sunday fair. It was a bloodbath; in those days, 'bath' was an unknown commodity. The Street and the Saloon changed its name to 'Bucket of Blood' and helped gain notoriety. Today, it still stands boarded up, waiting for an entrepreneur to rekindle modern tourism and a glimpse of what it must once have been like. The museum, the Saloon, and remnants of the run-down gas station on the old Route 66 and the Petrified Forest would greatly interest those passing through to make a stop before their destination. The map showed that the Little Colorado River was close by, and upon reaching it, I found a dry riverbed.

Back at the motel, I had an early night, determined to be on the road soon after daybreak. I handed the key to the manager and his assistant in the morning. They were both curious to see my trailer and asked me questions. Afterwards, he gave me $10 and said, "It'll be a long journey, have a meal on me." It was a noble gesture, and I thanked him and the young Navajo woman who was the assistant manager. She had filled me in on much of what goes on on the reservation. She said the older generation didn't want to change their way of living. They do everything traditionally, including carrying water long distances to irrigate their crops. The younger generation and most of the Nation's people are just getting on with their lives like everyone else.

Chapter 7: Making Tracks in the Wilderness

It was all quiet in the moody morning when I left Holbrook. The fleecy clouds raced across the sky. To be on the move again added a zing to my step, but the road was flat this time. I had chosen the motel at the edge of the upper end of town to facilitate my getaway. It was cold on the handlebars even with gloves on, for the temperature was no more than 37° F. I was ready to push myself to see how far I could go on the flats without tiring. Flanked by vast farmlands on either side of the Interstate Highway, white-faced, black-bodied cattle chewed the tall, dried winter grass. When looked closely, these grasses sprang out of the desert sand. They were in clumps about two feet apart, intermingled with tumbleweed. The Highway was busy twenty-four hours a day and seven days a week with huge fast trucks. I wheeled the trailer on the hard shoulder. The traffic was fierce and noisy. Each time one huge truck sped past, it pushed me forward, forcing my grip tight on the handlebars.

There were no "B" roads on the high plateau. No roads for bikers or walkers. I made headway at a good pace. Twelve miles later, a man approached me on one of the rare lay-bys and asked if I wanted a lift. I pointed to my caption, "NazacrossAmerica walking coast to coast across ten states." He parked and wanted to talk. He gave me a bottle of water and invited me to sit in the car. He was one of the Nation's people, a Navajo. This I thought would be an excellent chance to enquire and get views of his people. We chatted, and it turned out relatively trivial.

He seemed interested in where I came from and what I was doing. After a few minutes, I noticed a change in his mannerism. His questions became more personal, and his effeminacy much more apparent. I had put myself in an awkward situation. I acted fast and thought of a way out without causing offence or embarrassment to either of us. As a pretext, I said I wanted to show him a photo of my family. I went to my trailer, took a photo, and showed it to him via the car window. When we shook hands and said goodbye, he held my hand longer than he should have. His hand was sweaty, his fingers big and soft. He was embarrassed when I looked hard into his eyes. He then let go as though caressing it and drove away.

I allowed the incident to pass, pounded the road, and continued into my stride onto the long and straight highway. By late afternoon, I figured I had covered over twenty-five miles. The rain pelted down, and the wind howled. Trucks zoomed past, driving over the speed limit. It was close to freezing. I needed a place to pitch my tent, but the area was unaccommodating. Fenced off from the hard shoulder, with only a strip of land in between on a downward slope. Dense, thorny tumbleweeds littered the no-man-land. I had no choice but to continue until I found a convenient spot to camp. The rain turned to flakes of snow. The evening descended in the blue of twilight. I searched for a turning to get off the highway, and there were none.

On the threshold of darkness, the wind blew. It drove the temperature down to numbing all sensation. The frost paralysed my hands and feet. In the thin, gelid air of the high plateau, staying lucid became a test of my resolve.

"Walk faster, faster, I tell you." The Ape was back again, giving advice.

I shouted, "I thought I left you back on the way to Payson."

"You look like you might need help."

"No, I don't need help, not from you."

"Sorry to barge in."

"Damn, I hate your lisp, leave me be, go and climb a tree."

Suddenly, a car on full beam hooted behind me. A Patrol Police officer stepped out and said, "I want you off the road now."

"I thought, is he kidding me or what?"

I explained that Holbrook Patrol Police had permitted me and that he should check with them. He did, and he was on the phone for a long time, and every second increased the painful cold while I stood waiting, shivering.

"Okay, the station confirmed what you said. But I don't want to see you on the Highway. The weather is bad, and it's going to get worse. The trucks are driving too fast. Some of these drivers drink and drive. You could be killed at any time."

I was already meat from the freezer by then. I said, "You don't have to convince me, officer, but what can I do?"

"I'll take you to a motel."

It was an offer impossible to refuse, for by then, I felt as though my ears had dropped off. But before getting into the car, he said, "I need to search you for weapons."

I chuckled; my cheeks froze stiff. I said, "I have never seen a gun close up, let alone touch one, except in fun parks."

"This is what all the Brits tell me. I still must search you."

Sitting in his car was like having a sauna. Jason was a friendly and well-mannered man. He was in his late thirties, with bright blue eyes. Before he could ask me any questions, I turned my focus onto him. I asked if he was married. I learned this direct line of questioning while touring in India. It leaps the foreplay of ritual communication boundary.

"Ye, I've been married for thirteen years. I've got five kids, one on the way."

"So, you are building a football team?"

He didn't respond, but a broad grin lit up his face.

"It must be difficult for your wife to cope with the children while you are at work?"

"Her mother helps her. She lives next door in Scottsdale."

"What Scottsdale, Arizona?"

He could see my reaction. I was surprised by the distance between where he lived and where he worked.

"Life is hard. I'm doing my best to provide for my family even if it means being away part of the time."

"Have you always worked away from your family hundreds of miles from home?"

"I worked in San Carlos on the reservation when I first joined the police force. That was nearer."

I asked him about the Indians on the reservation, government help, and agencies dealing with the welfare of the nation's people.

"They've done nothing for the Apache. They're living in ghettos. There is a high suicide rate among the young. Drug use such as methamphetamine and alcohol were like chewing gum and drinking water."

"So, it's that bad?"

"I'm from New York. At college, they taught us that all the Indian Nations were treated well. I was shocked when I first got here to discover it was a damn big lie. Even babies are born addicted. There are other illnesses in the community, like diabetes."

"So, is there a general apathy towards the Indians, as you seemed to be saying? Are other tribes in similar conditions?"

"The Navajo and Hopi are living in a Third World state. I've seen it. They've poor housing, medical, and education in the middle of the richest country in the world. It's bullshit what they tell you on TV and in books at school. It's all bullshit. These are the skeletons in our closets, and we have plenty of others."

I needed to get off the highway, out from the wind and frost. Jason had come to my rescue. In our short journey to a motel, he spoke frankly to me without reservation. On my travels, I had many encounters. People have been upfront without concealing or disguising what they had to say. I find this attitude so refreshing in the USA.

At the motel, the manager, Mukesh Patel, greeted me and saw the flashing lights of the police vehicle as I unloaded my trailer.

He removed his glasses and asked: "Why were you arrested?"

His eyes held a sad look. I said with a deadpan face: "I was walking without headlights".

"You're a funny man."

"So, people keep telling me."

Much later, after sitting for thirty minutes under the shower, defrosted, I went back to see him to enquire about a place to eat. Again, he wanted to know why the police arrested me. I told him how it was.

"Why are you walking?"

"I'm doing it for good causes for children in need in Britain, and I like walking."

"You are crazy. You'll get yourself killed."

He shook his head in dismay. He didn't have an Indian accent from the subcontinent. Perhaps he was from East Africa. I asked how long he had managed this motel.

"This is my eighth year in Chambers."

With the wedding ring on his finger, I said, "How does your family feel about living in such a bleak place?"

"They don't live here; they are in Phoenix."

"Why don't they live with you? You must feel lonely without them, surely?"

"Yes, of course, I miss them; who wouldn't? I see them for four days every two weeks. The children need proper schooling, and Phoenix is their best place."

"You must miss your wife very much."

"Does it show?"

"Yes, in your eyes, in your posture."

It takes a unique character to make huge sacrifices when you are still in the prime of your life. Because of the nature and location of their work, Jason and Mukesh had become part-time family men.

Chambers was in the middle of nowhere, just a highway stopover. I rested well that night and thought about what it would have been like if I had been in my tent. I wanted to get on the road as early as I could. Mukesh wasn't around. Kim, the assistant manager, a young Apache woman with a pale complexion, helped me to find an alternative route to the highway. She spent forty minutes on the computer tracing the route to Albuquerque and writing it down.

"It would be longer with only five miles on the Interstate Highway," she said. "There was a problem on Route 66 Highway once. My father and I drove on the frontage road. It was easy. You must watch out for a few turns. The rest would be on frontage/service road to Lupton and to Gallup across the border into New Mexico."

Kim reassured me that I would have no trouble following the contours of the Highway flanks and the various roads that led to my destination. Checking the directions she downloaded, I realised Jason drove past Painted Desert on the way to the motel. Another missed opportunity Patricia mentioned.

It was cold, with a gusty wind that took away the thin film of warmth from my underclothes, which comforted me. The sandstorms began from the time my wheels turned. I had not recovered from the previous day's walk; my pedometer read was thirty-eight miles. It was just as well that the wind was not head-on as it was difficult pushing the trailer. I wanted to get to Chee Indian Centre, twenty-six miles away. There was nothing in between except farms fenced off with barbed wire. On the edges of those farms were small Indian communities of maybe a dozen houses every few miles. Often, there would be gaps, nothing for twelve miles.

These small settlements had dogs that came onto the road to bite me. They moved in threes, two attacking from the front and one from behind. At first, I paid no attention, but they became persistent. The one behind came too close, baring its teeth and gums. It frightened me. I got my flagpole and waved it like a tail. That did the trick. I did the same thing when the next bunch came along, and it worked. I regained my composure when I saw those guard dogs. I counted that they came to attack on seven occasions. There were many horses along the way; they thrived on this desert grass and weeds. Upon seeing my bright orange trailer wheeling along the frontage road, some came to accompany me. They gave me a look of curiosity, then went off at a canter as though wishing to race with me.

The gust and grit never let up throughout the day. When I reached the part where I needed to take the Highway, the noise and ferociousness of the passing vehicles made it very unpleasant. A huge truck, perhaps thirty metres long, went past me at great speed. It propelled the trailer away from my grip. It ended up in the tumbleweeds off the road with my food supplies scattered all over the hard shoulder. I fastened a rope onto the handlebars and tied it to my belt. I didn't want to lose control a second time.

I worried about another late day because of the sudden drop in temperature. I still had in mind the bad experience of the night before. The patrol officer, Jason, warned me about young 'Braves' getting drunk. He worried about my safety. I wanted to pitch my tent by four p.m. while it was still daylight. I arrived at the Chee Indian location at precisely four o'clock. They didn't have rooms, nor did they have a campsite. The facility sold local arts and crafts. I felt tired and disappointed and knew I had no choice but to push on some more. I asked two Navajo women at the counter how far it was to Lupton, the next stopover with a campsite.

One of them said, "Five miles."

The other said, "Maybe?"

An old Navajo man sitting with a cane in hand said, "Maybe more."

The double maybes suggested it would be more. I thought I'd get there by six and make camp. At six-thirty, there was no sight of Lupton. Twilight was setting in, and the temperature was dropping fast. Everywhere I looked seemed unsuitable. There were too many of those tumbleweeds and nowhere flat. Then, it was dark, and the frost dug into my bones. The almost full moon rose and lit the surrounding mountains. Everything I didn't want to happen converged on me. The numbness of my hands and feet muddled my thoughts. Walking after dark under the moonlight, suddenly, in front of my eyes, a dirt track appeared. I entered it and turned left, and there was a flat surface behind some shrubs perfect for a pitch. There was a pool of water about ten feet away. I set everything up but was too tired and cold to eat. I cleaned up, tucked myself into my sleeping bag, and thought how lucky I was to find a place.

Ten minutes later, a train passed by. I didn't know the rail track was some fifty metres away. The ground beneath me vibrated due to the mega weight of those wagons: double containers, one on top of the other. One train went by every twenty minutes.

I was in my sleeping bag at eight but could not sleep. In my tent, with the ground shaking under me, I imagined I was in a palanquin. In some ancient times, being carried off like a prince. The caravan crosses a vast desert lurking with danger.

In my exhaustion, I calculated that I must have walked thirty-five miles that day. My pedometer check said thirty-four. I felt bitten by the rime, and by midnight, I was frozen. I pondered for a long time and found the courage to get up and put on some extra clothes. It made little difference, and I regretted not bringing my heat pads. Each time sleep came, a train passed, shaking me out of my dream. Perhaps it was just as well. I couldn't keep warm, and hypothermia was a strong possibility. The next stage would have been oblivion.

I felt utterly distraught and craved a warm bed throughout the night. It was after six, barely daylight. My feet were blocks of ice, but my body was not cold and, with difficulty, decamped. I threw everything into my trailer in a disorderly fashion. I didn't have breakfast as it was simply too frosty. The pool of water near the tent was one block of ice. Despite my thermal gloves and double socks, I couldn't feel my hands and feet as I started back onto the road. I forced myself to run on painful, frozen feet. Slowly at first, then picking up pace as I gained warmth and momentum. It seemed a long time before my circulation came close to normal. Nature called when I thought I was winning the battle in these freezing conditions. I fought it, but in the end, I had to bare it all. It was like dipping in an Arctic Lake. I had to keep an eye on my middle leg if it suddenly fell off.

Lupton came into view an hour and a half later. On the approach, the morning sun on the mountain face was a surprise. Against the backdrop of the blue sky, my eyes were entranced by the tincture of pink terracotta layers. All the buildings were low against the mountain. Despite the activities in the area and the Highway running along its full length, there seemed to be an air of tranquillity in its vicinity. I walked past Yellow Horse and Tepee trading posts along Grant Road until I reached Speedy's convenience. It was a relief to get somewhere warm.

Speedy's was this great 'aircraft hangar' of a building where I took a long, hot shower and a huge breakfast. They had everything in the building: a supermarket, café, restroom, and shower area. It was a place for truck drivers and travellers to stop over, wash, clean their trucks, and sleep. Along the road was an all-Indian trade centre with traditional teepee dwellings but on a grander scale. They sold many local artefacts and goods. I tucked into a superb, hefty breakfast of hash browns, toast, beans, and two eggs. I couldn't resist three mugs of coffee. I felt clean and nourished as I hadn't eaten the night before. People reading the caption on the trailer nearby kept wishing me good luck and wanted to shake my hand and have a little chit-chat.

One man named Gaston (I recognised it as a French name, but he said he had no French ancestry) wanted to know about my trek and asked me questions. When I told him I started from Los Angeles, he took to me. I told him I couldn't find a place to sleep until late.

"Where did you sleep last night, then?"

"I slept in my tent, about seven miles from here."

"Jesus, it must've been cold."

"I practically froze."

"You are a lucky man. It was twelve below zero last night; it'll be the same tonight. Where are you planning to go?"

"Gallup," I said.

"Well, it's quite a way, close to thirty miles."

"I thought less."

"I can't be sure, but it'll be in that region. Good luck to you. Stay out of the cold now. Frostbite will put an end to your journey."

The sleepless night and the cold didn't play on my mind after my shower and breakfast. Gaston's reminder made me realise the potential danger of frost later.

On reflection, with my third cup of coffee, I had been in great peril and placed little value on the hazard. Yet that had happened on two consecutive nights. At first, Jason saved me; it was like a test, fraught with risk, as though it needed repeating. Consciously, this had not been my intention. Perhaps the thin air on the high plateau muddled my mind. The terrain was eight and a half thousand feet above sea level.

If anything, and because of my stubbornness, being saved by Jason curtailed a real possibility of endangerment. I was grateful for the moment when Jason came along. When something potentially harmful happens on one occasion, it could be deemed accidental. When it's repeated, there could be a case it was engineered, consciously or not. Why then go on searching for that threat?

This scenario didn't sit well and lacked clarity. This whole trek was full of hidden hazards. The terrain on this high plateau was flat, exposed, rugged, treeless, challenging, and dry. The ever-changing climate made the plants hardy, thorny, stunted, and deformed. The grim landscape was transformed by bitterly cold winds, searing heat, and snowfall. I immediately understood that the minute I saw how nature had arranged this harsh beauty of the wilderness and bleak view. Perhaps I dismissed too readily the depth of how the surroundings impacted and changed me. Subtly blind to the shifts that were taking place.

It occurred to me that the physical vulnerability I found myself once more took me to a wild dimension like its natural features. It broke down my everyday structured existence and shifted the essence of my equilibrium to the unfamiliarity between my sense of safety and suspension amid a potential catastrophe. This feeling of being close to a frontier's edge. In jeopardy, overwhelmed by tentative freedom without limits. It gave me a new mastery of self—an unexpected knowledge of my aloneness.

Chapter 8: Lupton, New Mexico

Dwarfed by this pink mountain, which spread along Grant Road for four miles, are massive cave-like cavities where the Indians once lived. There is one cave that was the home of Chief Yellow Horse. There were statues on the cave roof and sculptures of local animals, such as deer and buffalo. This whole area is in the middle of the Navajo Nation Reservation. Walking on these high plains eight and half thousand feet above sea level, the boundaries seemed immense. The magnitude of a patchwork dome sky was beyond imagination for a city dweller. At one point, the gradient of the road led upwards to other strata of the foot of the mountain range. In the distance, a car parked with two silhouetted figures standing as if waiting for me to arrive.

It was thirty minutes before I reached them, pushing my trailer uphill. The woman got into the car when I was a hundred metres away. I could sense they were wary of me. It must have seemed strange to see a man walking and pushing a bright orange trailer in the middle of nowhere. Yet I knew they would be curious; I was just a lone figure. They could have moved on or locked themselves in their car and paid no heed. I wanted to put them at ease. I parked my trailer, greeted them, and gave a spiel about my adventure, pointing to my caption. The woman wound down her window, and they relaxed and warmed up.

He introduced himself as Adam, and she said, "I am Evelyn."

I wanted to know if they were locals.

"We came down from Chicago," said Adam.

"Oh, getting away from the cold and the snow. It's a good idea."

"We are doing a tour of the country. We've been working abroad for eleven years. We wanted to see a few places before settling down."

They looked like they were approaching their late 40s and had no children.

"What work were you involved in?"

"I taught English," said Evelyn.

"I'm a structural engineer. We started in the Middle East, went to Malaysia, then to China."

"How did you feel being away for that length of time?"

"It's been a long haul," said Evelyn.

"We are happy to be back in the USA," responded Adam.

"I suppose you must find it has all changed."

"Yes, we're not finding settling in easy. Perhaps this little adventure will give us a new perspective," said Evelyn.

"Have you found any work yet?"

"We're taking time off, six months maybe. We'll check on that later," said Adam.

They were heading towards Los Angeles and were planning to make a loop via Las Vegas back to Chicago.

Adam said, "We want to see the country, places we've never visited."

They wanted to know what London was like. They spent two days in Paris before setting off to the Middle East and had been nowhere else in Europe. Without selling London too much, I told them it was one of the best cities in the world.

"We'll put London on our bucket list. What's your destination?" asked Evelyn.

"I made Norfolk in Virginia as my provisional end to the journey, but that's unlikely. I don't want to finish in a big city. I'll need to sit down and plan properly once I get away from these Rocky Mountains."

They offered me energy bars and soft drinks, which I declined, informing them sugar was bad for me. They were looking for a place to have lunch. I told them about Lupton, a few miles away, and mentioned the museum in Holbrook. We hugged goodbye, and they gave me their blessings and wished me luck. I am getting used to people hugging me, something I hadn't expected walking in America.

I galloped to Gallup. I wanted to double-check on the mileage Gaston had told me. A truck driver at Lupton told me nineteen miles. It turned out twenty-nine, and much of it was more of the same farmland, rugged landscape. My mapping and distance calculation turned out to be accurate. I never missed a turn. Just before entering Gallup, I walked through a Navajo village. It was made of small houses in rows smack in the middle of the desert. In the schoolyard, lots of children were playing. It was a desolate oasis.

A Navajo man holding a baby on the roadside said, "If the police catch you on the road, they'll arrest you."

I asked: "How far was Gallup?"

"It's about four miles. You'd better get off the road."

There was no sidewalk after the village. I had no choice but to keep to the road as I had until now. Later in Gallup, I met a police officer who advised me to stay on the pavement.

"It's safer there. The truck drivers are rough."

I asked him if walking on the highway in New Mexico was okay.

"No chance. Are you looking to get killed? You can check with the police patrol, and they'll tell you the same."

Like most towns, Gallup was spread out, about thirteen square miles with detached buildings, hardly a construction above one story high, except for some motels. I was not inclined to visit the town and certainly not by walking. I felt tired and needed a day's proper rest. One hundred and four miles in three days surpassed even my expectations. With a small rucksack and fair weather, a hundred miles in two days were possible, but it was a risk, nonetheless. I wanted to check into a motel as soon as I could. In the lobby, the desk was dealing with a customer. While pouring a coffee, a woman said, "I could do with one of those," and introduced herself as Jessica.

"I saw your trailer outside and was wondering."

I said, "It is what it says in the caption."

She said, "You look deadbeat."

I booked a ground-floor room. I sat under the shower for a long time before going to bed. I needed to check with the police patrol if it was legal to walk on the highway. I was in a different state, New Mexico. I turned on the TV and checked the news. The weather information came on. At night, the temperature would drop 10°/12° Celsius below zero (14°/10° Fahrenheit) for the next six days. I phoned the desk and asked for the number of the police patrol. The manager asked why, and I explained. He said he'll phone the police and let me know. Within five minutes, the phone rang, and the answer was a positive no.

Service roads were part of the way, but I would have to use the highway for a fair distance. In effect, The Highway Patrol made my decision for me.

Even if it was okay with the police, I was not prepared to sleep under these frosty conditions in my tent. I wouldn't have survived. I telephoned the desk and enquired about a bus to Albuquerque. The bus stop was in front of the motel on the opposite side of the road.

With this comforting news, sleep smothered me. Only an hour had passed when I woke up, yet I felt refreshed and hungry. My recovery period was remarkably good. I dressed and went to the lobby to ask if they could suggest a place to eat.

Jessica was there and said, "I know a good place. I wouldn't mind the company."

"Good idea," knowing she had a car, we wouldn't have to walk to the restaurant.

In the car, she said, "I just arrived from Santa Fe when I saw you in the lobby. Once a month, I visit my mother and sister in Flagstaff, Arizona."

"It's a long way to travel."

"I like to break the journey into two parts. It's less tiring that way. I don't like driving at night."

I wanted to know more about her, her children, and her husband, and she didn't hold back. She had fallen in love with her husband and married young.

"He was a no-good son-of-a-b……. He was a womaniser. He used to say my daddy taught me everything."

There was lingering anger. Her second husband died of cancer three years ago. She was now fifty and a little cynical.

"I've had no luck with men. They've been a pain. One moment, they love you, and the next, they eye someone else. I don't think anyone is left to suit me in this world."

"You don't think all men are alike, do you?"

"Well, maybe not all men. Some of them are dull-boring. I mean, just the ones who give me the eye."

"So, you like being chased?"

At that moment, she laughed, and her face changed, enhancing her appeal.

I said, "Men who chase women are on a hunting trip."

"Brother, don't I know it? They are the ones that are more interesting, more appealing. I guess for a time, I went chasing rainbows."

She had no children, "That was never possible."

I didn't press the point. I said, "These days, options are open to her."

"I have tried a few, but the men are fakes. They put up false pictures of themselves. Their résumé is shallow, unlike their bulging midriff. I arranged to meet a guy in a bar once, and I took one look at him and walked out. He was a good foot shorter than he said he was. His athleticism took refuge in his little finger. He wore an outfit where his jacket buttons were about to take a parachute jump. His thinning hair had an unnatural colour. That made him look like an overdressed poodle. I don't mind the effects of ageing. You know the rugged appearance, the receding hairline—the marks of a lifetime of living. But the eyes must show life, some intelligence trying to hang on. Not just a washed-up cowboy looking for a caretaker and a fuck. I hate swearing."

"Well, it's charming coming from you."

Jessica had vigour, which made her attractive. She had a friendly smile, and her voluptuousness made her more appealing. She was witty, a fast talker, and full of information. When I asked her about the Native population in Gallup, she responded that it was less than half, including Navajo, Zuni, and Hopi.

She didn't wait for my next question and said, "One-fifth of the population in the region now lives below the poverty level. There is a high rate of crime."

"Was that down to the locality being depressed?"

"The economy has never taken off. There was coal mining in the last century, but these mines were mostly closed."

We had been slowly driving on the famous Route 66 and passed a lot of restaurants and fast-food venues. I suggested pointing to one or two, but she kept driving. Then we arrived at the El Rancho Hotel.

"What do you think of it?"

It was a surprise and unusual style, like a prominent rancher's mansion. In the prairie, like in the film 'The Big Country.' It had a huge porch supported by square columns. Different shades of light surround the building to highlight its spectacle.

"This is a historic hotel where many famous film stars stayed and lived while filming in Gallup."

The films and stars rolled off her tongue like she was reciting poetry: "Films like the Ace in the Hole and Escape from Fort Bravo and actors such as Bill Holden, Kirk Douglas, John Wayne, Joan Crawford and Doris Day."

"This is where we're going to eat. Wait till you get a load of the inside."

"Won't it be expensive?"

"Don't worry; it's on me. Your trek is an inspiration."

As we entered the lobby, it was like being transported to the Old West. Indian-made rugs of some style hung on the balustrade of the mezzanine, which surrounded the downstairs lobby. The three-tiered wagon wheel chandelier hung at the centre of the ceiling. The ceiling was made of rows of roughly hewn timber stretched from end to end. Two heavier sets of timbers crisscrossed as means of support. It gave an impression of rail tracks pinned down as sleepers. Framed photos of Film Stars were scattered like a montage on the wall of the mezzanine. The furniture matched the nineteenth-century setting. The sombre colour of the décor created a mood of being wrapped in velvet and enticed into grander things to come. The interwoven muted pigment patterns of the Indian rugs on the floor were exquisite. They matched the furniture and the shade of the stair's carpet. The two arched stairs to the upper hotel rooms were lined with burgundy carpet. They were like those seen in Bollywood movies.

We entered the dining room; it was moody with a dark, varnished wooden herringbone ceiling and dusky tiled flooring. The walls were white, and plenty of lights created a quaint atmosphere for an evening meal. The restaurant was almost full.

"Are we going to have a bottle of wine?"

"I can't drink, and you're driving."

"A glass can't do you any harm. If you won't, then I'll skip it."

We ordered. She had steak, rare, and salad, and I had fajitas. She wanted to know more about me. At first, I tried to evade her questions, but she was persistent.

"Yes, from London, right in the centre."

"Were you born there?"

"I was born in Mauritius - a small group of Islands at the end of the universe."

"Where is that?"

"It's as far as you can be from the USA. Have you heard of the Dodo or Solitaire?"

"The dodo is a bird, and Solitaire is a game."

"The dodo is an extinct bird from Mauritius. Solitaire is also an extinct bird from its sister Island, Rodrigues."

"I thought the dodo lived on a deserted Island?"

"Yes, but the building of Empires killed the dodos, moved people, and turned the island into a melting pot."

"Oh, I get it. You mean like an experiment in Frankenstein's lab, right? The British did it here too, emptying their jails, Irish rebels, and half of Ireland and turning them into slaves before the Africans were brought in."

"You've done a bit of history."

"I got news for you, buddy; we aren't all as dumb as we look."

Her response tickled me, and I laughed out loud. We received some attentive gazes from the other tables. She came back to me.

"So, the British made you. That makes you more British than the British, a mongrel."

"Is that a compliment?"

"Take it as you like. We are all mongrels. Only those stuck up their dumb ass see otherwise. It's all coming out into the open with genome testing anyhow."

I hadn't thought of it that way because of the nature of the British Empire. People from far and wide were flung onto tiny islands, hence my background of Indian, Chinese, and African ancestry.

"When did you move to London?"

"We were part of the British colony, and my parents moved to England when I was little."

"How do you see yourself?"

"British, I don't feel like anything else."

"I should think so. You came out of it ok."

"What do you mean?"

"Do I have to spell it out to you?"

"Yes, your puzzle is too cryptic for me."

She paused and gave me a long, seductive look. Her unblinking eyes stared into me, and her alluring smile lit her face. For a moment, she looked down. Her long hair cascaded down over her cheeks. Then she looked up again and flicked her hair back into place. Her eyes were in the moody light, a darker blue unlike those I had seen earlier.

She said, "Skin deep; Frankenstein's lab did a good job on you."

The waiter brought the food. Her steak was large and sizzling hot, and her grilled zucchinis looked appetising. I was hungry, and my veggie fajitas brought a sliver of saliva to my mouth.

"Here you take those. I've enough on my plate. We can share the salad."

She gave me all her grilled zucchini. While doing so, she looked at me, unaware I could sense all her thoughts.

She said, "Did I embarrass you?"

"I don't blush. No, you didn't."

"What is it then?"

"I was hurt, and it hasn't gone away. It's still raw, a bit like your stake."

"Was it recent?"

"A few months, but it feels like it happened only days ago."

"When I saw you in the lobby, you looked down. Was it because of that?"

"Every day, there is a discovery. It has just come now because you've mentioned it. I have run myself into the ground to forget. If I am tired, I don't have to think. Thinking always takes me back to her. Her name is Mijo short for Marie Josephe."

"That's French. Don't take it too hard. We all get over these ditches. You are in a bog, stuck in a quagmire. Sometimes, the names of people tell you a lot about them."

"Do they, in what way?"

"My first husband's name was Gus Musthaveit. He says his original name was Mustavich. They couldn't spell his family name when they came through immigration in those days. He got stuck with Musthaveit and lived by its meaning, chasing every bit of skirt he laid eyes on. Marie Josephe, there is one to hang out to dry. In the bible, Mary married Joseph; perhaps she was too married to herself to see you."

She had reversed the table on me, making me the focus of attention. She was appealing and fun to be with. She made me laugh, and she changed my mood. She was generous and would have paid for a good bottle of wine if I had wanted to drink. There was an air of confidence and relaxed elegance about her. Despite two marriages and the trauma of having to go through the illness of her last husband, she had found her balance. She depended on no one.

When we left, it was only then that I saw the deer's heads, with antlers pinned to the leading posts in the lobby. Trophies and longhorns hung over the exit door. Cattle ranch emblems arched the entrance. Leaving the hotel and walking out onto the porch seemed like stepping out of a ranch house on the prairie.

Jessica wanted to give me a tour of the town. I wouldn't have seen its interior otherwise, at least at night. The back streets were like the suburbia of a fertile place with trees lining the streets. Shrub gardens were with modest prefabricated houses, paved sidewalks, and streetlights. Yet I knew it was a town in the middle of a semi-desert. The Court House was built in the Pueblo style with some form of early twentieth-century architectural touch. Jessica said the colour matches the surrounding mountains, dusky pink terracotta. Despite all its modernity, cars, neon lights, and asphalt roads, the general impression was that it was still an early twentieth-century town.

Jessica and I said our goodbyes as we were leaving in the morning. She said I could call her if I happened to be in her part of the country and gave me her address.

She added, "That's the story of my life. People I get on with are always going the opposite direction to where I'm heading."

It was her way of saying that she, too, had enjoyed the evening.

***

I needed to escape the freezing night cold of the high plateau. I had risked hyperthermia on several occasions with sub-zero temperatures. I had endured frosty conditions in double figures in the past few days. It proved beyond the risk I was willing to take, even if allowed on the highway.

Taos, New Mexico, became part of my destination. When walking up to Payson, Arizona, Morten contacted me via my blog. He was part of the Findhorn circle of friends (about two hundred and fifty of them live in the USA). The Findhorn circle had given me moral support and encouragement. Morton had invited me to stay for a while if I could make it to Taos.

The Findhorn Foundation is an intentional, educational community of two hundred-plus people who live in and around the village of Findhorn in Northeast Scotland. It was founded in 1962 in the Findhorn Bay Caravan Park by Peter, Eileen Caddy, and Dorothy Maclean. For over sixty years, the community has drawn together people from around the globe. People with diverse spiritual and cultural backgrounds. They practice and show how living and working sustainably, in harmony with each other and nature, can help create a consensus world. Many of the early members have remained close friends. And those in the US have an annual reunion in different parts of the country.

Morten mentioned some picturesque roads with villages from Gallup to Taos two weeks earlier. When I studied the map, I found that his proposed route led me higher. A further four and a half thousand feet and in freezing conditions. The villages for supplies were eighty to one hundred miles apart. That would have added a further hundred miles onto my journey. My original plan was to go to Albuquerque and stay on Route 66 as much as possible to Amarillo, Texas, in a straight line. That distance between Albuquerque and Amarillo looked grassy-dry, vast, and empty on Google. When I explained my predicament over the phone to Morten, he suggested I make my way to Santa Fe. He would pick me up from there and plan all the routes east together. He and his wife Kate lived in Taos, due north.

The bus left early, but coming out of the motel was numbing cold. The wind blew a bitter, icy chill. I felt my hair getting frosted, as though ready to crumble and fall into a heap on the ground. Inside, the bus was as warm as a hot thermal pool. We made a stop in Grant, a small town on the way. It was like being on a Western set except for the cars, the gas station, and the electric poles along the walkways. The backdrop changed to a prairie of winter-brown grass dotted with stunted pine and many scattered monument-type hills. The rocks in that part of the country were unusually black.

At the bus stop, Sam came on and sat next to me. He was eager to talk. My tongue was still asleep, but I didn't mind listening. He came from Texas, San Antonio, but he pronounced it as San Antone, munching the last part of the word. He said that he was delivering a car to someone in Arizona. The car had broken down about twenty miles before Grant. He was left stranded, got cold, and couldn't make a call as he was in a black spot. A truck later spotted him and gave him a lift. At the motel, he called home and was told to head back. They would have the car towed. I couldn't make an effort to ask him to where. Taking the car back to Texas would not have been a profitable venture.

He said it was his thirty-second birthday only two days ago. He kept his body shape well and had slight receding hair with a hidden handsomeness. He was polite and curious about my accent and what brought me to the USA. I wanted to place the focus on him and ask if he was married, the direct, intrusive Indian way.

"No, but I had a girlfriend for five years. We broke up four months ago. I am fixing to get married and have a coupla kids. First, I must save a few bucks and buy a house."

He had done car deliveries for three years. Did he think spending time away could have affected his relationship?

"Ye, maybe, spending time on the road, we kinda drifted."

After a long pause, his voice softened: "Friends have been saying she was naturally horizontal. That hurts."

He was still hurting, and I saw the sadness in his profile as he looked away into the distance along the highway. He became silent for a while and suddenly pointed to the car, "That's the car."

The car looked 'new' parked in a lay-by on the hard shoulder.

"Before they built the Highway, Route 66 was a two-lane road with many traffic problems and deaths. Getting stuck behind a truck could take thirty miles before you got past it."

The new highway was completed in the early 80s. I asked him how long the journey would take to get back.

"Two days plus. I got to change the bus in Albuquerque and make another transfer to San Antone. The buses don't leave till late tonight. I must kill time till then."

He went silent again, looking out the window. In the distance, a long train passed by on the sea of grass plain, and I counted the number of wagons it was pulling: one hundred and twenty.

Chapter 9: A Little Off-Course

I, too, had much time to kill. We arrived just after ten and missed the early train to Santa Fe. The next one was not due until late afternoon. It was fortunate that the train station was part of the bus terminal. I didn't have to venture out for miles looking for it. I wanted to visit the city, but storing my trailer proved problematic. My sole view was window glances as we entered the city and close to the station's vicinity. Albuquerque means White Oak. I never thought one day I would set foot here. The placename came to me from the song "By the Time I Get to Phoenix" by Jimmy Webb. Way back in 1975, a friend sent me a postcard from there.

Waiting in the lounge was tedious. The station was modest and modern, with only two trains going north daily. It wasn't easy to see why trains weren't the primary means of transport. I enquired why this was so. The man at the ticket counter said running more than two trains per day wasn't profitable. Providing a service for the general population didn't come into the equation. Two other people sat waiting. We got talking and lunched together. Debs, a grandmother, lives in Los Angeles, San Bernardino ("It's a rough place," she said). She was going to visit her daughter and granddaughter in Santa Fe.

She tires easily, "I've had two strokes and am on medication for high blood pressure and other conditions."

Her drowsiness caused her to drift in and out of our conversation. On one occasion, she told an interesting story.

"When I was havin' a stroke, I felt no pain at all. It ain't what people think. At first, I felt like an angel with wings floatin' in the wind. Then I was overtaken by a euphoric feelin', the best life experience I've ever had. It was like the ultimate orgasm in the last chance saloon."

It's the first time I have heard someone describe a life-threatening experience better than an orgasm. She became drowsy again after she took her prescribed drug. Slowly, she drifted out of our little talk.

Linda Santana made up our threesome. She had dark eyes, black hair, and unblemished skin. She was a bright young twenty-six years old and doing ecology work. Her friend was to pick her up in Santa Fe. She had a clear view of what she wanted and how to find the time to do it. Her home was also in Los Angeles. With her work, she moved to various states like Montana, Idaho, and now Taos, New Mexico. But she was itching to move again and was waiting to see where her next destination might take her, what journey awaited her.

"My parents were overly concerned with me and my siblings. It was stifling as we approached our late teenage years. It took a long time before I could break away. Since leaving the family hub four years ago, I have felt liberated. I have slowly made discoveries about myself that wouldn't have fit into the normal life pattern, or at least not now. I need to be involved in different aspects of work, meet new people, and enjoy the adventures that work and places offer me."

I mentioned the Camino de Santiago De Compostela to her and explained what a life-changing experience could be. She wanted to know more.

"Something happens inside, something extraordinary, and the effect will be unique to each person. You can be a believer or an unbeliever. The impact will be the same."

The train was on time. Linda, Debs, and I naturally moved into separate compartments. Perhaps we needed our own space. On the train, the landscape changed and became more familiar. The scenes of films I had seen in my childhood. The wavering hills in the background. The horses in the corrals. The little nineteenth-century haciendas in the foreground and the openness of the vista. In full view of the chilly, dry climate and the vast blue yonder, full of stars at night. It was as though I was on a steam train travelling in these parts in the days gone by. Only the train whistles, the specks of burnt coal, and the smell of smoke were missing. The journey was over two hours.

Morten was waiting for me at the station. We had a two-hour drive to Taos, surrounded by the sacred mountains. It's where the Rio Grande begins. I had talked on the phone and written emails but never set eyes on him. Our connection was instant.

"Welcome to this part of the country."

He gave me a big hug. He looked lean, grey-haired, and lively with the energy of a man in his mid-thirties.

Along the way, he told me: "This is the land of the Pueblo people. In the past, Taos was the hub of the trading centre. Many of the tribes came from far and wide to trade."

We had been climbing since we left Santa Fe between pine forests. The road was familiar to Morten. He knew all the contours as we wound our way up. He drove at speed, and the sensation sent me into a daze as if the world was passing by fast. Morten talked of the region; I listened but could not gauge most of his words. The speed of the car and his speech were synchronised. My reaction was too slow to pick up where I had left off. We climbed higher into thin air. Perhaps it was tiredness. We arrived late at their beautiful house, Pueblo style. Kate, his wife, was waiting to welcome us.

They had met at Findhorn, Scotland, where they spent a few years as part of the community. They married there and had their first child on the grounds of Findhorn. Morten was originally from Norway, and Kate was from Maryland, USA. When they moved on to settle in the USA, they first went to California. Later, they chose Taos as their preferred home. Morten was in the music business for a decade, but the stress attached to the industry made him choose a different path.

Kate and Morten, my hosts in Taos, NM

The large studio at the front of the house is where Kate and Morten produce their work. Morten said Kate taught him everything as he was in an impasse after leaving his profession. They are weavers. They create their fabrics using two air-pressured looms. The designs, embellishing, and patterns are their creations. They also generate the style of product to suit the woven fabrics. The whole creative process, from the original idea and choice of thread to the completed piece, is an art form. Even before the garments are sold and tried, they look alive, dazzle and drape so well on the hangers. But after thirty years, Kate wanted to leave it all and move on to something else.

"You know, when you've reached the end of something, you no longer have the enthusiasm or the energy to carry on. Morten didn't have an interest in taking over the weaving business."

My hosts were generous and kind and very relaxed people. They are both multi-talented and creative. Their house reflects the personalities that they had built.

It is spacious yet homely and decorated in white and pastel shades that blend into the classic Pueblo architecture. Their home furnishings were warm and instantly made you feel comfortable. In this part of the region, the Pueblo Indian-style architecture is famous. It's the construction where traditional houses or buildings are made with adobe. Mostly, they have round corners, irregular parapets, and thick walls and are kept in a natural, earthy look. The roofs are flat, with heavy beams unmilled and peeled. They support the structure with the protruding end of those beams shown on the outside. Modern construction uses modern materials but disguises the mode with stucco and tones yet strives to maintain the style.

The house blended easily with the broader landscape, as all Pueblo houses seemed to do. On the south side are three acres of land where they grow alfalfa hay, and these grasses were taller than people. I had read in Lewis and Clark (Pioneers who first went beyond the Appalachian Mountains in 1804) of the prairie grass being taller than man and stretched out like an ocean dancing in the wind. Taos is where one could imagine being transported into an image like entering "Lost Horizon" to seek Nirvana. The imposing presence of the Sangre de Cristo Mountains surrounds it. These mountains were held sacred by the Pueblo Indians for more than a thousand years. They are capped with snow in the vicinity of the blue lake. Still, there is concern about the lack of rain in this part of north-central New Mexico. Although it can get as cold as twenty-five degrees below zero in winter, it's a dry cold. The sun is always shining, and it is pleasant and mild by the afternoon in early spring.

After a good night's rest, Morten enthusiastically engaged me with the next stage of my travels. Soon after breakfast, he laid the maps on the table.

"We need to think clearly about this and not waste time."

We planned the route together in detail, looking at the difficulties involved, and found solutions to make the journey less hazardous. We assessed the trek. It looked daunting because of the long distance between villages and towns. I would need to stock up on supplies of food and water. Ahead was the Panhandle country of Texas. Dorothy, too, had shown concern about this leg of the journey when we were planning it back in California. She mentioned that she had previously driven through the Pan Handle and hardly saw any villages along the way. This section of the trek played on my mind, especially during those demanding moments in the Rockies, even though I had vowed to concentrate on one day at a time.

We planned a rough route to Michael Davidson's abode in Eupora, Mississippi, via Graceland, Elvis's home. (Michael had written to Morten earlier when he heard of my trek and offered to help. He was also part of the Findhorn group of friends.) When we went into greater detail calculating a set mileage per day, we realised it was a hazardous undertaking.

"The distance is too vast between villages, and you will need a gallon of water a day. It'll take you five days and, in some cases, seven days to get to a village for supplies," said Morten.

Since I could only carry three gallons and, if needed, make the water last five days. It made the trek grim and probably would put me on the verge of dehydration. I was in a mess. My mind was in constant worry.

Morten said, "Why don't you use a bicycle to cross the Panhandle?"

I gave it some thought overnight, and in the morning, we decided it was a good solution. I bought a mountain bicycle and attached the trailer to it. That way, the risks involved were lessened. Choosing a mountain bicycle was necessary because of the problem posed by the tumbleweed thorns. Ordinary bicycle tyres would be easily punctured. This changed the journey and made it different. I could do eight mph instead of averaging three and a half mph. In my mind, it brought relief. It had worried me ever since I left Holbrook. Rescued by Jason was a reminder of what could happen. The cold weather and distances between towns became a burden.

"This won't make your journey any easier. The roads undulate in New Mexico, Texas, and Arkansas until reaching the Mississippi River. The journey would be divided into walking, pulling the bicycle and trailer, and riding," said Morten.

In one way, the trip would be more leisurely, but in another, it would be more arduous. I would keep the bicycle until there was no longer a risk. The preparation and the thought of what was ahead made me anxious, and I had little sleep. Morten helped me prepare everything. He took me to a shop in Taos Plaza and advised me what I would need. I didn't like the look of the saddle, but the shop manager said it would serve me well in the long distance. When everything was bought and ready, I felt relieved on the eve of my departure. The next morning, Morten would drop me off in Cimarron village on Route 58, New Mexico.

Kate was quiet, like someone in deep thought, pleasant to talk to. While Morten was in the studio working, Kate and I went on walks together. She took me to the hills surrounding Taos on an old Indian path. We saw Taos from the heights, an extensive picturesque flat town in a valley surrounded by mountains. For the first time, a kind of relief came to me. It seemed as if I had been climbing mountains forever. They oppressed me and called for every sinew in my body to stay active and alive. The penalty for that was to experience pain in areas I never knew could exist. These mountains in Taos couldn't claim me and inflict their pains. It was I who had the power to assert. I couldn't be defeated; I earned the right to have these Sacred Mountains as a visual spectacle.

We talked about what it was like to live in Taos. We spoke of the issues that affected the community. The difficulties of getting people together to resolve problems such as water shortage. They first settled here some thirty years back: "It was hard, but we quickly made friends. That was vitally important." She took me to visit her friend who raised chickens; we drank tea and bought organic eggs.

I wanted to treat them to dinner in a restaurant. They invited one of their friends. Jane was from England but had lived in Taos longer than she could recall. There was still a twang of the English pronunciation left. That was our last supper together, and back at the house, Morten and Kate said, "I should be careful on my travels."

"I'm always careful."

Were they trying to warn me about certain dangers travelling in the southern states with my brown pigmentation? I put that question to them.

Morten said, "We are not suggesting that, but the possibility is always there that you could be in the wrong place at the wrong time. Be ready for what might lie ahead."

Early morning on the day of my departure at the breakfast table, Morten said, "I've found a better spot for you to leave from."

"Is it far from where we decided?"

"From Springer, New Mexico, you won't have to cross the main route there."

After three days, I was ready for the road again. The rest, the deliberation and planning gave my confidence an upswing. I couldn't wait to get back into the open and see what lay ahead. I set my alarm for six but stayed excited throughout the night.

Chapter 10: Stride on to Texas!

Morten decided it was best for me to take Route 56. We left early, before eight, after I said my goodbyes. We snaked down the long descent sandwiched between mountains and pine forests with whitening forest floors. It felt like we were gliding with almost no other cars. It occurred to me that the altitude was part of why I hadn't been breathing to my total capacity. The logic of it hadn't readily come to mind until then.

We passed a mountain, and Morten pointed out that it was the highest peak in the area, 13,500ft. Everything appears gigantic: the mountains, the valley, the space, as we motor down through the big country. After the ride imitating slalom, we arrived at Springer. Morten parked in a lay-by on a quiet corner. I unloaded my trailer, attached it to my bicycle, and bid a warm farewell to my friend. The cold wrapped around me like a soaked blanket. There was no snow on the ground, but a gale-force wind blew.

He said, "It's the windy season; it will blow for a month."

He watched me set off on my bicycle/trailer into the wind that blew from the south-westerly direction. A cold whistling air funnel hit me across the angle of my right shoulder. It took time to gain my balance as I zigzagged unsteadily along the bleak and empty route.

The road was up and down for the next twenty-four miles. Whenever there was a hill, I had to get off my bicycle and push until I reached the top. Despite the bicycle, it was clear from the outset that the trek would be challenging. Seeing buffalo on these vast plains was astonishing, which was a surprise. Never have I seen live buffalo chewing grass on the prairie. I aimed to get to Clayton, an old train-loading cattle town. It had its heyday in the early 1900s, but it has declined. The distance was eighty-two miles from Springer. It may take four days to walk in my present condition. I could make the trip in one day, but I forgot about pulling the hundred-and-ten-pound trailer.

It was a mean cold from the start. It became colder, and I was afraid to wipe my nose in case it snapped off. I kept my fleece jacket on. Later I had to put on my windbreaker, making five layers of clothes. After fifteen miles, I met a police patrol officer and asked if he knew where I could pitch my tent. I realised getting to Clayton was way beyond my estimation. Even in two days might prove difficult. The wind was fierce. It slowed me down to a walking pace.

"There is a rest area seven miles ahead, but not much protection from the wind."

I reached the rest area with park benches and tables made of concrete. I searched for a place near some bushes to set up camp. It was impossible, as the officer had said. The wind howled at me, saying, "Not here, son; this is a place for crows, cattle, and tumbleweeds". I felt tired; it was late afternoon, and the rough surface of the road and the weather condition had taken their toll. I couldn't take a break to eat a snack for fear of stiffening up. Even though the efforts of pedalling should easily have made me work up a sweat, I began to freeze. The patrol officer mentioned a shop about sixteen miles from the rest stop. A place called Gladstone.

"The people are good folks. They might help."

My bones sensed zero or below, and the light was fading fast. I rode all day except for a brief stop. Gladstone seemed that extra mile away. Maybe the officer's calculation was wrong. I attached a torch to my saddle. I sorely pedalled my bike. The saddle was stiff and cut through the inner part of my thighs. I ached and felt bruised.

Then it was dark, and Gladstone was just a shop with two gas pumps in front of it like an old disused petrol station. Everything was closed and dark. A house was on a hill behind the shop, like the one in Hitchcock's "Psycho." I pushed on up there and shouted, "Hello". A few snowflakes fell like birds' plumage from the black sky. Big Alsatian guard dogs might race towards me from behind the house at any moment. In flashing images, I saw my hands being eaten and blood gushing out and icing into hard globules falling to the dirt like marbles on the cold, hard ground. I shouted "Hello" for a few more minutes. Perhaps no one was at home, or they were too afraid to step out at night. Then, it occurred to me that they might show up with a gun. Then what would I do?

Dorothy once said, "People shoot first and ask questions later if you are on their property."

I looked around and saw a locked-up white building to the left of the shop and pondered, pitching my tent there. It would shelter me from the wind and leave early at daybreak before anyone would notice. The cold became unbearable. I was a solid block of ice. In that instant, death passed through my mind. I shouted at the top of my voice as if my life depended on it.

After a while, someone came out, a tall man with a cowboy hat on. I introduced myself and asked if I could camp behind his shop.

"You can pitch anywhere, my friend," pointing to the wide-open space.

"Can I pitch behind the shop?"

He looked closely at me and noticed I was frozen to the bone, my teeth chattering.

"You look like you could do with a hot coffee."

He invited me into the shop. The heater was on, giving out a deluxe warmth, but I remained cold to the bone.

He told me his name was Doyle Price. He had a full head of hair, a big man with a good, well-proportioned posture. "You can use the washroom if you want; it's at the back at the end of a hallway."

I washed my face and tried to defrost my hands. But I felt a burning sensation with pangs of pain, and my arms were weak without dexterity. I folded a towel over my hands and stuck them on the heater. I saw that the shop was a mini supermarket with everything in it.

"Are you hungry? I can cook something for you?"

I was hungry for something warm, but my upbringing caused me to refuse the first offer. It was a strange reaction of false modesty. In a time like this, I needed a warm blanket cover and to eat hot, comforting food. My response was robot-like, automated by my childhood conditioning.

"There is no need for you to go to such trouble."

"No trouble at all. I was going to make supper, anyway."

I accepted that time without timidity. He put the coffee on the stove in the shop and went to the house. I sat down and thought about how close death came in this big and empty place. He came back a few minutes later with a few pots in hand.

"Are you all right, son?"

"Yes, I am fine now. You saved my life. I wouldn't have lasted another fifteen minutes out there."

"I am glad you stopped by. I am happy to help."

The coffee was ready, and as he poured me a mug, it was black and thick.

"Here you go, son, get that down you. It'll bring you back to life."

The mug of coffee was soothing to my still-frozen hands. It was cowboy-style coffee. I had heard of it but never drank it. It was hot, thick, black, and bitter with a lingering caffeine aftertaste, and it tasted better than any brandy on a cold night. A couple of sips and the caffeine kicked in, and the thawing sensation was a relief.

"How d'you like our coffee?"

"I love it. It made me human again. I can feel my toes tingling."

"So, you've taken to it. It's got a kick. In these parts, you need something to get you moving in the early cold morning working outdoors."

In our conversation, he said he came from Texas.

"I came visiting' one day, and there she was, and I became her captive."

His wife was a local girl, and they had fallen in love and got married, and he moved to New Mexico instead of settling in Texas. His wife had the final say on that. He was a gentleman not just because he was kind but affable. His voice was comforting with great sincerity. He had called me son, but, in our ages, there was less than a decade difference.

Joe and Marlys, his son's partner, joined us for dinner later. They were in their late thirties, lived in Colorado, and had come to visit for a few days. They were out visiting friends that evening. The distance in the USA did not hinder family, friendship, or community life. It could have impacted if the price of petrol were not so low, making close contact less frequent. But again, the same fraternity existed a hundred years ago when the horse and buggy were the primary means of transport. People riding twenty, thirty miles or more in this expansive landscape to attend Sunday church would have been the norm. The worshipping of God was at the centre of this intimacy of human contact.

Doyle said a prayer before we ate. He cooked pinto beans, the most delicious dish I have ever tasted. Plus, a mixture wrapped in corn leaves was equally appetising. I didn't want to ask him if I could sleep on his shop floor where it was warm. I might have overstepped my welcome. In any case, he didn't suggest it. While pitching my tent in a sheltered spot behind the shop, a flurry of snowflakes glittered in the shop's dim yellow security lights. In the tent, it was well below zero. I was in and out of sleep. Despite the double socks, my feet remained frozen through the night. My crotch was sore, raw, and bruised by the unsuitable saddle the shop in Taos had sold me.

Doyle said goodnight while I was setting up the tent under the snowfall, and I contemplated while he was walking away how lucky I had been to meet such a man on this dark and icy night in the middle of nowhere. As he went past going to the house on the hill, he said, "I am an early riser, up at four." I replied that I would be up at seven to decamp.

It was a dry and frosty morning. It didn't surprise me not to see any snow on the ground. My feet were numb and uncomfortable. Those tumbleweeds piled up against my tent as I poked my head to look at the universe again. Thelma, Doyle's wife, walked by. I greeted her, and she looked at me with a solemn morning face.

She said, "Breakfast will be ready in fifteen minutes."

I hadn't expected that. She was a petite woman carrying a frying pan and a food bag. She walked briskly to the shop. As I decamped, I thought of the long journey to Clayton and doubted I could make it. There was nothing in between, and the wind was still howling.

Nothing is better than the smell of a hot breakfast on a frosty, windy dawn. At the table, I asked Thelma if I could get a ride to Clayton if I thumbed a lift.

Doyle answered: "I don't think so; it's Sunday. People would be busy preparing for the church gathering."

Then he said a little prayer before we tucked into our breakfast. I told them I was very fortunate for their hospitality. Last night, I couldn't think clearly, felt tired, ached, and was cold.

"We do what we can. Glad to be of help," said Doyle.

"Stay another day. You need the rest. We have rooms in the house. You would be no bother to us," said Thelma, still with a serious look.

My body needed to stay, but my mind wanted to move on. Unknowingly, I returned to projecting ahead instead of being in the moment. Besides, I didn't want to change their routine. We were in a good mood, and we chatted about my venture. Breakfast was delicious and satisfying: biscuits (a kind of scone) with white gravy and scrambled eggs on toast. Doyle had hot green chillies with bacon, eggs, and biscuits. This surprised me.

Doyle said, "We are used to eating chillies here."

Only while travelling through India had I come upon chillies with breakfast. Thelma encouraged me to double help, and I would not allow my polite upbringing to make me decline. She poured me another helping of hot coffee, cowboy style. Soon, it was time for me to leave. I gave them both a big hug and thanked them for their kindness. Thelma slipped twenty dollars into my hand.

"You will need a good supper where you are going," she said.

I felt so humbled by their kindness, and I was lost for words in my state of hypersensitivity. They hugged me, and Thelma said, "God be with you." Later, on the road, Doyle came to mind and what he said at the breakfast table when he asked me about London. I had given him my view of what the city was like. Afterwards, he said, "Here we are a little backwards."

***

My watch showed it was almost eight. The minute I stepped outdoors, I entered a cold storage world. It stayed frozen on the road until the afternoon when the temperature rose to 37° F. The wind chill factor made it feel more like it was sub-zero. My hands and feet remained numb. I pedalled as fast as I could to keep warm and made fine progress despite all the pain and discomfort inflicted by the saddle. It stayed overcast, and the cattle and horses stared at me as I rode by with my orange trailer. On either side of the road, tawny, tough, wilted winter grass carpeted the view until the dome of clouds descended to earth in the distance. Flocks of singing birds scattered when I wheeled past them.

Sometimes, I would get a good downhill stretch for two miles, free-wheeling, and then it would level off again for another mile. I thought that this was my lucky day. In two hours, I covered fifteen miles. I raced ahead and projected that I should be in Clayton by early afternoon. The route soon became unpredictable. Rough surfaces in parts made riding more arduous, and undulating regularity meant I had to walk and drag my bike and trailer along. Soreness and tiredness took over. I struggled to get to Clayton, arriving there in darkness at nearly seven o'clock in the evening, frozen stiff. My rear tyre went flat as I parked my bike against the motel wall. "Damn, those tumbleweeds!" I cursed. After my shower, I was smashed, didn't eat, and crawled into bed. I was up at six o'clock the next day. I needed to fix my tyre and count six thorns in the deflated wheel.

Although it was a restful night, I woke up with two painful lumps on my crotch, the size of ping-pong balls. The cause was the hard saddle. I needed a new seat. There was no bicycle shop in town. I walked about to see if I could find something to pad my saddle. On Main Street was a fabulous hardware store, R.W. Isaacs Company. Nothing had changed since the grand old Edwardian days. They stored all the merchandise imaginable. The people inside were friendly, and when one middle-aged server asked what I was looking for, he offered me a jelly seat cover.

"Ok, this might work, but I need to make sure since I'm going a long way."

"Where are you going?" he asked.

"To the Atlantic Ocean," I replied.

"My, oh my!"

Overhearing the conversation, the customers in the shop became friendly and curious. A small group of four gathered around the counter. One asked if I was from Australia, perhaps thinking I could be Aboriginal or maybe because of my 'strange' vowel sounds.

"London, England," I said. "And I don't resemble anyone." They looked surprised.

They giggled as though I was making a pleasantry. One man with his beard going grey, wearing a blue cap, asked: "What language d'ya speak in London?"

The question threw me. I didn't know whether he was being serious. He said it with a deadpan face. The expectancy of the others was like they were waiting to fit a jigsaw into a puzzle. The words wouldn't come out of my mouth fast enough. The man in a fawn jacket loaded another question onto me.

"Where d'ya learn to speak American?"

I was in a tight spot, and no matter how I chose my answers, it was bound to sound arrogant. I was just a lone rider for a moment on another planet. Inadvertently, to add confusion to the answer, I said, "The last time I checked, over two hundred and eighty languages are spoken in London. This might come as a shock to you, but English is the language of the land."

Blue cap man: "Ya don't say."

Those three syllabic words were enough to send me into vertigo.

"The American you speak is English."

Fawn jacket man: "Dawg gone; how did that happen?"

The server came to my rescue, speaking to the group, a kindly man: "Listen, Jack, every year we celebrate Independence Day, we fought the English for our freedom. They gave us the language."

They all seemed bashful after he spoke. Then the shopkeeper said, "I've some foam back in the other room. Maybe you can look and see what you can do, work it around the saddle."

I was glad he took me away from the attention. I bought a length of foam used to insulate pipes. I could fashion it to fit my saddle. It might ease the soreness around the inner part of my thighs. By now, I was walking like a jockey, bow-legged, and each step made me wince the pain when the upper thighs rubbed together. Provisions bought. I said goodbye to everyone. Upon leaving, puzzled, one of the gangs of four scratched his head.

Across the road, there was an interesting building; I ventured there. It was a classic nineteenth-century hotel, bar, and restaurant. It seemed untouched by modernisation, and everything was kept to a superb standard. I chatted with Jeanette Vigil Barras, who owned the Hotel Eklund enterprise. The saloon had a long bar which resembled an elongated Welsh Dresser. Behind the bar hung huge, panelled mirrors, two of which formed arches on either side of the bar.

Jeanette said, "The bar counter was designed with magnificent craftsmanship and was won in a poker game."

Three men were sitting at the counter, and a few others were at the far corner tables. We moved away from the bar, and she pointed to the ceiling.

"You see these two holes? These are bullet holes when one gentleman, a Democrat, got mad when Harding won the presidential election in 1920. He fired a couple of shots in the air, and we've left them there as part of the history of this place."

"Did they still carry guns in their holsters in those days?"

"Hell, I should think so," said one man at the bar.

"Black Jack Ketchum got his head torn off in a-hangin' in this town," said another.

The chandeliers and the lead-light windows were artworks of brilliant colours and design. The décor was done with taste, and my hunch was that Jeanette had a hand in everything on show. I should have had a camera with me.

She wanted to introduce me to her husband, Keith, who worked at a nearby small business. He was a man in his late forties, perhaps much younger than her. She introduced me to him as though he was her pièce de résistance. Her face bloomed, and her eyes sparkled. He seemed shy when he saw me. She mentioned my trek to him. He warmed up and informed me of a magnificent museum a block away. But I was too sore from venturing away from my motel.

Shortly after, Jeanette invited me to lunch at the hotel restaurant. As we sat down, she was immediately called away. I ate alone, and the large restaurant was empty. Eating without company is such an unappetising pursuit. I lost my appetite even before I began. My stomach had shrunk, and I was full halfway through. Feeling lethargic, I wanted to return to the motel and lie on my bed. I bade Jeanette goodbye as I passed the busy lobby. She wished me a happy trek, slipped twenty dollars in my hand, and said, "It's for your next meal on the road." I did not attempt to be humble.

Back at the motel, my do-it-yourself saddle looked like a treat, with all the comfort of a toilet seat, probably the best seat in the motel. Later, while checking my emails, I found Morten and Yvonne had been concerned about my lack of contact for three days.

Morten emailed me, "I called the state police since I hadn't heard from you to see if they could confirm you were safe. I was worried when you left. They said you were about twenty miles from Clayton at 16.00 hours. I can't imagine what you must have experienced along the way. The wind seemed to pick up; an inch of snow was on the ground this morning. I was concerned."

Family and friends in England, too, became worried about my safety. I wrote back, "The police found me buried under twenty feet of snow with a smile on my face."

I was unaware that the police had checked on me since they hadn't made contact. It must have been the same police patrol officer I had met three days before.

In the evening, while I pondered what to write in my diary, it dawned on me that perhaps as late as the early 1980s, the roads would have been just dirt. An old photo in a shop window showed Clayton at the turn of the twentieth century (Ketchum hung 1901), which was just a one-road cow town. The low buildings were partly brick and, to some measure, made of timber. The walkways were planks of wood – patios. Chimneys belched out black smoke, suggesting it was a coal-producing area. Coals for the locomotive were a vital necessity. As it was a cattle town, dry cowpats would have been used as cooking fuel. In the photo, oxen teams pulled heavy-laden carts. Mule's packs, too, were the means of transport. The dress code of those days was like Muslim women of today, with heads covered with cloth and dressed down to the ankles. Dust would have been everywhere, shoes and clothes covered with powdery grey chalk, one foot off the ground, maybe up to the knees. And if it rained or snowed, the roads would turn into mudslides.

No streetlights, in any case. Perhaps oil lamps hung sparsely. Clayton would have been like an island in this great field of tough grass and hard rocks. Even today, people passing through are the means of actual contact with the world outside. Television, cinema, or even newspapers could be a fiction of the outer world. I hadn't been here long enough to gauge what it's like living in a small community. From experience, a small society is gossipy. It would be difficult not to feel restricted when everyone knew each other. Jealousy and tension flourished, and anonymity did not exist in small societies. Status is determined by the amount of land or money one possesses rather than achievements. The land and money may have been passed down through generations. I drifted off into thought, and sleep came quickly.

***

Being on the road daily has its rewards. There is also a downside. The physical discomfort, the bonding with people, then moving on and leaving them behind. Not staying long enough to appreciate the actual value of a place brings forth a kind of sadness. The thoughts of going forward quickly change the mood. Being on the move, nothing is ever static or ever the same. The towns are new; the people are different and varied. I have noticed the difference in the drawl of the accents from state to state. The landscape and climate were constantly changing, leaving behind mountainous areas, deserts, and flat lands to undulating hills, with spring only a breath away. With the journey unending, it gave stimulation and a feeling of displacement. That made it boundless and appealing.

The crossing from New Mexico to the border village of Texline in Texas earlier that day was an easy ten miles. I did it in just over an hour. I stopped in a café. It had the décor of a 1950s look about it, run by six women. Business was good with people in and out. Two tables were occupied, one with two elderly local women and a gentleman. The other was with a group of people passing through. I ordered the homemade soup of potatoes/rice/spinach with a piece of toast and coffee. As I sat down, an attractive woman with a smile came from the group table and sat with me.

She said, "I saw you on the road two days ago. I'm Lola."

I said, "Dolores". But she didn't understand that Lola was a shortened version. She looked animated, not shy, and keen to talk.

"We were wondering what you were up to. You look like an awesome figure on your bike and trailer."

By now, I knew the word 'awesome' had become a byword. "Where are you heading?"

"Santa Fe, we are going to give it a try for a few months. We're from North Carolina. We've rented a house there until September."

She seemed hesitant when she mentioned Santa Fe. Perhaps she wasn't sure about it.

"Are you travelling with your family?"

"Just my husband and me; his mother lives in Clayton."

"Where are you going to?"

"We left Clayton this morning. We're driving around getting to know all the towns."

"How long have you been on the road?" she asked.

"Nearly two months. I started from L.A."

"Oh, that's awesome."

I suggested going to her table to chat with the others. She introduced me to her family and friends. There were eight of them. She was complimentary about me, which I didn't mind, as my ego needed a boost. Her husband looked a little shy and embarrassed. They were curious and attentive and asked many questions, as others had done before, about my trek and what London was like.

Lola was gregarious, easy, outgoing, and with a permanent smile. When they left, she hugged me, and they all wished me luck. They had barely left the man from the other table, came over, sat with me, and wanted to speak. He was a local farmer, Lance, and he wanted to shake my hand and wish me good luck, too, as he had overheard our conversation.

He said, "I have lived here near Texline all my life and never been to other places, not even in a big city in Texas. I heard you say you came from London. It must be crowded."

"Yes, like all big cities, but I am used to that and have lived there most of my life."

"I don't know if I could handle crowded places."

"Didn't you ever want to go east or west or to Mexico or Europe?"

"I guess I never gave it much thought. Not East, that jars with me. I never had it in mind to go elsewhere. This place still suits me fine. It's hard to describe it. It's like being in an old suit. Makes you feel comfortable in your skin."

I asked him about the two elderly women with him.

"They are my neighbours, and they have a routine of coming here for coffee and cookies and to talk a little. It gets them out of the house. They can't drive anymore. It's my pleasure to take them to town on some mornings. It gets me out just the same."

The elderly women looked quaint in their mid-fifties style of dresses with flower patterns. They had small, delicate mannerisms when lifting their cups of tea.

"I have known them since my school days. They were never married. I've lived here and worked on the farm all my life. I've never thought of doing anything else."

"Do you have any children?" I asked.

"No, my wife couldn't have any. She died a while back, cancer."

His eyelids took a bow, and his head bent forward slightly.

"I miss her. It's been four years. I try to stay busy, which keeps me from being sad and thinking about her. Finding new habits takes a while, and getting used to no one being there. You know, the empty house with all her things still there. After she died, I used to hear her voice when I came home if I had been out. For a few seconds, she was there, and then I knew she was gone."

"What was her name?"

"Kathleen. I called her Kath. The dogs keep me company, Blue and Bootsy. Homer died last year. He was an old dog, a German shepherd. Blue is a Dachshund, and Bootsy is a shepherd."

He looked fit and appeared younger than his peers. Staying active and doing physical work helped him to slow down his ageing. He was tall, clear-eyed, had a gentle personality, full head of hair, and looked a decade younger than he was. He asked me why I chose to make such a journey. I couldn't give him a clear answer except those on the periphery of my thoughts, which I gave to others.

He wanted to shake my hand and said, "Stay safe on your journey. It's been a privilege talking to you."

When it was time for me to go, the woman who served me put her arms around me and kissed me. She said, "Thanks for coming to the café. You brought in a good atmosphere." It was a great introduction, and welcome to Texas. I felt humbled by the warmth and simplicity of the reception.

The road was flat that day. I saw green pastures for the first time since I landed here in the USA—rectangular fields of ten acres and the massive irrigation equipment that was responsible. When cycling at a rhythm, I am, on occasion, distracted. It's a shame they haven't built small tunnels underneath the roads to create safe passages for wild animals to cross the dangerous roads. They ran across the road and got run over. I saw so many dead animals on the way. I passed a big deer, disassembled with blood everywhere; Coyotes, at least half a dozen, lying by the wayside.

The wind picked up, and it was blowing strongly. I made three miles an hour, less than on foot, and often walked and pulled my bicycle and trailer. I didn't feel tired, just annoyed by the drag, which slowed me down. The journey, which should have taken me six hours, took nine, with a lift at the end of the last four miles.

***

After a gruelling journey from Clayton, New Mexico, I reached Dalhart, Texas. I arrived late, close to seven in the evening. A nice Texan young man picked me up outside town and took me to a motel. He stopped by, "You looked tired." I was pulling my bicycle and trailer along as I was in too much pain with saddle soreness than anything else. He drove me to his motel, but that was full. We talked about my venture, and he seemed interested and noted down my blog. His dog kept licking at the back of my neck, tasting salt and making friends.

Dalhart is a cowboy-looking town. There are no pavements, just dirt underfoot and tumbleweed. Someone told me that tumbleweeds came from Russia. The drawl in the accent was different, too. It was a busy place with lots of shabby but expensive motels run by Indians from the sub-continent. I caught the manager not changing the bed sheets, simply dressing them up for the next customer. He hadn't noticed me being there. I left that motel immediately and searched for another. Raj, the manager of my next motel, was a pleasant young man born in Dallas of Indian parentage. He gave me a double room and helped me with the trailer to my room.

"I'll help you on your way in the morning."

"Do you know of a good place to eat?" I asked.

"What kind of food do you want to eat?"

"Indian," I said.

He laughed, "Funny man, not here in Texas. I'll have to cook if you want Indian food."

"Can you cook then?"

"No," he said.

"You are a comedian."

He suggested a Mexican restaurant that served home cooking and said, "It's dynamite."

I think he meant the chillies, not the after-effects. Mexican, it was that night, and I contemplated whether the jalapeño would prove to be a cure for my saddle sores.

I needed to rest my poor crotch for a day or two. It became uncomfortable having two ping-pong balls lodged between my legs. It was weird that my most agreeable posture was standing. Until then, I had no blisters or muscle problems. From a physical viewpoint, the muscle pains healed quickly, even when running on the empty way back in the Rockies. In Dalhart, my arse was just a "dis-arse-ter area."

In the evening, four builders in the room next to mine invited me for a beer. I was wary at first. They had a barbecue in front of their door. They turned out to be a friendly bunch of young Texans. They offered me a can of beer, which tasted great. I hadn't touched a drop of alcohol since arriving here, except the final night at Dorothy's. We chatted about my journey across the country. "Awesome", and wanted a photo taken together. They were all from Amarillo. They made a strange remark and told me that "people were not friendly" in Texas. Yet they were kind and amicable as the young Texan who gave me a lift. They showed an interest in my venture. They wanted to keep in touch and asked for my phone number, so I offered them my blog.

Michael Lawson, one of the guys, said, "We've been doing renovations at the hospital for over three months, and it looked like the job will last until Christmas. It's tough and dirty work."

"How often do you get to go home?"

"We break off early on Fridays and head home to Amarillo for the weekend with our families. We miss them and come back on Sunday late."

It would have been interesting to spend a few days in this town. It's not a pretty sight; it's quite beat up. There was a strong sense of being placed in an earlier era. The roads were battered by heavy trucks. The dirt pavements had no pedestrian crossings. The signal buttons at the traffic lights are broken. Texas is the second-largest state. Seeing so much neglect in this small part of the state was surprising. Everything looked odd and out of sync in the twenty-first-century modern state.

Two nights to get my backside/thighs fit again seemed enough. Well, not quite, for I still felt the lumps and twinges in the morning, although ready to leave. They were saying: "You mess with me, and I'll mess with you." Nevertheless, I was determined to go. Michael Lawson said the wind would be blowing north-westerly, which meant behind me on my way to Channing. I walked a mile to avoid the town traffic and took the hard shoulder. Once there, I drifted along like a sailboat. The wind took over, and I gushed forth. I could have made twelve miles per hour, but for the tumbleweeds. At one time, hundreds went tumbling across the road. They got entangled in my wheels and tried to puncture my tyres. I needed to stop each time to disentangle them. In one instance, I saw Daddy Tumbleweed followed by Mummy, then all eight little prickly weeds crossing the road. I, too, like that winged pigweed, went on rolling along.

Just when the going was good, something else created another hurdle. That was the way of the elements in this part of the country. Within a matter of minutes, a sandstorm had begun. Visibility was down to twenty metres, and sand penetrated everywhere. It was like being sandblasted. I reached Hartley, doing the first fifteen miles in two hours. I hid behind half a dozen gigantic grain silos which resembled space rockets. With difficulty, I could barely make out dim lights across the road. It was a gas station, and inside, a café. A big Texan stared at me as I stepped in. He didn't have a happy face. I went to the washroom, glanced in the mirror, and saw only a flour mill worker. My hair, face, eyebrows, and eyelashes were covered with fine sand and grit between my teeth. After a wash, I bought a coffee and an over-processed cheese sandwich. I sat down at the only available table with the Big Texan. He remained silent but kept his eyes on me.

I said, "Howdy," Texan style.

He didn't respond, still with his eyes fixed on me without blinking an eyelid. I felt lost for words. I lifted my cup of coffee and said, "Cheers."

Then he said earnestly: "What's you doin' walkin'?"

I told him of my trek.

"You got a screw loose, man, 'cause, in this country, people don't walk unless they're crazy."

I said, "Oh yeah, let me go and get a monkey wrench."

He laughed and loosened up.

"It's gonna stay like this until late evenin'," looking outside at the storm dust.

I realised I could not camp anywhere, and there was no motel in Channing where I was heading. That was only fifteen miles away.

"You'll have to go to Dumas twenty-five miles down the road east, where there are motels."

But my destination was south. To change course would add an extra forty miles to my journey. It ends in Amarillo, a big town, instead of Vega, with less hustle.

He said, "It's your choice."

He was right; I had no choice but to divert.

"The way the wind is blowin', you probably wouldn't need to pedal."

The big Texan chuckled when I asked him when would the rainy season begin. In his Texan drawl, munching his words -

"Texas has none, not in these here parts. Rain comes and goes, and sometimes, it just keeps goin'. It ain't rained since last August. Six inches of snow fell, but only about an inch had moisture."

That surprised me. I have lived in a temperate climate for over fifty-four years and always considered snow wet. There was a lull in the storm, and visibility was a hundred metres. I decided to make headway. He was right; I didn't need to pedal for eight miles. The sandstorm propelled me forward so quickly that I had to apply my brakes to stay in control. By early afternoon, I made the forty miles to Dumas. It was a four-and-a-half-hour bike ride, almost ten miles per hour. By the time I arrived, I had to strip off. The wind had died down, and the sun was blazing, with the temperature rising to 72° Fahrenheit.

I chose the Super 8 motel because they served me well in the past. The couple running it were Davina and Sanjay. They were welcoming and charming. Once they found out what I was doing, they did their best to help me. They wanted to contribute something in their own way. They gave me the room for the night for free. The room was the best I had slept in for a while, clean and large with crisp white bed sheets and white towels. They wanted to have their photos taken with me, so I obliged. It was a good end to a difficult day.

Davina & Sanjay in Dumas, TX

Sanjay was in the lobby of the motel the next morning at six. He was up early to wish me good luck and say goodbye. He had developed a strong bond with me, which I saw on his face as we shook hands. There was a sadness in his persona, in the way his eyes were fixed on me. It was as though he was mourning an old friend he would never see again. He stood watching me push my bicycle and trailer until I was out of sight more than a quarter of a mile later.

The morning was crisp and cold, and I expected a difficult day. Sanjay mentioned in the evening that the road from Dumas to Amarillo was hilly. I expected that I would have to walk at least forty per cent of the journey. I needed to get to Amarillo by the evening. I even contemplated arriving in darkness. There was no place to pitch my tent along the way. The landscape looked dry, with clusters of oil derricks bobbing up and down in the middle of the farmland. They looked like outdated machinery in the far distance.

Along one stretch of road, I saw a placard saying that cattle drive passed this way in the last century, and water stations were provided for the duration. The only means of livelihood in those days was cattle. The grass was as tall as the men driving the cattle. The tall grass has disappeared due to erosion, overgrazing, and sheep farming. Now, the grass is shorter, brown, dry, sparser, and hardier, partly due to lack of rain. I had mentioned the grass to the Big Texan; again, he had chuckled, "What grass"? They still have cattle ranches, but the economy is more diverse. The Texan had told me that apart from oil, "They grew corn, soya beans, petrochemical by-products, and gas, like helium." The vast plains are dry, with the grassland clutching to mortal existence. Some hardy shrubs looked healthy despite the harshness of the environment. If brought up in Europe, where the density of green vegetation is everywhere, it would be difficult to adjust to a land where a tree or any greenery was barely visible.

Two-thirds of the way to Amarillo, I met Armando Flores. He was the boss of a small gang of men building a bridge over a section of the road. I was tired and had pushed my bicycle and trailer for miles. There was a big hill ahead; I needed a break.

He came over and said, "It's looking tough. You think you can make it?"

He was gazing at the hill. I shook my head and wiped my brow. A wide, beautiful smile lit his face to display his bleached white teeth, as perfect as dentures. His grey patch of hair above his temple swept back like a mane.

He had the film star look with a body to match. He reminded me of Fernando Lamas, the actor. So, we talked. His phone rang, and his wife asked him to pick up some shopping on the way home after work.

Armando's reaction was that he never thought he would ever meet someone from England, let alone do what I was doing. England, to him, was somewhere in a storybook, as far away as one of Saturn's moons.

"I would like to go there one day. I want to go to Paris. I don't know if it'll be possible. I want to go with my family."

He had a boy and a girl. The boy was from his first wife, and the girl from his second. He said his first wife had died: "Eleven years ago. I'm still traumatised by it. We want no more children. Life is tough. It has taken us thirty years to get where we are. I want my children to do better than me."

We shared an orange, and the sun's glare was blinding and warm. He hugged me as we said goodbye and said, "I feel proud we met."

There was a hankering; he wished I had stayed a while longer. It had been a chance meeting, and he seemed happy then. I took energy from that and pushed on.

The hill was formidable, but nothing would slow me down on the way to Amarillo, not even my saddle sores. Much later, as I approached the outskirts of town, a cluster of cottonwood trees lined the road. They were the first trees I had seen in a while. They were leafless at that time of the year, reaffirming the dryness of the view. They resemble oak trees with similar bark and outer strength.

I arrived downtown after a five-mile walk from the city limits. I asked three people for motels. One Indian woman from the sub-continent who hardly spoke English told me, "Ready six o'clock, carpet putting down, no single room only double, thirteen blocks plenty motels", pointing north. I knew she was sending me the wrong way as I came from that direction. Besides, thirteen blocks were a long way to determine if she was right or wrong. I kept walking forward and met a Fed Ex driver. I asked him for directions. He pointed to the route, three miles dead ahead.

At the motel reception, Chris, a lively young concierge as well-tanned as myself, saw my trailer with my placard and danced, saying, "Man, that's awesome." I gave him one of my cards so he could follow me on the Internet. The next morning, in the breakfast room, everyone looked at me with big smiles and said, "Good morning." Murmurs and fingers pointed at me. Then, Chris promoted my journey to everyone who booked into the motel. I stayed for an extra day's rest. Although the ping-pong balls were now the size of small marbles, they were still sore.

When approaching the outskirts of the conurbation, I went through downtown Amarillo. It's an extensive town, as are all towns in the USA. The centre has a few detached civic buildings, banks, and businesses. I found it hard to find the hub and searched for a cluster of restaurants or clubs, cinemas, bars, or just places of entertainment. That core did not exist.

The heart was the highway as it was in India, except they were railway stations. Hotels and fast-food places hug the highways, splitting the town like a cross into four parts. The highway then became the pivot, a strange place serving the city, elevating that area, and yet was anathema to it, surreal.

I couldn't bring myself to understand the thoughts of city planners in the many places I passed through. I have not managed to get into the psyche of the town planners. It was as though they purposely created a place where detachment and alienation were their primary concern. All for the sake of fluidity of transport. Or maybe it's me since I am not a car owner. I don't have a driver's mentality or the willingness to journey long distances to places of interest or entertainment. Maybe it has to do with my life in the cosy metropolis of London. Everything was within a five-mile radius, with the world at my feet.

Why a romantic song should have been written about this city is beyond comprehension. Amarillo was not a romantic city. Its guts had been kicked out. When the leaves reappear in the coming spring, they might be less naked and harsh on the eye. The foliage should hide some of the blotches from view. It was almost the end of winter on the last day of March.

The people I met were charming, polite, and always willing to chat and be helpful. They were inquisitive, knowing that I wasn't from here but from another place. However, Europe seems remote from their awareness. That is not being unkind, and it is the same for everyone when we think of countries that are far away. But when I talked of London and Paris, I could see the glitter of romance in people's eyes. That's because of the images portrayed in the film, glossy magazines, and TV. I am only talking about my experiences in Amarillo, nowhere else. This view came from the responses of the people that I have met.

Again, I would have liked to have stayed longer to experience an inner view of the city and its people. But my time was limited. My impressions are just the personal photographs of someone clicking away as he passed by on the next part of a long journey.

Leaving Amarillo wasn't easy. In the lobby, Chris kept saying he would miss me and was sad about my departure. Each time I had to leave and say goodbye to new friends, this is how it was. The bonding with people was unconsciously intense. When it was time to go, everything surfaced. Chris wanted to help me take my bicycle and trailer out of the storage room. Then he cried and said he couldn't help it. I hugged him for a full five minutes before he felt calm again. I tried to stay focused on my route, but it wasn't always easy. On occasions, I would be disturbed the whole day, and it took a day's meditation to get over that feeling. Each parting felt like a loss. I suppose that must sound strange, but this was how it was.

In the morning, the wind blew hard once more. The breeze had been constant since I left Springer, New Mexico. "It's the windy season," the Big Texan had said, "and it'll go on for another month." I took the directions following a local map and got lost in town, then found my way again. As I pedalled, I couldn't get the wheel to turn one revolution - the wind was that strong. I needed to change the route. I returned to the motel and found Route 287 as an alternative Yvonne had suggested via the blog. This new route meant the gust would traverse my right shoulder, not hit me head-on. The saddle was still giving me discomfort.

On the blog, Morten mentioned getting an inner tube from a small barrow to tighten on my saddle. That idea had come to mind, but I couldn't find any bicycle or hardware shop in town. Claude, the next town, didn't have the size I needed. I had no choice but to plod on. The next day was sunny and warm with no wind. I left early, hoping to make good progress. On this road, I noticed the landscape had changed. There were more trees and groves of fruit trees in blossom. Further on, I saw cotton plantations that hadn't been harvested. It surprised me to see cotton planted so far north. These towns along Route 287, such as Claude, Clarendon, and Memphis (TX), were villages created by the 19th-century government policy to encourage homesteaders to move into the region. They were granted land rights of eighty acres per family.

My luck was in as the wind pushed me from behind when it came up just before noon. I gained courage and thought I might reach Memphis (TX), sixty miles away. By late afternoon, I accepted it was a futile thought. I was dead tired. Later, a 4 x 4 truck pulled up. An African-American woman asked me if I wanted a lift to Memphis, eight miles away. With my ping-pong balls still painful, I couldn't say no. Up and away we went, driving at speed. Michelle was in her fifties, kind, although her puffiness suggested an illness of the sort. She was a prison officer, born in Memphis, Texas, and married with two grown-up sons and thirteen grandchildren.

She said, "I started having epileptic fits and had to take time off work. I want to go back, but I need the all-clear from the doctor. It's boring being at home with nothing to do but potter around the house."

The loss of her mother had brought great sadness that prolonged her illness.

"Mummy was killed by her neighbour. They had known each other for a long time. He was a quiet man, never any trouble. He suffered from mental illness. Then, last year, he emptied his gun into her on a night when he went into a frenzy. I've been grieving for her death since and because of how she left us."

With a double dose of depression, she understood a little about her mother's death.

"I believe it was God's will to take my mother away. He called her. But it was the way she went that still bothered me. I couldn't understand why God chose such a cruel way for her to go."

She couldn't understand the contradiction. She could not think outside her religious upbringing to find a peaceful answer to relieve her burden. Perhaps society and the government should take the blame for not being able to provide a safety net for those with acute mental disorders by not making provisions for those people in need of safeguarding. She was incapable of seeing beyond her indoctrination and conditioning. The lack of foresight to understand that the wide availability of guns to those even with mental illness might give her a more precise picture than the wrath of God. I remained silent and listened.

"My epilepsy started around the time of mummy's death. I know she is finally in a good resting place. Bless her soul. We gave her a fine burial."

On the ploughed fields, the soil was reddish-brown and not as dry and sandy as the ones left near Amarillo. As we sped along in the 4 x 4, I noticed many trees still had no leaves. Soon, we were in Memphis (Memphis is an ancient Egyptian name), and Michelle dropped me at the Budget Inn, which is not one of my preferred motels, and wished me good luck.

All the rooms were vacant in the motel; it looked depressing. The man behind the counter, Mr. Patel, spoke little English and wanted only cash. He took the last of the notes I had. I remember taking everything off the 4 x 4 when I said goodbye to Michelle. I had my Atlas in hand. After my shower, I looked for the atlas, which was nowhere in sight. At the reception, Mr Patel said nothing was left on the desk. There were only the two of us, and I looked everywhere, and it was nowhere to be found. I had my suspicions but didn't want to believe he would have done such a petty thing as that. I felt upset and couldn't plan for the next day as all my plans with Morten were now lost. I needed to buy a new Atlas quickly before the shops closed. I hurried to the town shopping area, hoping to find that elusive inner tube for my saddle. The shop didn't have any. I went to the pharmacy and asked for one of those pumped-up doughnuts children use in a pool, but they were all too big.

A man called Terry chatted with me in the hardware shop and gave me a lift to the supermarket. He said I might find something in there for the saddle. On the way, he told me that Memphis was a thriving town until the 1960s, with a population of six thousand. Nowadays, the farming business is hard to get into. Businesses were shutting down, and the population had declined to two thousand.

He said, "It was expensive being a farmer. Young people can't get started. They leave after high school and try to find work in bigger towns or cities. I moved to Dallas to go to university. My father is a farmer; I didn't want to follow his profession. I wanted something else."

I asked him what he was doing so far away from his work.

"I'm in town visiting my ageing folks."

I asked him about his line of work.

"I'm in finance," he said.

Judging by his car, he was doing well. He wanted to take me to wherever I was going, but the motel was only a short distance away. Finally, he asked me out to dinner with all the flamboyance that seemed to ooze out of him.

It appeared that I didn't do well at reading his overtures. I told him bluntly that it was a dead-end road.

Memphis was built in the 1880s with the style of a turn-of-twentieth-century Western town. It reminded me of old photographs and postcards of places in the Edwardian era, except with an American flavour. The woman who greeted me in the pharmacy transported me to the 1910 period. Nothing about the town could place it in modern times. The feeling was of surprise at the well-kept period architecture and nostalgia.

Yet people are born, brought up, and stay here their whole lives. I met Michelle Bryant on the road when I got lost on my way back to the motel. She pointed me in the right direction. She was a schoolteacher with hazel eyes and auburn hair and had lived locally since she was four. She was interested in what I was doing and told me she had visited London once, over twenty years ago. She was married to a farmer and had three children. I thought that these were the things that would tie someone to this remote place. To live a life of simplicity, being a farmer, having children, having a stable relationship/marriage and a steady job. I couldn't imagine what it would take to find contentment with the conditions of living in a distant town surrounded by vast grasslands and nothingness.

Sometimes, I slip into a daze on the road, somewhere remote, with hardly any vehicles. A daydream of journeying to tens of places. To past scenes that play vividly in the recollection. It is as if the eyes and mind switch into reverse. The scene focuses on a few short 'movies' being played out on the screen in mind. Occasionally, they are interconnected; other times, they become detached and abstract. Then, when composure returned, I sensed that the ground beneath me influenced what frame of mood I felt drawn into. The emptiness of the land, its bigness, with a few stunted trees scattered here and there—verges of clumps of dry grass in the foreground and the uniformity of flatness in places. Then, a mound of earth showing signs of erosion breaks the monotony. The sky is vast, blue, always blue. The road was straight and black, like the shadow of a draughtsman's ruler leading to the beyond. Leaving Memphis and heading toward Childress, Texas, was like that.

My trailer's spare inner tube might do the saddle's job. I inflated and twisted it into a figure of eight, tied it together like two circle tubes, and fixed it onto the saddle. It felt comfortable, but I needed to pump it up every four miles. I was curious whether it was due to a missing valve cap, a slow puncture causing it to deflate, or just the sheer weight of pressure. In the meantime, it was doing a fair job, and my buttocks felt better. I got off early, leaving Childress and heading toward Quanah before seven. The day started off sunny but cold. After thirty minutes, heavy cloud cover brought on a much colder spell. My feet and hands froze. The wind picked up, this time coming right across my left shoulder. It slowed my pace to six miles per hour, and the road was undulating. I had to walk in the hilly parts.

I saw a dead eagle on the hard shoulder. It had a huge wingspan. A beautiful bird. How it died was hard to tell. At least half a dozen jackals were lying by the side of the road. The furs of these animals, with black and brown stripes, were well camouflaged in the grass of the winter landscape. They were all roadkill.

At first, I thought I saw snow on the ground. The morning was cold, and snow must have fallen during the night. Patches of white were still visible on the ploughed acreage. On closer inspection, I noticed that it was cotton. Cotton litter was everywhere, on the side of the road and in the fields, debris that got left behind after the harvest. The cotton plant is only about two-and-a-half feet high, and its stem is like that of dogwood - red. Cotton picking in the old days would have been very arduous. My historical knowledge informed me that the average life of a slave on the plantation was eight years when slaves were first introduced. If slaves tried to run away, dogs would chase and devour them. Or they would be whipped till their backs became raw and scarred. The runaways had their Achilles tendon cut. At times, even castrated. A vicious world.

How easy it is now, seeing machines suck up the cotton balls like a vacuum cleaner at a thousand acres a day, with a relatively low cost of gasoline for just one man to complete the task: the irony of time.

***

The signs say: 'No Trash in Texas', but deep in the countryside, people were rebellious. Perhaps it is boredom or parents and schools have not taught the children to respect the beauty of the countryside. The more untouched it is, the better it looks. But fast-food rubbish was everywhere, even in this remote part of the country. Litter lies along the road for miles: plastic bottles, juice cans, junk food takeaway packaging, beer bottles, coffee cups, and plastic bags. It makes the countryside look overcrowded, as if a football match had recently ended.

The landscape was much greener as I headed towards Quanah from Childress. Perhaps it rains more often, or irrigation was much more in use. The trees were in abundance. Here and there, laid in the fields, were old monuments of a bygone age. Remnants such as farm machinery are left to rust and rot in this windswept largeness. I saw ramshackle old houses built in the early twentieth century, left empty and abandoned throughout North Texas. They were simple buildings with an open porch and a pitched roof of corrugated iron sheets. These empty houses and their small eighty-acre farmsteads have disappeared, consumed by the larger farms. Someone said that in the 1930s, after the Depression, a drought lasted three years and almost wiped out everybody. The local people moved on to find a living somewhere else. It's what John Steinbeck portrayed in his novel, The Grapes of Wrath.

In the evening, a Vietnamese fellow with a room next to mine at the motel in town complained about the lack of entertainment. "There is nothing to do at night in these towns, no cinema, no music halls, maybe one bar and a restaurant, that's all." After dark, only ghosts roamed the streets.

In the morning, it was sunny, and the warmth felt good on the skin. A woman coming out of a supermarket said it would blow gusts of seventy miles per hour later that day. I hurried, got on my bike, and pedalled quickly. My destination was Vernon, thirty-two miles away. Six miles out of town, I lost my sense of place. Everything reminded me of Essex, England. The views were the same: green fields, hedgerows, patches of yellow fields - rapeseed cultivation; it felt like a late warm spring sunny day.

There was a distinct feeling of being in England again. I had not thought of England since my departure. The notion of not missing home might sound odd to some people. Being homesick was not something I had ever felt, no matter how desperate my situation was. I once knew somebody who went on a holiday abroad for a week and returned home after three days because he was homesick. Once, at a party in London, I chatted with a Russian woman and asked her if she ever missed being back home in Russia. She said she missed being home every day. She also missed the cold Urals climate and London was too warm. Home for people means different things. It could be the changing of the season, the familiarity, family, friends, routine, the smell of the place, the language, the food, and so on.

Why I never felt homesick is difficult to tell. Being displaced at an early age had something to do with it. I was told never to look back. I was conditioned then to appreciate where I was. To make the most of it, move forward and never regret what's left behind. I have missed people I met on this journey, however. They've all touched and made me think of them and are in my thoughts almost every night as I drift to sleep.

Every morning was a new beginning, a noble rebirth. Everything was different: the energy, the planned road, the new area, and the new people to meet and talk to. Often, a new state and the climate were changing and getting warmer as each day passed. I no longer wore layers of clothes to keep warm. I wore a short-sleeved t-shirt, and my tanned skin got even more tanned.

The wind didn't come. In the evening, I serviced my bicycle. The people at the motel in Vernon were kind and generous. They were from the Indian subcontinent and had lived in the US for twenty years. They were polite, welcoming, and hardworking, making my stay at the Green Tree Inn pleasant. I was determined to do extra mileage the next day to reach my destination – Burkburnett. Before I left, Raj (the hotel manager) and his wife wished to help me with my journey. "My wife wants to give you this $15 to buy lunch." Raj was adamant that I should take the main Route 287. But I wanted to travel the minor road, Route 240.

"What if something happens to you?"

"What can happen?" I asked.

"Your bicycle could break down."

"I'll repair it."

"What if something happens to you?"

He repeated the question. I understood his sentiment. He feared I would be attacked on the quiet road, though he didn't want to spell it out.

"I am healthy and have serviced my bicycle and trailer. Nothing will happen."

"You must please take the main route."

"I want to take Route 240, a minor road, away from highway traffic," I said.

He seemed frightened; his eyes flickered as if he was in a state of shock. I blocked out his fears. He watched me for a long time as I pushed my bike/trailer away from the motel until it was out of view. On Route 240, the new surface made it hard to pedal. I could only do about five and a half miles per hour, and it took me eight and a half hours to reach Burkburnett.

Burkburnett was a neat little town, pretty with sidewalks, the best I had seen since Taos. They have a population of about ten thousand. Unfortunately, they had just two motels. One was very expensive and looked pleasant. The other was less so and uninviting. I chose the less expensive one. I hated being there in that dingy box of a room. The internet was on and off, and a musty smell hung in the air and clung to its walls. It had been a hard day's ride/walk, and after my shower, lying in bed thinking of the day, and with Raj in mind, with pen in hand, this came.

Nothing

What is ahead?

Only forty-eight miles of gravel

Underfoot of my travels

My thighs grew big

Weighed heavy as lead

In my head

The cold wind blew

I would have turned blue

Save for my skin

Full of melanin

I talked and sang

Till the gale slowed down

And changed direction

It whistled back at me

Calling me Wolf

I pedalled and walked

In the silence of sounds

Except for the rasp of the squall

Ruffling my hair

Like it didn't care

The odd car whizzed by

Only four on Route Two Forty

My senses,

cast them into shadows

As if clouds raced by

in dark patches on the ground

The marbled clouded sky

fell to the horizon

A dome around the green fields

And the lone rider thought

"We exist in a goldfish bowl."

The metal farm gates

The ramshackle houses

jangled their rusted sheets of metal

Percussion of elemental passion

In the open stillness,

Everyone has gone. All left

Once, the route was crowded

Thousands came

Looking for black gold

Texas Tea

As they are charmingly called

Within a decade

they drank it dry

The electric poles

Lined the road

Crucifix crosses

Birds have no fear

Perched on live wires

Bats hang down

Gibbons-like

Suspended cadavers

The falcons flew fancy-free

As I whistled down the wind

It changed direction,

Propelled my fatigue away

Late in the afternoon

I had seen nothing, and no one

Save for a lost little rabbit

With a white undertail

Crossed my path

I thought about everything

Then, thought nothing of it

Nothing is not nothing.

The planned route was to go north into Oklahoma (The name is a Choctaw derivation of Okla Humma, meaning 'red people'). In Burkburnett, I didn't want to travel on Route 70 across South Oklahoma. The villages were small along the trek; they had nothing, no motels or campsites, and were miles apart. My contact through friends willing to put me up in Hugo fell through at the last moment. Oklahoma had also gone cold on me. (Much later, my contact said the people in Oklahoma wouldn't have been welcoming. I thought that was a terrible generalisation to say.) A quick look at the map gave me an alternative: Route 82.

The room nauseated me the whole night. I rushed out early in the moon's brightness while still dark. I made my way south to Wichita Falls. Entering its outskirts, I knew it would be one of those sprawling towns. I didn't consider it high enough to have a waterfall. The rain came falling soon after I booked into a motel. It lashed down for two days in torrential fashion. I've never seen a downpour with such ferocity without letting up. It carried thunder and lightning as though we were in a war zone. The threat of tornadoes was a genuine concern. There was nothing anyone could do. Everyone became stranded in their respective rooms, sleeping, reading, or watching TV. I watched three film noir on TMC.

After two days of unrelenting deluge, I was stiff and was glad to be on my way again. I wanted to compensate for the lost time and rid myself of the stagnant energy for two days.

Leaving town, I saw a small waterfall, man-made. All the water slid into another canal or river branch, which skirted a park and camping area. From a roadside view, it was a substantial town with plenty of fine buildings and forest/parkland. I still couldn't get my head around the thought processes of these civic planners and why they needed to split the city into four sections with two big highways crisscrossing each other. It might help the traffic circulation, but it is so ugly in its conception.

It took an hour to navigate out of Wichita Falls with the Monday morning rush in full flow and the effort of negotiating through the spaghetti junction. The temperature went up, and I was finally in my t-shirt, soaking up the sun and the humidity. Once on the route, I felt free and, in my element, exposed to the macro-world and cocooned by a kind of ethereality. I was there in my physical body but sometimes drifted into a dream and did not have that surety of a physical presence.

A couple of hours later, a 4 x 4 truck revved up from behind and pulled up on the grass verge beside me, and the man inside said, "How're you doing?"

It took me a few seconds to gain composure and study his face. Then I realised who he was when I saw the young Alsatian dog. Somehow, his name escaped me, although he had told me twice before.

"You don't remember me, do you?"

"Yes, I remember you," struggling to recall his name.

"We met in Dalhart," he said.

He was in his twenties, with a fine-looking face. He gave me a lift outside Dalhart. I was stunned to see him.

"What are you doing here?"

"I have been reading and following your blog."

"I hope you've enjoyed the stories."

"Ye, I've been checking on your route and looking at all the towns you've been through."

"Are you working locally now?"

"No, I'm still working at the same place."

"What, back in Dalhart? So, what are you doing here?"

"I wanted to see you again and hoped I'd find you. I knew you would be near here. Last night, I decided I had to see you again."

"Have you made this long trip just to see me, but why?"

"I wanted to wish you luck and to see if you're okay, safe."

"But you've come a hell of a long way."

"I feel like I've been travelling with you. Reading your blog spurred me, man. I wanted to warn you about some big towns in Texas. People get tanked up in the evening, and they might harm you."

"I'm careful, and I've had no trouble so far. People are kind to me."

"I also wanted to shake your hand, say goodbye, and wish you good luck."

We shook hands, and, in an instant, he left. Maybe he drove many miles to see me for this moment. He would certainly have lost a day's work. If he came from Amarillo, it would have been a three-hundred-and-seventy-mile drive. I felt humbled and remained in shock throughout the day. Perhaps he received inspiration through the writing of places I trekked and the talk at our first meeting about why I was doing this trek. He, too, possibly dreamed or fantasised about having a similar venture. He told me he hadn't been able to make such a voyage.

He gave me something more profound: humility, kindness, and empathy. He reaffirmed my faith in humanity as many people on this venture did. People like Morten and Kate, Doyle and Thelma and the Mormon priest John in Indio, CA, and before that Connie in California and many others. He stayed in my head the whole day. I kept asking myself why I had been fortunate to encounter many good people on this journey. Later, on my blog, he wrote and said his name was David Paul Moore and not Robert, as I wrote in my blog. How could I have made such a mistake?

The fifty-mile ride didn't seem long; the thought of David put me in a trance-like state. I arrived at another dingy motel, exhausted. I could hardly stay awake after my shower. I ate little, just fruit and some oats. Sleep came by eight. I was up at five and ready for a big day, thirty-eight miles to my next destination. I wanted to get out of that motel room anyhow.

A sign on entering the town the night before had caught my eye. It simply said Nocona Indians (Nocona was the town I stayed in). I became curious and wanted to learn about these 'unknown' Indians. Peta Nocona was the chief of a branch of the Comanche Indians. He had married a captive white woman and fathered three children. The town of Nocona was named after him. His first son, who later became chief, was Quanah (another town

I stayed in about 180 miles back). He also had a daughter named Topsannah, meaning 'Prairie flower'. His wife was Cynthia Ann Parker, of English parentage. She was captured as a young child and brought up as one of the tribe's members. Her father built a fort in the middle of Indian land, breaking protocol. The fort was attacked and destroyed, and everyone was killed except for Cynthia, five at the time. Nocona is a Comanche name; Noconis - meaning 'Wanderers,' a bit like me.

It is as though I had arrived at a different part of the world, for this area of Texas was fertile, unlike West Texas. Everywhere was green and dense, with a tract of forest incorporated into the individual ranches. The forests were of oak, not the majestic British type, more like the French sort. They were smaller with twisted branches, like a big apple tree, and with half-size leaves. There were elms as well, but I couldn't see any. In the view were pines and cottonwood and other trees I didn't know. It was like riding and walking in a vast forest spanned for miles.

Birds of prey hovered in the sky with their backs to the sun. They glide effortlessly in the mild wind. When they went in for the kill, they were like dive bombers. The grass verges next to the hard shoulders were carpeted with dwarf royal blue lupins and dwarf red flowers unknown to me. The road surface was difficult and hindered my progress. I had to double the effort due to the small pebbles, which created a drag, unlike smooth asphalt. It was undulating, much more than before.

It's funny how animals behave when I appear in view. The cattle became alert and ran along with me as I got closer. The horses did the same as before high up in the Rockies. A bay yearling galloped side by side with me. It might have to do with the orange brightness of my trailer. I saw a donkey shepherding cattle here. I had only ever seen that once before in Spain while on the Camino. Donkeys are such friendly creatures, my pet among all the animals.

All the little towns along Route 82 were pretty, each with its main squares with all the shopping facilities. I stopped in a small town called Saint Jo and went to a café/bookshop. It was a cosy and welcoming place, and once a week, they had a writers' group gathering. I spoke to a young woman running the enterprise named Alyssa Reynolds. She told me she wanted to visit Britain, France, and Ireland. She had been to Italy and Hungary when she was still at school, part of a choir. She has since recorded and put out an album. "It's on YouTube, check it out." She was polite and welcoming, which nicely broke my day's rhythm.

The day's journey took me to another small town, Muenster. German settlers arrived there in 1889 and built a village despite being hard hit in the early period when they suffered drought and lost almost all the buildings due to tornadoes. They recovered and had a thriving community of people. In 1926, they discovered oil, and the townspeople became affluent. "It's a farming town, and we deal mostly with farming equipment," a man told me. These were materials for the infrastructure of the region. As I passed through Lindsay, another town further on, I saw my first real armadillo, as big as a tomcat. It was lying by the roadside, roadkill. All these little towns looked similar. All with one main road with the same-named chain shops, and I rode along with a feeling of déjà vu.

The ideal distance for a day's travel was thirty miles. It would have been much easier if I hadn't had the one-hundred-pound trailer to pull. But it adds to the eccentricity of being on the road since it provided me with all my worldly comforts. That is the extra clothes, shoes, tent and sleeping bag, spare bicycle chain, and so on. I carried everything that fit into the small space and didn't leave a "carbon footprint" behind me, just like the Noconis in the old days.

I aimed to get to Gainesville from Nocona. I rode over hundreds of rosary beads thrown on the hard shoulder from Saint Jo to Gainesville, miles of them. I have seen this superstitious behaviour before in Mauritius, despite a notice in the cemetery which forbade witchcraft. People still perform rituals by exorcising a 'curse'. By leaving a series of coins on the ground at a crossroad or path, hoping someone would pick them up. The 'curse' supposedly would be transmitted from the sufferer to the penny picker. These kinds of rituals belong to the dark ages. It surprised me to see them here in the 21st-century USA. I couldn't ask anyone why the beads were scattered. There was no one in sight.

I also don't support irrational beliefs, as my wheels were trashed on these gravel roads. They got me to Gainesville, a substantial town, just. The town had its usual format: "hung, drawn and quartered" by highways. I chose the three to six o'clock quarter for a motel's location. I gave it a rating of one out of ten, which was generous. The microwave plate was missing. The shower half worked, and there were obvious signs that the bed had been sleeping in. The one point of credit was its locality. I didn't have to leave from across town for my route in the morning. The manager suggested the café next door for a meal. "Home cooking," he told me. The green beans were out of a tin, reheated, and so pale that my plate was their deathbed. The mashed potato was made at breakfast time, and the omelette danced doing the rumba, imitating a doormat on a polished floor. It helped me decide whether to stick with junk food or drown soberly with a drink. I chose the latter. I bought a bottle of Jack Daniels, only a miniature one, which cost me $2.29.

***

The sun's rays pierced through the slight parting of the curtain directly into my eyes. I staggered out of bed and rushed around, regaining my senses. I left after eight, late, in rush hour traffic. After four miles, I had a deflated tyre. Nearby, I saw a mechanic workshop and asked for a power pump to inflate my tyres to a maximum of 60lb psi.

The first ten miles proved a real struggle with heavy traffic and newly surfaced tarmac. I decided to take a minor road detour. I entered the village of Whitesboro three hours later, which meant I travelled just over three miles an hour at a walking pace. It was a neat, well-maintained village, with most newly painted houses. It was substantial, with four thousand plus inhabitants. The place was tranquil; unlike in West Texas, all the shops thrived. Every house along the four-mile stretch was detached and uniquely designed with well-kept gardens. If anything, the dwellings seemed a little too cute. I took a snack and a coffee in a shop which stood both as an old-fashioned butcher and a café. The cheese sandwich with relish and salad on homemade bread tasted exquisite.

The whole area was in the industry of horse breeding and training for shows. The horse ranches painted white and manicured resembled a classic film set. Mature pine and oak trees dotted the open corals, and the lawns were trimmed as neat as a bowling green. All the ranch buildings were pleasing to the eye. The wooden fences were pristine in all white. Those ranches went on for miles.

Six miles before reaching Sherman, my destination for the day, I arrived at another small, rambling village called Southmayd. As I passed by, someone called from across the road. He offered me a couple of bottles of water. He introduced himself as Marshall and said he was seventeen. He wanted to know why I was pushing a bicycle and trailer. He invited me into his house and introduced me to his mother, Michelle, and his grandmother, Janet. We chatted very amicably, and they became interested in my venture.

Janet, a young-looking grandmother, was not too well, "suffering from emphysema" after "a lifetime of smoking," which she now regrets.

"I have finally given up after my ninth attempt." She sat in a wheelchair: "I can't walk much now." She carried a fair bit of weight.

Her daughter Michelle was a nurse, and her grandson Marshall was still at high school. They offered me tea and, later, tons of food to take with me, but I was already overloaded and accepted a bag of fruit out of kindness. Again, I was continually surprised by the generosity and politeness of people I encountered across all the places I passed through.

At the front gate, I told Marshall, "You need to work hard at school, and you'll do well."

We shook hands and hugged each other. As I was leaving, he said, "I am undecided whether to join the army or the fire service after school."

I advised him to choose the latter. He was such a nice and pleasant boy, and the armed forces would have depersonalised him.

On the road, I felt disturbed. After leaving their living room, I saw at least twenty powerful rifles and other weaponry across one wall, neatly stacked in a line. This obsession took away the entire homely ambience. I shivered just glancing at them.

I finally arrived at Sherman, a large town with a population of over forty thousand. The town was split into four obligatory sections by a major route. I stayed in a lodge in the second quarter. Manisha was from Gujarat, India, and managed the motel Travellers Inn.

I asked her: "Is there any coffee?"

She said, "No," a minimalist exchange.

"Will there be coffee in the morning?"

"No", she said, keeping a straight face in the usual Indian way. Greeting customers, the American way with a welcome smile hadn't yet caught on with the hoteliers from the sub-continent.

"That means no dal puri for breakfast either, then?"

That cracked her up. She couldn't stop giggling, hiding her smile with her hand in a shy way.

She asked, "You like dal puri?" with a slight Indian head roll.

"I love it," I said.

"You like curry and rice?" again with a slight dance of her head from side to side.

"Yes, I love that too."

"I'll bring some to your room later."

"That would be kind of you. How much would that be, ten rupees?"

Struggling to hide her relaxed giggle, she said, "Nothing for you."

I thought she was being polite in our humorous conversation. Much later, she knocked on my door with her son and presented me with an Indian feast of rice, puri, vegetable omelette, spiced chopped potatoes, and Rasam (a spicy soup, the way my paternal grandmother used to make it.) It was a satisfying end to the day.

It was sunny at seven the morning after, and I felt perky. I hoped it would be a trouble-free day. Somehow, my bicycle seemed stiff and rigid to pedal on the road. I wasn't weak even though I had recently travelled through some tough roads. The wind whistled and blew against me from the start. I shouted aloud, "Not now; give me a chance to get going." The wind listened and increased its speed straight into the side of my face. I pushed on four miles per hour the whole day, the pace I would typically walk, and I wanted to get to Bonham.

I rested a little on the way to digest an apple and some dates. As a van passed, I heard a loud gunshot close to me. I was startled. Five seconds later, I wondered why I hadn't fallen to the ground. I lost my appetite. It was not the exhaust from the vehicle, as the noise had sounded exactly like a gunshot. I decided to get on my bike in case there was a deranged gunman about. The bike was doubly heavy this time, and a funny noise was dragging behind me. I stopped to look and understood that one tyre on my trailer had exploded. So, that was the sound of the gunshot. The inner tube was in pieces. Within thirty minutes, I had it fixed. I was getting good at that.

The last couple of days were easy going through the villages. I saw many types of animals: lamas, stocky muscled goats with long curvy horns, cattle that resembled the Highland cattle of Scotland, white sheep with black faces, horses of various breeds, Indian ponies, donkeys, and all those guard dogs that kept chasing me seeking to chew bits off my legs.

Waving the flagpole no longer worked.

The landscape was like the north of England or northern Spain - undulating, grassy, with alfalfa hay and taller trees. The tree I didn't know before in the forest was the pecan. Texas is a big pecan grower. I never realised that some pollination wouldn't need bees, insects, or birds. The wind pollinates pecan trees. It's logical and seems natural. East Texas also has many more rivers and ponds, unlike West Texas.

I found a good motel in Bonham, the Best Star Inn, at a reasonable price by the Patels. They were pleasant and helpful and gave me extra coffee and milk to take to my room. A couple of women owned a large restaurant fifty metres away. I chatted with a co-owner, Betty, earlier to see what was on the menu. It was Tex-Mex food, and they had a veggie section. She asked, "Where are you heading?" I told her to the East Coast, and we chatted briefly. When I finished the delicious dinner, her partner Linda said, "It's on the house." I must have a likeable face, two nights in a row, two excellent dinners, all free of charge.

So far, I had long left the Panhandle Plains. Once I reached Witchita Falls, I was in the Prairies and Pineywoods West region. The landscape became more fertile, with trees in abundance. I kept to Northern Texas close to the Oklahoma frontier to avoid big cities such as Fort Worth and Dallas. Leaving Sherman the day before, I slipped across the regional border of

Prairies Pineywoods East to Bonham, unaware. Again, the verdant vista changed. This time, late spring brought out a myriad of painted blooms. I saw cardinals and other painted birds and fields of bluebonnet. It was getting warm, and I cast off all my winter clothes. Paris, Texas, was my next destination. Spring fever was in the air, and I couldn't wait to get to the city's heart.

Chapter 11: Paris, Texas

The Wim Wenders film of the same name made Paris, Texas, famous. It's the kind of place where dreams can evolve. There is an Eiffel Tower with a Texan hat dangling at the apex. As the tourist brochure says, "Bonjour, Y'all."

I was forty-three miles away in Bonham and wanted to make it to Paris without arriving too late. I could make good headway if I left before seven in the morning. I switched to Route 82, and as it happened, the road was flatter and the surface smoother. By ten-thirty, I had reached the halfway point. The handlebars of my bike gave me trouble. I didn't have a set of Allen keys to tighten them up. Another faux pas was that each time I entered a Walmart supermarket, the thought of buying a set went out of my head. By that stage, I became worried and thought I might have to walk to Paris. Doing a Harry Dean Stanton with Ry Cooder strumming the steel guitar in the background. The Ape, which had long disappeared, was back and at it again.

"Where is he when you need him?"

"What are you on about?"

"Ry Cooder, to give us some of that steely Texas blues and some of that Tex-Mex sad lullaby, Cancion Mixteca. You remember, after watching the film, you had your handkerchief in hand."

Prairies Pineywoods East to Bonham, unaware. Again, the verdant vista changed. This time, late spring brought out a myriad of painted blooms. I saw cardinals and other painted birds and fields of bluebonnet. It was getting warm, and I cast off all my winter clothes. Paris, Texas, was my next destination. Spring fever was in the air, and I couldn't wait to get to the city's heart.

Chapter 11: Paris, Texas

The Wim Wenders film of the same name made Paris, Texas, famous. It's the kind of place where dreams can evolve. There is an Eiffel Tower with a Texan hat dangling at the apex. As the tourist brochure says, "Bonjour, Y'all."

I was forty-three miles away in Bonham and wanted to make it to Paris without arriving too late. I could make good headway if I left before seven in the morning. I switched to Route 82, and as it happened, the road was flatter and the surface smoother. By ten-thirty, I had reached the halfway point. The handlebars of my bike gave me trouble. I didn't have a set of Allen keys to tighten them up. Another faux pas was that each time I entered a Walmart supermarket, the thought of buying a set went out of my head. By that stage, I became worried and thought I might have to walk to Paris. Doing a Harry Dean Stanton with Ry Cooder strumming the steel guitar in the background. The Ape, which had long disappeared, was back and at it again.

"Where is he when you need him?"

"What are you on about?"

"Ry Cooder, to give us some of that steely Texas blues and some of that Tex-Mex sad lullaby, Cancion Mixteca. You remember, after watching the film, you had your handkerchief in hand."

"Get away from me. Go and dig some termites. That's why you have long arms. I left you for dead. I don't want your bellyaching to start all over again."

"You mustn't be too harsh on yourself. Even if I was dead, I have a twin brother."

"Oh yeah, what's his name, King Kong?"

"You know better than that. Rex Kong is a gorilla."

"Look, I am tired; I don't need this now. All you damn Apes like to do is torment me. You are the root of evil."

"You are wrong there, partner; we are the root of evolution."

At noon, the handlebars gave way and were loose. I felt resigned to walking the last twelve miles, pushing the bike and trailer. About six miles from Paris, completely unexpected, as if the universal energy was reading my thoughts, a 4 x 4 truck pulled up. He asked: "Do you need any water?"

"I don't need water, but I could do with a set of Allen keys to tighten my handlebars."

"I have them in my other car, but I would gladly take you to town if you wanted a lift."

How could I refuse? His name was Ron, and he looked in his early forties with a touch of tinted hair colour at the temple. A kind and generous person took me to the shop and bought and paid for the Allen keys. He insisted on doing so. Then he drove me to the main square and took two photos of me by the famous clock and the fountain.

"This is where everyone has their photoshoot; they'll make a nice souvenir."

"I think the film Paris Texas was shot here."

He said, "The film was not shot here. Most of the film's location shots were outside the town. There may have been a few scenes done locally."

There was much commotion in the square caused by an attempted robbery at the local bank. Some shootings had taken place, roads were closed, and many police were at the scene close by. A crowd of people gathered to watch the development near the building. We ordered coffee in a café close to the clock tower. Again, Ron insisted on paying for them, and we basked in the sun, sipping on our Americana. The whole scenery placed us on a film set. We were the extras waiting for a call. He seemed timid yet stared at me. With my initiative, we went to the motel I suggested. He wanted to help me more. Insisted on carrying my baggage into my room. He overstretched his generosity and invited me to meet his family. I thought perhaps that was a ploy. I felt tired and needed a shower and rest.

"I'll call the motel later and pick you up."

I thanked him for his generosity. As he left, he hugged me a little too close and said he would say a prayer for me. I became suspicious of his over-friendliness and motives; it was more than a gut instinct. I let it pass.

In the late afternoon, I took a ride into town. Paris is a pretty and sizeable town with twenty-five thousand plus inhabitants. For once, the town didn't have highways crisscrossing its centre. It had, instead, a circular road circumnavigating its outskirts. It is on record that the town burnt down twice, in 1877 and 1916. It has also suffered a disastrous tornado blitz and rebuilt each time. The old part of town was still intact, and it was worth the visit. Some original wooden houses added elegance to it. The cotton industry has almost disappeared. There is much more diversification, such as dairy farm products and tourism. The list is long.

With fortune or misfortune, I was stranded in the motel for two days after my initial short visit to town. The weather turned, and Ron didn't make contact. The gush of rain and the threat of tornadoes prevented everyone from moving. Outside the motel, it looked like a river had burst its banks, taking dead vegetation and debris. In the evening of day two, still grounded, I checked on the weather every two hours to see if the next day would improve, but the forecast was not good. Tornadoes were forecast.

The receptionist, Brittany, told me someone had passed through the motel two weeks before and was walking across the USA. "He was trekking from East to West, ocean to ocean." Our meeting didn't coincide. We could have exchanged a few ideas and found our motives for doing so. It wasn't meant to be. No doubt his experience will be life-changing. She gave me his blog, full of pictures of where he had travelled, but not much input in describing those places. Much later, via his blog, I found he ran into some trouble. He came within an hour of death and was rushed to the hospital.

At the beginning of his blog, he mentioned he had left his job, given up his flat, and was unsure when he would return. I sensed similarities between us. It is on record why I was doing this trek; deep inside me, I didn't know the real reason. Only something was amiss from my past. It was tentatively apparent why I turned my life upside down and caused great turmoil every decade. I don't know what I was searching for. Something was absent from an early age. It could be a thing I lost then or driven out of me. This trek was partly about finding that lost piece of a puzzle.

It rained again that evening, thick droplets, the like I hadn't seen since childhood. The fierce rain, continuous thunder and lightning drew me to open the door and look at what was coming out of the sky. Birds were unsettled on their night perch in the thick, leafy trees. The gushing cascaded from the motel roof, and the relentless downpour turned the driveway once more into a rapid river. There was the threat of a tornado mixed in with thunder. Had it come, the motel's roof would have been torn away. All the vehicles would have been turned over or fallen apart and dumped elsewhere. I was fortunate. It didn't come as I stood under the awnings and watched this spectacular show of our planet doing its thing. The static electricity from the lightning crackled the zinc sheeting of the roof. I ensured I had rubber shoes on and didn't stand in a puddle.

The show carried on for well over two hours. I went inside, listening to the rainstorm falling on the zinc roof. It reminded me of the times of old in the tropics when heavy rain would come suddenly and go on for days. We would be housebound, playing games, and then get bored. A build-up of dampness and fungus would begin to set in after five/six days of an incessant cloudburst. Perhaps a week later and only after hearing the twittering of bird songs would we know that soon the rain would stop.

A text from Michael Lawson woke me at seven in the morning. We'd kept in touch ever since our meeting in Dalhart. He said it snowed in Amarillo during the night, and it was cold. I looked out of the window; it was windy and misty. When I stepped out to test the air, it was freezing, with a strong breeze blowing. The mist was like a thin layer of smoke, a veil to the start of the morning. I asked the receptionist for the forecast. He said, clear but cold. I heard there was a ten per cent chance of thunder. I didn't want to be caught out in any change of conditions. The last time they forecast a seventy per cent chance of rain, it remained sunny the whole day. When they predicted a ten per cent chance of rain, it rained for two days. Not that they are often wrong in their forecast, but the weather in this part of the country is unpredictable at this time of the year. The condition can fluctuate sometimes, and anyone could get caught in it.

I decided to spend one more day at the motel to reflect. Many times, I wanted to give up on this trek. Like the time in California when I was so stressed that my body could not stop trembling. And my face looked like someone scared out of his wits in the mirror. I had terrible panic attacks and thought I would have a breakdown alone in the middle of nowhere.

I knew there would be difficulties on this journey. But had not thought of the overwhelming crevices which lay before me. Mel Coleman told me I must use adversity to my advantage. I went through a learning curve to understand that. It was slow coming, like gasping for breath at the deep end of a pool. It helped me to stay on this lone excursion and share the experience through my blog. The readers propelled me onwards. I Skyped people, phoned a few, and chatted, but it's not the same as face-to-face with someone and sharing. The people whom I have met gave me the human contact which I so needed. Without these meetings, I doubt whether I would have endured this travel.

Sometimes, it is easy to be on a couch and make deliberations detachedly. Being on the road gives you an alternate perspective. It takes different energy to filter through your lens, which feeds your brain and allows you to see the profundity of your actions. To comprehend it doesn't come all at once. It trickles through in dribs and drabs. Only with time and a retrospective view can anyone fully assimilate the impact it will or may have. I don't know what will happen at the end of it all. Perhaps this is a good thing.

***

Beth Key and her husband Abriam helped to break the monotony of being locked in the motel. They were from Arkansas, an attractive couple in their mid-thirties, and were on their way to a dog show competition. They were breeders and often entered shows in various parts of the country. We talked about my venture; they became interested and encouraged me to spiel. But I wanted to hear more about them. We were strangers, yet we connected in an instant. They were unsure whether their dogs would do well as one "was quite old and the other a puppy." Talking about the journey stimulated them, and we parted in good spirits. I mentioned that I could see them picking up prizes at their event. They had been unsure. Two days later, Beth wrote on my blog.

"Since we met you the other day – you inspired my husband and me…maybe one day, he too will make a journey like yours, but until then, we will continue to explore the world together … by car, of course, or maybe by bicycle. Completely unrelated, my oldest dog gained his championship that day after we talked to you, and my puppy received her Junior Championship …you started our day out with such positivity, and it ended the same. If you happen to come through Hope or Prescott, Arkansas, which is our neck of the woods …message me and let me take you for a meal! Safe travels."

After three days of being locked up in my motel room in Paris, I felt apprehensive. I was afraid I might have lost the edge of my fitness and confidence for not being on the road. The time seemed longer than these three short days. I had forgotten what the rhythm of being on the road was like. I said goodbye to Brittany, the receptionist. The full moon was ahead of me, some way above the cobalt blue horizon. I missed the lunar eclipse the night before - Paris was clouded over. In the misty dawn, the moon seemed opaque, like a rising sun behind thin clouds. I was heading east; later, I saw the moon behind me. I did not watch its descent into the horizon.

Clarksville was thirty miles away, and I remember Route 82 had been difficult. I hoped that it would be a comfortable ride. My luck was in. There was no wind, the road was flat, and I did well the first fifteen miles. It's cattle and forest country. The farms resemble those in Suffolk, England, with a patchwork landscape divided by oaks and pine trees. However, England would have more oaks, poplars, and hedgerows. The industrial pine forests were camouflaged by a façade of very tall, slim oak trees, with their girth no more than three-quarters of a metre in diameter.

Villages were scattered along the way, and the houses reminded me of those traditional Brittany houses in the west of France. There was a fifties atmosphere along the route, like the Island at the end of the universe. The only thing missing was the smell of ripe papayas and the sweet fragrance of a tropical landscape.

I paused halfway near a small village to have a bite to eat. A dog limping on one of his front legs came by. I gave him a piece of my bread, and he hung around. When I was ready to go, he wouldn't leave me and followed me for half a mile. I stopped and told him to go home to his owner. But he kept on looking at me with those sad, pleading eyes. I gave him my last buttered roll. While he ate, I steered fast till he was out of sight.

I made it to Clarksville in the late afternoon, walking a good part of the day's trek, much more than expected. Clarksville was a small village of three and a half thousand people. The population used to be fifteen thousand in the 50s when it was prosperous, and cotton was still king. Now, it has but two industries, both related to farming. Jobs are scarce. John Smith, a man I spoke with who resembled John Lee Hooker, the blues singer, told me that all the young people moved on to Dallas and elsewhere in search of work.

"I was born in Clarksville." He was a man of seventy-plus. "My parents were born here. They worked in the cotton mills all their lives. It was hard in those days. They struggled." He didn't want to elaborate. "Everything has changed."

We stood outside a school; he pointed to it and said, "I went to that school when I was a boy, and now I work for the same school, and I have done so for thirty-five years."

He was a caretaker. After a while, he became silent and looked at me with suspicion. I ventured out more than usual, even though there was little interest. I stayed out of my motel room, which felt cramped and over-furnished with bulky 1950s furniture. I had to walk through a maze to get to the bathroom and back to bed.

I needed an early night. New Boston was a long way ahead. I calculated it was about forty-three miles away and a bit more from the motel area. Sleep didn't come until past midnight. I was on the road by six-thirty. Everything piled up against me from the start, gradually worsening as the day passed. The route surface was of recently laid chippings, and it took twice the effort to do half the distance on a well-surfaced road. The wind smacked into my face, and significant roadwork meant no hard shoulder to protect me from fast-moving vehicles. I felt so unsafe in some places that I walked instead of riding my bicycle/trailer.

Since leaving Paris, it became a long ride through dense forest, except for some clearings for cattle farming. Every twenty miles, there was a sawmill. On the way, a placard advertised "Cedar, Pine, Cypress, Oak and Hardwood" for sale. Amongst these trees, the chorus of birdsong followed me everywhere I went. Their harmony altered the atmosphere and filled the air. It sent me into a meditative state. East Texas seemed very fertile; no wonder many wars had been fought and much bloodshed. It is worth more than gold or black gold. Davy Crockett passed through these same roads with his Kentuckians on his way to The Alamo.

I was still in Texas, but it was difficult to believe. Water was everywhere: ponds, brooks, rivers, creeks, and lakes. People in this region love their catfish and prefer them spicy. I have seen people eating chillies, and lots of it. I would be wary of the side effects the next morning. On the way near a river, I saw two large terrapins. They dived into the silted water as I passed by. I didn't expect to see these amphibians here.

There were times when nothing happened on this journey, but later that day, the road became busy with no hard shoulder and was dangerous. On the opposite side, I saw a man walking with his bicycle and trailer like mine.

We stopped and looked at each other. Out of curiosity, he crossed over, and we talked. His name was Patrick, and a little cocker spaniel sat in his trailer. He was a man in his late fifties, perhaps younger. His face looked much older and weathered, but his body was lean and fit, defying his age. He had journeyed around Canada and the USA for eight years with his dog. He was from San Diego. Why had he stayed on the road for so long?

"I can't live in one place."

He wasn't married and didn't have children. Did he miss anyone?

"I miss a few people, my sister and brother and their kids."

That was why he was heading back to San Diego; then, he would move on to Oregon.

"Don't you have any friends? How do you keep in touch?"

"Old friends, they've gone their way getting on with their lives," and added, "I meet good folks and get on with them wherever I am."

He seemed well-spoken, university-educated perhaps. I asked him how he managed to survive.

"I do voluntary and paid work when I can get it, mostly from churches and campsites. The churches are helpful. They give me food and a place to stay, but I have my tent. Sometimes, they would make me a donation for the effort I put in."

His last job was working at a campsite for six months.

"They gave me food and lodgings, but after a while, I wanted to move on. They begged me to stay. It was peak season. I stayed longer than I wanted to. I guess I came cheap."

"Did you feel hard done by?"

"I didn't expect anything except food and a place to stay."

"But they asked you to stay. You rendered them a service."

"When I left, the man wanted to give me $350 as a donation, but his wife told him to offer me $250 instead. I bought a few beers for a treat, and now I won't run out of cigarettes."

He appeared healthy, and so was the dog. He offered me a cigarette, but I declined. He reminded me of a friend, John G., with the same beard and looked in his eyes. John G., has since died of respiratory failure. To take my mind off the last few miles of this arduous passage, I reflected on how Patrick escaped the system and lived a life of his choosing: independent, solitary, determined, adventurous, and dynamic. I thought about his age, his health, and his future. There was no point; I didn't want to project anything about him.

I reached New Boston utterly exhausted. After my shower, I could write nothing on the blog. I planned a short trek of twenty-five miles for the next day to reach Texarkana on the Texas-Arkansas border and then perhaps write something worthwhile. I woke up in the middle of the night, felt refreshed, and checked the clock. It was well past three. I sat up and wrote about Patrick.

His eyes were sad, yet they seemed alert when he suggested places I could stay. He was tall and had stubble on his face, which indicated maybe he shaved every three days or more. I pondered on what caused him to drift for over a decade. He mentioned that he worked in education but volunteered with no details, a teacher perhaps or in the administration. When I pushed him, he reluctantly said, "I was tired of it all."

My deceased friend John G, who had also been in education, head of the literature department in a private school, had become "bored with it all." He descended into drugs and alcohol. When his marriage broke down, he found another companion who was a frequent drug user. Despite everything, he was articulate and a well-read man with a devious sense of humour.

In our second year at university, he said I should stand for President of the Student Union because I would win a clear majority.

"What made you say that?" I asked.

"The Left likes to believe they are progressive. As an exotic, you would make the perfect token candidate."

He then let out a big, belching, throaty laugh at his spontaneous dig at the union and no doubt at me. Death came too early for John G, in his late forties.

Sitting on my bed in the early hours, I wondered whether Patrick had a similar experience of broken relationships and lack of stimulation at work. Instead of drug and alcohol abuse, he escaped into the open and became a drifter. A drifter was only an outsider's view. No doubt, he was searching for something and would have been prepared to take away the bedrock of his own house if it lay between what he wanted out of this life. Was he joyous in his liberation in adopting the wide-open space and the solitary existence? He would constantly be a stranger to everyone. Even if a close encounter were to happen, there would be this battle of yearning between the pleasures of the soft flesh, the mutual bonding, and that of the voyage. Later, maybe fear might have set in with echoes of entrapment and routine. The desire to vanish can be overpowering, and the unfamiliarity of a long haul, often different, constantly new, can be the pursuit of actuality.

I wasn't sure whether this reflected my adventure. The overlap of connection between Patrick, John G, and me, for we all had this strong desire to escape, each in our own way. Then again, being on the road was in every way living in a spectacular resort of the outdoors. And being part of the open every day and night, under the big sky in the big country, came as a huge reward.

Dawn filtered through the aperture in the drawn curtain. I was packed and ready. It was a short distance to Texarkana from New Boston. I had been looking forward to the trip, but the route made it tough. I thought I'd arrive by eleven but didn't reach my destination until nearly two. My calf muscles paid the price for the imaginary extra mileage. My first motel didn't accept bookings until three. I went across the road and booked into Day's Inn, which was more expensive as they didn't have a single room. The double room was almost twice the cost. The manager was pleasant, talkative, and not a Patel but from the Indian subcontinent. She left India when she was twenty-one and lived in Leicester, England, for eighteen years before moving to the US.

"I feel settled here and cannot imagine being anywhere else."

I asked her if she had missed anything about India.

"I go to India whenever possible, which isn't very often. The last time I was there was five years ago. I miss my family and the food. I'm not a good cook."

"Don't you miss the atmosphere?"

"No, I'm settled and comfortable here. India is too much of a dirty place."

"Did you see India that way when you were living there?"

"No, when you are in the middle of it, you are blind to many things."

So, it was a retrospective view as she elaborated further about being outside India for more years than the country of her birth. India has changed, I said.

"Yes, in many ways, but not India, I knew. I've left it all behind."

I felt that perhaps I had asked too many invasive questions. She seemed more like a Mauritian than an Indian, quite an extrovert in her persona, not restricted by the mores of her upbringing, bubbly with a veneer of Americanism.

In the morning, I enquired whether she knew a shorter way back to Route 82. When I checked on the map, she pointed me towards the long route around. Everyone thinks in car terms and not walking or cycling through shortcuts. I decided to leave early and retraced my steps to Route 82. It came to a point where I missed a turning. I asked a couple for directions at a crossing at a small junction by the railway station. They were Josh and Diana. A friend called Josh across the road, but Diana stayed with me. We chatted in the glorious morning sun. She explained the route to me; we stood on downtown Main Street, which was once the hub of the town in the old days. Only a strange silence inhabits its deserted past glory as in other places. Now, the activities were by the highway as in other towns and cities. Josh and Diana were "going against the grain", as she puts it, trying to bring "some motion into old downtown." Some beautiful buildings on Main Street were left empty. A re-gentrification could bring back life to the old centre again.

"We've made a start with the Silvermoon."

It was a grand place, not architecturally, but in size, with many activities, such as a theatre, a huge wedding reception hall, and a conference room. They owned the property.

"We are involved in the community project which will get the hub of the old town back to the way it used to be."

I suggested encouraging street cafés, bars and health food shops, a gym, and a literary venue mixed with an art gallery might invite the more entrepreneurial public to rejuvenate downtown.

"Some of these suggestions are already in motion."

Josh was a judge, and Diana taught classical history and Latin in high school. She was a thoughtful, open-minded Christian, and it was a pleasure talking to her. We chatted about several topics, including each other's backgrounds. She chose her words with care, and there was precision in the way she spoke, with a flow and knowledge that Latin contributed to the poetry of her speech. We talked about my journey, and inevitably, Jesus entered our conversation. I told her I was a humanist and that reincarnation was not part of my philosophy. She was a devout Christian without being an evangelical. She wanted to pray with me for my journey to the ocean. I said, "I could meditate while you prayed." She agreed, and I did so.

She mentioned God twice in her long prayer. As I saw it, her incantation was more like poetry, her chosen words, not a prayer. She voiced an impeccable fluidity of words that held such beauty under the morning sun. It brought wellness in me through the asset of her language. Everything about it was spontaneous: the journey and my quest to achieve it. Seeing the moistness of happiness in my eyes, she hugged me hard, and her eyes glistened, too. It was a special moment for both of us.

Afterwards, she looked me straight and said, "What do you think will happen when you die?"

"I am not afraid. My flesh and bones will be dust and remain part of the universe like all atoms," I said with conviction.

"Why have you given up on God?"

"I was a Catholic. As a boy, I served mass every morning, five days a week, and the priest took it out of me. When I think back, it was a two-way process; God gave up on me too."

"In what way did the priest affect you?"

"He used to beat me for asking impertinent questions. Like, what if God doesn't exist? As I grew up, I found the explanation that made sense."

She said, "Once a Christian, always a Christian. God will not let you go." Then she added, "What if you find yourself before God?"

"I would do battles with 'Him' for eternity so that 'He' would know not everything he created was perfect."

I was being confrontational. But I understood that death of consciousness was at the core of her question. So, I added, "My consciousness will be like before I was conceived."

She didn't show surprise by either of my responses, but I noticed that momentarily, her speech flow was less fluid. Despite her beliefs, I saw in her a great humanist, much more than the gentle persuasion that pervades her Christian intentions. We touched on many subjects in the hour we spent together on the street corner. Somehow, we created a strong, amicable closeness with mutual respect in that short period. And knowing that our integrity did not diminish despite our differences in religion. The fear factor, which so many religious people are contaminated with, did not exist in Diana's persona. She was solid in her convictions and confidence, although I couldn't enter her faith. We hugged for the last time as the sun reflected a golden glow through the floss of her hair.

Back on Route 82, I was sandwiched between forests on both sides of the road for the first fifteen miles, between tall Oak, Scots Pine, Beech, Sycamore, and others. The route snaked through the woods. At times, it seemed I was in a virgin landscape in the past century of Europe. There was nothing obtrusive to alter that view except for the road surface and the occasional passing vehicle. My bicycle/trailer was like a chariot gliding through the magic of it all. Through the drama of seasonal change, the birds, the towering trees, and the variety of their tender green leaves. The air was warm, fresh, and unpolluted. Each time a lorry full of felled pines passed, it left a lingering resin odour in the air and my lungs.

Fifteen miles later, the forest ended, cut down for lumber. The land lay fallow and not replanted. Shrubs competed haphazardly. The land looked odd and ravaged, and I felt naked; the road changed, now straight for miles. Then it was farmland on either side, cattle country again, not the tiny patchwork but on a larger scale. Later, the road changed again to a zigzag south-easterly direction for ten miles. Once more, it was back to forests on both sides of the road, which gave me a sense of being lost in the wilderness.

In the afternoon, I crossed the Red River, which in parts is as wide as the river Thames, London. Red because of the earth in this part of the country, and the silts gave it its tincture. A while after, I was in Lewisville, Arkansas, the poorest village I have come to since being here. I saw dilapidated, rusted houses that were still lived in. Everything was in decay, including the oil tanks and derricks, some of which were still in working order. Many broken-down cars and trucks are piled high in someone's land or junkyards close to the road. This setting could have been anywhere in a village in an African bush. Five miles later, I was in Stamps, where I rested for a few days. These are small communities, fifteen hundred people or so per village. Someone told me that fifty per cent of the population in these villages couldn't read or write. "Kids are put through the school system, but nobody cares how they come out." It's the backwater - a 21st-century society with a school system that produces ready-made cannon fodder.

Chapter 12: A Little Meditation

When setting out on a long journey, planned or not, it inevitably gets diverted for unforeseen reasons. The harder I struggled, the luckier I got. Yvonne, putting up my blog back in London, let it be known on the Findhorn circle that I was trekking across America. Morten Nilssen first contacted me while climbing the Rockies to Payson, Arizona. He kept in touch, encouraged me, and made suggestions. He even mentioned people I could stay with in Albuquerque, which ultimately didn't come to anything. Unbeknown to me, he was busy getting in touch with other members of the Findhorn community. He Spread the word to those who might offer to put me up for a day or two if I happened to be in their vicinity. Meanwhile, the news circulated in the circle. Many people took to follow my journey, encouraging me and making comments. Even before I met Morten in Taos, while I was still in Show Low, he had written to Michael Davidson in Mississippi about my venture.

Michael had said, "He can stay as long as he wants out at the studio (schoolhouse); very beautiful; very rural, a real artist's retreat, but warning, it's a long way to go for the eggs and orange juice. We will be delighted to have him. I could put him on a job; the only problem is that I move around because I'm the boss and cannot always pick him up. Has he any craft skills? If he can and wants to work, I can have him make the mud on one of my projects."

I would've been too tired to mix mud (concrete/cement/plaster). I didn't need a job, but I was glad of the offer of a place to rest somewhere along the way. In a sense, and because of the people of the Findhorn community, my pathway was determined and geographically planned by their kindness. I have always been on the move eastwards, making pit stops from the time I left Arizona. My original 'plan' was to cross New Mexico after Albuquerque into North Texas, then across Oklahoma and Arkansas, see Graceland. To then cut across Tennessee and North Carolina and touch the ocean there. After crossing the Rockies, I knew that going over the Appalachians would have tested all my resolve. Michael's invitation not only changed the direction I was heading but relieved many of my anxieties. Once I reached Morten in Taos, we based all our planning on the routes on how to avoid difficulties and reach Michael in Mississippi. On the way, I changed some designated routes due to the sandstorm, the wind, the rain, and the threats of tornadoes.

Since departure, this continuous daily push, doing an average of twenty-three miles when walking, rids my body of all the toxins. Though at times, I had no choice but to eat junk food. My daily intake of water was four litres plus six pieces of fruit. All this and the exercise of being on the road and the stimulation of it all raised my fitness level to a height that, for someone my age (66), I never thought possible. I became fitter and mentally sharper than I had been for years. I lost ten pounds of worthless weight, looked lean, and the whites of my eyes were clear. My hair and my nails grew at a faster rate. I endured terrible conditions on the road, yet I didn't suffer from any illness (except for sunstroke in Phoenix). The only thing that bothered me was a little dexterity problem with my hands, and that was due to the constant tight grip on the handlebars. I wasn't anxious about it and knew it would return to normal once I rested.

Before I left London, my doctor warned me about the breaking point of the body mechanism. The limits a body can endure. He said, "No matter how fit someone might be, even for super athletes, there was a ceiling to the stress level. It normally occurs between two thousand and two and a half thousand miles of durability testing."

Once I reached Michael Davidson's home in Eupora, Mississippi, I would have completed two thousand miles. I have proved that the ageing process is mainly in the mind. We've been made to think that way. Yes, our hair goes grey as we age, our eyesight weakens, our skin sags and our bodies stiffen. We are less able to do tasks than in our mid-twenties. All of this is true. We cannot put back the clock, but we shouldn't resign ourselves to the fact that our days are done once we reach a certain age. So far, the trek proved that I have the same capacity as when I was in my mid-30s, and I found myself in better shape and fit then, too.

I had gruelling days on this adventure and did an average of forty-eight miles on the bicycle daily. And pulling my one-hundred-and-ten-pound trailer. When calculated, it meant riding/walking one hundred miles daily on a free mountain bicycle. At the end of some days, I found it too tiring to concentrate or write. Instead of diminishing, my body's recovery rate recuperated faster than ever, as though nothing had happened the day before. Each morning, I woke up fit and without any ailments. But specific indications around my thigh muscles spoke to me: "Look, man, if you don't give me a rest soon, I'll give up on you." So, I listened, and I understood what my body needed. I was close to a good, long repose.

This has been my experience; when you think you are incapable of doing anymore and are at the end of your tether, you can do much more than you think. That 'Ape' inside, which refused to disappear, held me back. Always getting ready to take a short way out of a situation and tested me to reach my full potential. I have killed my Ape, well, one of them, maybe?

I contemplated using this recovery period to read, write and explore places like the Mississippi Delta, New Orléans, and Graceland by bus. Also, use this time to write a blog worth reading for the people who followed me. In the meantime, I was still a few days away from Michael's house in Walthall, Mississippi.

***

Leaving Stamps, Arkansas, I noticed a significant rise in African Americans. It was as I expected on the approach nearer to Mississippi. Getting to Magnolia was a long ride, up and down, which meant walking and pushing. It gave my thigh muscles a chance to recover and my forearms a rest from the handlebars. My body could relax more, allowing me to have a bite to eat while on the move. I was once more among forests for many miles, which was the way of the journey for the next few days.

Luck trekked with me like a shadow. Not once was I caught out in the rain, and when the downpour came, it was with a vengeance. There are no differentials for rain here, drizzle, light rain, or showers. The sky opens and sends everything down with a spectacular explosion of thunder and lightning, which may last a day or three. There were threats of tornadoes while en route. With sheer good fortune, I escaped the wet whirlwind. Until then, the sun had not been a bother, just warm enough to enhance my already deep tan. But there were a few problems, like the road surfaces, especially the newly laid ones. Those made it laborious, causing a real drag with the thick tyres of the mountain bicycle.

The wind against me was a major issue, forcing me to divert my route. The lack of a hard shoulder made it very dangerous on many occasions. The vehicles were driving fast, and dead animals scattered with razor-sharp splintered bones raised to spike my wheels. The undulating landscape of New Mexico, Texas, and Arkansas and the curse of those tumbleweeds. They punctured my tyres on so many occasions. In this remote part of the country, there were only tiny villages of a dozen houses every so often. Occasionally, a gas station with a 'food' store, then nothing for miles until a big town. Being caught out in this open country could have been harmful. It was necessary to check the weather forecast three days ahead.

***

Magnolia was a university town. It is strangely located as there were many ways to enter it, and all were uphill gateways. I didn't feel like going up a hill only to find it was the wrong side of town to get to a motel. I stopped by the university and waved down about twenty vehicles to ask for information, but no one obliged. I didn't understand why. Perhaps I looked down and out, although I tried not to look like one for appearance's sake. I took a chance and pushed up a hill and asked an African student for the whereabouts of any motels. He didn't know where the centre of town was. I moved on to a police station, and no one was there. Magnolia was like a ghost town on Easter Sunday. I kept on pushing forward until a police car hooted me from behind. I quipped about aliens kidnapping everyone in town on Easter Sunday. Neither of the officers showed me their teeth. I hesitated about telling them a joke to change the severe mood on their faces - "What did the policeman say to his belly button? You're under a vest," then skipped it as I deemed it might backfire. They checked me up and down silently as though I was a body snatcher with a zombie look. They whispered something to each other and stared at me again.

"Is something wrong, Ociffer?" I quickly corrected my mispronunciation. "I am looking for a motel."

They read the caption on my trailer. Then they pointed down a hill and drove off without a word having been spoken.

This Patel was doing well; he owned three motels on the same street. In the USA, Indians from India and Uganda only have one name, Patel. Patel rhymes well with motel and cartel.

At first glance, Magnolia seemed like a wealthy town surrounded by farmland. The university buildings were designed in Classical Greek architecture, giving a prestigious appearance from the outside. The town is substantial, with many churches and large houses. I wasn't sure where the people disappeared to as I could see no one to talk with. I only had the motel receptionist exchange a few words. I asked her about the red flowers I saw all along the roadside from Texas to Arkansas. I wanted to know its name. She couldn't tell me. No one I asked knew either. It was surprising how so few people paid attention to the flora in the place where they lived. I found it quite frustrating on my travels, trekking in my ignorance. Yet, I could recognise certain flowers and trees in Texas and Arkansas but knew nothing of others. Later, I learned more about flora such as Pin Oaks, Water Oaks, and hardwood pines that a nail would not penetrate when dry, like the Casuarinas. I eventually found the name of the red flowers by the roadside, whose name had puzzled me for weeks - red clovers.

A long three-day meditative journey was from Magnolia to Eldorado, Crossett, and Lake Village on the Mississippi River. The distances between each stop were long and tiring, but meditation made it possible to absorb the shift in the changing countryside. The transformation came with stimulation. I learned the names of each creek, river, slough, bayou, wash, and brook. I was no longer ignorant of their difference. It had been the same with birds. As I went by, I made inquiries and was lucky to have found someone who gave me a poster with local and migratory birds of the region. His name was Cole, and he lived on the west side of the Mississippi River.

He became interested in birds through his father and has studied them ever since. I placed him in his seventies, upright and sporting a grey beard, and his eyes glittered as though, with time, his youth had refused to desert him. He pointed to the names of the colourful birds I saw along the way.

He said, "Most people don't know these birds; they are dead to the world of nature, busy just making a living."

Some were migratory birds from down Mexico going to the Arctic Circle. I am now familiar with birds like the Painted Bunting, White-Eyed Ibis, Purple Gallinule, Roseate Spoonbill, Barn Swallow, Least Bittern, and Little Blue Heron. I will forget them all again as I have forgotten the names of many of the towns I passed through. But they made an impression on my memory, if only briefly. I shall keep a photographic recollection of them and understand that I have been part of the landscape that belongs to them.

The oxygen and the aura of the rustling of the leaves, the forests nourished and visually stimulated me. Being in the countryside was overwhelming, simply too big an impact to explain. The lush greenery against the open sky with hardly any human habitation, surrounded by nature's sounds, can frighten anyone if they fear being alone for long periods. However, remove your fears, and it becomes an everlasting journey into its emptiness. There are alternatives to that experience if you've spent time in the calmness of a desert in the spatial immensity under the Milky Way. Or if you have been in the middle of the ocean on a still sea as motionless as the surface of a mirror with nothing in sight. All three spatial exposures bring out a special sensation. As a traveller, life could be fulfilling. I count myself fortunate to have chanced upon all three.

I arrived at my motel in Crossett, exhausted. After a shower and a meal, I went to bed early. The next morning's journey played on my mind and could prove too much as it would be a fifty-mile trek. Thunder, rain, and lightning were due for the following evening, with nowhere to sleep in between. I needed to make it to Lake Village on the west bank of the Mississippi River. When I woke, it was before five in the morning. I was raring to go as if I had had a massage and had rested the day before. I was on the road at six-thirty and reached my destination earlier than anticipated mid-afternoon.

I assumed Lake Village was a resort, yet it was like any other town I passed through. I took a cycle ride along North Lakeshore Drive. I expected to see a marina, and perhaps there would be cafés, restaurants, and bars beside the shore, even a music venue, but I saw none. It was a residential area overlooking the great water's edge. The area had modest houses, well-kept gardens, and other grand buildings with large, manicured lawns and mature trees. The view of the river and the sky was a breathtaking window of a water meadow.

Chapter 13: Mississippi

Seeing the great Mississippi River at dawn was a magical, surrealist experience. It was magical because riding on the flat road was like gliding after all the undulation left behind. The approach to the river was like seeing a new continent for the first time. The inflamed clouds beyond the tree line and the entire sky were lit to a new dawn. Everything seemed out of proportion, and the air was full of expectation. It was surreal, for I had never experienced such an enormous body of flowing water inland in all my travels. Forests surrounded it on either side, and gaps in the woods showed flat land for miles.

Eight miles later, I came to Greenville Bridge, which I assumed was the Mississippi Bridge leading into Mississippi State. The bridge was the longest I had ever had to cross, at two-and-a-half miles in length. The colossal steel and concrete structure showed the ingenuity of human creativity in all its complexity. And despite it being an arrangement of man's endeavour, in abstraction in the grand scheme of things, it blended well into the magnitude of the panorama. It was impossible not to stop, meditate and admire. Watch the sheer volume of water under the bridge and consider the river's width that once would have been tens of miles wide. Later I found after crossing over that I had not left Arkansas. Mississippi was still a handful of miles away.

The State of Mississippi is one of the poorest in the USA yet one of the most fertile. Wood was a primary industry and still a significant employer.

Mississippi has grudgingly parted with its past of attitudinal and racial segregation. It is known that the State gave birth to American music, Blues, rock and roll, and more. The list of Blues singers read like an epitaph on the pages. It was also the birthplace of the greatest entertainer and music ambassador - Elvis. The State has also produced writers such as Tennessee Williams and William Faulkner. It hasn't been short on actors or personalities, people like Morgan Freeman and Oprah Winfrey.

A little while after I crossed the bridge into Mississippi, I came across a 19th-century riverboat parked as a museum. I went a couple hundred metres past it and then decided to return and visit. The women at the desk, Cathy and Casha, told me it was a replica of the riverboats that would have navigated up and down the river, trading, gambling, entertainment, and bussing people around. I asked them how much they were affected by attitudes to politics and people in this area where they and their families spent their lives.

Cathy said, "Our parents protected us as children. We never met face-to-face with racism. Our mothers and fathers suffered all that."

"Didn't you ever hear people talk? How did that affect you?"

"That didn't bother us; we gave as good as we got."

"Some people like searchin' for trouble, and the Po-leece like to give them a helpin' hand," said the man standing in the corner.

"Listen, Joe, you go about your business and let us talk," said Casha.

"You know, they like to show who is boss," said the man as he left, referring to the Police.

"What was that about?" I asked.

"He is an old man; he'd trouble with the Po-leece a while ago. It left him bitter," said Cathy.

"They gave him a whuppin', and he hasn't been the same since," said Casha.

"Are the police still like that?"

"I can't say they are, and I can't say they ain't," Casha said.

"We've never been in trouble. We keep ourselves as good people as our parents brought us up," they said in unison.

So, I asked them how they felt now. Cathy replied religiously that people don't have an axe to grind.

"Whether people like it or not, everybody must compromise and be part of society. Everyone must deal with their situation and issues and get on with their lives. It's what the Lord would want."

I could see on their faces that they had kept their dignity. They had moved away from the history of segregation. What was in the past lay buried like the dark, sacred possessions of the older generations and their attitudes under their headstones? There will be an overlap in the next generation. Old dispositions don't die off as quickly after four hundred years in the making.

The impact of the modern technological world and the willingness of people to change have resulted in a metamorphic society. The old order can only be considered the remaining debris in modernising fallout. There will be remains of ripples to re-enact past outlooks like crackles in dying embers.

In Indianola, I wanted to visit the B.B. King Museum. Cathy and Casha told me it was a worthwhile visit. It was impressive, a maze with a theatre at the hub of the building. Many stories were told by historians and musicians of the time, with videos showing how BB King started his career in childhood. There were photos, posters, and pictures everywhere, each telling a story. Many memorabilia were on display. They even had a photo of Elvis with other musicians. It would have taken two days to see all the displays. I had only two hours to spare before closing time. I was leaving in the morning.

The museum unfolded the evolution of music in the region and what life was like in the Mississippi Delta in the south. The hardships endured by African Americans. When I passed through Indianola, B.B. King was still alive. Every year, he gives a concert in Indianola to benefit the locals.

The downtown area of Indianola was small, with grand-looking buildings but in almost miniature forms. In the old days, the plantation accommodated everything. It was the workplace, the hospital, the houses where everybody lived, and their purlieu of leisure activities was all there too. After 1880, there was a great movement of people. With the new order after the Civil War, many left the large plantations to seek work elsewhere and settled in small towns like Indianola. The museum was near Church Street. In the old days, the Street was the place to be on a Saturday night where music, dancing, and gambling occurred. People came from the countryside, travelling many miles to get there.

Soon after I had left the museum and had just arrived outside my motel, a drop of rain fell on me. The skies opened with lightning and thunder while at the reception having a coffee. It rained for five hours. Again, I found myself lucky not to be out in the downpour.

Michael and Belinda, friends of friends from the Findhorn community in Scotland, arranged for me to stay at their place. I had spoken to Michael, and he wanted to pick me up the next day from the motel. I thought this was fine since I wouldn't have to cycle for thirty miles without hard shoulders. In Mississippi, there was no hard shoulder over the bridge, which made it dangerous. I had a few near brushes when the drivers blew their horns to frighten me.

Michael was late arriving. Work had delayed him. I had looked forward to meeting him. He was a big man with blue/grey eyes, a very jovial person. We got on well from the start. He took me back to the museum after we left the motel and told me how it had been one of his restoration projects. He did work in a bar next to the museum, too, which didn't look too impressive on the outside. It seemed more like a warehouse made of tin with no windows apparent. Next to the bar, eight silos stood rusted like abandoned sculptures, with creepers getting a stranglehold on parts of them. Inside the bar was a real surprise. It was like an auction room with many nineteenth and twentieth-century paraphernalia—a slick nightclub with some incredible decorations creating the mood for evening entertainment. The manager welcomed and treated us to a beer as Michael explained what the building was like before the conversion.

A while later, we drove on to Eupora. A short distance away was the village of Walthall, where he, his wife Belinda, and their daughter Mary lived. Belinda was a charming and intelligent person with a dynamic lifestyle. She runs a business that employs twelve architects and was also the mayor of the village of Walthall. Their teenage daughter, Mary, had the energy of two people and, with singing lessons, could have become a soprano. Michael was into everything spiritual, and polarity therapy was central to this. He also ran an architectural restoration business. They have a splendid house with a sixty-five-acre garden with two mini lakes stocked with fish, two cats, and two dogs.

On my day of arrival in the evening, they took me to a dinner gathering with friends set in a Regency house in Columbus, Mississippi, where Tennessee Williams was born – a mere 50-mile drive. The houses in the town have maintained their magnificence. Every house was kept in pristine condition. The impression it gave was that they were all recently built. Ten of us attended the dinner party. The hosts were Robert and Holly. Robert was the Executive Director of the American Institute of Architects (AIA) and a friend of Michael and Belinda. Also, there was Jim and Peggy West.

Jim was the Dean of the Department of Architecture at the Mississippi State University. Helene Dreiling was there too, and she was the President of The National American Institute of Architecture.

There were moments when I felt I was being transported back into mid-nineteen-century Mississippi. I was in a 'happy' mood with one glass of wine. The house was restored to its Regency-style décor, including the wallpaper.

Robert said, "We found a section of the original wallpaper and had it reproduced, which was some feat and involved considerable cost."

The conversation flowed around architecture and restoration, and Jim West took centre stage and talked about the lack of funding affecting various university faculty departments. Michael and I drifted out of the main conversation, and I wanted to know more about why he took up polarity therapy.

He opened, "I had gone off the rails for some time. My life and family were affected. I over-indulged in too many things, which impinged on my body and my mind, alcohol, for instance. My Findhorn experience helped me to find the right method. I took up polarity therapy, and it gave me a ladder to climb out of my deep well. I no longer touch alcohol and have been dry for five years. I exercise daily in the pool and participate in a nationwide live online mind and body session."

"What is polarity therapy?" I asked.

"It heals and stimulates energy flow within the body and the mind. It focuses on bodywork, counselling, a balanced diet, and polarity yoga. It's not like other forms, such as Hatha yoga. We use gentle rocking and stretching movements and vocal expressions to allow energy flow. My weight and movement gave me a problem, but I found a solution by exercising in the pool and participating in group therapy."

The wine flowed, too, and I overindulged just a little. I remained lucid after three glasses of Prosecco. The food was southern cooking, of which the main course was chicken done in prunes with rice and green beans served by two charming African American women. Holly took me to the kitchen and introduced me to the two women. She gave me a tour of the house and explained how she and her husband put a lot of thought and energy into the restoration work. They researched the design, paint, materials, and furnishing such as chandeliers, curtain rails, doorknobs, and a variety of glass panes in the bathrooms of the period. The contrast and combination of materials were exquisite in all the décor.

I was treated with great Southern hospitality. I made a few women blush and laugh by kissing them on the cheeks when I greeted them. They weren't used to this etiquette as we are in Europe.

Throughout the evening, I kept having these flashbacks as if I was being transported back to the early 19th century because of the house, the décor, the furniture, and all the paraphernalia from that era. Maybe the wine, too, had helped me to gain perspective. I asked Robert what it must have been like then.

He said, "The land was stolen from the Indians by the low price they paid for it as the Indians didn't understand the true value of money."

Then we were interrupted, and he went to attend to a matter. The history of violence took place when the primaeval land changed ownership. First, by deforestation, and later, people who worked on the land were in chains. After the Civil War, which was the most violent in history until that time, the subjugation of the people continued under the Jim Crow laws, which lasted until the 1960s. In law, society had to change. The attitudinal change took longer and was more painful.

The party at Robert and Holly's was a great surprise on the day of my arrival. It was a welcoming gift. The gift that I received in the post was also unexpected. Silvia, of the Findhorn circle of friends, having read my blog, sent me a book by Robyn Davidson 'Tracks'. It's about a woman who, in 1975, walked from Alice Springs in Australia to Hamlin Pool on the West Coast. Her walk covered 1700 miles with three camels and a dog. It was a gift worth waiting for, and I looked forward to reading it.

No hangover the next morning, but nettles ran up and down my throat the whole day. Morten from Taos wanted to visit Michael and Belinda for a Findhorn reunion. He contacted me while I was in mid-Texas, saying he wanted to follow in my footsteps on the motorcycle. He would try to arrive in Eupora on the same day as me. He, too, was invited to the dinner gathering. He had followed my journey, giving him the itch to be on the road. We expected Morten to arrive in Eupora on Friday, 25 April. On the day of my arrival. Morten planned his route from Taos, New Mexico, to Mississippi, riding his 750cc Triumph Tiger motorcycle, and followed my route. Unlike me, he had many difficulties. He ran into a sandstorm where visibility was barely twenty-five feet and had to stop for a day. I faced a similar situation after Timeline on the border of West Texas, but I was lucky enough to find a diversion into Dumas. Morten had no such luck. Sand infiltrated everywhere, into him and his motorcycle chain.

The following day, hailstones combined with rain and wind and the threat of tornadoes slowed him down and delayed him further. He diverted away from the bad weather and took an alternative route. He had hoped to reach us by Friday for the dinner party, but that cost him an extra day, and he arrived the next day. He looked tired, but two beers later, he returned to his usual self, joking, laughing, and telling stories. Michael, Morten (and Kate, and Morten's wife) are old Findhorn friends. It had been a while since they had last met. They needed good banter, so I took a back seat, observed, and listened. They were both in their element, sharing an episode of their time at Findhorn, reminiscing over their experiences in the 1970s when they were both in their mid-twenties. It almost took me back and placed me in that community of people.

Morten and Michael had much to parley as we drove in Michael's backyard in a buggy. He showed us around his sixty-five-acre garden. He said, "In the woods and in the mud, there are coyotes, turtles, badgers, snakes, where many animals made their habitat." Michael talked about building a bridge over a creek. This was what I felt was happening between all of us. I had only met Michael the day before and Morten for the second time; they hadn't seen each other for a while.

The following day, we were all subdued as the threat of tornadoes was on red alert. We remained indoors. Some of Belinda's cousins came over for safety, and we all chatted and played games. Throughout the day, we thought tornadoes would hit us. We were lucky, while other parts, such as Tupelo, the birthplace of Elvis, suffered devastation. As the news came on, we heard that over forty people had died in the disaster as it swept across the country. The next day was no better, and we were all worried about Morten's trip back to Taos. He needed to return home for urgent business with only three days to spare. He planned how to dodge the weather. Eventually, he was on his way. He wrote later that it was colder on the way back and close to freezing when he got home two days later. He followed my route to Mississippi except in reverse, from Texarkana westward.

He went through the landscape I captured on my blog, except at high speed; his trip was different. "I don't think people can understand the 'slow' experience, the smells, the sights, and the road. What you (I) covered in three days takes a half-day in a car: that's the reality. I don't think people can slow their minds down to that level. We have grown accustomed to speed and expediency in all aspects of life."

***

For two weeks, I was at a standstill. I didn't feel motivated. It was a winding downtime from my exhausting trek from Los Angeles. On the road, the thought of being tired came after a day's journey, then only briefly. Michael helped by taking me along to see all his projects. Belinda was always busy at work, even in the evenings at home. We visited many parts, and I was fascinated by the drive. Michael gave me a guided tour, touching on the history of the places we passed. Sentences would roll off his tongue about the struggle of African Americans. As we crossed a bridge, he suddenly said, "This is where they dumped Emmett Till in the river in 1955. Or that recent development in Mississippi or tarmac roads only happened in the 80s." It never ceases to surprise me what a densely forested state Mississippi is still.

We went to Jackson, where he had a survey to do for three days, with the four-star hotel all paid for. Michael worked during the day while I toured on my bicycle and explored uptown Jackson. In the evening, we would go downtown and tour around and have a meal.

While riding on the first day, a police officer pulled me over and asked about my helmet or lack of one. It was illegal for me not to have one. The police officer did not charge me a fee ($75) but directed me to a bicycle shop in Ridgeland called "The Bike Crossing." In the bicycle shop, they told me that the law had changed after much debate due to victims of accidents suffering devastating brain damage. Using helmets decreased the severity of the injuries that the riders incurred. Rather than terrible brain injuries, riders often have only cuts and bruises, according to the medical emergency unit at the local hospital. This law only applied to Jackson City and not the state of Mississippi.

Besides the helmet, I needed to raise my bicycle handlebars by two inches. The staff in the shop were friendly and wanted to know where I was from. We struck up a conversation about my trek. They fixed my handlebars for free and wanted to shake my hand and wish me good luck. Kimberly Tolliver, a young woman of about twenty-two, helped me to select a helmet. We chatted, and she wanted the address of my blog and asked: "Where are you heading?"

"I intended to visit Graceland before leaving for Alabama," I said.

A sparkle spread across her face, and she said, "I have been obsessed with Elvis since I was three years old."

"He has been my idol since I was eleven," I said.

She wasn't a local girl but lived fifteen miles from Jackson in Madison. I asked how long she had been working in the shop.

"This is just a temporary job until I can enroll at the University of Mississippi Medical Centre."

"What do you plan to study?"

"I intend to do a course in Radiologic Sciences." Before I inquired what that involved, she asked: "Have you been on the Natchez Trace Parkway? You would enjoy the quiet scenic scene by bicycle."

Later, I checked it on the map. It's a route stretching south of the Mississippi to Nashville, Tennessee. Originally, it was an old Indian trail used by early settlers along its Trace. It was turned into a national conservation area, and the route is over four hundred miles long. The Trace and its alignment were handed to the generation of today. It remained almost undeveloped and unspoiled along with its entire distance. Many sections of the original footpaths are still visible to observe and hike the Parkway's right-of-way. I had completed about ten miles of the route when I met a gentleman along the way in one of the rest areas. We spoke, and he mentioned that Elvis's car had once broken down on the Natchez Trace. He had hiked and ridden the Trace for over twenty years. Often, he felt that he was back in the earlier days of the pioneers: "It's so peaceful without the modern-day jingle-jangle; you can only hear the sounds of rustling leaves, creaking of branches and tweeting sounds of birds." He looked a fit man, perhaps in his mid-fifties, with a full head of hair, greying. His name was Matt.

When asked, he said he had no children. "The planet is overcrowded as it is, don't you think?"

I offered him an orange, and he took it, looked at it, spun it around, and said, "The world is a great big orange."

"What do you mean?"

"It's sweet and sour at the same time," he said and laughed.

He handed me back the orange and said, "I have a sack full of snacks. Thanks for the offer."

He wanted to go, and I wanted to talk some more. So, we talked.

He asked, "Are you from Australia?"

"Yes, only in spirit."

"I'm from England, though I left Mauritius when I was young."

Before I could explain, he said he knew of the island. That surprised me.

"I was stationed in the Diego Garcia archipelago during my naval force days and met many Mauritians working there."

"Did you know that a population of Islanders lived there?"

"I heard they had people on the islands long ago."

"The fifty-two islands were part of Mauritius and used as a leper colony in the 18th, 19th century."

"So, they had sick people living there. Did they all die?"

"On the contrary, the population grew and supported healthy inhabitants of two thousand by the mid-sixties."

"What happened to them?"

"Before the islands' independence, the British wanted to separate Mauritius and lease Diego Garcia to the USA. The Islanders refused to leave. The British threatened to bomb these Islands if the Islanders did not leave; at least, that was the story at the grass-roots level."

"So, they gave up their homes without a fight?"

"They were forcibly evacuated like cattle, leaving all their possessions behind, to a tin ghetto in Mauritius."

"Are they still in the ghetto?"

"I'm not sure. Many committed suicides or went into prostitution and drugs. There was compensation owed to them, but they were swindled by the different administrations of the day. Little of the reserved funds ever found their way to the Islanders. They have disappeared from the face of the earth as a cohesive group of people. There may be some second generation dotted about."

"It's a terrible thing when you are weak. You don't have leverage."

"I remember in the early 80s, an Islander used to protest in Parliament Square in London, holding a placard saying, "Free Diego Garcia." He once told me people would approach him and ask, "Who is this guy, Diego Garcia?""

Matt burst into laughter and said, "I lived a dual life on Diego Garcia, one on land and at work, the other under the sea where I found a different peaceful existence."

For him, it had been an unexpected haven away from a military complex guided by rules and regulations, punctuality, and discipline.

"Without having this other world to explore, the atolls would have been claustrophobic."

I wanted to know more about his background and why he had joined the Navy. And how long had he been in the force, and what had he been doing since he left? He looked uneasy, and I felt that perhaps I was being too inquisitive. He asked me many questions, some personal, and I was open to him. In conversation, it seemed fair that I should have been able to ask him a few. There was a look of timidity on his face when I asked him whether he was married. He gave an embarrassing laugh, got up, and said he had to go. Meeting me had been pleasant. He wished me luck on my travels. He was riding with his back to me at a distance in no time. I sensed a vacuum of human emptiness all around me.

I wanted to explore Jackson City by bicycle and did so after a long ride into town. As I entered the suburbs, I noticed the Brittany-style houses, all detached with long front lawn gardens. The streets had sidewalks. They were tree-lined, not wide and alienating as in Phoenix, but with much more of a European street view. The city still had the grid system, though.

Jackson is a beautiful city, clean, neat, and organised. The city's architecture varied, such as the turn of the 20th-century building of the law office Ogden and Associates on E. Capitol Street. Its red-brick construction and pairing of tall arch sash windows are magnificent. In the centre stood great modern innovative structures such as the Jackson Convention complex, where the geometric angles of the building dazzled the eyes.

At odds was the need to introduce Greco-Roman revival architecture with some simplified rococo and baroque style, such as the Governor's Mansion and the Old Capitol Museum. Others were scattered around, showing incongruity in the density of the city's vegetation. Somehow, it seemed out of sync in this state. In an absurd way, it would be like a giant tepee set up in the middle of Hyde Park London; nice to look at, but out of place. There were other peculiar buildings, too. Two that stood out seemed to have been influenced by the Mussolini architectural style. They were the William F. Winter Archives and History Complex. The building on the grounds of the Governor's mansion was a sharp contrast to the mansion. They were both of very similar architecture: rectangular, with several square columns, imposing, monolithic, and with regimented uniformity, a minimalist simplicity. The one on the Governor's grounds had carved a huge caption "Peace shall come to those who strive for peace" on its face. It would be impossible not to see the peculiarity in its architecture closely linked to Italy's style in the 30s in any prominent schools of thought.

I wouldn't say I liked the feeling of being in front of these buildings. They were imposing and menacing, not to be entered. These classical-looking buildings were like museums, a spectacle – detached and alienating from the reality of ordinary citizens. They were like tiered wedding cakes in a bakery window simply for display.

It was a sunny, warm, and pleasant day and a great time to be out and about. Enjoy the pristine sidewalk under the shade of splendid trees that forested the streets. Yet, my day touring the city surprised me that I only saw two people out in the open. One was about to enter his parked car, and the other was in the suburbs cleaning his vehicle. It was an empty, spooky city with the humming noise of vehicles on the roads. Perhaps it was I who was the real phantom. I stopped near an outdoor restaurant crowded with casually smart-dressed working people at lunch, I presumed. I asked, "Where is everybody?" making a gesture of out there. There was a momentary silence, and people looked at me as though I was mad.

Then someone shouted, "Here, having lunch," which brought laughter, and someone else yelled: "On holiday, and they ain't coming back."

It was like a comedy show, and I was the straight guy. Three people sat at a table nearby; two men and a woman invited me for a drink. They wanted to know about me, and before I could decline, a man at another table commented: "They will stop him for drunk riding." It was all part of the fun. I couldn't get a straight answer about why no one was walking in the city. Except: "Why walk when you can drive." For me, it made little sense.

It was the dodo syndrome all over again. It would be remembered that the dodos flew to the Mascarenas Islands thousands of years ago and found plenty of food and no predators. The necessity to fly was no longer needed. Over the centuries, their wings got smaller and their bodies larger until they could no longer fly. Men, the first predators who went to the islands, hacked them to death for their oil and meat until they became extinct.

I left with a few shouts of "Good luck, man, and "God bless." This bigger picture appeared as I rode the streets to head back to the hotel. The city was not designed to make it easy for pedestrians. It's stretched out, shops or malls are too far to walk to and likewise, for businesses. Delivering parcels by hand or an important document by walking to the next building may prove difficult. Parents would not be able to walk to a playground with their children. Driving there was the only option. Then, park in the parking area, let the children play on swings and slides and drive them back home. It seems to defeat the purpose of enjoyment and exercise. Many streets have sidewalks, but they are for aesthetic reasons, like a cherry on a cake. Yet, at first, it hadn't seemed that way. The trees on the streets and the sidewalks brought me closer to familiar surroundings. Now, there were no bicycles on the roads except a lone rider in an unfamiliar landscape trying to make connections in alien surroundings.

It was our last night in Jackson, and Michael invited Belinda to join us to dine in town for the evening. Steve Kelley, who was the project manager, joined us. I felt it was only fair that I should pay the bill as I had been so well received since my arrival in Mississippi, and besides, Steve treated us to a meal two nights before. The restaurant was in downtown Jackson, and the décor, the lighting, the cosiness and layout of the tables, and even the menu card were exquisitely done. The wine and the food matched the excellence of the atmosphere. Inevitably, the conversation flowed around architecture and its financial involvement. I drifted in and out of the chat.

A man further along at another table on the other side of the aisle drew my attention with intermittent laughs. He sat with five other people and was the focus of attention, dressed in a tanned linen suit except for his tie, which was as loud as his laughs. His silvery hair added a further ten years to his birth certificate. I noticed that he dissected his piece of chicken or duck, putting the bones in a neat pile on a side plate. The carbohydrates were separated by an aisle on his plate away from the protein before he ate. I tried to place him in a profession. I thought of him as a butcher but then saw his delicate hands and decided he was in the entertainment profession, perhaps a comedian. And dismissed that, too, as it was unlikely that comedians would laugh at their own jokes. I placed him in textile retail or the fashion business. By the end of the evening, his cheeks had blushed like the rosé wine he drank.

The waitress was abrupt in her manner; she reminded me of Jackie Brown, the actress. She served us with an air that she was above her customers. We were the last to leave the restaurant, and when I paid the bill, I left what I deemed was an appropriate tip, which in Europe is between five to twelve per cent unless it was included in the bill. In her abrupt way, she handed me back the tip. I gave it to her again, and for the second time, she returned it and turned her back on me. I looked at the others and said, "Did I do anything wrong?"

Belinda said, "She shouldn't have been rude to you."

Michael explained, "The normal tip is fifteen to twenty per cent. That's the basis of her wages."

Not used to the customs, I explained in Europe that a waitress has a basic wage, and the tip comes on top as an extra for services rendered. If a customer felt satisfied with the services, the server might receive twelve per cent. If the service was below par, the clients could use discretion and give a reduced amount or none. I was both embarrassed and annoyed. Michael said he had settled the tip when I left the restroom.

I said, "I hope it was only fifteen per cent," he chuckled.

The next day, I drove Michael's 4 x 4 truck from Jackson to Walthall. It was my first time at the wheel since I entered the USA. Driving was easy as the roads were free from traffic. Michael caught up with his sleep on the way back.

It never ceases to surprise me what a wonderful ambience of tranquillity the garden and the house of Belinda and Michael had on me. The effect was immediate upon entering the driveway, the tall pines, oaks, pond, and flower gardens to the left. The house with a grey painted roof and a large porch sat back from the quiet country road in Walthall village. It is a large house; everywhere inside seemed spacious. Although it's a three-bedroom house, it has nine rooms total, plus a basement section Belinda built in case of tornadoes. There is a small pool on the north side of the house, an idyllic setting for a mad trekker like me to take a deserved break. On most occasions, I was alone with the two dogs and two cats to keep me company. Michael and Belinda were at work, and Mary was at school. I was free to do as I pleased: read, write, swim, walk around the estate, fish in the lakes, walk in the village, or potter in the house. It was a time to heal my body from its tiredness.

Within two days of returning from Jackson, Michael mentioned a meeting in Mobile, Alabama, about a job if I wanted to go along. I couldn't refuse. On my bucket list, New Orléans was one of the places I wanted to visit. The difficulty of getting from A to B was not easy. Public transport did not exist, and to hire a car and spend a few days in New Orléans would have proved too costly for my budget. To my regret, I jettisoned the idea, but Mobile was an opportunity to see the southern coastline. Besides, I knew Michael needed company, and he wanted to show me that part of the country.

We were on the road early as it was a two-hundred-and-sixty-mile drive to get to the coast. Later, we stopped at a café for breakfast, each eating two rolls. Michaels was bacon rolls and mine were eggs. The rolls were very soft and made for people with dentures or to chew with their gums.

I drove; it was all flat land, green, with no ruggedness, desert, or mountains. The texture and mood of the landscape eluded all senses and remained detached and alienating. The vehicle comforts and protects, and every pulse can be felt. On a long drive in a moody trance, which numbs the sensibility, even though in command, at times, there is uncertainty. A thought came to mind – "Am I doing the driving, or is the vehicle in command?" It was as though a spectre existed in the machine.

We arrived at Michael's appointment building with five minutes to spare. Michael seemed undecided about whether to take on the project, as it was far from his usual work area.

He said, "Some of my men are married and have kids. It would only be workable for them to go home at weekends. That might prove too much. On the other hand, I could regroup the team and hire single men. Reliable, skilled tradesmen are scarce. This job could last a year and be very profitable."

With a dozen men gathered for the meeting outside the designated building, he asked me to park the truck and meet him in the square nearby in a couple of hours.

I parked the truck in Bienville Square, and what a fabulous square it was. It was that perfect time around nine in mid-May when the sun caressed the skin like a warm embrace. The air was still, and the aroma of croissants and coffee emanated from the café.

The majestic live oak (Quercus Agrifolia), the fig leaf (Ficus Benjamina), and other trees filled the square. The sun's rays through the leaves cast mosaic shadows onto the ground. Men tidied up the garden whilst the red squirrels were busy at the treetop, munching and dropping leaves and small branches to the ground. Cast iron benches dotted the square. People sat bathing in the sunlight with their colourful clothes. It was a morning ritual, replenishing their vitamin D, eating, drinking coffee, reading the paper, chatting, and laughing. Others took their dogs for walks, rode their bicycles, or exercised. A grand cast-iron fountain in the square, maybe forty feet tall, shaped like a wedding cake stand of four tiers, and the cascading waterfalls were like a bridal veil.

I carried no city map and hadn't read up on it. Since coming to the USA, I haven't researched any city, town, or outback. I planned no selected route. I wanted a fresh experience with no corrupted thoughts or influence from others. Michael wanted to go south to show me Dauphin's Island by the ocean. I had little time to venture around.

With less than two hours to spare, I walked along Dauphin Street, which led from the square, and what a street it was. I knew that New Orléans had French influence. I have seen photos, documentaries, and films like King Creole and A Touch of Evil. I studied the history of the USA. It was pleasing to discover that Mobile had a great French spirit. Dauphin Street had been preserved in all its magnificence, and the street reminded me of the French Quarter in New Orléans in films. The street, restored and gentrified, is strewn with bars, cafés, restaurants, boutiques, cinemas, and clubs. It was the heart of downtown and seemed lively with a great feel-good factor. The only thing missing was the sound of the French accent and an echo of a French melody. Only one other place took me back to what it could have looked like in days gone. That was Tamatave in Madagascar, where the port town had a similar architectural taste, although it was seedier.

A while later, as I arrived at a crossing, stood, and admired the surroundings, a man took a photo of me. He smiled when I looked at him and introduced himself as Jordan. He said he was from New Jersey and that his hobby was architecture. He had visited New Orléans and wanted to see Mobile for a few days.

With a voice full of wonder, he said, "Have you ever seen a place like this?"

I said, "Yes, Tamatave in Madagascar."

"No kidding, the French have been everywhere."

"Yes, even in Polynesia doing the hula in grass skirts."

He laughed. He asked what I was doing in the USA after hearing my accent. I told him of my trek. I knew his response - "Awesome man, awesome", while his thick one-lane eyebrows did the tango on his forehead. He wanted to chat more, but we had little time left as we returned to the square. He told me about the varied architecture of Mobile. The late Victorian revival, Spanish colonial revival, Beaux-arts style, Greek and

Roman revival, Gothic, and plantation-style houses. The names slid off his tongue like a priest reciting Latin prayers in my recollection of mass back in the days.

We shook hands, and Jordan wished me luck for the rest of my trek. He suggested having lunch together, but it was still early. Michael wanted to drive down to Dauphin Island and spend time there and picnic on the beach. Within a few minutes, Michael arrived. He wanted to leave straight away on Route 193. He was unsure whether to take on the project, and that played on his mind while driving. Michael reminded me that we were in Alabama. It hadn't occurred to me that we had crossed the state line. Earlier on, we went through De Soto National Forest to reach Mobile, and the name brought back memories of De Soto's men escaping down the river to the coast away from fierce Indian pursuit.

It is documented that Indians chased these men on a crusade under De Soto's command (1541) in search of gold and were prepared to butcher their way to find Eldorado. His name lived on, and now we were in the State of Alabama, and more memories came flooding in of the calamities of the 1960s civil rights movements. The stubbornness of Governor George C. Wallace, a liberal in the 1950s. He later turned segregationist for "Today, tomorrow and forever" for opportunistic reasons. He repented in his later years, and people were forgiving. In college at the time, in London, we watched television programs in class in the afternoon. They showed documentaries based on global political turmoil, and we had seminars on world affairs afterwards. The protest and the brute force used in Alabama in a documentary had seemed alien to us. We were made to believe that the USA was the land of freedom.

A third of our class was of Caribbean descent, and we all felt embarrassed and didn't know how to participate in the discussion. None of us had ever tasted the raw violence of an apartheid society. The frequent use of the N-word in the documentary made people wince. It's creepy how brutality and casual hatred can transmit themselves across the globe. It affects people in a lasting way no matter how far they are. As if the forces unleashed were all binding and that no one could escape their tide. De Soto and Governor George C. Wallace brought strife, disharmony, and violence to this part of the world. Obsessed by their desire for power. Perhaps this part of the world's recorded history was 'cursed' from when De Soto set foot on its shores in 1539. Only in the 1970s could it be said that the constitutional laws of the US lifted this 'curse'.

Michael and I grabbed a packed lunch on our way to Dauphin Island. Upon arrival, we changed into our swimsuits and went to the pier for lunch. It was hot, and we sat in the shade and ate. Michael was quiet and contemplative, deliberating whether to take on the project if offered. Lunch was filling, and he fell asleep on a bench.

Relaxing on Dauphin Island (Alabama)

Belinda & Michael's home in Eupora, Mississippi

I walked to the end of the pier, and the expansive view of the Gulf of Mexico lay before me. I hadn't seen the sea since I left Los Angeles. The sea there was unexpectedly cold, and a chill in the wind as Dorothy and I walked along the beach in Santa Barbara. Here on Dauphin Island, the air seemed more tropical. It was only May, and the temperature was already in the 80s Fahrenheit. The sand was white, and the beach stretched for some miles. But unlike a tropical beach, it had no coconut trees or windbreaker pines to provide shade and create a contrast in the landscape. The broad span of beaches banked into the dunes. Large apartment buildings immediately after, about three hundred metres from the beach, were a visual architectural catastrophe. The building structures, at least the view from the beach, seemed monolithic and plain. They were rectangular functional concrete mass. A few people were on the beach, and the usual sound of gulls in the air was missing.

Four years before, a great oil spill in the Gulf stretched from Texas to Florida and polluted the beaches along the coastline. The fishing industry in the area collapsed, and businesses of all sorts were affected or lost. From the pier, the beaches looked unsullied. Later, Michael and I walked down along the water's edge. It was clean and warm, and any trace of the spillage had long been cleaned up. The beach was back to how it used to be. We both dived into the water, and the sand at the bottom was white. It was like being in the tropics or a warm bathtub. Any residual pain I might have had after the long trek soon disappeared.

I asked Michael why he thought there weren't many people on the beach; he said, "It wasn't holiday peak time."

I said, "It was hot, and not everybody takes their holiday at the same time."

July is the height of the holiday season, but even now, many holidaymakers should have been visiting the Island.

He said, "People have been afraid of the spillage and the damage to health it could cause."

"But it's all cleaned up now."

"People don't want to take chances. They'll find alternative places for their vacation."

One disaster leads to the next, then another. The birds have gone, the people no longer come, and businesses struggle. That ripple effect again emanated thirty-five thousand feet deep on the ocean bed.

I was at the wheel for the three-hundred-mile drive back to Walthall. Michael fell asleep within ten minutes as we left Dauphin Island. The sun was strong and dehydrating, and perhaps lunch and the meeting in the morning had taken their toll. The drive was smooth and simple, just a straight road with two connecting routes. The traffic was light as we glided all the way. There was an urge to be on the road again. The sea had lifted all the tiredness from my body. It was coming to my third week at Michael and Belinda's. They had been kind and generous with easy-going personalities. I felt as though their home had been mine.

Chapter 14: Graceland

While contemplating my journey, Michael and Belinda announced they would take me to Graceland. I was in shock. I had to ask them twice to be reassured. I was a child again. I was resigned to not making it to Graceland due to transport difficulties. I couldn't sleep and woke up the following day feeling like I had been at an all-night party. I was human again after a solid breakfast of two cups of black coffee. We left soon after, on the road sandwiched between what seemed expansive forest walls. The sun glittered through the leaves of the tall oaks and pine trees.

Belinda switched on the radio as we drove on Route 51 towards Memphis. Along the journey, Elvis was singing from his station. It was a surprise that a radio station was dedicated solely to his music. Elvis sang across Mississippi, Tennessee, Arkansas, Louisiana, and other states. It was a long way north. The music put us in the mood during the one-hundred-and-forty-mile drive. All along, there were large tracts of farmland and forests. In the 1950s, when Elvis started, the roads would have been dirt tracks, and in one of his interviews in the early 1970s, he said that in the early days, he performed in many small towns in all the surrounding states. DJ Fontana, part of the Blue Moon Boys, Elvis's band, was his drummer and said, "They travelled for days cooped up in the car." Sometimes, they would stop and walk their different ways to cool off.

A little under three hours later, we were in Graceland. It was like a circus with buses and car parking on a considerable scale. Tourists in groups with their guides talking and meandering, going into detail about Elvis, did this and did that, which was stifling and sent me into a daze. I wanted to be alone, but there was a bustling crowd. Once in the house, I separated from the herd and went on alone. I never saw Elvis perform live. He hadn't toured outside the USA except in Canada in his early days in 1956. I didn't have the finances or the space to see him on stage in Las Vegas or anywhere else while he was alive. No one knew he would suddenly die without doing a world tour. Many of his fans would have paid for a ticket even if the price had been exorbitant. In Europe, he would have been a sellout. The whole world missed out on his live performances. This visit into what was his private domain came as a late reward. Everything was smaller than I anticipated it would be. Though the photos suggest otherwise, the main gates were big enough to drive a bus through. At the front doorstep, I had a turn, my head spinning like I was about to levitate. The moment overwhelmed me.

Once inside, I became a trespasser, an intruder, uninvited, entering someone's home like a thief to steal a look into the privacy of the greatest superstar. There was emptiness all around, not as I imagined it would be. The thought of walking in the shadow of my idol, a step at a time, thinking perhaps an engram echo would have recorded some of his aura in these walls. All I sensed was, "Elvis had left the building". I didn't want to stay there.

The house was modest and had simple decor except for the jungle room. The furniture was of sculptured animal figures, kitsch ahead of its time, reflecting Elvis's "perverse" sense of humour. The ceiling made of pleated fabrics had at its centre a round cushion. The effect was like the sun above and the pleated fabrics beaming out sun rays. In the TV room, the mirrored ceiling created an illusion of a much larger room. In it, four TVs were placed in a line on the wall with comfortable sofas to watch. His favourite program was Monty Python. The upper parts of the house were off-limits, the staircase quite narrow. There were six rooms, not counting the upstairs, including the kitchen. Everything was left as it was at the time of his death. Time remained still with little removed or updated. It was like entering a time warp, the best luxury anyone could afford in its day.

The whole place lacked a feminine touch. His mother died in 1958, only a year after he purchased Graceland. Priscilla lived there for over a decade, yet she left no imprint. It was all about Elvis.

I felt like a prowler and went through quickly. Outside into the sunshine, I shivered, yet it was 30° C/86° F. I passed into another section which had been added to the east side of the house. There, displayed some of his awards, platinum, gold, and silver records, and the clothes he wore in the early stages of his career. There must have been two thousand platinum, gold, and silver records and so many other awards on display, with videos showing his very early performances to the very last.

In the garden, the swimming pool was to the right of the exit of the gold records chambers. A medium-sized pool, nothing big, nice shape though, like an exaggerated figure of 8, with the bottom part larger. His racket room was about forty metres from the back of the house on a downhill slope. A vast, thick glass wall separated a section from floor to ceiling where he had a piano (There were three pianos in the house altogether). It was where he did all his practice. He sang his last two songs before retiring to bed the night of his death. The racket court was transformed into a spectacular mausoleum for all his costumes (He had two hundred in total with various colours), jewellery, many awards, and guitars, with four screens playing Elvis live on stage in Las Vegas. That whole building, once inside, reminded me of the tombs in the Valley of the Kings. An impression that Elvis was surrounded by all his artefacts as did those Pharaohs in ancient times, only for the new generation to rediscover him.

I felt nauseous and stepped outside into the rear garden where horses were galloping in the acres of grassland enclosed by white fences. I checked on a building that looked like a cabin on the west side of the ground. It was not part of the tourist trail, just a disused building. Peeping into its window, it had remained unused for a long while, with a desk, chairs, and metal cabinets. Then I remembered the wall panelling. It was his father's office, and he filmed an interview there when he came out of the army in March 1960. He looked polished then, and his hair returned to its fair shade. Elvis dyed his hair black from 1957 until he died for aesthetic appeal. He was a picture of health, looked confident, and articulated with a touch of shyness that added to his attraction. When asked at the interview if he planned to stay in Memphis and keep Graceland? He answered, "I'll keep Graceland for as long as I possibly can." He kept his promise even in death.

On the last part of the Graceland trail, I went to the meditative garden, where he spent much of his time meditating and reflecting. It is his burial place, alongside his mother, father, aunt, and a headstone for his twin brother Jessie, who died at birth. Staring at his granite stone, I lost it. I wanted to be sick. I moved to the front garden. The tall and plentiful mature trees made it peaceful, where I was most at ease. I don't know why this grieving came at me thirty-seven years after his death. Death comes in small stages, with its crackling signature from within all of us. When he died, I blocked it off. I was worried about my pre-university exam results. I was indecisive about returning custody of my two daughters to their mother. My mind was full and stressed, and Elvis's death remained stifled in me. I knew that I shouldn't have gone to this mausoleum. As Elvis fans, we all have images of him, alive and vibrant on stage and in films. He was a giant, "The King", and he got bigger; even death could not kill his flame.

Elvis's burial place in the meditative garden

Outside Graceland, on the other side of the road, there were so many things to see: all his cars from the 1950s. He had sprayed a pink Cadillac and a purple one, a white and a black Rolls Royce, and many other cars as if he had missed his childhood toys as he was poor. A whole forum dedicated to his birthplace, Tupelo, in Mississippi. There was an opportunity to visit inside his two aeroplanes. Each time, when coming out of a forum, a gift shop, or a boutique, lay waiting. There were many restaurants, and the King's dish was on the menu, but I didn't fancy it, for it was full of calories. Then, there was his radio station, which we listened to on the way. I went in and spoke to the DJ Bill Rock, and he allowed me to say a few words and a dedication, "Loving You", which he played later. He asked me why I chose that record when there were so many others to choose from. We were leaving; it seemed right at the time. Elvis sang in a very early version I had never heard before - jazzy, with backing and all. Brilliant!

Many of his early unpublished recordings played on the radio, and some were done with a jazz touch and deep blues, which the station was playing 24/7. On the way back, we stopped at his ranch where he used to have all his horses - Ranch G, G for Graceland. Someone said Priscilla Presley never liked staying there. There was a small, modest house in the foreground of the ranch. He sold the ranch in 1970. The trust fund was trying to buy it back and restore it as a heritage site. I asked one worker in Graceland how many people visit Graceland in one year. She said, "Perhaps a million and increasing." Elvis is richer dead than when he was alive. He has sold more records than any other artist, over 1.5 billion. Even in death, he remains a commodity extraordinaire. The Elvis machine will keep going like a train on a railway track without brakes because people of all ages and all nationalities are flocking to Memphis.

In 2026, fifty years after his death, the actual cause will be known. It's only an instinct, and all Elvis fans who felt the embryo of his voice and music implanted in them will sense he may have taken his own life. He found a way to end the nightmare of his suffering. A short meteorite sensation to stardom that lasted just twenty-two years but went on beyond all we could have imagined long after he left us. He was a happy person in public and gave a tremendous thrill to many people worldwide with his interpretation of music. He gave us all a great gift and infected us with everlasting joy.

Chapter 15: Mississippi Blues

Michael and Belinda thought it would be a good idea if I spent a day and a night in Clarksdale before going on a weekend trip canoeing and camping on the Great Mississippi River. Before they headed back to Walthall, they showed me and suggested a few ideas of what I could do while in Clarksdale. Michael talked of canoeing and camping on the river since my arrival. He insisted that this was a chance not to be missed, and he was right. He arranged for me to stay at Quapaw Canoe Company Lodgings and paid for everything. I felt humbled by Michael and Belinda's generosity since I arrived at their home. I had three rooms in the lodgings, a kitchen and a living room, as no one was there. There was no TV or Wi-Fi, but it was a comfortable place. Later, John 'Driftwood' Ruskey came to see me and spoke about the river venture. He is the person who started the Quapaw enterprise. I slept the night there and didn't go out as I was still affected by the emotions of Graceland. The evening was quiet, and I wrote in my diary and purged myself from eating. I drank herbal tea instead and went to bed late.

Early in the morning, the sun was shining, and I bought breakfast at a supermarket and walked around downtown Clarksdale feeling my way. It is a town in Coahoma County, Mississippi. It was land inhabited by Choctaw and Chickasaw Indians, where De Soto was laid to rest. Clarksdale was made famous by the Robert Johnson song Crossroad. It's the town where Sam Cooke and Ike Turner were born, along with many blues singers. And where Muddy Waters lived and worked for most of his life. Mississippi is where the blues came from, up and down the state. Clarksdale was where everyone wanted to be to get a small recognition before moving on to Memphis and later Chicago. Route 61 passed through the town, and people moved north during the 1940s to work in the big factories in Chicago. They left behind a way of life, the cotton fields' culture, and sharecropping.

Many were blues singers who worked on the plantation to sustain a living. People like Muddy Waters drove tractors during the week and played the blues at weekends. Thousands migrated north to the Windy City and passed through Clarksdale. Highway 61 was the only road going north, and it was not tarmac surfaced but a dirt track. It was a bustling city in those days, but the changing economy profoundly affected business and the eventual running down of downtown Clarksdale. It has stood still, and new functional buildings have sprung up, but a stroll along the streets shows there is still seediness downtown. Finding a new prestigious building with a well-kept garden opposite the warehouses wouldn't be surprising. Factory buildings of the 1920s adjoining those newly constructed social houses or apartments. This shabbiness, a lack of uniformity in the construction, and the overhead mass of electric cables kept the blues atmosphere and gave it a more aesthetic appeal. There were quite a lot of empty shops in need of modernising, but the town planners were doing great things here.

They have the best Blues Museum in the world, and Belinda's architecture business helped to restore and extend the museum. The museum has a first-class display of the history of the blues. As far as I could make out, I counted ten blues venues. The exterior of these buildings looked seedy, and in some, the proprietor spent big on the inside and created a great atmosphere. This is what they were doing. They were in the process of reclaiming their cultural heritage, which had been ignored in the past. Huge restoration projects were underway to maintain the vibrancy they once were. Everyone was into Blues, and people worldwide came to enjoy these cosy clubs.

Morgan Freeman co-owns a club called Ground Zero next to the Museum. A German man who visited Clarksdale became so passionate about the place and the music that he gave up everything in Germany. He came and created a Rock and Blues Museum, which is now a great tourist attraction. An old Cinema, Roxy, was turned into a venue. In the entrance foyer was a slick bar with a few tables and chairs in the main hall. The rest was a brick shell. The roof replaced with glass immediately gave the impression of being in a derelict building. The latest sound system and lighting were on the stage, where the old screen would have been. It makes the place very inviting. I was lucky to witness a rehearsal, and the acoustics rebounded off the walls. The façade of the building was left untouched with the old Roxy name in its original form with a certain amount of rust showing through, placing it in a time warp of bygone days.

I walked the streets without purpose for curiosity and seeking visual stimulation. But it was not that kind of town, for the heart of it was in its soul – Blues. Blues came out of the spirit of the people through their sufferings. It is this thought which came that a healing process was taking place after long periods of indifference. Blues emerged; it came out of Africa, dating back 2,000 years when the land of the Pharaohs was black in the times of the Nubians.

I listened to a recording from a London library some thirty years ago which traced the origin of the sound of Blues in the ancient Nile region. It sounded nothing like the blues except as a continuous pulse of today's beat. Blues were transported across the ocean with the Africans in chains, but it beat like a free spirit inside and on the cotton fields. It went on a journey and found a new form, merging aspects of Irish folk songs and finding its own essential identity. Blues metamorphosed over centuries, and each generation contributed to the innovation of its sound. From the single acoustic guitar of Lead Belly of the 1920s/30s to the 1940s when the electric guitar was incorporated. The Blues is all about the condition of Blacks living in America. Whether it is expressed from a personal point of view of lost love or a general condition of suffering, the songs are always melancholic and express the inner soul of a person or the general condition of everyday living. It is a passionate expression of grief, love, or sorrow.

On the streets of Clarksdale, hardly anyone was about, reminiscent of a day I spent in Jackson. The odd car would pass, and there were people in the shops in ones and twos, but no more. There wasn't the hustle and bustle of a town on any day as one would see in England, yet it was a Saturday. I wanted to speak to someone local, but no one was there. I went to the library and met Sheila, and she gave me some time, and we chatted. I asked her where everybody had disappeared.

She said, "Clarksdale has seen a huge migration from the past, but the population was never that big. The present population is less than eighteen thousand. About one-third were less than twenty years old. People are just going about their business."

She asked what I was doing in Clarksdale. I told her of my visit to Graceland and about Michael's idea of me making a canoe trip on the Mississippi River. She then told me that a trust is trying to buy back Elvis's old ranch to turn it into the Elvis experience.

I said, "The old house on the ranch looked run-down, but the bridge he built is still intact."

She said, "The Elvis Trust will restore the small house and make the ranch accessible to tourists." Then she added, "Elvis performed in Clarksdale before he was famous in 1955 together with Johnny Cash and others. We are researching further on the subject to add to the history of Clarksdale."

I went to four venues that afternoon/evening. I started in a bar down Main Street, Delta Avenue, where the décor was done in a slick modern style. Two guys were singing country rock. I drank a local brew, and the atmosphere was convivial, with the small crowd lively. Then I moved on to an outdoor concert by the Blues Museum. A substantial outdoor stage is set up with a group performing Rock/Blues/Reggae. The was good, and the crowd was having fun. It was more of a family outing, with fathers carrying their children on their shoulders and others holding stools or chairs.

An hour later, I went on to Morgan Freeman's Ground Zero club. The outside looked run down, white paint peeling off the red brick façade. The windows had not seen a coat of paint since before World War II, with the blinds in tatters, sticky labels, and graffiti peppered the glass. It was difficult to see what was on the inside. The porch had sofas and armchairs as though they had been dumped off the streets and then recycled. A vague attempt at flowerpot arrangement, all in a line as though they were ready to march out like drilled soldiers with green berets. It was an introduction to kitsch art at its best. I dreaded stepping over the threshold.

Once inside, it was like stepping onto a film set. The lighting display was fabulous, more than a Christmas tree. The décor was crazy and cosy, perfect for a night of blues. The place was full of paraphernalia, such as an old saxophone, T-shirts, framed photos of Blues singers, and hanging trinkets. Thousands of signatures framed the graffiti walls, such as, "I woz there, and so woz dodgy Dave." The tables had 1950s plastic covers with colours imitating the American flag but with maple leaf patterns. The stage was bare, and I was standing there with emptiness. It was early (nothing began until ten in the evening), but the bar and food were available. I met a

Spanish couple at the bar counter, Sebastian and Immaculada. Sebastian didn't speak English but was a cheerful figure.

I asked Immaculada about her name, and she said, "I don't like it. You can call me Imma."

To be stuck with the name Immaculate as a child seemed daunting. They were both at university and drove across America to see as many places as possible.

"Doing a Thelma and Louise?" I suggested.

"Oh no, more like cruising with Seb and Imma," she laughed.

They started in New York and wanted to finish in New Orléans.

"We sleep in the car most days, but every three days, we go to a motel to get a good night's sleep and a shower."

They had a terrific adventure. I invited them to stay in the spare room at the Quapaw, but they already had a room booked for the night. We drank together and left to go to 'Reds', which Mark, my guide for the river trip, recommended.

All the venues were near each other, only a stone's throw away, unlike any other place I had been to since I arrived in the US. We were there at nine, and the music was in full flow. We could hear it from down the road. As we reached the door, it was electrifying. The venue was atmospheric, taking you back to some imagined 1940s set where BB King might have played. The musicians never stopped playing until three, with just a short break. The man/boy on lead guitar and vocal named Kingfisher was fifteen. Another man/boy on drums named Hollywood, also fifteen. The bass player was twenty-three and was named Jimmy Big Richard Johnson. I had a hunch he preferred Richard used in its shorter version. The atmosphere was riveting, and the venue was packed with people coming from miles around and from abroad, England and Australia. The place was not big, perhaps large enough to accommodate fifty people, and it looked like a warehouse for bales of cotton. The bar only sold beer. Those young musicians will make it big. The only thing is that it was better to shut your eyes when using the lavatory.

I stayed in Reds until the early hours and drank more than I should have. In the morning, I was to be ready by nine for the weekend canoeing and camping trip. I was afraid I would not wake up in time after "drowning my sorrows" for the last two days. But I was up like a robot at eight. I felt I had aged overnight, but I ran downstairs and was ready to go by 8.50 a.m. Mark 'River People' as he calls himself, and two other tourists were already there getting the equipment organised. Mark was our guide, bright, knowledgeable, and very eco-conscious. He writes a monthly blog for a magazine about adventures on the river. He talks of the river from the time of the great glacier meltdown thousands of years ago. It had made the expanse of the river a hundred miles wide and created floodplains on either side of the banks. Today, the river is only three miles at its widest. And land on its banks has been reclaimed, and levees and dams built. Still, wildlife was everywhere, such as otters, deer, beavers, muskrats, and other mammals along its banks. More than one hundred and twenty species of fish make their home in the river, as well as mussels. Birdlife seemed in abundance, and forests spanned for miles.

I had traversed the large, wooded land since north/mid-Texas. It was to my surprise that it stretched to this river. If a patch of land were left fallow for a year or two, it would turn back into a jungle. This was how fertile the soil was by the great river. The twenty-foot canoe carried us, and all our supplies and the equipment weighed fifteen hundred pounds. It glided through the still waters of the Mississippi River effortlessly and in silence. The great body of water offered those in its vicinity a gift. That is calmness, yet wrapped in nature's sounds: space, spectacular views of the immensity of the sky, and the voluminous tranquillity of slow-moving water. The surrounding woodland is dense and tall, reflecting on the water like an immense protective wall.

The canoe rowing came without effort with the four of us on board. We moved smoothly; everything passed by like the river itself. I wanted to swim after we rowed for ten miles and chose our designated island for the day. Mark decided to stop on Island 64 and pitch camp there. The water cleansed my body, but within minutes, I was out. It was icy coming straight from the mountains up north. The other group members were a father and son on a weekend outing, John and Jesse.

John wanted to give his son a treat on the great river. He was a chatty fellow and talked about anything. He couldn't stop talking. Jess, nineteen, spent most of his time on his mobile phone trying to contact his girlfriend, but he had no joy with the satellite reception. "Like all teenage boys, they become restless when not near their girlfriends." John was making fun of his edginess. Mark suggested we explore the island while he lit a log fire and prepared lunch. Father and son made their way while I pitched my tent on the beach close to the water's edge.

Later, I, too, went out exploring. I saw tracks made by a jackrabbit, a deer, and a sidewinder. Shrubs of blackberries, loganberries, and many grapevines were dotted along the way, with bundles of small grapes hanging down. The tall pines, cottonwood, and willows made the island seem tropical, surrounded by white beaches. In contrast, the banks of the Mississippi were of thick mud two feet deep. It was sticky and difficult to wash off unless scrubbed hard with sand with the feet planted in the water. It was like glue. Back at the campsite, the wind had picked up. My tent at the river's edge seemed ready to take off. I needed to relocate it to a sheltered spot among the small willows away from the beach.

We gathered around the log fire in the evening while Mark prepared dinner. John brought out his moonshine, and I needed the "hair of the dog." I took a gulp and wasn't sure whether I felt better. He gave me another. I sipped on it more quickly that time. And it got me out of my silent mood as my lingering hangover receded. John was in good spirits, gulping his

Bloody Mary. He preferred that to the moonshine or the vodka which he brought. Jesse didn't want to drink, and Mark wanted his after dinner.

John loosened up considerably after a few glasses and told us he had been married three times – "Not much luck with women. They wanted more than I could give them. The fucking bitches took me to the cleaners, and it wasn't enough. They wanted my balls."

I wasn't sure whether he included his son's mother in the equation. On the surface, he didn't sound bitter, more a resignation, having lost a series of battles without understanding why. The experience was never shared. He gave, they took, was his overtures. He talked about animals too, always catching that big fish, shooting that wild boar or deer, or "that son of a bitch jackrabbit got away." Jesse was a copy of his father.

He said, "I once bet $25 I could shoot five birds in less than a minute."

I butted in and asked him what he did with the dead animals.

He replied, "Nothin', just left 'em there."

I left it at that. It was storytelling time. I knew he was boasting, trying to copy his father. Throughout the day, I had seen flocks of geese painting their black silhouette on an open grey mass of clouds. If Jesse had had a gun, he would probably have taken potshots at them and laughed at his marksmanship.

Mark came in and talked about conservation. He had fluency in the way he could change a topic that was going the wrong way. He cared about the environment, and he lived by his actions. He picked up tin cans and plastic bottles that people had left or had drifted downriver. He put them in a bag, later to be disposed of. He ensured that the driftwood he used for the log fire was not part of a fence treated with a chemical solution. He was forty-four and had no children. I asked him if he wanted any, and he said, "Yes, but with a good woman. Time was running out."

The wind whistled hard and fanned the blaze, carrying the echo of my voice away in the crackles. We remained silent for a while.

The barges lined six deep and seven in tow, locked together, moved upriver all day and night. The enormity of the cargo seemed impossible. Each barge, perhaps one hundred and fifty feet long and twenty-five feet wide, was being weighed down by the tonnage. The log fire blazing bright red lit everyone's face. Alcohol flowed; jokes and stories carried the laughter into the night. The oxygen and late night at Reds caught up with me. I went to my tent and listened to the echoes of laughter and voices as I drifted to sleep. In the middle of the night, the distant rumble of the barges woke me. I unzipped my tent, and the explosion of stars in the night sky stunned me. It was overwhelming with stars; I wanted to see a meteorite or even an exploding star.

The evening wind had died down, the forest in an ensemble, and the nocturnal chorale was unimaginable. I was unfamiliar with this part of the world and could not make out any of the sounds.

I walked to the fire, and the big log was still burning, glowing red under a film of ash. Mark came to mind, and it seemed he had found peace. He was a professional in what he did and understood the river as if he was born there, yet I knew he was from somewhere else.

I wondered why Mark had added the name "River People" to his name. Those river dwellers of long ago must have camped on islands such as this one and gazed at the night sky. They would have lit a fire as Mark did with driftwood and told stories that had a different meaning to our world. That afternoon, Mark picked up modern debris left behind. To those river people in ancient times, nothing would have been imported; all things belonged to their enclosed world. With no contact with the world outside except perhaps a neighbouring tribe, everything they knew would have been of their invention, their design, and all biodegradables. They were the masters of their entire universe. Their world was shattered, and they lost their wholeness when outside contact broke through and intervened. Their way of life was reshaped forever.

We were up early, and dark clouds covered the sky. It felt like the rain was on its way. The fire was still alight under the ash. After breakfast, we broke camp double-quick and moved on. The rain threatened to come, but it never did. Mark wanted to show us some impressive trees growing in the water. We moved from Mississippi onto the other side of the riverbank in Arkansas territory. We glided into the shallow water of the tributary under giant trees, such as bald cypresses whose great girth was like an upside-down cornet just above the water. Other trees, such as the golden leaf water oak, whose reflection in the still dark water resembled a painting. As we went further in, we saw a corroded refrigerator and a rusted old car from the 1930s. Other debris, such as dumped kitchen units and polystyrene, is no longer white but sullied, covered in rotting leaves. How did it all get there? Tornado dumps, perhaps? We drifted silently in the canoe.

The fifteen miles to our pick-up point was a calming cruise. We felt privileged to have had the opportunity of a lifetime on this expanse of the river. The only thing that was missing was the blue holes. There are huge swimming pools at the centre of the many islands. When the river gets high, these islands get flooded, sometimes almost bursting the levee. As the river recedes, water is left in deep pools, and the fine silt filters through the sand and clarifies the water. The white sand below and the sky above make the water appear blue. Fish and turtles are often seen marooned in them. These are the best places to swim. I didn't get to see one, but the others walked through the mud on the bank of the river and took photos of one near the levee. After Graceland, I became dazed for a second time by the splendour of the Mississippi Delta.

Michael was due to pick me up at the Quapaw Canoe headquarters but didn't arrive for a while after. This gave me time to chat with John

'Driftwood' Ruskey, who owns the enterprise. John came from Colorado two decades before to learn how to play the Blues from Johnnie Billington, an old master blues musician. He learned the Blues, but Johnnie Billington taught him more than that. Johnnie taught him how to plant the seeds of his learning, which he has done ever since.

He returned two years after he did his music tour around a few countries and, with patience, set up the Quapaw Canoe Company. He wanted to influence the youth and involve the local community in his attempt to keep the wildness and magnificence of the Mississippi River. He wanted to extend what Johnnie Billington taught him. He runs the society and leads tours in kayaks and canoes with his associates like Mark River People, Markvicus Dinky Jones, John Maddog Fewkes, and others. The youths learn to build canoes from trees by hollowing out the trunks and assisting at every stage with the product of canoe building. John and his team of dedicated people wanted to give back to the community, especially the young, a direction of how important it was to have a vision of their lives. They need to understand their environment and preserve the wildness of the delta. Everything they did was hands-on. It involved hard work and dedication. The youths love taking part in the making of adventure and creativity.

John took me into the "cave". It was the basement where all the equipment was stored and where he used to sleep when he first arrived. It was a treasure trove, a library full of books from floor to ceiling, guitars, drums, hats, driftwood, and maps. John had drawn himself and painted.

There were so many artefacts picked up from the river. Every piece drew your attention, and you wanted to touch them. John is a calm and charismatic figure, and he has surrounded himself with thoughtful, caring leaders.

I asked him why he took to the river.

"It was constantly changing, and unless efforts are made to preserve its wildness, industrialisation will slowly creep in, and it was important for everyone to understand this. Whatever you learn in life, it is important that it is passed on to the next generation. Otherwise, it dies with you."

This idea of death seemed to me to be a recurring theme. The death of the river people, the systematic removal of the old forest and replaced by an industrial forest except for a thin strip in the immediacy of the banks. Big changes, such as great mounds of the levee to control the floods, dams, and the machinery of commerce all along the banks. This great river was the lifeblood of all the communities which lived along its length and all the wildlife that depended on it. It would be madness if its citizens were to stand by and allow the economic system to push ahead and destroy this living artery of the United States.

Chapter 16: Au Revoir Mississippi

It was time for me to leave Michael, Belinda, and Mary in Eupora, Mississippi, and move on again to continue my journey.

Belinda & Michael's home in Eupora, Mississippi

I needed repose to give my body a break to recover. Time was irrelevant on this trek. I wanted to keep to my schedule, and at the beginning, that played on my mind. It was different once the journey took over and entered another dimensional zone. The relationship with your world no longer applies. In mind, in a delayed reaction way, all the rational, behavioural conformity is stripped away. The garb which everyone wears to be part of that tribal whole vanishes. Society expects conventionality; everyone acts accordingly. Not here on the road, in the forest or in the desert. Something alters with a feeling of liberation, a natural to the landscape. Many things taken for granted became obsolete. Only three things were necessary: food, health, and shelter. Everything else crucial was free: air, conversation and connection with people, courtesy, laughter, and tears.

You could be trekking for days, seeing no one and nothing. This changes how you view yourself in this universe—the self you have inhabited for the years of a lifetime. You strip yourself of all things until you are psychologically and emotionally bare. This is not a conscious decision but a slow process in changing conditions. The environment that impacts you can be so massive as if an implosion in the great silence of your existence had taken place.

It is difficult to decipher this feeling and articulate it now. It isn't easy to comprehend everything precisely. Perhaps some insight could be shown by pointing to an example. A person reading a poem must gauge the written words or listen to an audio recording and assimilate the meanings. The understanding is based on this recognition. In between these words and lines, there is nothing but space. Those gaps are not empty, containing hidden, parallel, and parabolic undertones. It is up to the reader to see these spaces as meaningful and discover their deeper meaning.

Being liberated is to be in these empty spaces, in a challenge, to redefine yourself, and by virtue, undermining who you were. Few people ever get the opportunity to challenge such depths. Nothing remains static. Nothing is permanent; you must return to the wider world to fit into that societal conformity and all that goes with it. Except you now have this dual understanding of yourself. After a lifetime of conditioning, you have managed to view the hidden side of another you.

While walking through the Bible belt, I encountered numerous evangelical people. Those old philosophers who constructed the books and wished to create gods also wanted to bring their gods from the heavens back down to this world as alien invaders in the form of body snatchers. How clever they were to have succeeded in making God an invisible entity. For we are all great creators and big dreamers. The God we pursue will forever be elusive. An idea came to me on one of the most demanding treks I had to endure when I almost broke down. I was in the Rocky Mountains and wondered where the concept of the Trinity came from. This triple phenomenon is an entity of the Christian God of the Father, the Son, and the Holy Ghost. We could find a meaningful answer only in the great depth of thought and perhaps exhaustion. All prophets and sages go to the mountains to seek "spiritual guidance." Moses and Mohammed did it, as did Jesus. He spent forty days in the desert to speak to his father. As those sages in the Far East, the Himalayas and the Pueblo shamans had done in sacred mountains in Taos, New Mexico.

Mountains and deserts oddly influence the human psyche. In utter exhaustion, an internal battle occurred in these mountains in the Rockies, where the effort to walk fifty metres demanded every ounce of energy. A contest between the physical self, the mental capacity, and emotional defiance. In these interdependent components of self, the triangular energy flow was measured and balanced. When an imbalance occurs in this trinity, the other two parts compensate for the lack of energy movement. If two parts shut down, the third must bear the brunt of all the current. If all three shut down, a complete breakdown occurs or death. These mountains could test the limits of anyone's resolve. In my case, mentally and physically, I was spent; emotionally, I refused to lie down, even if it meant death. Logic or common sense had long since disappeared into the great blue yonder. How clever those ancient philosophers were to give us the true meaning of the saying that God the Trinity was within all of us.

So quickly, I had all the difficult parts of the journey rescinded into my memory. But now, on the eve of my departure from Mississippi, I was anxious. Three weeks since I had been on the road, my fitness level was questionable. It was as if I was starting all over again. Summer was in the air, becoming humid and hot in the 90s Fahrenheit. In the wide-open space, mosquitoes were a menace day and night.

I was ready to go again when heavy rainfall delayed me a few days. It wasn't easy saying goodbye to Michael, Belinda, and Mary. I enjoyed being with them. To think that I was a stranger a few weeks before, they treated me like a family member. They were generous, and I felt relaxed while I was there. We talked, and they filled me in on the culture and history of Mississippi. They took me to parties and restaurants and introduced me to their family and friends and the pillars of their community. They gave me an insight into the work they were both associated with.

We attended one of Mary's school concerts - she was part of the school band; she plays the clarinet and piano at home or practices the piano with great energy. Given the opportunity, she has exuberant vocal cords and could be a soprano. She loves singing, but her teenage hormones were playing havoc.

On one of those evenings when we all went out to dinner, I was introduced to Sea Ryder. She worked at a Big Creek restaurant a dozen miles from the house. Belinda thought it would be of mutual interest if I met her as she had also done a trek across America. I took her phone number and said I would phone her before leaving the region. It was an uplifting experience meeting her in Big Creek while Michael and Belinda were in New York. (I looked after the dog and the two cats while they were away.) Sea travelled with two horses and made a loop from Maine to California and back again. It took her two years and a month. We chatted for three hours in her newly gained home in Big Creek in Mississippi. She bought the house for $10k while she was doing her trek. She met someone in the middle of nowhere who offered her a house on the cheap and got her mother to deal with the contracts for the property while she was still on her travels. It was an ideal offer; she needed a place for her horses. She also needed sanctuary to write in relative isolation.

It was a modest wooden house in the style of the region. No one had lived in it for a while, and she was refurbishing it a bit at a time. The garden was a fair size but not large enough to accommodate her two horses. She had them in a coral about a mile further down the road. She kept chickens and two goats. She and St. George, her partner, had already begun a vegetable patch. When I arrived, she was in the bathroom. St. George entertained me and made me tea. She called him Saint because he had been good to her, helping to renovate the house. He had helped her move in, always doing something in and around the house and grounds. When she came into the living room, she looked radiant. She was taller than when I first saw her in the restaurant. Her stature, well-spoken and relaxed manner surrounded by all her books gave her an attractive, out-of-the-ordinary aura.

I wanted to know what made her make such a long and arduous journey on horses.

"I have been around horses since I was sixteen. Caring and handling them would have been the least of my problems."

"Why did you take this four thousand five hundred miles trek?"

"It was something I wanted to do for a long time. Perhaps it was a teenage dream, but it got stuck. You move on with your life, get involved with living, and it's all forgotten. Later in the lull of a moment, an urge to do what you've always wanted to do comes at you."

At the start, she wasn't on her own.

"Fortunately, it began with my best friend and three horses. It was her idea as much as mine. We started well. She was more of an extrovert and dealt with people easily. They warmed to her, and it was easy for us to find places to stay and set up camp. I would take care of the animals and prepare food together."

Did you decide upon a division of labour from the beginning?

"Yes, but that didn't work out well, and after a month of stress, the journey became overwhelming for her. We weren't getting on. We were constantly arguing. She decided to leave."

You said stress. In what way did she feel stressed?

"We were both tired. In the beginning, after two weeks, you begin to understand what you've taken on. The sheer distance involved. It affects you mentally and physically in ways you wouldn't dream of."

Her leaving must have upset you. Did you want to pack it all in?

"No, I wanted to continue with the journey. My mind was made up. I cried a lot. The tension had been building up. I hadn't expected her to leave so suddenly. I wasn't afraid of being on my own. I didn't have the skills she had."

What skills didn't you have?

"The skills to deal with strangers. I'm not good at talking to people. Maybe it's the vibes I give out. People don't respond well. I got a lot of negative responses."

Her statement surprised me. She was very charming, and in my encounters on the road, I had only positive experiences. I put this to her.

"Perhaps it was because you are not an American. People are more receptive to someone from Europe. You are a man, and I am an American woman with horses. It doesn't have the same favourable appeal."

I was staggered by what she said, for I would have thought the opposite.

"I asked many farmers if they could put me up because one of my horses became lame. I told them I needed nothing as I was self-sufficient. But they all turned me down. A while after, I felt exhausted and desperate; it was nearly dark. I chanced on this farm run by three Mexican brothers, and they offered me a barn. They were hospitable and allowed me to stay for three weeks until my horse recovered. They took care of me. I met a few good people, but not many. I cared for the horses, and the healing took longer than expected. It is different when walking, pushing a trailer, or riding a bicycle. If something breaks down, a punctured wheel or a broken chain, you fix it. It might take an hour, and you get going again. Animals are like children. You must feed and water, groom them, and they need special care from head to hooves."

She said that on another occasion, approaching a town, word had gotten around that she was looking for a place to rest her horses.

"This elderly woman was searching for me, driving around town to find where I was. Eventually, she did. She wanted the grass in her large backyard grazed to keep it tidy."

All the time while we talked, George sat and listened and did not utter a word.

"This is the first time I have spoken about the trek to anyone. George has heard none of this."

He looked captivated by her coming out of herself as she was in free flow.

"It came to a point when I had had enough. I wanted to give up many times. I went beyond exhaustion."

But she had promised to finish and give a talk at the end and held on to her promise. The last five hundred miles proved too much even though she completed it.

"I became ill and was in bed for two months, unable even to care for myself."

I sympathised with her feelings since the desperate moments occurred in the first part of my journey. I came to the point of breaking down and wanting to give up so many times and again in the Rockies. At that time, I had no notion what the ending would be like since I was only a third through my journey. There was composure in her as though she had discovered hidden secrets about herself, things unknown before. She held a contented look with an appealing smile. Maybe it was because she had met George or unlocked something missing in her life. I asked her how she felt about moving away from a city in Maine, leaving her family behind, and setting up a home in Big Creek. She had no immediate friends apart from George.

"People are friendly in Big Creek and have helped a lot. I made many friends when I needed to. I like it here. It's peaceful, and I can have the space to write."

She was where she wished to be. The journey taught her that. Our time together went by quickly. What were her plans?

"I'm writing a book, making discoveries in my new surroundings, and doing the things I missed out on. Simple things like gardening and growing my vegetables. But the goats ate all that we planted three weeks ago." She burst out into a belly laugh.

She was serious about her writing and disciplined. She wouldn't see anyone in the morning until after one, only on certain days. Some of our experiences were similar but, in a great measure, different. Our time ended, and George took a photo of us together. We didn't talk about important issues such as her internal journey. Perhaps she would have wanted to keep that for her book. Still, time was cordially spent in her charming company together with George. Sea writes poetry, too, and has spent time in Europe, a year in Ireland, isolated with a group of writers in a rented house on the west coast. She told me she loved the rain there, which was a surprise as it never stops.

Walking and riding is the best way of learning, giving me time to think, observe, listen, and reflect. My blog had over two thousand encouraging followers, urging me on till the end. They came from around the globe: Africa, Australia, Britain, Canada, Europe, Latin America, Mauritius, New Zealand, South Korea, and the USA. So far, the journey has been challenging and testing. I was sixty-seven with onset diabetes, but as fit as a thirty-year-old and young-looking, so people kept telling me.

I couldn't sleep the night before I left for the coast. The road was a stage. I was nervous and excited and felt in awe by what was in the offing. While lying in bed, I thought, Atlantic Ocean, here I come.

Chapter 17: Trail in the Southern States

Out in the open and on the road again forward into the unknown. I was apprehensive; it had been a long time. On my own into the elements. I thought that all would be fine after my first day's trek. At first, it was as if I hadn't been off the road.

I was wrong. After a few miles, I understood that picking up from where I had left off would be hard. Our memory has a way of erasing and healing what was arduous. It does this by bringing to the fore times when you were robust against the formidable terrain and strain. Towards the end of my first two thousand miles, I felt strong. I was in an advanced rhythmic stage, clocking up fifty miles per day four days before reaching Eupora. Back on the tarmac, I became exhausted after just twenty-five miles. The humidity was draining, and it was the start of summer. I was less fit after my four-week break. I hadn't put on any weight and didn't look out of shape. It was not entirely to do with inactivity but more with a lack of rhythmic flow.

Ever since I started on this journey, not once could I have said I had a smooth run. Every day of trekking was full of surprises and difficulties. If it was not raining, it was the threat of tornadoes. I have been in high winds where Plan B was put into action, changed route, and recalculated my distance. My knowledge did not develop at an even pace in all areas. It advanced, dragged its feet in others, and even moved back. I tried to be kind to my ignorance. As the season was changing towards summer, I felt uneasy about what I would find ahead.

It was an exhausting week in Alabama. I hadn't expected the problems ahead, just ten miles of hard shoulder on the two-hundred-and-fifty-mile ride. I had to share the main road walking/biking with traffic. Unless riding a super bicycle with small panniers, cycling is never easy. Even then, there will be some pushing and walking to do. The roads are not flat. A superbike will have thin tyres, bringing huge problems of their own, which could easily puncture. All the roads are hilly and mountainous except for fifty miles on either side of the Mississippi River. On an average trek of thirty-five miles, only two might be flat. On a typical day, I would bike downhill and walk uphill, towing the 110-lb trailer. The road's gradient at speed in a car seems imperceptible, almost flat. On the approach of a hill, the climb gives an optical illusion as if it flattens out. Not walking or on a bicycle, for every hump impacts the muscles and ligaments of the trekker. The busy road didn't intimidate me during my week's trek across Alabama. I kept in a rhythm with the flow, stopping when I needed to and using my road sense.

The weather was beautiful, with brilliant sunshine every day with a temperature of 90° F/32° C. The humidity was at a high of sixty-five per cent, draining as the sun beat down. I remembered something old. As a child, sleeping when it was hot at night in the tropics was difficult. We didn't have modern cooling facilities then. To sleep, I scratched my skin gently to create goose pimples. It was my way of cooling off. In no time, I would fall into a deep sleep.

The first three days on the road, the humidity was high, and I knew I shouldn't drink liquids on the trek as this would make me sweat more. I drank a lot before setting out and a large amount at the journey's end. But in the intense heat after 10.30 a.m., my mouth became dry, and the saliva tasted bitter. I was tempted to drink a little. I sweated more and craved water. When my urine became bright yellow, I rested in the shade and drank a small quantity. I was careful; I carried supplies of electrolytes.

I learned more about how to cope with heat and clamminess. I was awake and up at 4:30 a.m. and on the road as soon as it was light. I learned something from other pilgrims while doing the Camino de Santiago in northern Spain. I watched the enormous sunbeam through the tall trees and foliage gaps at daybreak. Between forest walls, the treetops touched the sky. As a lone trekker, I rode under the canopy of a blue causeway. The road ahead and behind dissolved into a density of green, like drawn curtains across a living ocean of minted air. Scented by a mixture of flowers, pollen, bark, and resin, infused with the moisture of morning heat.

Camino trek Northern Spain.

The humidity brought all kinds of life into the animation. The mooing of cows, dogs barking, the crowing of the roosters, the long and repetitive song of the mockingbird, crows imitating Indians on the warpath as in the movies, the screeching of the grackles, a myriad of bird songs, the hissing of the cicadas and crickets. The whole planet was waking up simultaneously, and every living entity was being unspeakably themselves. And I passed silently, listening to it all, placing me in my element.

Everything we create on this earth goes against the elements. The earth and the atoms return everything to broken down matter, dust. We do our best to preserve them, a constant battle. Aren't we all recycled material? From my reading, I only know half a dozen tribes of people on the globe that blended into the environment and did not try to change it - the Aboriginals of Australia and the Apache Indians of Arizona are two examples. They succeeded in being part of difficult landscapes and thrived in them. I thought hard about this, and one's sensitivity deepens on a walkabout.

Something clicked and took the mist from my eyes. Throughout this journey, I had been defying the elements – seeking comfort from old habits. Such as yearning for a bath in the middle of a desert. Although my doctor had advised me that I could have a sand wash if it were clean and fine. On the terrain I had trekked through, it was sub-zero, and now it was sweaty hot. I had learned to accept it for what it was. Go along with it, letting the sweat drip, allowing the heat to take over, relax and be in harmony with the climate and be part of it. Above all, enjoy its sauna/steam effect and not struggle against it. I did ninety-seven miles in two days and was less stressed and tired. Two days earlier, after forty-five miles in the blazing heat, I had the energy to do it again. I was uplifted, relaxed, and contented without knowing why - just feeling alive like all life around me.

I went to a buffet restaurant late afternoon in Eufaula, Alabama. People wanted to chat with me; maybe it was something about my accent, different. They asked me whether I was a Puerto Rican or an Australian Aborigine. So, I told them what I was doing, and the information passed from table to table. Other people got involved, and soon, all the tables were chatting and throwing questions at me. The staff, too, became involved, and the kids wanted to shake my hand. We chatted, and I cracked corny jokes such as "C'est la vie, as the Germans say", and they laughed. The entire place became animated. This kind of thing can only happen here and nowhere else. This journey had taken me into a labyrinth of discoveries. I discovered brutal truths about myself, and even humble pie tasted good. Fear was the key. Once this was disregarded, then anything and everything was possible. There must be willingness, audacity, spontaneity, and daring; we would remain meek and careful without these. And never be inclined to take a challenge to adventure.

I left Alabama and the beautiful town of Eufaula two days later. It was a magnificent town with all its nineteenth-century architecture intact. The tree-lined roads were the best I had seen. Even though they are inhabited on weekdays, grand houses are open for visitors. Most houses in the old part of town were built in 1830/the 1850s. People can walk and enjoy the scenery in this old part of town. The new part had no sidewalk; it was just the usual shopping mall and car parks, the occasional grass verges in front of business buildings but treeless. Quite a splurge on the landscape, designed with little imagination.

The news came as a shock. The planners and politicians of Eufaula, straight from the mental asylum, want to construct a four-lane road right through the middle of the most picturesque boulevard in the old part of town. The plan was to remove all the trees in the median part of the road, those on the sidewalks and the sidewalks. It will all be done in the name of progress. But the smell of political corruption permeated the town all over. In the old quarter, leaflets pinned against trees in a protest denouncing the project were everywhere. It's astounding that such municipal vandalism could be contemplated in this place. Once the heart and soul of this pretty town are obliterated, its cultural treasure will be lost forever.

Eufaula is a frontier town flanked on its east side by a great lake and has a marina for water sports, leisure activities, and fishing. Across the long bridge on the other side of the lake is the State of Georgia. Georgia seemed less affluent than Alabama. At least, that was my first impression. In bigger cities like Atlanta, it might be different. But soon after crossing the bridge, the houses were poorer—the semi-shabby look of the towns, with more outdated, rusted vehicles on the road. The number of closed-down businesses was more apparent, in contrast to Alabama. Even on the bank of the Eufaula Lake in Georgia, no effort had been made to create a holiday resort of any kind. This could have been a great leisure playground, stimulating business and work, thus regenerating the area.

I also found the vegetation wilder in Georgia, almost jungle-like in density. The earth was red, it rained a lot, and plants got out of control quickly. The wheat had been harvested. In the fields, the corn was tall and flowering. The crops of peanuts, soya beans, and others were more than two feet high, not even mid-June.

These southern states of Mississippi, Alabama, and Georgia are about three times the size of England, yet the total population is fewer than eighteen million people. There is so much emptiness, vast forests, and wildlife. In 1983, I craved space and a little tranquillity in India. Nowhere could I find such a place? Everywhere was like being at the end of a football match, even in the countryside. Here in this region of the US, I had the same feeling, except, instead of people, it was trees, tall, reaching for the sky, dark and majestic. The towns and villages buried within them were like distant hamlets.

Jay, originally from Mozambique, of Indian descent, educated in India and has lived in Leicester, UK, for twelve years. And now, here in Alabama, for the past thirteen years, he has been doing well for himself, managing a motel. He told me that families here have no man in the house, role models, books, or encouragement to seek a broader horizon. A lot of African

Americans were doing well. There were those stuck at a dead end with no inspiration. "For many, it has become a land of apathy, a comfort zone within poverty."

On a trek, it's easy to understand certain aspects of such a huge place as the USA. Living in a small town, where many are scattered and far apart, poses different problems. If there was little work to be done locally, there was no choice except to move out to a bigger town or city. It wouldn't be an easy thing to do. There was this thought of leaving close relatives, friends, and community behind.

There would be a need to find a new abode, commute long distances, and see family every other weekend as Mukesh and Jason Cardoza did in Arizona. Even if willing to comb a broader radius to seek employment, consideration of transportation and the cost of running a vehicle will have to be calculated. Those with adequate education might achieve this. But a segment of the underclass goes back generations across ethnic lines and is stuck in a localised view of the world. They don't have the capacity or know-how to escape their predicament. Some people possibly never went outside a ten-mile radius of where they were born. Political circumstances in the past subjugated, stifled, and curtailed people's aspirations across these southern states. Education, or lack of it, has created invisible shackles. Drug abuse may be endemic in some sections.

Jay's Asian background would have greatly emphasised education, as he was now doing with his children. In an Asian setup, failing in academia would shame the whole family greatly. The pressure to succeed is always intense. Jay had crossed the frontiers of half the world and chased his goals. He could move on if he thinks it would benefit him and his family. His worldview and perspective differed from those in the town where he found himself. Many of the people looked depressed and not healthy, like in the town they lived in. But they were always receptive, and the world I went through was only a walk or a bike ride away.

Anywhere in any southern state, a walk or a ride away would be right in the middle of the forest or a hidden plantation. Days after leaving Eufaula, on one occasion, I was on the road, surrounded by woods. Throughout my journey, I drank only water. The pine resin smell in the air left by the passing timber trucks irritated my senses and made me crave a sweet drink. It was like my thirst was being answered when a gas station appeared in view on the other side of the road out of this forest wilderness.

I entered the shop, and four or five other customers were there. I picked up a can of juice. The cashier wouldn't give me any attention. She seemed preoccupied with happenings outside through the glass window. A queue was behind me. I heard murmurs and turned around and saw everyone gazing at figures outside. I, too, became curious. I saw three young men in jeans and sleeveless T-shirts, tattooed arms, unshaven, each with a can of beer in hand, pointing at my trailer. They were making comments and laughing. I checked the people behind me again, and they looked worried. The young woman at the cash register seemed concerned. A thought flashed through my head what Morten and Kate told me back in Taos, New Mexico, about "being in the wrong place, at the wrong time." I considered the worst scenario possible was for someone to challenge me. I would have to make a getaway back into the shop. Perhaps take a good hiding. But witnesses were about. That could prevent them from being too ruthless. It was an uncomfortable thought. I didn't want to think of the worst because, until then, no one had posed a threat to me. It didn't make any sense why these three men outside should. I brushed the introspection aside.

I drew the attention of the cashier to pay for my drink. She looked worried, and as I left the shop, fear showed on the faces of the others, too. Once outside, the men looked at me. I assessed which was the 'leader'. I approached him, grabbed his hand, shook it to say hello, and told him of my journey from LA. I talked in detail about the distance and the difficulties I had had. I spoke of the journey's aim and where I planned to finish. I pointed to my caption and told them I was doing it for three charities. I didn't let go of his hand. Perhaps three or four minutes passed. When I ran out of things to say, I released his hand. I did all this by looking at him directly into his eyes without blinking until I finished. He looked at me silently for a few seconds, grabbed and hugged me, and said, "Awesome man, awesome." The other two wanted to shake my hands, and they looked humbled. We chatted for a minute; they worked locally, delivering building materials. I asked them about the morning beer, for they each had a can in hand.

One said, "Can't do without breakfast, man."

Their accent made it difficult to tell whether they were from Mississippi, Alabama, or Georgia. We then parted, and they left, wishing me, "God bless man, good luck". As I was getting ready, I looked behind into the shop. The customers and the cashier had a look of amazement on their faces, with their mouths gaping. I gestured to them, and a couple of them waved back. Soon, I was on the road again. My instinct had been right all along. I didn't want the influence of others to sway my perceptions, even if they showed concern for my safety.

I wanted to get to Cuthbert in Georgia. I was tired; the rain was on its way, and I didn't want to get caught out in it. The forest gave way to farmland in places, and the forests were no longer disguised with oak trees on the edge of the road. Instead, they showed the full industrial view of planted pines in straight columns like scaffolds, some young, some ready for harvesting. The town came into view in the distance, and I felt like a child wondering what surprise awaited me.

Upon entering the outskirts of Cuthbert via Route 82, the Victorian houses looked impressive, with wide-manicured gardens and mature trees in the foreground. Nearer to the centre of town, the buildings were compact and smaller. The colours were drab; the town deserted, and its hub - the god of the town elusive. The main square was empty. I approached a man alone, standing by the Dawg House restaurant. I asked him where everyone was.

He said, not in a rude way, "Mindin' their own business, I guess", in a southern drawl.

"But there aren't many businesses around."

"Well, it's like I said."

I wasn't sure where my line of conversation was taking me. I asked him if he knew where there was a motel. He pointed to the road left of the square.

"Well, if you go down this route, keep goin', about four miles, you'll see maybe two or three motels. But if you go down this road (pointing to the right), go about two miles, then you'll see one there."

Before leaving, I peered into the restaurant window, and it was empty. The first item on the menu on the wall said Dog. The first word, hidden behind a flue, presumably was 'Hot'. If someone unfamiliar with Hot Dog had seen this, they might have thought they would serve dogs on the menu. Dog with cheese, Dog with chilli, Dog with slaw, Dog with kraut, Corn Dog, Scrambled Dog. The only thing missing was Dog Biscuit. Instead of the impending rain, the sun came out, it became hot, and I said to the man: "It's a dog's day afternoon." He looked at me, puzzled.

In the motel, I checked on the internet to see where the 'buzz' was in town. Where it was all happening, or at least a restaurant with a nice atmosphere as in Eufaula. There was nowhere to go and few places to eat catered fast food, as with the Dawg House. They were all shut. The main square I passed through was the hub. It was soulless. People 'retired' there, and nothing ever happens. The tourist information said that Larry Holmes, the former boxing heavyweight champion, was born there, and so was

Fletcher Henderson, the jazz musician. I became restless. My Wi-Fi connection was lousy. The TV weather forecast said it would rain in the afternoon the next day. That was also the forecast the day before, and it turned out sunny. The Turner Classic Movies channel was playing a Hollywood classic film noir with Dana Andrews and Gene Tierney. I had seen it more times than I could remember. I wrote in my diary instead and purged myself of a meal that evening for the third time on this journey.

Chapter 18: On the Road Again

To be out and about is to take risks, especially if the plan is to do it for eight months or more. There was a motto in my mind: if the will is there to change anything, then go all the way. Commit to it one hundred per cent, whatever the circumstances. Being on the road is a way to unearth a path to living. There is no hope of finding an answer to that critical question concerning one's destiny. But something has gained a strong focus, and it rubs off on others, and they rub off on you. An energy flow happens, and people become responsive, as in the incident in Eufaula in the restaurant. And with the many people I have stayed with and met since the start of this journey. The road is both natural and a metaphor. You may think you are on the road somewhere and navigating from point A to B, which is real. But it is the elements and the road itself that guide you along and determine your destination. In the metaphor, you are no longer the factor. Unknowingly, you become a passenger being taken for a ride.

Out trekking is not only being in the outer landscape. You are in a constant meditative trance with no one to converse with except your inner self. Even when meeting people, it is only fleetingly, as if they weren't interruption at all, that it had only been a dream, a mirage. On two occasions, something confounding and extraordinary happened, once in the Rockies and the other on the road between the forests in Georgia. It isn't easy to convey as recollection can be elusive. In both incidents, I was conscious throughout the episode. I was in control of all my faculties.

The mood of meditation took me back to my childhood. Two dreams have been repeated ever since. One haunted by the fear of failure. The other was the amazement of levitation. It was while daydreaming on the road sandwiched between forests of oaks and pines. I thought about the forest and its usage (timber, employment, wild animals, absorption of carbon dioxide, water management.) Yet. I preferred to avoid regimental planting.

While crossing a threshold, just one turn of the wheel into the acoustic sound of life's orchestra. I entered a realm of every imaginable living thing without human sound. Not thirty metres away, a man stood looking straight at me around a bend. He was alone with no form of transport. I stopped and walked towards him with my bicycle and trailer. He had a strange expression as if he wore a mask. But the contortion of his face when he spoke revealed it was his true feature. I thought that perhaps he had been in an accident and had had plastic surgery. But I didn't see any scars. His face was not unpleasant. The two things that stood out were his ears and eyes. His ears were small, bat-like, and his eyes were translucent and slightly apart. A clear, indescribable 'blue' ring circled his pupils. He was saying something in a strange language without vowels. I couldn't understand a word. When I asked him to repeat what he had said, I could hear my voice in stereo. It was as if my utterance was coming from him.

The symphony of nature increased by an octave, and I was cocooned. I was part of and attached to everything around me for the second time on this journey. He enticed me to do as he did, standing upright and then leaping two feet up in the air vertically. Then he did it again, encouraging me, both feet together, hands straight down to my sides with a sudden leap. I remember how I did it in the recurring dreams of levitation. With eyes closed and knees bent, I pushed up hard. It felt light, with no gravity. With my eyes open now, I was above the trees. He showed me how to lie flat, face down like swimming, and move in any direction, up, down, or sideways. I was like a dolphin in the ocean of still air. Everything was interwoven in a patchwork of a sea of shades impossible to describe—colours I had never seen.

Once more, I needed to experience the hurt of being alive, and I bit my tongue hard, felt the piercing pain, and tasted blood. It was not a dream; I had taken no drugs or medicine. This was happening. I didn't want to go into the thought of an alien encounter. I understood the mechanics of engineering too well. The distance of light-years, the ageing process, food, and breathable gas of sorts to be lured into that mode of thinking. Besides, as seen in The Wizard of Oz, he looked nothing like a sophisticated alien, more like a scarecrow.

These thoughts occurred in the initial moments. The deep urge was to let go with a sigh of the last dying breath and not to resist. The fantastic feeling of rolling into solid air, defying gravity, imbued with an orgasmic sensuality that seemed to go on and on. I floated like a feather in the wind, except there was no air current, and the leaves were motionless on the trees.

A while passed, and he came to say something in his manner of bafflegab. He sounded like a singer rehearsing before singing, vibrating his tonsil and tongue on different notes. The only thing I can vividly recall was the smell of his breath. It was a smell that can only be described as fruity, the lingering smell of jackfruit or ripened Noni fruit (Morinda citrifolia). Something that remains long after it has been thrown away, like a smelly cheese such as Vieux Lille.

I looked at him, and he descended with ease, and I followed him, and we touched down. He asked me to close my eyes, showed me how, and placed his palm on my eyelids. A warm sensation engulfed my face. I wanted to stay in its warmth. Then I opened my eyes; the sun was bright, and he had vanished. I stood and looked up and saw where I had been high up on the canopy of green against the sky blue. And the road ahead was straight as a contrail of a jet stream.

I wasn't afraid of going insane this time. I read how messianic figures such as Moses, Jesus, Mohammed, and other sages went into the desert, wilderness, or caves for long periods and spoke of communicating with an extraterrestrial order. My learning and studies have taught me not to look into the expansive space of the universe to resolve a complex problem. But to search for the answer in the universe from within. I didn't want to announce that I had seen God and that he looked like a scarecrow. He had spoken an unearthly language and taught me to levitate above the treetops.

Nobody would have taken me seriously. I may have been offered the gift of a sleeveless white jacket instead.

Throughout this journey, I stuck to a vegan diet. It suited my onset of diabetes, kept me lean, and my sugar level was normal without any medication. There were times when other choices weren't available. Often, when I reached a small town or village, the only eating places were two famous fast-food cuisines. One goes by the name of a Scottish Highlander, and the other is akin to Royalty. The burgers tasted nothing like beef, the fries were made with artificial potatoes, and the relish hid the taste.

It occurred to me what might have produced these phenomena: my diet and fasting the night before. Each of these extraordinary events took place after a purge. And alongside the fact that, on average, I walked twenty-three miles per day. If my body produced endorphins, could it have induced other, natural, more powerful chemicals, taking me into an alternate zone/world? I needed to consult experts on the matter, but for now, being on the road and levitating suited me just fine. What will the experience be the next time? I couldn't wait.

Chapter 19: Georgia

The day after coming down from levitation was like a daydream. Perhaps it had all been a dream. I don't recollect having seen anyone or any vehicle before reaching Dawson. I left Cuthbert after eight a.m., and the journey was only twenty-five miles. Yet, I didn't reach there until after four in the afternoon. That was a journey of three miles per hour. It was exhausting and hot, and the rain didn't come. I was hungry and peeved that I had to settle for the Scottish Highlander's menu. I skipped visiting the town as the map showed similarities to others, and the tiredness put me in a stupor.

In my diary, I tried to write about the levitation experience in my motel room. Like a dream, aspects of it are forgotten, and recollections vague. At the time, so many fantastic things occurred that I could bring little back with me except for remnants and distant thoughts pieced together. I had smelled nothing unusual, only the pine resin, which always hung in the air long after a truck of lumber had passed by. Was I hallucinating? Had the resin vapour doped me? I wrote in my diary: Why was I still feeling the pain where I had bitten my tongue? Could I have been conscious and yet hallucinating at the same time? Or are we able to shift to a different space in time when the right 'key' is found? I wrote, "I hate the mystic appeal to this; I hate that angle of a cop-out."

It must have rained in the middle of the night. It looked overcast through the window. The forecast was rainy for the latter part of the day. Leaving

Dawson, I wanted to get to Albany, Georgia, before getting drenched. To be caught out and get soaked is not fun as it makes going on the road heavy. This would reduce any intended distance by half. Upon leaving the motel and over the first hill, I approached dense fog with visibility down to fifty metres. The early morning drivers didn't reduce their speed, rushing to work. Two miles further up the road, I was stopped by David, a police patrol officer, near a lay-by. He was polite and said he wanted to tie reflectors to my trailer and bike to ensure I was noticeable from afar.

He took the initiative, "Three cyclists died a month ago on the same spot you are standing on. It was carnage. Bits of flesh lay on the very spot."

I didn't feel at ease standing in all that spilt blood. It gave me a weird sensation. My breakfast wasn't sure whether it wanted to settle down comfortably or go out for a jog. I was already anxious in all that fog. But David kept on talking about it to put fear in me. To make sure that I understood the dangers. All the while, I thought of those young men between twenty and twenty-three, training for a sports event and everything to live for. One moment, they were in their prime, and next, it was horror. The great holes they left behind in their families, close friends, and girlfriends. All these people will live the rest of their days with something missing, with a heavyweight in their hearts. As we stared at the fast-flowing traffic, some cars didn't even have their headlights on.

David commented, "Some drivers are still in their dreams rushing to work, forgetting to turn their lights on. It's what happened when those cyclists got killed. The driver swore he had his headlights on. It was a foggy morning, just like today. It was likely he switched them on after the accident. He probably had drifted into sleep."

He suggested waiting until the rush hour had died down. The coming of the rain played on my mind. The sky looked heavy and dark in that density of fog. The rain was not like anywhere else I had ever seen. If it comes down, it would be like a cascade with thunder, lightning, and wind, and it could last for a day or three. The roads would be impassable, just a rapid river. Anything can happen in the middle of it. Walking or biking would be madness. A while later, I contemplated going back to the motel.

"The fog is beginning to lift," David said.

The visibility was three hundred metres in the direction I was heading.

"I'm going to take a chance and go ahead."

"Why take a chance? But it's up to you. It's dangerous, but if you must go, good luck. Be careful and phone the emergency if you get in trouble."

I had three close shaves with those heavy trucks zooming past me with barely six inches to spare. One time, the drag velocity propelled me so fast forward, heading me into a ditch. By luck, my reflex was fast, and I applied my brakes and almost toppled over. On another occasion, I was singing, but after a close shave with a wing mirror and swearing countless times at the speeding truck, my mood dropped like a brick.

The rain didn't come, and soon after, the sun shone. I thought that, rather than making it to Albany (twenty-five miles), I should carry on to Sylvester (fifty-one miles away). I was lucky as most of the road was flat, with just half a dozen hills to negotiate. The temperature rose as each hour passed until I was dripping with sweat. Tiny flies started buzzing around my face, looking for salt.

Since leaving Mississippi, I haven't been able to set up camp. The heat and humidity were paradises for all insects, especially mosquitoes. Standing in one spot for a snack was like queuing as a blood donor for the little suckers. They even tried to penetrate through my trousers to get at me—no chance of wearing shorts despite the sweltering heat. At the end of each day, I needed to shower and wash my outfits. Until I reached Mississippi, camping had not been difficult as the conditions had been favourable. I used wet wipes to freshen up for two days while camping, and on my third day, I took a shower at a motel. Camping in the southern states in the summer is virtually impossible unless on an organised campsite.

Camping on the Mississippi River

My estimation was seven miles per hour for that day. Sylvester town seemed far away, and towards the end, I felt drained. A thought troubled me that perhaps I had taken the wrong road whilst daydreaming. Eventually, a sign of a town appeared, "Welcome to Sylvester, the peanut capital of the world."

On my approach to town, two police patrol officers pulled me over, and they were friendly. We chatted about where I was heading, where I came from, my trek, and the motivation for the journey.

Then, after some twenty minutes, the older officer asked what seemed out of context: "Have you got a baby in the trailer? It's illegal. Unzip your trailer. I wanna see if you're telling the truth."

Somehow, that line of thought seemed strange. While unzipping my trailer, I joked, ' I dropped the kids at the pool.' That didn't go down well. At a guess, that officer was in his fifties and the other, a rookie, was no more than twenty-three. The older officer had a permanent grin and a calculating look in his eyes. At the same time, the rookie had an air of enthusiasm, which pervaded his eagerness to preempt the next course of action. A while later, after our "friendly" chat, the older officer said, "I wanna check your ID, " as I was ready to leave."

I was surprised, considering how chatty it had all been. Still, I gave them my driver's license. They both looked astonished, although I had told them I was from England.

"I wanna see your passport."

"Isn't the license enough?"

They remained silent and stared at me.

I tried to crack another joke and said, "Yes, sir, boss."

That didn't go down too well, either. Perhaps it was the way I had said it. The permanent grin from the older officer turned into a sour smile. I gave him my passport. He went through it, page by page.

The younger officer said to the older one: "It would be complicated if we wanna do something."

I made it as though I hadn't heard what he meant by that. "Let sleeping dogs lie" passed through my mind. The older officer returned my ID with a sarcastic grin. I looked him straight in the eyes without blinking. Then, seconds later, he said, "Good luck."

I asked, "Could you point me where I could find a motel?"

He pointed down the road: "Three miles on the left side of the road."

It was three miles on the left side of the road, and the manager, Ojay from Gujerat, India (where else?), another Patel, was welcoming. I thought they couldn't be very inventive with names in that part of the world, like the Smith and Jones. He saw that I looked tired and offered me coffee, but there was none in the pot. He didn't have a room on the ground floor but offered to help me take my trailer to the next level. I told him I would manage. He made me coffee and said he would give me a $15 reduction as the trek was for charity. He kept on asking me if I was okay. I must have looked haggard. He was a nice man, sympathetic and generous.

The main produce of the region was peanuts, cotton, wood, and melons. They make boiled, fried, roasted, roasted/salted peanuts with and without the shells, peanut oil, peanut butter, and chilli peanut salsa. Peanuts were used in many other food products. The other products were versatile, too.

It poured spectacularly as I was ready to set out for a meal. At the reception, Ojay said the Scottish Highlander's eating place was next door: "I could lend you an umbrella to go there."

Joking, I said, "The meat was not halal."

He said, "Ah, I'll get my wife to cook you some rice and bring it to your room at no cost, no trouble. It's on the house."

What a treat, an unexpected Indian cuisine in the middle of the USA.

I hadn't witnessed ordinary rain since I had been here. I phoned Michael in Eupora, and he told me it rained for four continuous days during the week, always with thunder and lightning. So much water; no wonder the trees are so tall and straight. It bucketed down in the evening. The lights went out in my motel room. I had no Wi-Fi, air conditioning, or TV, and it was hot. It was a restless night, too humid to be still. The lights came back on at three in the morning.

I was lucky as most roads were flat, travelling to Sylvester. The next day payback time came. There was a hill every quarter of a mile. It meant getting off the bike, pushing uphill and pedalling down to Tifton. There was a change in the landscape with more acreage of plantations along the way, with the forest receding into the distance. The vegetation changed to subtropical. This region was scattered with palm trees, bananas, bamboo, buddleia, oleander, tall hibiscus, and Mediterranean clematis.

Although the journey couldn't have been more than thirty miles, it became difficult. When I reached Tifton, going under a bridge of Route 75, there was no hard shoulder. The traffic was busy, and I became stressed. The sun beating down shattered me. I huffed and puffed up a small hill near the centre of the town, and a car as big as a truck pulled up. A woman said, "It looks like you need help."

"Well, I wouldn't say no to a lift to a motel."

"Let's load you up, and I'll take you there."

Once inside the car, she said, "You ain't gonna attack me now, are you?"

"I was thinking that of you."

"Oh, my lord, I didn't mean to be rude. We've crazy people in this town. Where are you heading?"

"I'm going to the coast."

"Oh my god, you're crazy," laughed and then asked, "Where are you from?"

"England and I'm on a charity trek, at first it was by walking but now by bicycle and on foot. But right at this moment, in your car."

She coughed a laugh and said, "Now I understand why you are tired."

"Do I look tired?"

"You did when you were walkin'. Now your face looks all right. You could do with some food because you look a little skinny."

"I'll take that as a compliment."

She laughed loudly and said, "You're a sweet man."

After I booked in at the motel, she invited me to dinner to taste "our southern cooking." I said I needed a shower and time to wash my clothes and take a little nap, to call on me in two hours. She agreed and came early after an hour, and I wasn't ready and hadn't had my shuteye. She seemed eager.

"I invited a couple of friends to meet us at the restaurant."

Then her phone rang, and her friends couldn't make it. While driving to the restaurant, I noticed how huge the car was without my trailer and bike inside.

I said, "Why did you choose such a large vehicle?"

"I like big cars; they make me feel safe."

It was a buffet restaurant offering southern cooking. The menu contained excessive meat, although there were enough vegetables and salad. It was a help-yourself buffet and 'eat as much as you like.' It was a busy place with a great atmosphere, and the staff was welcoming. I chose a vegan mixture, which is plenty for an evening meal. My companion had a plate of meat.

Up to that point, we hadn't exchanged names. She introduced herself as Jamelia.

To make light conversation, I said, "Did you know the name is derived from Arabic Jamilla?"

"Oh, my lord, I thought it was Christian. My grandmother chose it."

"Do you know the meaning of Jamelia?"

"No, I don't."

"It means beautiful and lovely."

"Oh, my lord." She seemed overjoyed.

"What do you do for a living?"

"I've been in the army all my life but recently retired."

"Were you an officer?"

"I made the rank of Sergeant."

She had hurt her back after an accident and couldn't walk for three months.

"I suffered a lot. I thought I'd never walk normally again, but it got better. It's stiff in the mornin', and it takes me fifteen minutes to get movin'. I've got to do the exercise the physio gave me before gettin' out of bed."

She looked in her mid-forties and still fit. Now, she was onto her second plate of meat. She wanted to hear about my adventure.

Afterwards, she said, "You've urged me to travel. I've been thinkin' about buyin' a small caravan trailer and travellin' over the country. But I couldn't find the courage. I need someone to travel with."

She needed a purpose for doing so and had had two significant relationships, but they hadn't worked. She had no children as she never wanted the responsibility.

"I'm close to my brother, my sisters, and their kids."

She felt rewarded enough to have them around.

"Have you ever considered going abroad, visiting other places, and seeing the world?"

"I never thought about it. I don't have friends there. I don't want to travel on my own."

She had never thought about venturing outside of the US. She was in Germany with the army a long time ago. She went onto her next meat plate:

chicken coated with batter and breadcrumbs. Her first plate was beef, then pork.

"I love eatin' food," she said, eating like a person who hadn't eaten for a few days. She was a tidy eater, placing her bones, fat, and gristle on one side of her plate. She had learned discipline in the army and carried that onto her plate. She didn't chew her food very much. I looked at all that sinew that would transform her figure in a short time. She was small in stature, and I wondered where it all disappeared. She finished it all with a huge ice cream, syrup, and other concocted monsters of a dessert.

She looked at me and smiled, "Aren't you gonna have any I'm buyin'?"

"It's on me, my treat for you for saving me from exhaustion. I feel full just looking at your plate."

She laughed and finished only a third of her dessert.

Back at the motel, she insisted on buying me breakfast in the morning. I said I was planning on leaving early. The thought of breakfast on a full stomach after eating brought an immediate block about food.

She said, "What if it rains?"

"I hadn't had a chance to check the weather. Let me see the forecast. It's going to rain until nine in the morning."

"See, we were meant to eat breakfast together."

"Okay, at eight, and don't be late."

"I'm army; I'll be right on the button."

In bed, in my diary, I wrote: "Jamelia is searching for a companion." She must be at a loose end outside the army and recently retired. She had a disciplined life and a set routine. Now, she found herself in a new set-up with different demands made on her, in an unfamiliar routine. Time becomes a killer, boredom can easily creep in, and life skids into quicksand. She was still young and could make a new start in life. What enthusiasm does she still possess? She had the boldness to pick up a total stranger like me. Daring, enthusiasm, and adding to that motivation and the willingness to go all the way to one single pursuit might shift her into another arena.

I woke early, and the rain had already stopped. I wanted to be on the road before the traffic started, but I had promised her breakfast. She came on time as she said she would and looked clear-faced after a good night's sleep.

Unlike her, while shaving, the guy in the mirror looked at me with a stupid smile. I understood his thoughts, "You need more sleep, buddy."

She had the full, 'I'm ready for the marathon' breakfast, consisting of bacon, eggs, biscuits, gravy, hashbrowns, and coffee. I had two pieces of toast and two cups of coffee.

"Is that all you're havin'? Eat some more?"

"I eat little and often, and it's early."

She looked at me and saw that I was staring at her.

"I know what you're thinkin'; I burn them real quick, sir."

"You must, to stay in such good shape."

She eventually wiped the plate clean, "Let's go and load you up."

"Whatever for?"

"I'll take you to the coast."

"I'm here to walk and ride for charities, remember? It's one hundred and forty miles away from the sea."

"Ok, I'll take you to the next town."

The traffic had built up, and it was heavy with no hard shoulders. "Just drop me on the outskirts of town, which would help."

On the way out, she was quiet, and as we reached the highway, she pulled up in a lay-by, and we unloaded my bike and trailer. I glanced at her, and she looked downhearted. I grabbed her and gave her a warm hug.

"What are your plans? What are you going to do?"

She was in a sombre mood, "I don't know". After a pause, "Wait, take my number; ring me when you get to the coast."

Her sad face stayed with me as I rode thirty miles to Willacoochee. With my heightened sensitivity, I felt her mood. I get the same sense with each encounter. Occasionally, I would be in tune with their feelings even when they hid them. This was my experience, and Jamelia and I only met for a few brief hours. She was kind, looked after me, and was ready to help. There were no ulterior motives. I didn't read that from her. Maybe she wanted to drive to the coast for a day's adventure. To do something different, to be somewhere new with someone for comfort and security. To travel for the first time to a place she had never been and all the magic it could conjure. This was in my meditation on the tarmac of Route 82, heading east to Willacoochee.

Under the hot conditions, the thirty-mile trek would have been just right. But something about the town made me suspect that a motel might not exist. Checking was impossible. The internet connection was down during the night. I gave myself an option of the next town, Pearson, a further twelve miles away, just in case. As it so happened, there were no motels in Willacoochee. Passing through was like travelling to any other village. It had these long industrial units, no doubt a necessary blemish on the land. No effort was made to hide their ugliness like a toothless smile gaping. Some appropriate vegetation might have done the trick.

Later, I arrived in Pearson, hot, tired, and bothered. I went straight to the only motel. To my surprise, it was fully booked, with nowhere else nearby. Forty-two miles had exhausted me under the 100° heat. I asked the proprietor if I could pitch my tent at the back, hidden somewhere. He gave me the Indian head roll, moving from side to side, almost apologetic, with a low voice, "Sorry." I think he genuinely was sorry because he saw I was deadbeat. I had to re-psyche for a further thirty-one miles to the next town. I convinced myself I could do this and sang even though that was the last thing I wanted to do. I chanted at the top of my voice like a tenor in defiance.

The sun was beating down on me, and at two o'clock, it was the wrong time to get a darker tan. The old Noel Coward song came to mind. The beast from the tarmac rose, the sun scorching, and I felt sandwiched like a hot dog on a bicycle. I stopped after fifteen miles and drank the last of my water. While getting ready to go again, a vehicle with a young man at the wheel saw me at a distance. He increased his speed and came straight for me at the full dash. I could see that he was trying to frighten me. I stood my ground without flinching on the narrow strip of the hard shoulder. He swerved, with only a few metres to spare, while I stared straight into his eyes. I thought, 'Bollocks if I'm going to give an inch.' I didn't need that; I suspected he would check me in his rearview mirror. I remained motionless and gave him no satisfaction. What occupied me at this stage were my trailer tyres blowing out because of the heat and melting asphalt and the miles still ahead. Up to that point, I had covered fifty-seven miles with another fifteen before my destination. A little breeze developed, and I became refreshed. A short while after, it clouded over and wasn't as hot. I took encouragement from that and rode harder.

Waycross had been beyond my calculated distance, and the exhaustion overwhelmed me when it finally came into view. I sat under the cold shower for thirty minutes. I couldn't eat, was overtired, and was restless. The next day was already on my mind. Brunswick was the target, sixty-two miles away with nothing in between. I was worried about my recovery rate. Could I regain sufficient energy to do that long haul? Waycross wasn't appealing for another day's stay, and nothing in my reading convinced me otherwise. The receptionist at the motel assured me the road was flat. Two other people said the same thing. I was determined to leave Sunup.

At two in the morning, I was wide awake. I shot out of bed just after five and recovered from my tiredness. After having an excellent breakfast at the motel, I was on the road at seven. The sun was well above the horizon. The scenery was flat, nondescript, like a continuing shadow. It set me in a dreamlike state, a robot on a bicycle. Trucks hooted at me for encouragement, and I waved back. Late in the afternoon, I reached the outskirts of Brunswick South, stopped at the first motel, and crashed out.

The morning is the best time to smell the air, with the warm sun on the skin. The birds sing, and the dew-filled leaves glitter under the early light. It's also the ideal time to think. I decided that I would leave everything in the motel in Brunswick. I unattached my trailer from my bike, took an easy ride to Jekyll Island and touched the Atlantic Ocean.

My bicycle glided the eleven-mile trip to the sea. To reach the island, I had to pass through a six-mile causeway. On either side was marshland with tall grasses, where rivers meander through mud. At first impression, the causeway was awash with colours. On either side of the road, on the verge, myriad wildflowers dazzle the eye. White and yellow butterflies glided over nature's artistry.

There was a barrier at the end of the causeway to Jekyll Island, and I wasn't sure whether I needed to pay to go on the Island. The Welcome Centre or Tourist Office was adjacent. I went in to find out. At the desk, people were well-mannered and hospitable, noticed that I was not from this part of the country, and enquired.

"I'm from England, more recently from Los Angeles."

"Did you fly over or drive all the way?"

"I walked and bicycled here to the coast."

"Oh, my goodness, you must be tired."

"Yes, just a little. I had a good sleep last night."

Other clients nearby began to ask questions. A little girl overheard what was being said and told her mother I had trekked from Los Angeles. This got a few people curious and chatty.

One woman asked, "Weren't you afraid someone might have harmed you?"

Then another, "Didn't anyone trek with you?"

The commotion must have filtered through to the inner office. A woman walked toward me through a door from the back and said, "Good morning, I'm JJ."

JJ

"Ah, Jesse James, I presume."

She laughed and said, "Johnette Jones."

"Johnette is an unusual name?"

"My father wanted a boy, and I turned out to be a girl. He wanted to name me John, after his father. He named me Johnette."

"It exists in French as Jeanette, but I have never heard of the English version. I must look it up."

There was a charisma about her, striking looks, large medium brown eyes which looked directly at me. In an instant, I felt a connection. Throughout the journey, I shared energy with people, making links with them. But here it was as if I had always known her, an emotional familiarity, something emanating from her straight into me. There were no walls between us, no formality. She was easy to talk with, light in personality, and joyful. It was a vibrational stream. We were on the same wavelength, an instant attachment, something irrational in my thinking. But many occurrences on this journey ceased to surprise me. We chatted for fifteen minutes, and I felt the bond was unexpected and mutual.

"Is there a campsite or motel on the island, and is the sea far?" I asked.

"We have many motels and a campsite to the north with all the facilities and places to eat. I can give you all the information you need."

We discussed my venture, and she asked for my blog's address. She wanted to know where I trekked to reach the Atlantic Ocean. We parted company, "I'll call tomorrow and pick up maps and other information which might be useful. Perhaps you could suggest areas of interest to visit?"

"I'll have them ready for you."

I didn't want to break away from the ambience of the Welcome Centre. But I needed to touch the sea half a mile off. The long beach was empty when I reached the Atlantic Ocean, with no stray dogs. I went on to touch the water. It was warmer than I had expected, tepid. I made it to the end of a dream, which had been a fantasy for all these months. I stood before the endless ocean waves, sky, and golden sandy soil. The enormity of the landmass I had left behind came crashing down. Looking at the tiny granules, I fell to my knees, grabbed a fistful, and understood I was no longer dreaming. It was my reality. After all the hardship, I made it. I couldn't hold back the tears.

The one hundred and eighty-six miles in three days had affected me. Later I wrote in my diary, "I'll hide for a while on Jekyll Island."

The thought that I should have made this odyssey now seemed maddening. It was time for rest, not because I was tired. Tiredness was not a factor once the psychological barrier of the trek was overcome. I needed to take in the lasso of the journey and let it sink in. My emotions had been uncontrollable by the ocean. It was because of my mixed feelings, for I didn't want to disappoint anyone. Last of all, the people who followed me on my blog and the charity people too. Some feelings were held in check to keep the equilibrium of expectations. This journey kicked up the unexpected, and anything at any time could have happened.

I sensed nothing out of the ordinary, for I still had time on my hands until September when my visa expires. It was the middle of June, and I had the energy and enthusiasm to do it again. I had accomplished what I set out to do. I wanted to leave everything open, and the final journey would unravel when the time ended.

I wrote to the people on my blog and told them I still needed their support. I didn't know whether to holiday on the island or to push on some more. They were tremendous and uplifting when I needed them most. Many wrote back once I had reached the ocean.

"The journey was done. There was no need to put yourself through further hardship," said by many.

Many offered me congratulations. These were only but a few.

Chrissie Davis wrote, "Well done, what an achievement!"

Mike Ranson wrote, "Time to relax!!"

Adrian Kay – "Well done, a splendid effort."

Marie-Josephe – "Magnifique! La, le mot n'est pas trop fort. Quel periple plein de richesses!"

I told her, "It's funny how things fall apart and come together interestingly."

Before I left England, I had considered finishing in James Town, the place of the Pilgrim Fathers' first attempted settlement here in the USA. Later, I changed my mind and thought of Norfolk since it looked like a big city on the map. It ran in a straight line from my starting point in California. I later discovered that it was a busy naval town, and I felt it wouldn't have been an ideal place to finish the journey there. In the end, the people's generosity and their invitation guided my route and determined where I should meet with the ocean. It was appropriate to have concluded the coast-to-coast trek on this exquisite island.

My Alter Ego.

Nobody Walks in America
Part Two

Chapter 20: Jekyll Island

After two thousand and eight hundred and seventy-six miles of trekking from Los Angeles, I reached the Atlantic Ocean. On many occasions, I was put to the limits of my endurance physically, emotionally, and mentally. Running counter to that, I also experienced great hospitality from various people who comforted me and gave me the strength to carry on. Strangers I had never met invited me to their homes, fed me and treated me courteously and kindly.

Once I touched the Atlantic Ocean, I settled on Jekyll Island. Cosy in my tent, I began meditating on the time I had left, ten whole weeks before my return to London. On reflection, I felt sandwiched between sitting on the beach and enjoying a luxurious vacation or pushing on all the way to Maine. In the end, the momentum of the journey from Los Angeles and the rhythm of the daily experience of new places and encounters swayed me to push on.

I devised a plan to hit the Maine coastline as a target, adding a further fifteen hundred miles from my original aim. Jekyll Island, in the meantime, was my short stay in paradise.

Jekyll Creek and the inter-coastal waterway separate the island from the mainland. The marshland, the creek, the island, and the surrounding sea are massive wildlife sanctuaries. In the south, dolphins can sometimes be seen. In the north, there was the space to promenade Driftwood Beach. The beach is full of sculptured twisted tree trunks, limbs, and exposed large root systems of upturned trees. Their bark was stripped, washed over by the sea and sand, and bleached by the sun to resemble the skeletal remains of dinosaur-like creatures. On the western side were the long golden sandy beaches where most hotels and restaurants were situated. There were several hotels on the island, plus a campsite and rentable apartments/beach houses. The island is unspoiled. The thickness of vegetation is remarkable; almost every tree has a majestic look. Live oaks with their dangling lichen tresses. Tall straight Scots Pines, so huge in girth yet swaying in the breeze. Others contrast the architectural leaves of the fan palm against those of bamboo. They were tall and luscious, ready for a pandas' feast, but there were no pandas on the island.

There were facilities for cycling and walking and miles of tracks created for holidaymakers, so there would be no use for cars. This made the island a tranquil place, a sanctuary for meditation. It's hot and humid, which is healthy for the skin and removes body toxins. Yet, no one is exposed to direct rays of sunlight. Almost all the tracks for trekking are under the canopy of these marvellous trees.

To my surprise, I expected the sea to be fresh or cold. In Europe, the Atlantic Sea is always cold. Not here, where the sea is as warm as a tropical lagoon. The beaches are clean with fine golden sand with facilities for showers and toilet all along the waterfront.

I rested, explored, and enjoyed my time there. Mostly alone, rediscovered myself and listened to what the place gave me. Tranquillity and time to heal. It was a location where there was hardly the sound of human activity, no humming of traffic or horns—the noise we take for granted in a normal town. I rode to a lookout point near the marshes. A secluded enclave where Jekyll Island Garden Club donated a bench. It was there that I put down notes in my diary. I could hear the hissing of the cicadas and many bird calls. The gentle breeze rustled the bullrush's tall grassy leaves, swaying in a dancing fashion.

There were squirrels and birds of different plumage on the island. One afternoon, I heard a drumming sound on the campsite near my tent. It was as though someone had hollowed out one of those huge pine trees seven floors high and had placed an animal skin on the top part and turned it into a drum. It gave out a loud drumming echo that sounded like an amplified bass of the Indian Tabla. I needed to find out what it was. A man said that it was a bird. What bird, I ask? Woodpecker was the answer. I have seen a woodpecker pecking away, but that was different. Peckerwood it remained.

Two deer and a raccoon crossed the road on the first day on my way to a promenade. It was my first sight of a raccoon. What a sensation. Something jumped inside me, the same feeling I had after seeing Lemurs years ago. Two raccoons on my patch in the campsite went through my food bag on the second day and stole my breakfast and lunch. The next day, I tied my food at the end of a thin branch in a plastic bag to stop them from getting to it or breaking into my tent. When I returned from the beach, I saw them devouring the last piece of my bread. They had managed to get to the end of that thin branch. I watched them; they looked like a cross between a cat and a fox, with hooped tails, off-white and black and almost as big as a fox.

They left me with a present. In the middle of the night, I felt two little lumps on one of my testicles. I checked with my torch and discovered the raccoons had brought ticks into my tent. I knew the connection with lime disease. I tried to pull them off, but they had their 'claws' well dug in. I put a drop of tea tree ointment on each, and within three seconds, the bloated 'little suckers' dropped off. "Tomorrow, I'll give those damn raccoons a ticking off," I thought.

In trying to read an enormous book given to me by Sea Ryder, I could never get through a chapter without falling asleep. The book was brilliant, but it had to compete with sleepy time during the day's life murmuring and the overlap of the awakening of nocturnal life. The resounding reverberation of these orchestras and the oxygen in the air drowned my senses to sleep. I managed one chapter in three days.

It was two days before I had planned to leave. I felt refreshed and thought I would catch up on my reading by my best-liked spot on the bench beside the marshes. By the end of the day, I had managed two chapters without falling asleep. Near twilight, the pale blue sky changed to orange, setting fire to the distant horizon. The muddy marsh water turned terracotta, then violet in the fading light. Grackles, mockingbirds, and many others would sing in a screeching chorus to celebrate another approaching night.

The following day, I wanted to prepare for my departure north. I took everything out of my trailer and discarded what I no longer needed. In doing so, I discovered the atlas I had lost in a hidden pocket. And all the notes for direction Morten and I had planned. I felt terrible for having done a mental character assassination on Patel, the manager of the Budget Inn, back in Memphis, Texas. I had blamed him for taking my Atlas.

Already on my mind, I was in the mood for the wheels turning and into the momentum of step by step, seeking each time to reach the next stage. After the rest, I was mentally easing into the trek. Initially, I felt in tune with all the facts about myself. But I was often surprised. The journey turned out beyond what I had hoped, Yet I still needed to gain more knowledge of the geographical and meteorological maps. I started as an ill-informed traveller and what lay before me. Making it thus far was an education beyond expectation.

Chapter 21: Making Connections

Throughout this trek, I offered friends and anyone who followed the journey to join me for this unique experience, even for a week or two. No one took up the opportunity. Work or family commitment, perhaps fear, and the daunting journey might have dissuaded them. While in Mississippi, I reconnected with a friend from my university days. We hadn't seen each other for over thirty years. Miriam was a New Yorker but now lived in Florida. She wrote that she would reschedule her work program and join me for a while in Mississippi. She suggested visiting New Orléans, which was on my bucket list. A few days before she was due to arrive, she cancelled.

Several weeks later, she texted me on my second day on Jekyll Island and wanted to join me for four days. We discussed booking a motel in Brunswick town near the Island to be near each other. She planned to arrive on a Thursday when I thought I would be back on the road. It was a surprise, for I had given up hope of seeing her due to her busy work schedule; she teaches.

I bid goodbye to JJ at the Welcome Centre that Thursday morning. We took photos of each other as souvenirs. Rarely do you meet someone where there was an instant coming together. We hadn't seen each other outside her workplace then, only on two previous occasions. There were no words of intimacy exchanged. Yet in our silence, a gravitational pulling together exists, a hyper-awareness of each other's presence. As we parted, I felt this melancholic presentiment running through me, yet knowing I would not see then violet in the fading light. Grackles, mockingbirds, and many others would sing in a screeching chorus to celebrate another approaching night.

The following day, I wanted to prepare for my departure north. I took everything out of my trailer and discarded what I no longer needed. In doing so, I discovered the atlas I had lost in a hidden pocket. And all the notes for direction Morten and I had planned. I felt terrible for having done a mental character assassination on Patel, the manager of the Budget Inn, back in Memphis, Texas. I had blamed him for taking my Atlas.

Already on my mind, I was in the mood for the wheels turning and into the momentum of step by step, seeking each time to reach the next stage. After the rest, I was mentally easing into the trek. Initially, I felt in tune with all the facts about myself. But I was often surprised. The journey turned out beyond what I had hoped, Yet I still needed to gain more knowledge of the geographical and meteorological maps. I started as an ill-informed traveller and what lay before me. Making it thus far was an education beyond expectation.

Chapter 21: Making Connections

Throughout this trek, I offered friends and anyone who followed the journey to join me for this unique experience, even for a week or two. No one took up the opportunity. Work or family commitment, perhaps fear, and the daunting journey might have dissuaded them. While in Mississippi, I reconnected with a friend from my university days. We hadn't seen each other for over thirty years. Miriam was a New Yorker but now lived in Florida. She wrote that she would reschedule her work program and join me for a while in Mississippi. She suggested visiting New Orléans, which was on my bucket list. A few days before she was due to arrive, she cancelled.

Several weeks later, she texted me on my second day on Jekyll Island and wanted to join me for four days. We discussed booking a motel in Brunswick town near the Island to be near each other. She planned to arrive on a Thursday when I thought I would be back on the road. It was a surprise, for I had given up hope of seeing her due to her busy work schedule; she teaches.

I bid goodbye to JJ at the Welcome Centre that Thursday morning. We took photos of each other as souvenirs. Rarely do you meet someone where there was an instant coming together. We hadn't seen each other outside her workplace then, only on two previous occasions. There were no words of intimacy exchanged. Yet in our silence, a gravitational pulling together exists, a hyper-awareness of each other's presence. As we parted, I felt this melancholic presentiment running through me, yet knowing I would not see her again. I didn't want to leave, for I was going against everything that stirred inside me. Leaving was like suffocation. We hugged, and at that moment, I searched for an explanation for my mood. Something involuntary came out instead.

"Never suppress your true feelings. Don't restrain your individuality."

I was already in the motel when Miriam arrived. She looked well as though the thirty years had passed hardly imposed the stress of life on her. We spent an hour chatting, telling each other stories. We reminisced about when she studied in London as an American exchange student at the university. She asked me about a mutual friend, Ewan, whom she had a crush on, who now lived in Australia. She told me that she was divorced with two independent grown-up children.

"My marriage didn't work out."

She also revealed that she had an affair with another mutual friend, John.

"That hadn't worked out either. I was hurt by it."

Even at the time of our meeting, she was still not over it, and nearly a year had passed.

"I feel lost and want to move on, but I can't."

The tears streamed down her cheeks.

She wanted to visit Savannah, about eighty miles north on the border of South Carolina. And I, too, was eager to see the town. All along the way, we talked about the thirty years which went by so quickly. Yet, we were in our twenties again in the car and travelling. There was an ambience of contentment, having adventures going to places we hadn't seen. At speed, it was like gliding in the wilderness sandwiched between forests. Occasionally, there would be a small clearing and a few low-built houses with cars or trucks in the driveway as if to break the monotony of columns of woodland on the ocean drive of Route 17.

Suddenly, her mood changed: "Where did it all go wrong for us?"

She was voicing the tristesse that a marriage or a partnership prerequisite should last a lifetime. The feelings between two people should never wane. They should be constant, as it was on the first day they met, with stars in their eyes. The cells in their bodies hadn't changed, and the accumulated experience shouldn't have made them travel along different paths.

"A marriage or a long-term partnership should be sacrosanct, no matter what."

"What made you say that, after all, you instigated the breakup of your marriage?"

"Over time, I ended up with the thin end of the straw. For a long time, he put me down. Reconciliation became almost impossible."

"What do you mean by almost?"

"We had sessions with the marriage counsellor. He said I was to blame, and he was adamant I was the guilty one."

"Did you love him?"

"No, not at that point. I was his trophy which he placed on the shelf as his long-ago conquest. I found out in one session that he had an affair during the pregnancy of our second child. It made me numb."

She went silent after that as though she had found the answer to her question. But I also sensed it wasn't the marriage she was referring to, but the love affair with our mutual friend John that was still hurting her. It was as if the two experiences, her marriage and affair, had interfused in her mind.

She opened, "The hurt I was feeling didn't go overnight. It lingered, festered, and ate up my life force. I went into overdrive and depression. As each day went by, I felt engulfed by it all. I tried to do everything possible to distract myself from thinking about it. My mind played tricks, and sometimes, in a moment, I had terrible mood swings. My belly wanted to burst with pain so acute. I felt a haemorrhage was about to tear everything apart."

Her tears would come flooding out once more.

"I didn't realise you had kept in touch after university."

"I hadn't seen John for twenty-odd years, but he wrote. He wanted to see me, and my marriage was over, although my husband and I still lived in the same house. We met in New York, and I went to meet him at the airport. I was shocked. He looked nothing like I remembered him. He had a fat gut and wore dark clothes to hide his shape. His teeth were black and yellow with smoke, and he had a few days' stubbles that aged him even further. He looked a mess."

"What drew you to him then?"

"Slowly, I became enchanted. He was charismatic and used to write me long love letters and poems after our first meeting. He was overwhelming, passionate, and had a body smell that turned on every light inside me, which was exactly what I needed."

To change her mood, I said, "What fragrance, stale tobacco?" She laughed and eased up a little as we drove on.

Savannah was a feast for the eyes. It was the most beautiful city I had ever seen during my trek. Anyone interested in 18th and 19th-century architecture must put Savannah on their list of places to visit. These grand houses are set in tree-lined streets with no less than twenty-two spectacular squares in one square mile of gardens. The town gardens are adorned with live oak trees and many other species. There were beds of flowers with park benches to rest, admire and take in this extravaganza of the Georgian city surrounding. It was hot, but we walked under the shades of those trees and visited street after street just for its visual pleasure. We chose a rooftop restaurant overlooking a square at lunchtime and ordered a chilled rosé wine with our meals.

Her phone rang, "I bet it's John. I don't want to answer it."

She guessed right; John was phoning from the other side of the Atlantic. She sipped her wine, and tears rolled down her cheeks. Watching her and how she sipped her glass with her head bowed. More tears cascaded beyond the convex of her dark glasses. In an instant, I had a memory flip back to my youth. I must have been eight years old. Only grandmother and I were in the house having lunch. She had cooked rice, fried fish, and some vegetables. But the food was dry. She didn't like saucy food, for it reminded her of "duck's dinner all squelchy." In the middle of eating, she stopped and made salsa. I asked her for some, but she said it was too hot and gave me some tomato sauce. Then tears poured down as she ate. I asked her what was wrong.

"The chillies are too hot."

"Why don't you stop eating it?"

"Because it tastes so good," and carried on eating, cried, and wiped her nose and eyes.

Burning love inside Miriam brought longing and tears to her eyes throughout our lunch. She only drank one glass of wine. I drank the rest of the bottle and was still stone-cold sober afterwards.

She suspected, "He phoned to know what was happening between us."

He knew from an email that I was seeing her. Through him, I reconnected with Miriam when I had asked for her address and phone number before leaving London.

We drove back to Brunswick and talked about John until morning. She never ceased crying. I received a phone call at seven the morning after. She was in the breakfast room waiting for me. I thought I was in a dream. The alcohol had an after-effect. It was the first chance since Mississippi that I consumed more than a glass of wine.

At the breakfast table, she was still shedding tears. We needed a distraction from doing something physical and agreed to spend the day on Jekyll Island. We packed lunches, took our bicycles, and thought we would spend the day cycling, exploring, and relaxing on Driftwood Beach. I wanted to see JJ again, and this was an opportunity. At the Welcome Centre, I introduced Miriam. It felt good to see JJ once again with her welcoming smile. She gave us maps to tour the Island and made other suggestions. She also suggested that an evening meal in downtown Brunswick might be worthwhile. I was unaware I was stalling and chatting with JJ until Miriam dragged me out.

Made it to Jekyll Island (Georgia)

Relaxing on Driftwood Beach, Jekyll Island

On the beach, after lunch, Miriam explained how it had all gone wrong with John.

"We arranged to meet in the south of France and spent time together. It was difficult for both of us living here in the States and for him in Barcelona. We decided that I would spend time in Europe. He would then go to the States for part of the time until we found a solution to be together. South of France was a disaster."

"So, it was already going wrong even then?"

"His previous relationship hung over him, although he was adamant that it had long been over. She kept on phoning him while we were there. He insisted it was me he wanted. He came to the States several times after that and told me he was still committed. But I noticed he became less passionate, more standoffish. The last time we met was in New York. We bumped into his old friend, and the two got paralytic on Jack Daniels. They talked about soccer the whole night. It was our last night together, right?"

Tears rolled down her cheeks again, and she continued with an affected voice in staccato.

"He almost missed his plane back the next morning. How could he have done that to me? He no longer writes poetry. He writes about mundane things and soccer. I have no interest in soccer whatsoever. And it's only a line or two as if to say I haven't forgotten you, soothing his guilt trip. He has backed off from everything he promised he would do. You've been friends for a long time, right? What's he like?"

"Do you want me to give you an insight into what he is like?"

"Yes, I do."

"You are both my friends. How can I be fair?"

"I'm not asking you to be fair. I need another angle of what he is like."

"I can give you a man's view from a friend."

"Ok, shoot."

"Look, as far as I remember, he was fond of women older than himself. He was not attracted to women of his age or younger. That might have changed over the years; I'm not sure. I knew his image was to portray himself as loyal and monogamous. But I've often heard of his promiscuity."

"So, was he a womaniser then?"

"I can't be sure of that. I've only heard of these rumours from gossip. I can tell you this: he made a big move in his early twenties by going to live on the continent. He has established himself in a comfort zone. That took a while to achieve. It would be impossible for him to take a big leap at this stage of his life. Quitting your profession, friends, and family takes great nerve and courage. To leave all you've built for three decades and move into an unknown quantity on the other side of the Atlantic. It will take more than just love. It demands fearlessness."

"I thought I knew him. I feel so let down."

"Look, John doesn't possess that in him. Perhaps he loves you, and once, he tried to talk about it over wine and a bottle of brandy. We didn't get far. His image got in the way. We ended up drunk with bad hangovers with empty bottles by daylight, maybe above all, he wanted you most. But he was too anchored to leap to your call. His youthful exuberance had long since evaporated into his daily preoccupation with living. You must have been aware of that?"

"I don't know. Maybe he had another existence on the other side of the Atlantic. I have only this one picture of him. Now you are giving me another."

"How do you rekindle what is already lost? It could be because he loves you and thought he would make a final stance in his late summer years. Then realised he couldn't and let you go in the way he did. He drinks and smokes a lot, all the signs of suppression. He possibly knew he couldn't stop being promiscuous. We all strive for consistency and continuity in our behaviour, don't we? We mask ourselves with various guises to fit in with the code of how we should be. This rule doesn't always apply when it comes to our emotions."

In my experience, in moments of intensity, our passion swings up and down like a conductor's baton. One moment, we are in sublime heaven and the passion of The Swan in love's levitation. Next, we are trapped at the bottom of a deep, dark well, as if caught in Bernard Herrmann's symphony piece in the morbid theme of the cutting atmosphere of the violent violin and the moody descending bass cello sound into darkness.

She went into silence and understood it was over. It had all been a guessing game, hanging on to something that wasn't there. She understood she had to go through the suffering. But time was not moving fast enough for her to appreciate the healing waves. Doubt haunted her; she loved him and disliked him at the same time. Everything sweet and beautiful now seemed brief and bitter. Forgetting lingered on and possessed her.

She loved Jekyll Island and wanted to return the next day. We bicycled on hidden pathways and read every placard with snippets of history. At lunch, we became extravagant and had coffee and cake at the Jekyll Island Club Hotel. Later, we sat in the garden under the shade of an old oak tree and ordered drinks at the bar by the pool in front of the hotel—a fabulous location for a relaxed chit-chat. Miriam had a gin and tonic, and I had chilled wine. It was hot, and the cool drinks went down quickly. We ambled to the bar and ordered another. The young man with an impeccable smile, a youthful version of Robert Redford behind the counter, gleamed at me and said it was the compliment of the bar. I thought it must be our lucky day. Miriam's mood changed. The gin gave her a tonic, which brought a sparkle to her eyes, and her full lips had a sweet, permanent smile. The conversation was no longer centred on John. She talked about taking a trip to Italy. A change of environment might do her good.

She commented, "Rome is like an open museum. Every building, every street captures your imagination."

On our third drink at the bar, it was still free. The woman with medium blonde hair and a sexy smile behind the counter beamed at me.

I whispered to Miriam, "Everybody else is being charged. Why are we getting treated for free?"

I looked at the woman serving and made a shoulder gesture as to why.

"We heard about your trek. Awesome."

That word again felt pleasing. News must have got around during my stay on the island. I had spoken to a few people making casual conversation, but I never expected the news to have gotten around. A man in a light suit with an open-neck shirt sitting at the bar wanted to shake my hand. News, I thought, travels quickly.

Late in the afternoon, we said goodbye to JJ at her workplace. She had read some of my blogs and made complimentary comments. We agreed to be pen pals, and she hugged me and kissed my cheek. Something happened at that moment that moved beyond attraction, an uplifting. I didn't want to leave. I'm not too fond of goodbyes. It had been a happy time for me on Jekyll Island. Was I ever going to see her again?

Miriam was leaving the following day. I would be alone again, disconnected from my journey, having not been on the road for eight days.

The thought of being alone saddened me. In the morning, Miriam bid me farewell. For the third time on this journey, I was left behind. It was eight before I made the road. The traffic looked daunting, heavy, and noisy. Every vehicle was in a hurry, and before I put my foot on the pedal, a panic attack gripped me.

The motel manager agreed to give me back my room. I tried to contact JJ but couldn't get through. The shaking wouldn't stop like in Desert Hot Spring all those months ago. After, she answered my text, supported me, and asked me to go to the Island as she was working. It was impossible; all the energy had drained out of me. After a shower, I returned to bed, regained my composure, and fell asleep. In the afternoon, a deep and melancholic mood gripped me. I wanted to be sick and felt wretched. After, I gathered, it was not only being alone that caused this pensive mood but that the endorphins had eased out of me.

Elvis once commented that he became nervous each time he got on stage. The routine didn't take away the tension. He needed to do his best each time he faced a new audience. They demanded that of him. For him, it was like being on stage for the first time. Being on the road was like being on a stage. I was ready for it because our universe kicked up a different brand of elements my way every day. There was an inner tempest brewing, and I knew little where it would take me. Perhaps the last four days of intensity with Miriam took their toll. The path northward and the subliminal mutual connection away from JJ affected me. I tried to meditate in my motel room in that storm of emotions. Drifted over this silent confrontation in the space where the essence of my body took the lead over everything else.

I lived my life in real-time on the road, for tomorrow doesn't exist. I understood the magnitude of refined, sensitive thoughts. All my worldly possessions were in my trailer. None of the materials I left behind counted anymore. I knew I possessed a strong sense of direction and being alive. Perhaps it was a part I was unfamiliar with and didn't fully understand. The knowledge of being in exile gave me another perspective of myself, of who I was. My predicament obliged me to deal with all situations at every moment without depending on anyone. It became vital not to operate through a delayed action plan and fall into a mañana attitude over anything. I needed to be attentive and deal with any matter on hand immediately. This idea of living in an astigmatic world was no longer valid. The focus needed to be total.

In bed that afternoon in the motel, I checked my blog written the previous week. I read the good wishes and congratulations of the followers of the trek. There have been over two thousand of them supporting me from all over the world. One from a person whom I had never met called Palestina Bnc from Punta Arenas, the southernmost city of Chile.

There were many comments made to say well done, such as "You've been a tremendous inspiration to me;" "Your journey has been amazing so far…and what you write makes me feel like I am there;" "I never get tired of reading your posts;" "a real Miracle to cross a continent …suggest leave walking the Atlantic to someone else;" "fantastic … what a feat;" and "Is it finished, or are you going on?"

I gained courage from all the feedback and was ready to push on. With my mind made up when reaching the Atlantic, I wanted to go further. My enthusiasm for the trek only increased. Many people along the route invited me to stay if I passed their way. Throughout the journey, people were kind, and many invited me to spend time at their place instead of going to a motel or campsite. I was getting invitations as far as West Virginia and Maine. I felt I could go all the way north by hugging the coastline. The map no longer played a major part in my direction. I was unaware of what was ahead and made it a point not to spoil my surprise. I wanted the experience to feel like I was entering a terrain like Marco Polo had done in the 13th century on his way to China. An area of darkness. My only trepidation had to do with what I was leaving behind.

I often felt alone on this trek as I did then in the motel room. Without all the support, I would have felt like the last person living on Earth. It is difficult not seeing or talking to anyone for days on end. There were times like that. These were the most difficult because, towards the end, silence can be terrifying. Sometimes, one day in solitude can be intolerable. In an exhaustive state, the mind dances around with hyperactive emotion. Upon reading people's comments and emails on what I wrote on my blog, I am brought back down to the centre. It was unexpected. They carried me forward and kept me strong. Perhaps everyone who read me gained something, too, walking alongside me, as JJ said, like my shadow. There was a magnetic pull from JJ, and I wasn't sure whether the feeling was mutual. Before leaving, we exchanged email addresses and phone numbers. She promised she would follow me all the way.

Chapter 22: Towards South Carolina and Beyond

When I left Brunswick, it was almost dawn, and the traffic was light; when I reached Route 17 towards Savannah, it was in full flow. I had woken up from a dream about JJ. We had stood on a bridge, and mist rose from the estuary. She spun in my head again on the road while I drifted further away. Every impulse demanded that I turn around and head back to Jekyll Island. Instead, I kept with the flow of traffic going north. There was a sense of pulling away from her alluring grasp. A huge truck waited until it got near me before blowing its horn, almost frightening my breakfast to jettison. I screamed out loud at the universe, "You have to put me on the right track here."

It was eighty miles to Savannah, and I wouldn't make it in a day. After eight days off the road, by the early afternoon, I ached all over. It was the perfect bugs' climate, and mosquitoes don't sweat. The temperature rose into the 90s Fahrenheit with humidity to match. At the midway point, a campsite came into view. There was a car at the front of the house and a notice saying to go to the back, but no one answered. I waited for half an hour. The campsite was deserted, so I ate a sandwich to kill time. The mosquitoes buzzed around, looking for an afternoon meal, too. Their chances were slim. I went back to the road and saw a man pulling a heavy load nearby. I asked if he knew of a motel in the area.

Scratching his bald head, he said, "Now I can't tell", and told me, "We ain't got no motel here 'bouts, back fifteen miles, I estimate there's one.

There yonder (pointing to the north) 'bout twenty-five miles in Richmond Hill, there's a few, ah think?"

Backtracking was out of the question. Another twenty-five miles would test my endurance. The mosquitoes always tried to bite my neck, mini vampires, daytime feeding.

I asked, "Why aren't they biting you?"

He laughed out of an almost toothless mouth.

On the outskirts of Richmond Hill, I passed the South Savannah Camping Site and thought about staying the night. Then I recalled the mosquitoes coming through the vent in my tent and decided to avoid the torture. The day's journey was monotonous. It was the same pattern of landscape mile after mile. Tall pine trees sandwich the road. Beyond that was vast farmland, some of which was made into managed forestry, all fenced in. It was all humanised and domesticated, yet it hadn't always been so. Most of the area would have been virgin land a hundred and twenty years ago. Towards the ocean was marshland, parts of which were un-spoilt and broke the monotony of the day.

I needed a comfortable night's sleep for the distance that lay ahead. In Richmond Hill, there were more than half a dozen motels. Finally, I entered the lobby, and the man at the reception greeted me the American way with a big smile.

"Mr. Suresh Patel, I presume?"

He looked surprised, "How did you guess?" with an American accent.

"Ah, I am a clairvoyant."

"You mean you can see in the dark?"

"Adding numbers together has been my favourite pastime."

"You must be John Smith."

"So, you are a good putter, a hole-in-one."

He smiled, offered me coffee, and was eager to talk about England. I wanted to know more about him. He was single but planning to get married "soon".

"Is it going to be an arranged marriage?"

He hesitated, then said yes, "but I chose her."

"Have you met her yet?"

"Yes, we studied at the same university in Mumbai."

"So, you met her through casual acquaintance?" more hesitancy from Mr. Suresh.

"Our families are friends, and thought if I went to the university there, it would be helpful."

"Helpful? In what way?"

With a big smile, "Understanding the culture better and economically made more sense."

"What course did you do?"

"I studied for an Honours degree in Business Studies."

"What about her? What is her name?"

"She did chemistry. Her name is Sobha."

His beaming smile was infectious, the white of his eyes glistened, and a full head of thick, jet-black hair was tidily groomed. He could easily have fitted into Bollywood stardom. His degree will tie him into the family motel business. There is continuity and security in that format of close family and community ties. He 'chose' or was culturally conditioned to live in a predestined world with all its limits. Perhaps it would have been too difficult to break away from a traditional norm. To shift into a socially unconventional 'free-spirited' unorthodox lifestyle would be an alien thought. Pluses and minuses exist on both sides of the fence in our lives. It is a choice between a world of solidity and one of the frontiers and inexactness.

The following day, Mr. Suresh was at the reception and wanted to wish me luck on my journey. He seemed puzzled by my venture. "Why had I taken the risk" of so many unknown factors? I had no time to explain why and how I had chosen to live my life. We shook hands, and he said, "Be careful", with a slight Indian head roll, which he no doubt had picked up while studying in India. The gesture was unconscious, maybe his way of showing a brotherly affiliation. He came out to watch me set off on the road.

The outskirts of Savannah came into view after a detour off course, and Route 17 ended abruptly. After making inquiries, I found my way again via Route 80, which took me into Savannah onto Martin Luther King Boulevard. I had the sense of feeling lost in the middle of town. As I was about to head to the information office, I spotted a sign saying Route 17 across a huge, suspended bridge. I felt private contentment. All my thinking, inadequate maps, intuition, and awareness had guided me to the correct route, as they often did on this trek.

The Talmadge Memorial Bridge, less than two miles long, separates the states of Georgia and South Carolina. On the other side was Speedway Boulevard, aptly named. The road was the worst I had seen for the next thirty miles. There were potholes, cracks everywhere, and no hard shoulder. People blew their horns perpetually and drove faster than the speed limit. People honked to wish me luck through all the places I had trekked. Not here; they kept their hands on the klaxon to frighten me off the road.

Later, on approaching Hardeeville, one woman stepped out of her car full of children and swore at me.

"Git off the fuckin' rout' you cart pusher; you nearly made me 'ave an ak-ci-dent."

Stunned, I timidly uttered, "I've every right to be on the route. You should have indicated and passed me by. You need to calm down; there are kids in the car."

Suddenly, she went ballistic on me. I knew it was a mistake to mention anything about the children. Their eyes were all gazing at me. The words slipped out; it was too late to suck them back in. Her face reddened; her lips pursed, holding on to the volume of abuse that was about to add to the already 'radioactive' atmosphere. By then, her hair had fallen on her face like she had just come out of a headlock in a wrestling match.

"Why don't you get your ass into gear, you Yankee fuckboy, and head the fuck back north where you belong, you cocksucker."

The word flabbergasted was an understatement, "Okay, lady, get it all off your chest, and I'll remain silent."

Instantly, I felt I had made another mistake. It was an unconscious provocation. She looked and sounded like a Pit Bull Terrier. Her eyes bulged out, her mouth gaping wide open, her shoulders robust as if ready to pounce. Her words were so damning.

"You fucked up shit, you freakkin' jackass. You, you banana eater, banjo-eyed son of a bee-ch. This ain't no rout' for a fuckin' roadrunner. Your rout' sense is dumber than a tick on a dead dawg."

I had no idea that spoken English in these parts could be so creative and rhythmic in anger. I stood and thought, "How beautiful the universe was at that moment," while her rant surpassed the hundred-decibel level. If only I had a recorder. Each word acted as a delay to the time before she gave up on me. It seemed impossible that someone could have said so much in that stretch. She hurried back to her car, slammed the door shut, pointed her middle finger at me through the window, and then sped away. The children at the back of the car (infants, really) looked curious and slightly stunned. A girl, perhaps eight years old, gazed at me with big, blue, shiny eyes as though she was looking at Father Christmas.

That day, four men and two women clashed with me, winding their windows down and swearing out loud. On one occasion, a man kept his hand pressed on the horn and braked hard just behind me, leaving the smell of rubber in the air. I stopped and parked against a post on the grass verge. He stepped out of his car. He was smartly dressed in a light grey suit with a shirt and tie and started a rant.

"Get your dumb ass outta the fuckin' road. This ain't no place to take your brat to a fuckin' picnic. (He must have assumed my trailer had a child in it.) This ain't no Alabama backwoods, you bullfrog. You son of a ..."

Before I could say anything, he stopped mid-sentence, returned to his car, and drove away. The thought of madness crossed my mind. It wasn't easy to comprehend the logic of his action or reason. It wasn't my day. I needed to calm down. I composed myself and sipped some water. I took out something to eat and scanned over what had happened. Nothing made any sense. Only when I was leaving and backed off from the post, where my bicycle leaned against, did I notice the sign above, "Please share the road with bicycles."

Barely thirty minutes had passed, and a Police Patrol officer pulled me over and said, "I want you off the route'," pronounced 'rout'.

His whole posture and speech gave out an image of toughness.

"Here we go again," I thought. "I have every right to use this route. You can't tell me to get off it. There is no alternative."

He looked like he had been in the army – upright, stern, no-nonsense.

"I want to see your ID."

I was going to say I am from Planet Earth, then decided he might not have taken too kindly to that. I was already wound up by then. The one thing that I can't stand is direct orders. I gave him my driver's license.

"That's not enough. I need more official documents."

I wasn't prepared to give ground. "Look, officer, it has my photo, date of birth, address, British flag, European Union flag, and validation date. What more do you want?"

"I want your passport and your entry visa."

I thought that I had better calm down. I was liable to get arrested. While I opened my bag to get the documents, he stepped a few feet away and was on guard. His hands were close to his hip like a cowboy ready to draw. I could only assume he was ready for me if I drew a gun.

"Give me a minute; I hid it somewhere," while rummaging through my bag. "You're not in a hurry, are you? I'm having trouble finding it."

I remained calm and didn't get annoyed while dripping with sweat from the 100° heat. Somehow, I couldn't locate it hidden in a pocket somewhere.

"What was the last place you stayed in?"

"I stayed in a motel in Richmond Hill."

I finally found the passport in my secret pocket, which I had forgotten. He checked my passport and kept on looking at me up and down.

Abruptly, he asked, "What's your name?"

I thought, strange, he was back to bullying me again, "Are you kidding me? It's all there in the passport, staring at you. Remove your dark glasses."

More aggressively now, he demanded, "What's your name"?

Then, with a raised voice, "How old are you"?

I could feel the heat rising. That's it; I was about to blow my lid.

"Look, officer, are you having me on? It's in the passport, and you are looking at it."

Calmly now, he repeated, "How old are you"?

I shouted my age at him. Checking every page after, he handed me back my passport and then said with a surprised smile, "I wouldn't have believed it."

He took his shades off. It was like he had taken his mask off. It transformed his face. He was fine-featured, with piercing brown eyes, short afro-hair, and now with a pleasant smile. The change took me off guard.

"I hope I look like you when I reach your age. No wrinkles, fit lookin', what's your secret"?

"Are you sure you want to know?" I said it with an air of sarcasm. I was still annoyed, but he didn't catch on.

"Ye, for sure I wanna know."

"You might not like what you hear."

"Try me; what's good for you, gotta be good for me."

"You better write this down: junk food, late nights, bad sex, drugs, and rock and roll, and not always in that order."

That reduced him to an outrageous belly laugh. In that instant, our moods towards each other changed.

"All you Brits are a bunch of comedians."

I had heard that before from another officer. Why do they think that Brits are comedians? So, I put the question to him.

"We like to watch British comedy on TV."

"Really? I thought you Americans would find our sense of humour too dry. So, who do you like best?"

"Many people like Ricky Gervais, John Cleese and David ...."

He was searching for a name. I said, "Cameron."

"No," pondering with his hand on his chin, then said, "Frost."

"I had no idea David Frost was a comedian."

"Ye, but he died."

"Who do you like best?" I asked.

"Craig Ferguson and John Oliver crack me up. John Oliver has a way with words."

Soon, he seemed concerned for my safety.

"The reason I stopped you was to tell you we've bad drivers on this route, and every day, someone gets killed. They drive fast and pay no attention. They drink and drive, get racy tearin' up the rout', and pay no heed to anyone. Just be careful. I'll be lookin' out for you."

I saw six crosses along the stretch of road with wilted flowers, fallen petals, torn pieces of clothing, and the odd single boot or shoe lying by the wayside.

"You must have seen bunches of flowers laid out?"

"Yes, I have, and each time, I felt a chill pass through me near those sites."

I was more aware now of my vulnerability. He shook my hand and wished me luck. His advice and warning made me more vigilant.

Within a few miles, I heard a loud, screeching emergency brake from behind me. I reacted quickly and stopped on the grass verge. The smell of burnt rubber tyres in the heat filled my nostrils. A car that had lost control sped past me and careered off the road onto the grass median. No other cars were in view from behind or on the opposite side of the road. There surely would have been a catastrophic accident. It took the driver over three hundred metres to steady his vehicle, veering left and right, wrestling to get hold of the steering. At times, the vehicle was tilted, moving on two wheels. My heart went into overdrive. I needed a long break to calm down and determine what happened. The only explanation that made sense was that he had fallen asleep on the steering wheel for a few seconds. Or he was on his mobile phone, saw me at the last moment, braked, swerved, and lost control. Luckily, no other car was behind him. It was getting late, and I had lost time. Since morning, the road has proved difficult and stressful. It was tiring; after sixty miles, I needed a shower and a bed.

***

Charleston, South Carolina, wasn't far, perhaps ten or twelve miles. But I wanted to get off the road. It was getting near twilight. I passed a motel and kept going as it didn't look appealing. Then, a furlong later, I decided it couldn't be worse than lying in my pool of blood and returned. Mr Patel was too glued to his phone to welcome me properly. I had to draw his focus. He gave me a room down a flight of stairs, at the back, near a car park. The rear of the building was seedy, a run-down warehouse look concealed by its front façade. I knew I had made a mistake when I walked into my room. There was no internet, no refrigerator, no microwave, or telephone. The door didn't lock properly and was, in any case, flimsy. The room was tiny. I had to leave my bike and trailer outside. I went to see Mr. Patel. There was no reception room, just a small space to stand by a window as roomy as a phone booth.

"That's the only non-smoking room left. I can give you your money back."

He knew full well of my tired condition; soon, it would be dark.

"I can't give you a reduction," with a blind look.

I was good at bargaining, but that wouldn't have solved any of my problems. Besides, it was cheap enough, and I was too tired to push the matter further. He kept busy thumbing his mobile phone. His eyes never looked at me once while we talked. He looked bored at his job, irritated. I placed him in his late twenties, already with two young children by his side. Both boys, an image of their father with dark eyes, light brown complexion, and heads thick of jet-black hair.

The walls were thin. I could hear everything from either side. On one side, a couple was arguing. The woman's voice was slightly deeper. The man, with a tremor, perhaps older and feeble, and the argument continued.

The woman said, "Ah shoulda left you long ago."

The man asked, "Why didn't you and gone with that sonofabitch. Ah hear he done gone to jail for cuttin' up his woman. Should count yourself lucky."

The woman said, "Ah ain't been lucky since Ah met you."

That was only the beginning. I found myself in a real dilemma sandwiched between two theatres. On the other side was a young couple I met outside on my way in. They looked mid-twenties; he was African American, tall, and lean, and she was Caucasian blonde with green eyes. They made love throughout the late afternoon and evening, with loud murmuring noises like a scratched 'Je t'aime' record. Their headboards banged against the wall with the rhythm of their movement. Between lovemaking moments, the young woman had conversations with her mother. It was clear that her mother was worried about her.

"I'm just fine, mamma. Yes, I have eaten. Please stop tellin' me to come home. He is not like that. He feels he won't be liked. I'll come home later. Soon, mamma, I'm not ready now."

Later, the young man expressed his apparent inferiority about her family rejecting him, saying, "They see me as ugly."

I tried turning on the TV loud enough to drown the noise from my no-man's-land. When that didn't work, I switched the air-conditioning on. That did the trick, except for some low background noise and the rhythm of the headboard. It was all silent by midnight, and Serge Gainsbourg's erotic rhythm had paused for intermission. Peace, at last, sleep came like nights on the equator.

In the early hours, bedbugs chewed my ankles. I applied tea-tree ointment and went into my sleeping bag. I couldn't wait for the morning. I was on the road in the dim dawn light. I left the keys and a note to Mr Patel in his letterbox expressing my concern about uninvited guests emerging from the mattress. I wanted to spend a day in Charleston. As on so many occasions on this journey, I was lucky. Several motels were nearby, and I chose the Super 8 as it was newly built with luscious gardens on three sides. They kindly offered me a room, unusual as it was early morning. I entered the shower faster than a goose glide-landing on a frozen lake. I applied tea-tree oil to my whole body and washed my sleeping bag.

People tend to compare Savannah and Charleston. They are both beautiful places. Savannah could easily be in Brittany, France. The houses are very much French-influenced architecture. A lot of the houses were grand, with impeccable gardens and verandas. Every street has mature oaks, pines, majestic magnolias, and flowers. Each street had a median strip, also planted with trees and flowers. It's unusual for not even in London such plentiful squares could compare. Miriam and I had walked on the cobbled streets of Savanah near the trendy, bustling markets just a few days before. I couldn't capture its ambience due to our intensive conversation.

In contrast, Charleston went from one tragedy to another in my reading. War, tornadoes, hurricanes, and even earthquakes ravaged the town for over four decades. It was rebuilt time and again. Some houses look pre-Georgian, but most were of that period. Also mixed in, in many areas, were Brittany-style houses. The narrow streets of downtown Charleston sheltered the vegetation from the occasional harsh elements. The flora, therefore, thrived well, such as the varieties of palms, live oaks, and others that gave it a semi-tropical Mediterranean setting, yet without a doubt, it has an English/French flavour.

Downtown, they have a long indoor market of Victorian design with a classical Greco/Roman façade where they sell arts and crafts. The market was packed with traders and vendors selling their work or that of other artists. All the products were exquisitely packaged.

I met Laura, an attractive artist with long dark hair and dark eyes. I asked her why she had a Christian statement on all her work since the paintings spoke for themselves.

"I had rejected Catholicism for twenty-five years, and a year ago, I saw the light and my mistakes. Now, I wish to express this newfound vision in all my work. The captions are there to put the paintings in context."

"Have you ever heard of the expression, in the 'Garden of Good and Evil'?"

"I have, but never gave much thought to it."

"Do you think Eden was a garden of good and evil?"

"No, since it was Paradise. Adam and Eve lived there."

"If you remember, Satan frequented there too in the guise of the snake. And it was the snake that tempted Adam and Eve to eat the forbidden fruit. Hadn't God commanded it so?"

She remained silent as if trying to comprehend this idea. To break the silence, I said: "There are many contradictions in what we do, what we say, and what we hold as sacred. It is always healthy to explore these ideas and see what is at the bottom of them."

"I am an artist; I let my feelings flow, and from that outpouring, my work emerges onto the canvas. I have faith in what I believe. I cannot go into a deep analysis of my beliefs."

"Doesn't that make faith a barrier to a deeper understanding?"

She looked upset by my question. There was a sense that I had put her in an awkward situation. It was a logical and linear pattern of thought. The intention was to avoid getting on that subject anyhow. But her paintings focused on religious themes and invited would-be customers into her arena. She came back to me.

"It is up to you in what you believe. I searched for a long time. Logic and common sense cannot co-exist with intuition or within your emotional world. Someone showed me how to keep faith in Jesus, and doors opened. I felt at peace for the first time. It's impossible to explain. Don't you have faith?"

She turned the tables on me. I wanted to part with a change of mood.

"I was born into Catholicism, but the priests prized it out of me by the time I was twelve. I don't need religious beliefs."

"Oh, how sad!"

Her response tickled me and made me smile. She smiled, too, and the moment was right to alter the subject's mood.

"Is it acrylic you have used on these canvases?"

"It depends, on this one, it is oil, and that one is acrylic, and this one here with the Madonna is acrylic, and the child painted in gouache."

I had seen the Madonna and the child messiah painted in black in Ethiopian paintings but didn't expect it here. I asked her why she had done that.

"I am an artist. I experiment with paints and textures. I painted the child black because he is the son of God. Black is not a colour, but it absorbs all colours. Like God absorbs everything everywhere, it helped to give the painting depth and focus. People can read what they want in a painting as they do with the Bible. What do you think?"

"I like it. It's provocative. I'm still not sure about the captions, though."

We shook hands, and a stall further up drew me. Arun Drummond, the stall owner was attractive, fine-featured, articulate African American, selling paintings and printed cards. On display were paintings by John W. Jones, although other African-American artists' works were also being sold.

John W. Jones paints ugly. All his paintings were haunting. I felt taken by the crushing 'beauty' of his concept. One painting called "Slave Harvesting Cotton" showed a man on the plantation, his hair uncombed and matted, his face burnt and raw from overexposure to ultraviolet rays. His hands were as dark as his boots - jet black. He was picking cotton from the thorny shrubs with drops of blood tinting the white bulbs. The man's clothes were much too big for his undernourished body. His head seemed oversized and disproportionate to his frame. But for this figure, the vast fields with tall trees spreading far into the distance look like a biblical paradise. With bent knees, stooping back and drooping shoulders, the man looked like he was in the throes of de-evolution.

I discussed some of Arun's paintings, including those I felt had missed the mark. He explained the context and clarified the objective of the images. Another painting depicted a slave picking cotton with a great smile, happy in his work.

When I questioned that, Arun said, "That image came from an old Confederate currency note to make propaganda to the North, to show how happy the slaves were at their work."

John W. Jones' paintings map the history of the region. All his paintings were provoking and challenging. I thought they were a statement, the ugliest images from an artistic viewpoint I had ever seen. A dark past buried deep in history, re-emerging on the psychedelic canvas in the contemporary light of day. We live in paradise on our little planet, but we know how to turn it time after time into hell.

While talking to Arun, Paul Silver joined us. He had silvery hair, a robust figure, a happy face, a permanent smile, and deep blue eyes. His stall was on the other side of the aisle. He noticed my accent was not local and wanted to know more about me. I informed him of my trek, and he became animated. I asked him what he was trading, and he took me over to his stall and showed me his paintings, mostly landscapes in wild tropical variegation. We were about the same age. We chatted about the origins of words, why he became a painter, and what he had done before. We had a lot in common.

"Every decade or so, I would move on to do something completely different."

"Why?" I asked him.

"Once I feel I have reached the limits of a project, I become bored, need a new challenge, and move on."

Suddenly, Laura appeared, and Paul, cracking a joke, said, "Let me introduce you to my mother."

"Too late. We've already met."

Somehow, the conversation turned to God again, started by Paul, and Laura added her bit to fire the discussion. I declined to take part.

I said, "It's a very pleasant day. Let's not talk about politics and religion. This will change nothing; you will stick with your beliefs, and I will hold on to mine."

With a smile, Laura told him about my venture. Paul replied we've been speaking about it. Afterwards, Paul became insistent; he wanted me to shout, "Please, God, help me during my trek." He hollered it so loud that the whole market in our vicinity heard him.

"Please, Paul, don't ask me to do that."

"Why? It's a marvellous thing to do."

"I couldn't do that because if I fail, I will want to take responsibility for that failure."

He repeated it louder so that everyone in that market section got his attention again.

He said, "Say it, say it loud, please God help me on my journey."

It was like a congregation watching a live sermon. I felt annoyed with him for having drawn so much attention to our conversation. I didn't need to prove anything in front of an audience.

I gave him a stern look and said, "I'm a humanist, Paul. Believing in an extraterrestrial order would be like believing the moon was made of gorgonzola."

Laura left abruptly. Her dimples disappeared. She said, "I gotta get back to my stall."

Standing tall and towering, hair like a biblical patriarch, Paul half turned his back on me. I moved to face him and held out my hand to say goodbye. He took what seemed a long time before he clasped my hand. I didn't let go of his hand. I stared straight into his blue eyes; they appeared grave and glistening. My reaction had upset him, and then a reluctant smile came down his face. I hugged him and went away. His evangelical insistence disturbed me. It hadn't occurred then to ask him, "What if it had been the other way round? Would he have swallowed my version of the universe?" I couldn't understand that closed tribal mentality of his reasoning. Once outside, I allowed the sun to appease my mood.

I felt angry and hungry, too. I came upon a restaurant by the seafront recommended by the motel staff. It was near the pier, a great place with a fabulous sea view. The restaurant was big and spacious, and the atmosphere was superb, with white and rosé wine glistening at the tables. The aromas of garlic and herbs swirled in the gentle sea breeze through the large windows. The windows and doors opened onto the seafront. There was a balcony patio area with tables and chairs under umbrellas packed with clients. The chiming of glasses and lunch on the well-prepared tables, white cloth, and silver cutlery made the ambience fabulous on that summer's day.

It was busy, and I told the hostess, "I could share a table if there weren't any available."

She said, "We will consider that", and led me to a table for four. The server dealing with me was of Sicilian descent.

To make light conversation, I said, "I have a couple of Sicilian friends whom I visit in Sicily for walks, wine, and seafood,"

She pointed out, "Two Sicilians are sitting behind you."

I turned around, and they had heard us talking and introduced themselves as Pepi and John. They were from New Jersey and came down for a wedding and a change of scenery. It was her grandparents who had migrated to America.

"We are all mixed now. I am part Sicilian/Irish/Czech."

John's family originated from Napoli, southern Italy. He had a dark complexion with blue eyes. Pepi had full lips and an outgoing personality.

She asked me about my doings here. I told them what I had told others. They seemed fascinated by the places I travelled through.

Pepi said, "We've been planning for years to do an adventure of this sort by car. Running a business takes so much of our time. We are in textile."

John took a back seat in the conversation. They had finished their meals and were waiting for the cheque.

"We would like to contribute to the charities." They later contacted me for my campaign donation details.

When John and Pepi left, a well-spoken woman introduced herself as Cyan came and sat at my table.

She said, "I have been looking at you for a while."

She was slim with dyed shoulder-length blonde hair and hazel eyes. Her figure suggested plastic surgery on her upper body. I felt caught out, and to snap out of my surprise, I asked if she liked the landscape. She rolled her eyes at me with a pleasing smile.

"Do you know the meaning of your name?

"No," she said.

"It means a time traveller in the spatial light, turquoise."

Her face lit up, and she smiled with her lips pressed together. She was with a group of friends at another table ten paces away.

"Tell me, what made you come over to my table?"

She uttered, "You are the best-looking man I've ever seen. I wanted to meet you."

I was flabbergasted, "Are you serious?"

"I mean it."

"Damn, I must learn to look into the mirror more closely."

"Don't do that too often, in case you fall in love with yourself."

"Now you've deflated me."

At the time, I thought if I wrote this down on my blog, people would slaughter me for being vain. She invited me to her table to join the others, Patricia, Lisa, Diane, and Megan, with Cyan and myself, making the table lively enough to get a lot of attention from neighbouring clients. After initially focusing on my being there in the USA, I wanted to hear about their adventures. They had all been longtime friends from college, although Patricia and Megan were sisters. They were in Charleston for a wedding (a popular place to begin a 'lifetime' commitment) and planned to stay on for a week and visit Savannah too.

"Where are you all from?" I asked.

"Elizabeth, New Jersey"

"I've never heard of it."

"It's a kinda suburbia city," said Lisa.

"Isn't that a contradiction?"

Diane commented, "Ye, a city where nothing ever happens."

They all laughed, and I missed out on the in-joke. Their laughs expressed the confidence they had around each other. They were attractive women in their late thirties/early forties, with everything going for them: maturity, experience, and good looks. It was an elegance that came from within more than skin deep, with a touch of eroticism which women in their twenties seldom possess. Lisa wanted to know if I was married.

"I've never married but looked forward to the day."

They had all been married except for Diane, who had affairs and relationships when it suited her. She was a lawyer.

"Work is very demanding, and men are shitty sometimes like some clientele."

Patricia and Megan had married two brothers, but they were both divorced.

"We got bored," as though speaking in unison, I didn't ask whether they were twins.

"They liked ball games, and if they weren't at a match, they would sit in front of the TV with a beer can in hand, switching channels with the volume loud. Nothing motivated them."

"Not even sex," said Megan.

"That was like taking the dog for a Chinese singing lesson in the park," said Patricia.

I was puzzled for a moment, and they all laughed again.

"Do you like ball games?" asked Patricia.

I hesitated for an answer, and they laughed even louder. Cyan discreetly grabbed my hand from under the dangled tablecloth, squeezed it, and held it. Her rings pressed against the knuckle of my fingers. We talked and laughed for nearly an hour, and their cheque came as did mine, and they insisted that they would pay for me. They wanted to meet in the evening, and we exchanged phone numbers. As it happened, they were staying at a posh motel a car park away from my own. Throughout the time, Cyan didn't let go of my hand. Her hand became sweaty, and it felt awkward. My emotions were somewhere else back on Jekyll Island. We left the restaurant together, they went to their car, and I wanted to walk. The sun was beating down, and I had forgotten my hat at the motel.

Later, when I returned, I became feverish. Having wine at lunchtime had the effect of running down my energy. I developed a headache and wasn't sure if it was the alcohol or the food, as a fever gripped me. My stomach didn't trouble me, and then it occurred that I must have been in the sun too long. I phoned JJ and told her I was ill.

She replied, "I wish I were there with you. Why haven't you made contact? I miss you."

"I had been in a black spot with my phone until now. I haven't been able to stop thinking about you. Do you think I am crazy?"

"What is there to be crazy about? The feeling is mutual. I had a vision that I would meet you a while ago. I couldn't say anything before. I needed time to digest it. I can't speak any longer. I'm at work. I'll phone you later."

It was the first time that she had expressed her feelings. There had been a silent understanding between us that was more than physical attraction. Such a strong pull between two strangers would have been strange, but it felt natural.

In the evening, Cyan telephoned, and I told her I had sunstroke, blowing hot and cold, weak, and my saliva tasted bitter. Within a short time, she knocked at my door. She wore a dress that would point anyone's eyes to her cleavage, which made her look ready for a rave. I was laid out with a splitting headache.

She sat near me on the bed and held my hand. "What can I do for you?"

"I need something to stop this fever and headache. I'm cold and can't stop shaking."

She bought me painkillers and wanted to stay awhile to "talk". My headache eased, but I didn't let on. It had been a chance meeting, and sometimes the attraction works both ways, a holiday romance. It wasn't working for me, though, and JJ's 'sorcery' had a hold on me. If anything were to happen now, it would feel like a betrayal. I was ill and could have done with warm comfort and being looked after. It was the wrong moment, and the timing was out of sync. She left after a while.

"Today is not my lucky day."

All I could say was, "I'm sorry." In the morning, I got a text: "Good luck - C". I responded, "Stay happy, N."

Every day, upon waking, the guy in the mirror would say, "It's time to go," and then the shivering would start all over again. The painkillers stopped the headache but didn't stop the fever. It came and went. On TV, a hurricane threatened the coastline. I monitored its development. It took four days before I was confident about making the journey north. The hurricane vanished into the ocean. I studied the map and knew where I was heading. Time in my motel room allowed me to write a long piece for my blog. I received many comments, one from JJ saying, "Wow! Like I have told you before, I think you are awesome."

The encouragement from the blog gave me the impetus to shake off the tail end of the sunstroke. I was myself again, and early in the morning, I was back on Highway 526 to rejoin Route 17 and bypass the congestion in Charleston. Within twenty minutes on the highway, a Patrol Officer pulled me over and told me to leave at the next exit. I did so and was lost in the suburbia of North Charleston without a detailed map of the area. It was early morning with the odd one or two joggers on the road doing their morning exercise. In my anxiety, I needed someone's help to point the direction to Route 17.

The area looked wealthy, with large gardens dotted with mature pines, oaks, and magnolias. I saw a supermarket hidden by vegetation sectioning the car park. The young man inside could not help me but said he would ask his manager. Ten minutes later, a man with a shirt and tie introduced himself as Kevin, "I am the manager. How can I help"? I explained my predicament, and he said to give him twenty minutes, and he would take me to Route 17. He explained that there was no other way except via the Highway, which would take us almost a full circle to Route 17, about sixteen miles away. He gave me the key to his 4 x 4 to load up. How trusting is that?

While driving, we chatted. "I'm married with two children and have lived in Charleston all my life."

He wanted to know about my venture. I gave him a brief account in the short fifteen-minute drive. He helped me to unload and wished me luck. Then he said wait a minute, got into his car, and returned with a small box.

"Take these healthy bars; they contain dates and nuts. They'll give you energy when you feel low."

I thanked him for being kind, trusting, and considerate. He gave me a firm handshake and said he needed to get back to work. In no time, he was gone, and he took away all my anxiety. In a day, I wouldn't even remember his features. He had gone out of his way to help me more than I could have expected from anyone. I looked at the box he gave me and thought I'd have one bar to get me on my way. I opened the box and saw six bars and a $20 note underneath.

Chapter 23: Wilmington North Carolina

The intention was always to head north. Friends had been in contact with the Findhorn community. Discussions had taken place on the net. Some members offered accommodation if I passed near 'their neck of the woods.' In any case, my flight back to England was from New York in late August. It was still July. It made sense to head in the direction of invitations. Besides, it would take me to a part of the country where I probably wouldn't have ventured.

In the meantime, Richard Overton contacted his friends who lived in Wilmington. (Richard Overton is Yvonne's brother. Yvonne was the person who put all my journals on my blog in London and relayed to friends and family news of my safety when I couldn't make contact.) Paul and Barbara (Richard's friends) had read my blog. They contacted me and invited me to stay if I needed a rest.

I took their offer and headed to Wilmington. I knew that the road ahead would be difficult. I would have to travel long distances in the summer heat. The temperature was never below 35° C/95° F. The summer months from June to August are known as the 'gates of hell'. I figured out I could do the one-hundred-and-eighty-five-mile distance between Charleston and Wilmington in three days. My trailer would be heavier because of the water I must carry. It was not unusual to consume a gallon a day.

Leaving Charleston to go to Georgetown was a hard day's stretch, edged by forest and farmland. It was like travelling through a tunnel of a steam room. On any day, from six in the morning and on the road for thirty minutes, my body became drenched with sweat. After a while, if the roads weren't too busy with morning traffic, I settled into a trance-like state. I glided into a meditative mood that often took me back to my past. It never ceased to surprise me how many discoveries I made on this trek. I learned that trekking could be the best form of education.

Late in the afternoon, I reached Georgetown, and after winding down, I wanted to see the Historic District. The streets were busy, and the restaurants were making a fine trade. Venturing onto the Harbour walk, I could see Lafayette Park from across the river. What a coincidence that this area should remind me of Poole Harbour, Dorset, England. The island opposite Lafayette Island resembles Brownsea Island. Andy was in my meditation en route, a friend who died fourteen years since. He drowned near Brownsea Island. A week before it happened, he had given me a souvenir, a piece of triangular metal, a talisman, with an etching 'Marinero', part of the boat he had built. I carried it with me on this journey. He wanted to sail the seas but didn't learn how to swim. I went to the motel, took the Talisman, and returned to the harbourfront. I imagined Andy's face smiling at me, saying, "You made it." I threw the Talisman as far as I could into Sampit River and muttered: "This is for you, Andy; part of your creation made it too, like those long-ago pilgrims."

I walked back to the motel with Andy still in my mind. The manager, Sanjay, approached me and wanted to talk. I was reluctant to do so, but he became insistent. He was inquisitive to the point of annoyance. When he caught on to the idea that he was being ultra-intrusive, he changed tack and asked me about my plans for the next day. I said I was heading for Wilmington. I turned the conversation to him and asked him if he was of the Shudras caste to see if he would be annoyed. The labour caste was a low pitch for him, in my estimation. Most Indians would be hurt if you placed them in a lower caste. At a guess, he was likely to be from the Vaishya, the merchant caste, one above the Shudras.

He said, "Caste doesn't mean a thing here in America."

Now, it was my turn to say, "Did you marry someone from your caste?"

"Yes, yes, I had to respect my parents, and in India, things are different. Here, everybody needs to change."

"In what way do people from the subcontinent need to change?"

"Look, let me put it this way: I might have walked around in my dhoti in India, but it would be out of place here. Whatever works for us, we learn to accommodate it. Like the dhoti, if it doesn't work, we get rid of it."

"I thought Gandhi went to England in his dhoti, spinning wheel, and goat's milk?" I said.

He laughed and didn't respond for a while. Then he said more than I had expected, fluent in how he spoke, and his outlook was pragmatic.

"Some family members and many friends have married outside of their community. Hindus marry Muslims, and others marry into the general population: African American, Caucasian, Hispanic or Asian. Some people don't even know which caste they are from. Within two generations, it's not talked about. We move forward or remain stuck in old ways that don't suit our new life. As you must have seen, people of each community mingle among their own. This possibly has to do with a cultural attachment, language, food, religion, and so on."

His facial features lacked appeal, but his energy made him attractive. He came to the USA as a young adult and looked to have established himself. His mild Indian accent had a gist of the American twirl wrapped around certain words. He wanted to invite me to a barbecue gathering and meet some friends the next day.

"It's the Fourth of July, and there will be plenty to eat and drink. You must come to celebrate and don't worry about paying for the room tomorrow. Your legs must feel the pace, and it's our holiday."

"Our holiday," he seemed well adjusted to being an American citizen. I had forgotten what date it was, and the Fourth of July was mentioned by JJ a while back, but it had gone out of my head.

"You will have plenty of opportunities to meet and talk to people, which will be good for your blog."

At first, I had taken an aversion to him, and now, with his openness and warmth, I accepted his invitation.

He phoned me at ten the next day and said he was ready to leave as we had a two-and-a-half-hour drive to our destination. I got him to open up and talk some more on the way.

"My wife can't conceive."

"Has she tried IVF treatment?"

"Yes, she tried it once, and it didn't happen. It doesn't always succeed. She is nearly thirty-nine."

"How is she taking it?"

He went into a long silence. I didn't pursue an answer. We had been on the road for a while, and I paid no attention to the direction of whether we were heading north, south, or west.

Then, with a tremor in his voice, he said, "She has been gone for a month visiting her sister in New Jersey. We haven't spoken for a week."

Again, he remained quiet for a while. I sensed that he was downhearted and needed company. He had been animated the evening before and was willing to talk about anything. I needed to snap him out of this mood, get him chatting, and be lively again.

"Where did you study?"

"I went to East Anglia University, England. I met Mansur Uddin there. You will meet him at the celebration, a shy fellow, and he is also from the subcontinent. He was a village boy surrounded by paddy fields and muddy rivers. He used to reminisce about the time when he ran around in his bare feet and lungi. A fortunate fellow: he had people in high places. He is peculiar but a good friend."

"Why peculiar?"

"He must eat rice and lentils every day. He says he gets constipated otherwise. Withdrawal symptom, he calls it! We all had very little money at uni. He used to say that he could cook tin sardines in twenty-five different ways with spices. His hair was long, like a hippy, but he went bald even then and used to do a comb-over to hide the bald patch. He looked comical. He studied philosophy, which was unusual for students from our subcontinent studying abroad. They tend to go for medicine, law, engineering, or business. These days, hotels, computers, or banking is the big thing."

"What did you study?"

"Mathematics came easy for me. I didn't need to swot a lot."

"What did you do after your studies?"

"I returned home. I had a job waiting for me in government, and marriage came along. My wife's family wanted us to go to America. Her people here were in the motel business and wanted me to take over. The business was expanding. It's been eighteen years since. Asians do well here. We are business-minded, and we work hard."

"It has been a land of opportunities for you, then?"

"I have been lucky. My parents worked hard for me because they thought I was a clever boy and sent me to university. I obtained a good degree. I was in demand. All I wanted was a government job and a nice family. Look, I have no money problems, but I do miss home. I miss my old parents. I miss the smells, bumping into people, and the spirit of the place. All the bustle of the streets, the markets, the festivals, the sounds and loud colours of the sarees. So many kids are neglected in this world. We can't have any. You don't always get what you want in life. Do you understand?"

"Yes, I do, although I've never felt the way you do. You can take vacations, can't you?"

"Yes, but America is busy. Work all the time."

Then we veered onto a leafy road off the main route and drove until we reached a large wooden cabin standing on stone piers by a lake. There, in the ground, stood very tall trees with dense dark green leaves, their girth thin like cable posts. Brown fallen leaves of the previous autumn were swept onto the stone bed surrounding the trees. The driveway and parking area were all tarmacs. The next cabin was some distance away, hidden by the vegetation. Outside, a long table was laid out with plates and food pots, and the barbecue smoke gave it a camping atmosphere. The view of Murray's Lake was true splendour.

There was a group of six people sitting, chatting, and laughing. Sanjay introduced me as the man who was trekking across America. I didn't want the talk to be around me. I took the initiative by saying, "Have you known each other long?"

A man with a moustache introduced himself as Doug. "This is my wife Sandy, who yesterday went blonde. I woke up this morning and thought I had entered the wrong bed last night. Over there, the man with the outdated beard is Pete with his lovely wife Laree, who recently had plastic surgery."

"Stop your fooling around, Doug. Excuse his rude manners; he is drunk already, and it's only one in the afternoon," said Sandy.

"I apologise, Laree, no offence meant."

"You said it to embarrass her in front of a stranger," said Sandy.

"Listen, sweetheart; I said it because it rhymes."

"I'm Veronica, and my husband, John, is the quiet one around here."

"He is from London doing this trek across America for charity," said Sanjay.

Doug said, "Anyone who can trek across America deserves a medal."

"What made you do it?" asked Pete.

"I don't know; it's a difficult question to answer. I have so many reasons. A simple answer would be that I love adventure, passion, and physical pleasure."

"Have you reached your destination?" asked Veronica.

"No, I plan to stop in Maine."

"Man, you've still a long way to go. How many miles have you trekked so far?" asked Pete.

"I don't know, maybe three thousand plus. I haven't added them up yet. The last time I looked at my pedometer, it was 3.3k miles."

"How much walking have you done so far?" asked Laree.

"I think about 1.9K miles or thereabouts."

Doug made a long phew sound and said, "We did our walking in the army. I haven't walked since. Why walk when you can ride?"

He was still at it, making fun of everyone and lighting the atmosphere. The sun was blazing, and under the shades of those trees, it was a perfect summer's day. Before Sanjay took me away to introduce me to Mansur Uddin, Doug said, "Tell Mansur to go easy with those chillies. I don't want my ass burning up in the morning. Last time, he'd me sitting on the pan for an hour."

Mansur Uddin was busy preparing the barbecue. He no longer supported a comb-over; his head polished as a well-displayed eggplant. He wore an apron and a dishcloth thrown over his shoulder. He seemed jovial and greeted me warmly.

"Sanjay told me all about you last night. Interesting! How are you?"

"I'm fine. It was good of Sanjay to invite me. I needed the extra day's rest."

Sanjay left us to talk and went into the cabin. Sanjay had mentioned that Mansur Uddin lectured at one of the provincial universities in the west of England.

"He retired after his wife's death. He suffered a great deal for a time but met Hilda on an internet dateline for academics. She teaches English and Drama here in South Carolina. He can't do anything wrong in her eyes, and she loves his cooking," Sanjay mentioned on our way here.

"How have you been coping with living here in the States? Sanjay mentioned you came over four years ago."

"It was strange in the beginning. I've lived in England since 1975. When you know you must live somewhere else, you adapt as quickly as you can. But in some ways, I am still finding my feet."

"Was it difficult dealing with the immigration department?"

"It might have been, but I had a little money behind me."

"So, money moved mountains for you?"

"Yes, but I was also married to Hilda. One would not have sufficed without the other."

He lifted the barbecue lid, and the light vapour of sizzling meat filled the air. The dry rub spices exuded an aroma of the cooking, bringing on an involuntary faux pas. He sneezed aloud all over the barbecue and never gave it another thought. It was just as well that I was a vegetarian.

"Let's go inside. I need to put on the rice," he said.

There was an odd urgency in his movement as though the preparation to cook the rice was of vital importance. Hilda was preparing pinto beans in a large kitchen with Sanjay. She looked at me with beaming eyes. She was tall and slim with reddish hair and a very welcoming personality.

"We've been talking about you," she said.

"Good or bad?" I asked.

"Oh, just indifferent," then she laughed.

"Honestly, it is a truly amazing trek you've done so far."

"I've thought little about it. Doing it takes up time. To overthink would mean winding down. I don't want to wind down yet. I didn't mean to interrupt you. Carry on with what you were talking about. We can talk later."

Then Sanjay said to her, "Sumitra has been seeing a therapist. Her sister suggested it."

"It's an excellent idea. It might relieve some of her anxieties and tensions," said Hilda.

I turned to Mansur Uddin, and he looked like a man absorbed in preparing his food. He placed the rice on the cooker and lit a slow fire, then lifted the lid on another pot, dipped a wooden spoon into the lentils, and put it straight into his mouth with a slurp, tasting it. Then he added more salt, stirred it a little, and licked the spoon. He did this twice, plunging the spoon deep into the pot each time.

After, he turned and asked, "Do you want a glass of wine?"

"All right, can I have white wine if there are any chilled?"

"Let's sip it outside and check on the barbecue."

Lifting the lid, "This batch is cooked. I'll put on another load."

The lake looked inviting for a swim, and the temperature was already 90° Fahrenheit. In the distance were two canoes rowing along. The aroma of spices drifted in the open air, and I heard another loud sneeze behind me. No doubt Mansur Uddin added extra ingredients.

"Bless you. The delicious smell is making my belly rumble," said Doug from afar.

A short while later, we sat down, sipping our wine. He asked, "Are you going to write a book about your journey?"

"People have asked me to, but I need to assess whether I have the mental energy to carry it through to the end. I'm living only in the moment. I'm still on the journey."

"Have you written?" I asked.

"Yes, a few academic papers and three novels."

"Were they well received?"

He seemed hesitant and rubbed his nose like something was making it itch.

"The last book had positive reviews in the South Asian circle back home. It revolves around the liberation movement."

Unconsciously, he picked a piece of dried mucus from his nose, rolled it into a tiny ball, and dropped it on the ground!

With a sudden jerk, "Let me check the barbecue."

He flipped over the ribs with a fork in his left hand and used the fingers of his right hand to turn over the chicken, then shouted to Hilda, "To please switch off the rice."

A short while later, Hilda said, "Come on, everybody, the feast is ready."

I was in a quandary about eating, and Hilda suggested having a portion of her cooking first as it was all vegetarian. A huge relief came over me. She gave me a plate of pinto beans, a tortilla, and some salad that she had made.

Mansur Uddin, busily eating, "You must taste some rice and lentils after."

He ate with relish with his hand, mixing the rice and lentils, turning them into a small ball, and slurping it into his mouth. He ate intently, licking his fingers like a man who had missed his supper the previous day. We lifted our glasses and toasted a happy Fourth of July. I skipped eating the rice and lentils unnoticed.

"This is great, Mansur, so delicious. I wish I could cook like this. Where did you learn to cook?" asked Pete.

Everyone hummed in agreement, and Mansur, efficiently licking his fingers, did not respond absent-mindedly. It was a lazy afternoon with old stories being retold and jokes with fits of laughter. The beer and wine flowed, but Sanjay didn't drink, and I had only one glass of white wine. In the late afternoon, Sanjay wanted to get back. We had a long drive, and it was six.

In the car, he said, "What did you make of the crowd?"

"A very nice bunch of people, but I'm no good with crowds. I am a one-to-one person."

"What did you think of Mansur Uddin?"

"He looked like a man in love."

"He is, but he is also depressed."

"Why do you say that?"

"He hasn't been able to write since his first wife died. It has been six years. People said she was the brains behind his writings, and now he seems lost. After she died, he became depressed, and I invited him over. He came and spent a month here. I thought he should look on the net for a partner. I sent him a link to possibilities in this region. We talked day and night about everything. His wife's name was Tonia; she was of Spanish origin. He admitted that he had never allowed her to win one argument in twenty-five years of marriage. He regretted she went to her grave without asking her for forgiveness."

"If others said she was the brains behind him, he'd unlikely have won all the arguments. Developing such an idea takes a huge amount of arrogance and narcissism. He must have felt safe in his trenches."

"What trenches, in what sense?"

"If you barricade yourself, you are digging your own grave."

"Yes, he is intelligent but very childish sometimes, like a boy who needs to win every game."

"She took away all his inspirations with her, too. How did she die?"

"She died of a complicated illness."

The drive was tiring. We said no more until we reached the motel in Georgetown. He knew that I was leaving early in the morning. His eyes looked tired with dark shadows beneath and sad. Perhaps he was now that he found himself alone again. In my room, I looked up the meaning of Tonia - it said 'Priceless'.

***

I checked my blog in the morning, and JJ commented, "Crazy man! Do you think I would let our friendship fade away now that you've walked half the world to find me? I will always be your shadow."

The bridge crossing the Great Pee Dee River and the Waccamaw River was over a mile long over the Ocean Highway. It had taken me a while to sleep during the evening after the long drive. But I felt fine in the morning like I had been on holiday. I was up early, and Sanjay was not about. I was on the road by six, determined to beat the traffic. I crossed the bridge with virtually no hard shoulder. A placard informing the Cofitachequi Indians lived in the area before European settlement. Nowhere could I find anything written about them - a people gone extinct without a trace, except for a marker by the wayside of the road, like a tombstone.

Within a few hours, it became clear that this area was a holiday resort, and I aimed to get to North Myrtle Beach. The traffic was heavy, and eventually, I left Route 17 and travelled on Ocean Boulevard, which hugged the seafront. The famous part of this long resort was Myrtle Beach. It reminded me of Montpellier, except the French have that touch of panache that no other place could emulate. A lovely stretch of warm sea and fine white sand that was idyllic at that time of the year. Unfortunately, it was in the middle of the peak season, and the hotels were full or else very expensive. The campsites were fully booked, too, leaving me with the dilemma of pushing outside these resort areas.

By early evening, I was lost, heading towards the outskirts of North Myrtle Beach and having to double back three times to find my way. I was running out of body fuel until patrol officer Drabble saw me sitting on a grass verge in a village green. I was trying to work out my route on my inadequate map. He pointed me to the right road, a few miles from the highway, where I would find a motel. "It's a new one." He asked me about my name, where I was heading, and where I had come from. When I told him I had journeyed from Los Angeles, he whispered, "Wiseguy." Then, "I wanna see your passport."

Myrtle Beach S.C

He checked my visa, and my port of entry was Los Angeles. He handed me back my passport and wished me luck with a smile. I was apprehensive about the motel being fully booked. The motel's garden looked pristine, the motel new, and the man behind the desk smiled at me as I entered.

I looked at him; "Mr. Patel, I presume."

"No, my name is Gupta. I have a room for you at a reduced price, only ten bucks less," giving me the Indian head roll.

"Why," I asked.

"Officer Drabble said you are coming. He phoned."

Gupta was all smiles, and he gave me a nice room. I couldn't say anything to him except thank you. I was spent. I seemed to have a knack for choosing motels where the walls tend to speak. These walls can tell many stories. One of these days, I will sit down and write a novel about war, peace, and love in motels hopping across the USA. There is much room for a Shakespearean drama with great comedy and tragedy.

Crows are early risers and hungry birds. Unless you are up at the first blush of dawn, you will never experience them scavenging on dead animals' road kills during the night. Their beaks are as skillful as a butcher's knife, leaving the bare, splintered bones to bleach in the hot sun. They flew away from the carcass as I trekked past them in the blue light of the morning. By midday, it was scorching, and Wilmington was still hours away. And when finally, Wilmington came into view, I faced an impossible crossing. The Memorial Bridge is a kilometre long, with no hard shoulders. The traffic-heavy with big trucks and fast cars. Whenever a driver passed me, I could read his face saying, "Get off the frickin' bridge, you damn asshole."

Once on the other side of the bridge, I was bewildered by loops and turnings, left and right and two lanes going straight on with traffic right up my tail. It was too difficult to make a snappy decision. I knew I had to turn left at some point, but it was dangerous. I stopped in a lay-by instead, allowed for a gap in the traffic, and moved on to a left turn.

I arrived in Wilmington bathed in sweat and delusional. I lost my way a little despite Paul giving me clear instructions on how to get to his shop downtown. Two women assisted me with their mobile phones to find the shop. While I sat on the pavement, pouring cold water over my head from the bottle they had offered me.

Myrtle Beach S.C

He checked my visa, and my port of entry was Los Angeles. He handed me back my passport and wished me luck with a smile. I was apprehensive about the motel being fully booked. The motel's garden looked pristine, the motel new, and the man behind the desk smiled at me as I entered.

I looked at him; "Mr. Patel, I presume."

"No, my name is Gupta. I have a room for you at a reduced price, only ten bucks less," giving me the Indian head roll.

"Why," I asked.

"Officer Drabble said you are coming. He phoned."

Gupta was all smiles, and he gave me a nice room. I couldn't say anything to him except thank you. I was spent. I seemed to have a knack for choosing motels where the walls tend to speak. These walls can tell many stories. One of these days, I will sit down and write a novel about war, peace, and love in motels hopping across the USA. There is much room for a Shakespearean drama with great comedy and tragedy.

Crows are early risers and hungry birds. Unless you are up at the first blush of dawn, you will never experience them scavenging on dead animals' road kills during the night. Their beaks are as skillful as a butcher's knife, leaving the bare, splintered bones to bleach in the hot sun. They flew away from the carcass as I trekked past them in the blue light of the morning. By midday, it was scorching, and Wilmington was still hours away. And when finally, Wilmington came into view, I faced an impossible crossing. The Memorial Bridge is a kilometre long, with no hard shoulders. The traffic-heavy with big trucks and fast cars. Whenever a driver passed me, I could read his face saying, "Get off the frickin' bridge, you damn asshole."

Once on the other side of the bridge, I was bewildered by loops and turnings, left and right and two lanes going straight on with traffic right up my tail. It was too difficult to make a snappy decision. I knew I had to turn left at some point, but it was dangerous. I stopped in a lay-by instead, allowed for a gap in the traffic, and moved on to a left turn.

I arrived in Wilmington bathed in sweat and delusional. I lost my way a little despite Paul giving me clear instructions on how to get to his shop downtown. Two women assisted me with their mobile phones to find the shop. While I sat on the pavement, pouring cold water over my head from the bottle they had offered me.

A little girl about seven years old with them said, "Don't waste the water."

I said, "It's not being wasted; my head needs it as much as my body."

"Silly, your head doesn't have a mouth; it can't drink?"

"My hair is like little straws."

She stared at me, puzzled, then said, "No, they are not." That was a serious statement to answer in my dehydrated, delusional state.

"You got me there, pardner."

She said, "You are funny."

I made my ears move without grimacing, and she laughed. When I looked cross-eyed at her, she laughed even more. Eventually, they had Paul on the line, who gave them directions. It was a short distance downhill towards the river on a quiet road. I found him waving at me frantically as I descended at speed. Luckily, he had a shower in his grand boutique bazaar that sells goods imported from Bali and elsewhere.

Paul & Barbara were friends of Richard Overton, who now lives in Malaysia. They were business associates from when they lived in Bali and ran an export agency. Getting first-class friendship treatment, having the space to relax, and fitting in with them felt good. They were fantastic hosts in their beautiful house. After my first day's recovery, Paul took the next day off work to be with me. He wanted to talk and show me around. He took me to the park near the estuary and the open sea. It was another scorching day. Barbara reminded us to take water, but we both forgot. It's easy to forget things when the weather slows your faculties, and general lethargy creeps up.

Paul & Barbara my hosts in N.C

The park was dotted with tall thin pines with lichen clinging to their barks and carnivorous plants scattered in between. Paul wanted to show me the Venus flytrap, but we couldn't find any. Then we came across the Pitcher plant, indigenous to North America. Inside their tubes was a gel substance that trapped sand insects and dissolved them. They come in different sizes and shades. Later, during the walk, we lost our path. We ventured into the tall grass that grew in the muddy part of the beach, finding our way back to the car park. Huge grey pelicans flew low above us in groups of a dozen or more. They resembled Concords, hovering in the wind current without flapping their wings. They looked imperious and odd, like flying dinosaurs.

Paul and Barbara were pleasant hosts. We hadn't met before. They both had a previous marriage, but, in each case, it hadn't worked out, and neither had children. Paul had a kind face with a serious look.

He said, "We met inside the Canadian border in a small community of people in the north-west. We got on well, and after a hard winter, we searched for warmer climes. We ended up here. We lived in Bali for a while, and this was how we started our business."

"Was it difficult to get it going?"

"Yes and no. There were always problems with customs, transport, late arrival, and damaged merchandise. Overall, we've done well out of it. We started over twenty-five years ago, and we are still at it. Over the last few years, the business has slowed down."

"What do you think is the reason for that?"

"Since the crash, people have tightened their belts, and the business hasn't been able to get back to the same level. The market has become saturated too."

"What are your plans?"

"We've thought about selling up and moving on. Get rid of stress. It's not so easy to do. To move on to do what? Retire to live a life of leisure?" Then he laughed and reiterated, "It's easier said than done."

Americans don't stop working. They work until they can't physically cope with their load. Or they retire after they've reached an age limit and search for a new job and sometimes two. It's as if they've too many bills to pay, or as someone pointed out back in Texas, "Why retire when you can still earn good money?"

In the evening, Paul and Barbara invited two of their friends for drinks and introduced me to Sally and Lowell. They were great people to talk to and open-minded. Sally had wavy shoulder-length argent hair and was a biologist and a superb artist. She gave a piece of her work to Paul and Barbara. A big calabash painted exquisitely with Aboriginal-style images of turtles, alligators, and lizards. It looked like a precious piece of antique China. It was exquisite to look at, touching, and feeling its artistic elegance. Meeting someone who can excel in science and the arts is always pleasant. Lowell worked in the nuclear plant a few miles away but had since retired.

I would have liked to have spent more time chatting with them. I never saw them again after that evening.

Sally and Lowell talked about politics a lot. I had raised a question about US society based on merit.

"It's far from that. There's a lot of nepotism and underlying racism still at play." Sally said.

I said, "In my experience travelling through the country, not an utterance against my person. In fact, in my case, the opposite was true. People of all backgrounds helped me, welcomed me, gone out of their way to cater for me."

Through my observations and intuition, the people at the grassroots level were more willing to live by and accept the fluidity in a multi-community society than those who held power. People in power in management, media, powerful institutions, and politics are out of touch with ordinary people. This trek has given me that angle with a different lens to see what those in the "ivory tower" can never comprehend. Perhaps they wouldn't want these dynamic changes. A fluid connection among the populace might ebb away the very authority they possess to keep society fragmented. The more divided society, the better it would be to keep a hold on to the status quo of a power base.

Paul went to work the next day, and Barbara spent the day with me. We talked, and the talk was like meditation as we walked on the local beach. We spoke of the journeys we all had to go through and are going through, with many impasses along the way. The two of them have reached such a point about their business. They are responsible for a large house and what interest remains in their lives. They have a very special kind of love for each other.

"We are both tired. You know it's a crucial time when we get to this age. We must dig in and search for what is important. Find something that'll give us enthusiasm for living. Not merely passing through life and existing in it.

We all need to bite into something hard and to stimulate to take us to a new threshold."

I understood what she meant. There are three ways to live a slow death. One is to wallow in the boredom and routine of life without dynamism. Two is to hold on to a secure life even when a relationship is without love for fear of the unknown factor. And three, because the interdependency in a 'marriage' was so bound up that both have lost their individuality and the fear of living separate lives, be it alone, was death itself.

Throughout my time there, we had relaxed evenings. Barbara cooked some lovely meals with Paul helping, and we drank some excellent wine. I let go after not drinking for such a long time. Not once was there a hangover.

These months of travel taught me that three days was the limit of a stay; otherwise, it would become difficult to pick up my rhythm again. Paul and Barbara had said I could stay for as long as I wanted. On that Saturday evening before my departure, they took me out to a Thai restaurant in town by the sea. We decided I would leave early Sunday morning, and Paul dropped me on Route 17, well away from the Wilmington traffic. It was sad to say goodbye to them; as always, I was in mourning throughout the day on these occasions. That is the part that is most upsetting, departing. When you begin to know people, you must leave them, as if cast away in a rudderless boat in the middle of the ocean. You see nobody; you talk to no one; your jaw gets tired of the lack of movement, and your sentiment travels adrift.

The novel, 'Cape Fear' was written and set in these parts. I saw Cape Fear River on the way into town. It was also an area with much piracy in the 18th century. Black Beard used his marauders in Cape Fear. It might have got its name because of those brigands. I wrote on the blog that he had returned and reincarnated into a fellow with a white beard and deep tan, riding a bicycle & trailer, except the locals don't know it yet. Ou ahrr! And what treasures do they have hidden in these here parts, me hearties? JJ wrote a comment, "You are the treasure."

Chapter 24: A Change of Direction

Heading north after leaving Jacksonville and New Bern, the home of Pepsi, I came across the longest bridge I had ever crossed. The Neuse River Bridge was two-and-a-half-mile long. The traffic was light at six in the morning. I wanted to get ahead and reach Washington, NC, forty miles away. The weather forecast was for rain in the afternoon.

Paul had written and said, "It rained heavily in Wilmington, the river burst its banks and water covered half the garden, almost reached the house."

As often, when rain was due, the clamminess rose, the sun beating down, and it felt like an open sauna. It's great for the skin. It relaxes all the aching muscles if the skin is not overexposed to ultraviolet lights. It took getting used to being sweaty and sticky in that environment. The clothes cling to the skin like the thin needles of the Jumping Cholla cactus. Every so often, I would have to stop and drink water or chew on some dates and nuts to give myself a break. On that day, on such an occasion, cars hooted at me as they passed, encouraging me. A grey-haired woman, elderly, drove past, heading towards Washington, NC, and waved at me as she went by. I waved back. A few minutes later, a car stopped in the lay-by next to me. The grey-haired woman opens her window and hands me a bottle of water.

"I saw you standing there as I passed, and you looked thirsty. I had to turn around to give you this bottle. I saw you earlier a few miles back while talking to my friend."

I took the bottle and told her I had plenty in my trailer. She wanted to talk, and she seemed troubled.

"I felt in my heart that God wanted me to turn around and come see you."

"It's nice of you to do so. I am fine, just a little hot."

"Have you been travelling long?"

"Yes, for the last five and a half months from LA on foot and, as you can see, also by bicycle."

Her eyes were ice blue, sincere, and her voice gentle. There was a resigned tone in its vibration.

"Where are you going?"

"To Washington, the town ahead for today, but I hope to make it to Maine eventually."

"My goodness! Why are you doing that?"

"Well, for charity and adventure. I don't truly know. I need to think about that. It must seem like madness under this scorching sun."

"You know, I was on my way to the doctor. He has some test results for me. I am a little early and, on the way, I couldn't stop thinking about you standing there. You cut a lonely figure. You looked lost. I wanted to stop the first time, but I carried on. Something caused me to go back to see if you were okay. I'm not in a hurry to get my results. I don't have a good omen about them."

"What is your name?"

"Barbara, Barbara Pankhurst."

I grabbed her hand and said, "I'm passing you some good energy. I've been fortunate on this journey so far. You have your path to travel. We've both come a long way. Everything will be fine. Today has been a good day, hasn't it?"

She smiled beautifully and said, "God bless you and good luck on your journey."

I let go of her hand, and it felt like my hands were on fire. It startled me. She waved at me as she drove off. With her image in mind, I remained still momentarily, looking at her car disappearing in the distance.

The road was straight, with forests and farmlands on either side, framed with the canopy of an impending sky. Throughout this east coast trek, there were more plantations than forests, even though forestlands were still abundant. I also saw vast areas of swampland and a significant volume of water in the wide rivers and lakes. In North and South Carolina, corn, wheat, peanuts, soybeans, sweet potatoes, tobacco, cotton, marijuana (for medicinal purposes), and other crops are planted in enormous quantities. I also saw ditches surrounding these crops with rows of bulrushes, or at least I thought of them as bulrushes. I found out, though they looked similar, they were, in fact, Cattails. My untrained eyes were not able to differentiate between the two.

Later, I stopped near a man in front of a workshop made of corrugated sheets in the middle of nowhere. The building was surrounded by plantations, fifteen miles from Washington, North Carolina. It was the middle of the day, and the heat was at its peak. I wanted to ask him for the name of a plant in the field that puzzled me. Jared was his name. He offered me water and something to eat, but I had eaten a sandwich and fruit not long before. We chatted, and he was polite and friendly. He was de-hulling the beans he had planted. It was done by a simple, low-tech rotating machine which took one-tenth of the time to make a bushel of beans by hand. He showed me how it worked by turning a crank that spun a drum.

"I keep a couple of pigs to recycle the hulls."

He showed me his garden with rows of beans, sweet potatoes, cabbages (he gave me one to eat raw, and I did), corn, tomatoes (he gave me four), pecans, and so many other vegetables. The garden was about three acres.

"This workshop was a big bar back in the 1950s. Night trucks made stops to quench their thirst. The road would have been dirt tracks back then, and a beer or two would have gone down well during the hot summer months."

He gave me water and electrolytes and said, "You might need those."

He wanted his photo taken with me on his phone. After he said, "You better hurry. Rain and thunder are coming."

Jared was forty-three years old. He had a bad accident, broke his leg, hip, and shoulder, and was on a small monthly benefit. He did what he could on the three acres to supplement his income. With partial disability, he learned to work with wood, making benches and wells' folly.

He offered me to stay the night, "I have a spare room in the house."

He tried to telephone his wife to come and meet me. She was in the house but didn't answer his call. "She must be in the washroom." I thanked him and said I was on a mission to make a certain mileage. As I was leaving, I noticed children's toys on the grounds near the house. I never found the name of the plant I was searching for.

The rain came down an hour after I reached the motel. It didn't just come down. It was like watching a spectacular show of thunder and lightning. The wind blew thick drops of rain at a forty-five-degree angle. That curtailed my plan to skip Washington to the next town, Williamston, a further twenty miles. The clouds became darker, and the rain forecast was right. It had been a wise move to stop in Washington. The sun and the steam effect had been draining anyhow.

Earlier in the day, I made an emergency stop due to a large pothole when my bike slipped on the surface. I fell to the ground and hurt my right knee. It was my first mishap on the journey. The pain went away after ten minutes. At the table in my hotel room, writing notes on the day's events, my knee looked swollen with pulsating pain. Thinking through this pain and the landscape I saw of the day, how difficult it must have been in the old days. Clearing acres after acres of land, ploughing the fields, sowing the seeds, irrigating, and harvesting the crops – back-breaking work when nothing was mechanised. It was astonishing to see this human idea of creativity, vandalism, and remodelling of the land, as though we were the gods, then repeat that process again and again.

The bicycle fall left a lingering pain throughout the night. I was ready to go the following day, but the weather looked heavy and menacing. The forecast predicted an eighty per cent chance of rain. My mind was made up; I stayed put in the motel. In any case, my knees were hurting, one in sympathy with the other, and they needed a rest. I used the remedy Michael gave me in Mississippi – pain-relieving Wok Lok oil - a pleasant smell that also worked.

Thinking ahead, I wanted to push on to my next stop, which I planned to reach Fairfax in Virginia outside Washington DC, where a Facebook friend of Jim O' Keefe would receive me, Mike Ranson. Jim was married to my cousin and had followed me on my blog. He told Mike of my journey. Mike wrote to me and invited me over if I was passing near his area. I needed a change with more interaction with people. Feeling strange and isolated, I calculated that reaching there would take over a week. And I was optimistic the route would not be as busy as it had been over the past two weeks. That morning, I received an email from Mike suggesting a new meeting location. We decided on Culpeper, Virginia, although I was wary of the number of ridges in the area. I mapped out my route and kept on Route 17 to Fredericksburg, then along Route 3 to Culpeper. It seemed easy on paper, but I sensed it would be a lot of sweat with a bicycle, trailer, and on foot.

Steve & Mike Ranson, my hosts

I wanted to get out of my motel room. The clouds were not dark or light. They almost camouflaged the doves perched on a branch against the backdrop. The ground was wet in patches after the rain during the night. In some puddles, deposits of engine oil had fallen in droplets. One was round like the sun, surrounded by a halo of rings of various shades fraying at the edges. They were metallic, like the plumage of a peacock.

I was determined to see downtown Washington, and if the rain came, I thought it would be like water off a duck's back. Main Street was well preserved like the towns of old England. The narrow streets and pavements were well restored, and shops maintained and appeared wealthy. I turned off into Market Street, hoping to see sellers at their stalls. But any market which must have existed had long since disappeared with the coming of the shopping mall. Instead, I saw grand houses Brittany style set back in pristine front lawns well-groomed. The only marred view was the mass of overhead electric cables.

I shouldn't have looked up for a large drop of rain fell straight into my eye. The sky opened, and there was nowhere to run for cover. The rain came down, and the back of my saddle was like a rivulet, funnelling water to the part that never gets to see the moon. Everything coated to my skin, the opposite of water off a duck's back. I got back looking like a wet chicken.

Back in my room, I felt subdued. I had gone through a kind of mood change for some three weeks. I was not sure why this came about. The enthusiasm was only half there. When I spoke to Sea Ryder back in Big

Creek, Mississippi, she mentioned feeling that way after three and a half thousand miles. She completed her four-and-a-half thousand miles loop on horseback. With her heart no longer in it, she became ill and persevered for the last thousand miles even though she did not want to go on any further.

I felt the same anxiety as I had reached three and a half thousand miles. I knew I wouldn't stop. I didn't know how to do that. It affected the way I wrote my blog. Days would go by, and I wrote nothing. I didn't want to repeat anything that was already written. Perhaps it was because the journey from 'ocean to ocean' had been done, and the extra 1600 miles northwards no longer held a mystery. I may have been tired and displaced the fatigue into an emotional response because I was too stubborn to give in. I wasn't sure whether it had to do with the intensity of the past two weeks affecting my mood change. Was it because I was drifting ever so far away from JJ?

She texted, "I don't know why we have this link ... reincarnated souls? Thank you for coming to Jekyll Island. I need you more than you need me."

I recalled reading Robyn Davidson's Tracks. In the most challenging part of her journey in the Australian desert heat, she was accompanied by an Elder of one of the Australian Aboriginal tribes. It was a great learning curve for her, more so because she wanted no company early in her journey. Much later, after she had the companionship of the Elder for a hundred miles, she didn't want him to go. She became captivated by him. He opened for her a whole way of seeing. I have been on the road longer than time seemed to suggest. I, too, wished I had a travelling companion I could relate to and bounce off in times of difficulty. But I have had no such luck. It's only now that I realise how difficult this journey has been. The full volume of it hasn't quite sunk in. Perhaps long after the journey was made, the feat of it all would come home to me. It took Sea Ryder a year before she could speak to anyone. I was the first person she spoke to and talked about her journey. The effect of her journey had been profound. I have yet to find out what it will be like when it ends.

The discoveries and surprises on this journey have created a shift in the shape of my being through my emotions, physical energy, and mental capacity. The comprehension of it all does not present itself in a prominent, conscious way. Sometimes, weeks would go by before I felt any of the impact. It might take a word or a sentence from someone as a key to make something fall into place. Only then could I comprehend that the path, this trek, the decision to come here, to face all this full-on, was worth more than I could have expected. It felt like I was being propelled into the deep space of my interior. Everything had been unknown, and my fitness level, energy flow, and enthusiasm were rejuvenated. It seemed strange that I should be experiencing this phenomenon at this late age. To have a clearer vision and regain all my youthful energy when the opposite was meant to happen with the descending years.

On the road, in the flow, full of expectations and surprises, I set out to Windsor and Suffolk on the border of Virginia. With good navigation, within three days, to reach Gloucester Point, fifty-five miles away. The traffic was easy, not hectic. The air, dense with unpolluted oxygen, filled my lungs with excitement. The odd car would toot at me encouragingly. I would make a few stops here and there and chat with people. They would 'bless' me and wish me good luck on the rest of my journey. A cycling club of about thirty cyclists headed in opposite directions waved at me. I floated on my magic bike, full of contentment. The twenty-mile to the long bridge took less than two-and-a-half hours. The bridge frightened me. All bridges are dangerous places. There was little room for bikers or walkers with the bridge traffic so fast and the wind current strong. The James River Bridge was five miles long, and the hard shoulder was wide enough to fit half of my trailer. I did not like being there. I couldn't ride at speed. It would take me over an hour to cross. It was the longest bridge in the world before 1920. Zach told me that.

When I had done two miles, he pulled up with his truck and said, "It's illegal to ride on the bridge."

I said, "I saw no signs."

"It's there, but I'll give you a lift because it's too dangerous to cycle over."

I took the offer with relief. I asked him if it was seawater under the bridge. He said it was fresh water. I thought that a river with a width of five miles seemed unbelievable. At the bridge's end was a beach with many people swimming and sunbathing. Zach dropped me off in the parking lot attached to the beach. I thanked him for saving me.

"You're not the first biker I've rescued, and you won't be the last."

He liked my fashioned grey beard; his was all over his face – 'ginger'.

Ten miles later, I wanted to check my direction as I saw no signs after following my limited map as far as I could. I saw a grand hotel and stopped for some information. At the desk was the assistant manager, an African-American woman with explosive eyes and an attractive aura. She greeted me in a welcoming manner.

I said, "I wanted to ensure I was heading in the right direction."

"Yes, you are on the right route. Are you looking for a motel? Why don't you book a room here?"

"I'm on a trek with a limited budget. This is a grand hotel way beyond my means."

She became curious and wanted to see my bike and trailer. She came back with a surprised look and took my blog's address. She disappeared to check my blog while I poured myself a cup of coffee in the lobby. When she returned, she was all smiles and took to me.

"Why don't you stay here for the weekend?"

"I have told you I couldn't afford the room here."

It would cost nearly $250 per night for a double room. She looked at me with those eyes and said, "We would like to offer you the room for free for the weekend."

"Are you teasing me?"

"As you are doing it for charity, we want to help."

I accepted in an instant with a wide Cheshire cat grin on my face. Once in the room, I was gobsmacked. It was a suite, a large bedroom with a TV, a kitchen fully equipped, a living room with a TV, a makeup/shaving area with a mirror and sink, and a separate bathroom. The space was huge, and I had the facilities of an indoor swimming pool and a gym – not that I needed the extra exercise. Later, when I looked at the price list at the back of the entrance door, it was $350 per night for the suite. My eyes almost dropped to the floor like marbles. I felt lucky that day – the lift across the five-mile bridge and this offer.

While shaving, the guy in the mirror said that I deserved this. I winked at him. He hasn't always been polite to me. A few days since, in Washington, when drenched, it was he who had coined the phrase 'wet chicken' at me. A little while back, after I reached a motel exhausted and in the middle of shaving, he poked fun at me. While checking my reflection for imperfection, I have tried to stay, dare I say it – young. But as anyone would know, as each day travels rapidly, grey hairs suddenly appear and say: "Hey, how do you like your new look?" I usually execute the little bastards with a pair of scissors. But lately, they've been ganging up on me, whole tribes of them appearing overnight.

I did an excursion around town looking for a music venue I had not seen since leaving Clarksdale, Mississippi. I saw a huge advertising board saying that Ringo Starr and Jeff Beck would perform in town. I had seen the same advert in the Myrtle Beach area. The thought came to me: is Ringo still beating his drums? The next day at breakfast, I got chatting with someone named Biggs, and he was. I asked him about the music venue and Ringo's appearance there. He said that he had seen it.

"He is a crooner now."

I almost had a tear in my stomach. "You're having me on!"

I rested well over the weekend and planned to go fifty miles that day. I checked on Google for the availability of motels. Before that, there was one more bridge– this time only one mile long. It had a wide shoulder, and I was there early enough to beat the heavy traffic. I felt strong all day, and the cloud cover helped me from being overheated. There was less moisture, and I didn't sweat. JJ and Barbara mentioned there would be less humidity beyond North Carolina. Somehow, when I arrived at my destination, Saluda, there weren't any motels. The next town was Tappahannock, thirty miles away; Google had let me down again. I took information from a gas station where someone thought a motel might be three miles in the opposite direction. I took a chance and ventured out, only to find wide-open spaces. Doubling back added an extra six miles to the day. There was only one thing to do. I pushed on and completed eighty-nine miles that day (an equivalent of two hundred and ten miles on a free bicycle without a trailer). My luck was still holding. The motel manager, Neil from Gujarat, gave me a reduction when he saw my NazacrossAmerica caption on my trailer.

That day, I was on the road from six in the morning until almost eight in the evening. After a shower, I searched for a place to eat, and only the Scottish Highlander's rapid cuisine was open. They had no vegetarian menu or French cuisine except for French fries. Instead, I opted for oxygen in the open air with a whiff of gasoline fumes.

My hunger challenged me at four in the morning. I allowed myself two portions of oats, dates, bananas, nuts, and water. I was ready to go by five-thirty, but it was still dark. I waited and watched the news and checked on the weather forecast. I couldn't wait to be out in the open and on my way to Fredericksburg. The landscape changed and became hillier and steeper. Inevitably, these conditions meant pushing and pulling both bike and trailer, which sometimes proved almost impossible.

There were many names on placards by the roadside that told the story of the local Indian tribes which once lived in the area. The Rappahannock found themselves between new hostile settlers and other Indians dispossessed during Bacon's rebellion in 1676. The Rappahannock was urged to merge with another tribe, the Nanzatico, or move further down the Rappahannock River. The new influx of immigrants shifted the stability of the huge area from Maryland, Virginia, and further south to North Carolina. Once the protocol amongst the Indian tribes was destabilised, it created suspicions and mistrust between all the tribes.

Other tribes lived near the Rappahannock River, such as the Portobacco Indians. They were farmers, fishermen, and hunters. At one point, they were joined by the Rappahannock, thus creating a safer environment against attacks from other tribes, such as the Senecas. They occupied the land on Portobacco Bay until 1704, when the English colonists, claiming the land by patent, drove them off. I think it is called land stolen through 'legal' means. I wished I had time to research what happened to these lost tribes. From my vague recollection of history at university, annihilation occurred during the rebellion, where men, women, and children of the Occaneechi tribe were savagely butchered. Their shadows were still there to see all over this land.

Fredericksburg was a large town, busy with traffic and a nightmare for cyclists. It was hilly and bustling. I left at daybreak and headed towards Culpepper, where Michael and Steve Ranson were picking me up. They lived in the interior near the Appalachian Mountains in Shenandoah County. Getting to Culpepper was one of the most arduous journeys I had had to make on this trek. The ridges between were almost impossible. I must have lost half my body weight. The roads were continuously up and down, and the climb almost defeated me. I was halfway to Culpeper and needed to take a rest more than ever. The weather was hot, 95° Fahrenheit, sizzling.

That day hadn't begun so well, for I checked the direction twice and still took the wrong road. It was three miles later with a downhill gradient before I realised my mistake. I had to haul myself back to the starting point. Afterwards, it felt like I had already made a day's journey. This sometimes happened when the road signs were vague and misleading. By then, it was nine in the morning, and the traffic was flowing fully. I was only five hundred meters from where I had left at 6.15 a.m. Route 3 had a good hard shoulder, even though it was an uphill start. Later, the struggle with the hilly roads became even harder. Suddenly, out of the woods, barely ten feet ahead, a huge deer zipped past me, trying to cross the dual carriageway. It got to the grassy median in a panic and onto the other side onto oncoming cars. Two fast cars missed it by sheer luck; the third should have noticed it and stopped. The dreamy driver, too slow on the uptake, probably busy on his mobile phone, was blind. The deer crashed against his oncoming vehicle, somersaulted fifteen feet in the air, landed with a bang on his bonnet, and fell onto the road.

I dropped my bicycle and ran across the dual carriage road, cars tooting at me. Its front legs trembling, I gathered them together to stop them from shaking. I caressed its neck, and the two big doe eyes stared deep inside me. It tried to breathe, but the impact must have crushed its lungs. All I could hear was a suffocating inhalation. A short time later, which seemed ages, the shaking stopped. The warmth of its body and the vibration seemed to have transferred to me. The young couple from the car were in shock. I pressed them to phone the police. I left them, crossed the roads, and got on my bike. The collision stayed on my mind—the grace and majesty of this living animal and its sudden end.

So quickly, like the blink of an eye, the shock impacted me. I, too, had become shocked by the incident and numbed as I rode on in a state of surrealism. The sweat and tears washed over my face until I could no longer ride. I stopped and poured out my shock to JJ through some texts. She tried to calm me down, but I was too far gone. I have seen many dead animals on the road: snakes, turtles, wild boars, coyotes, possums, armadillos, carrions, and so many others. Never have I seen one that was living one moment and dead the next in my arms. Much later, maybe three hours had passed. I saw a truck with an open trailer pass by with the animal in it.

Twelve hours later, having reached the motel in Culpeper, in utter exhaustion, I poured out my emotions to JJ again. It helped, and after a shower, I fell asleep. Only an hour had passed, but it seemed like I had a full night's rest. I stayed up; the image of the day played on my mind. Light flashes made me open the door; thunder and lightning raged in a downpour.

Chapter 25: The Appalachians

It's fascinating to observe how our world has a constant duality. There is night and day. The nocturnal world and those of us in the sunlight of the day. The plants we eat from below and above ground. This idea of good and evil shifts through in our imagination; we are the only animal on the planet always pushing the boundary while every living thing is busy being themselves. We party all night, illuminating the planet with artificial light—people working night shifts and living the wonder of life after dark.

It was daylight; I had left the TV on all night after feeling exhausted. The news was on; a woman in black was walking in the US and had completed a thousand miles. She was getting tremendous responses from everyone as she went on her journey. She didn't speak to anyone. She was like a mysterious figure, walking in silence, mourning, into the unknown. What is the unknown? It is the steps outside our boundary. A personal journey into the landmass she may have decided upon. In doing so, she traversed an inner journey into an area of darkness, hoping to find a path, her light.

It's an odyssey that goes further than the limits of our existential experience. To go beyond what we think we can reach until we arrive at a point where we can no longer go on. Then, to push on some more. If we fall short, it would not be a failure because, along the way, huge discoveries would have been made. An inner revolution would have taken place where many aspects of fear would no longer find a place to hide. It forces us to reevaluate the whole philosophy of our lives. It illuminates us to reject many notions of our culture, which we had aspired to through our conditioning. We understand how to re-draw the frontier we wish to continue to live by in our remaining years. It makes us look at the duality in our inner and outer layers. It makes us understand that no matter how convincing and elaborate the singularity of an idea may be, there will always be an alternative to that singularity.

It had been a hard trek from Fredericksburg to Culpeper. Michael and Steve drove for two hours to pick me up from a motel on the outskirts of town in the middle of nowhere. They hadn't had breakfast, but we couldn't find a place to eat all along the way to Mount Jackson. Steve needed to return as he was camping with his son and grandsons. The ridges to Mount Jackson were phenomenal. It would have been outrageous to have made it to their place. Every descent faced an uphill like a fun park big dipper. Our vehicle drove like a pendulum to their house.

Still without breakfast, as soon as we reached base, we helped Steve load up for his four-day camping trip. Steve was Michael's older brother. Michael wanted a change in his life, and Steve invited him to stay in the Shenandoah Valley. Michael had only moved in from Philadelphia the week before.

He vacated his room for me and slept in Steve's. It was a modest, calm house with a large garden full of wildlife running around munching on the planted vegetables. Steve harvested many vegetables before he went.

"You guys had better use them."

We had squash, spaghetti squash, tomatoes, zucchini, eggplants, beans, and others to eat. One of the neighbours came to say hello out of curiosity and brought honeydew melon for us. All that was missing was wine, and we bought plenty.

On the house's front porch, while drinking our wine that afternoon, we faced the panoramic view of the Appalachian Mountains in the distance. We could see the Blue Mountains, farmland, farm animals, forests, and birds. They descended in flocks of a thousand and took turns to feed on flies hovering on cows' dung. As vehicles passed, the people in them waved - just locals living nearby curious at two new faces in the neighbourhood. As the sun set, it became slightly larger, with the red/orange disc painting the sky with varied hues. I counted many shades - from red to dark grey as the sun plunged beyond the mountains. The swifts swooped low in the twilight, feeding on insects with precision and diving to their targets. Fireflies or will-o'-the-wisp illuminated in darkness in waves - specks of incandescent. "This is God's country," Steve had said before leaving. As Mark Twain might have said, God created Shenandoah Valley first, then paradise.

It was holiday time, as though Michael and I were on vacation in the Appalachian sipping on glasses of red wine and prosecco. We told each other stories of excitement, intrigue, and romance. Tales told many times over the years. Except once more, we repeated them with a new freshness, more polished, as we've become more mature. He prompted me and egged me on. Likewise, I did the same. We cooked and ate and drank some more until it was early morning. In that single evening, both Michael and I were like long-lost brothers. We clicked on most levels. He was pleasant and polite with a very dry sense of humour. He was finding his feet in a new location. He had lived his life in Philadelphia. He wanted to see whether he could settle high up in Patsy Cline's country.

All his life, he had been a city man. Like many of us, marriage hadn't worked out, and he had a grown-up daughter and son. I wondered how he would fare moving from the city to the countryside.

"I'll try it for a year and see how it pans out. I plan to move my work here soon. I'll move back if it doesn't work out,"

He could conduct his business on the phone and via the computer. He had a modern outlook on everything. He was not standing still, and he had other projects in mind that might help him settle in his new locality. In the afternoons, he rode his 1100cc Harley Davidson motorcycle and encouraged Steve to buy one too. For Steve, it was as if he had discovered new wings and was elated by his 750cc Honda.

We both went to Harrisonburg, a university town with plenty to do. It has a mixture of old and new architecture, which blends in well. We shopped for food and wine and did a business transaction. We had a document validated by a Notary, which would have cost £100/$143 in England, but here, two dollars was the charge. We made discoveries in the town after spending time in a large bookshop. I bought JJ a birthday present, a Pablo

Neruda book of poems. After, we had lunch in a restaurant on the rooftop overlooking the city.

In the spur of the moment, Michael said, "I need someone in my life. I find it difficult to meet up with the right person. The people who go for me don't appeal, and those I'm attracted to are attached or don't see me."

"Have you tried online dating?"

"Ye, there is something weird and exact about it. They take your details and try to match you with people they think will suit your profile. It isn't very reassuring when you meet them. There is something very dishonest about the whole thing."

"I know of people who made out. A couple of friends of mine married the people they met online."

"Maybe they got lucky. Some people do. I haven't been that lucky."

"One of the best ways to meet people is through family acquaintances and friends."

"Ye, it's the best way to lose family and friends when things fall apart, right? I'm just procrastinating. People take sides and play the blame game. Kids get squeezed when pots and pans go flying against the walls. Squeezed between full-blown egos, a Sammy might end up as Salami."

"It sounds like you're speaking from experience?"

His eyes lit his deadpan features. As if there was no bitterness from his past, it had all been left behind. He was being ironic and funny with a straight face. I felt that part of his reason for moving in with Steve was loneliness.

I said, "You could travel to Mauritius and visit Jim O'Keeffe, our mutual relations. He would welcome you, and you would enjoy it there. It's refreshing to go far away from what you are used to. It gives you a different view of yourself and might bring out another you whom you didn't know was there. Who knows what might happen?

"All right, you've already made your first move from Philadelphia to here. See how you feel after your first year. You will be settled if you've found what you are looking for. If not, then places like Mauritius, Thailand, Indonesia, or Europe are all there for you. Everything is waiting. You need to make a move that first important step."

Steve returned after a few days camping and introduced me to his son and two grandsons – good-looking boys. They didn't stay long as they had a five-hour drive back to Philadelphia. They had already made a long journey to the house, and now this long drive was still ahead. Long distances to Americans don't seem a problem. It's routine, so unlike the way we think in Europe.

Steve likes to potter around and can't stay still for too long, except when he watches the news late in the evening. I can't recall seeing two brothers who get on so well together. Steve, for the past twenty years, has gained writing skills. He wants to start a writing class. He read me three of his stories, sitting on the front porch while Michael and I sipped our wine. The stories came over as insightful, impressive, and funny. He is already an accomplished writer.

Michael and Steve were generous people, and to trust a stranger like me and offer their hospitality was overwhelming. The whole community around Mount Jackson was like that. The picture I received was much more than friendliness. It was like a family of people living in proximity. They would come over to say hello or come to make an offering. People like Patsy and Curtis (brother and sister) live two doors away. They would bring cans of vegetables which they planted and have canned themselves. They cultivated their garden, ate, and sold their produce all their lives. This is how they've lived. Curtis was seventy and Patsy sixty-six, and they had a large garden to maintain. Where do they get their energies from seemed beyond belief? Patsy likes to chat and would appear at any time of the day. Everybody loves her in the neighbourhood. Both she and Curtis were brought up on a farm and have lived within a mile of where they were born.

Patsy Cline (the singer) was born not too far from there. The neighbour next door, Roger Miller (not the singer), and his wife came to say hello and chatted with us. Buck, a chicken farmer a quarter of a mile down the road, stopped to introduce himself. This was how it was: friendly, caring, and always ready to help. There was a vague remembrance in my childhood of the family entourage supporting each other. Sometimes, the neighbours did likewise.

People ate mostly meat, beef, pork, and chicken. The meat counter at the supermarket might be twenty-five metres long, while the fish would only be frozen. Two hundred yards away from the supermarket, a fishmonger called Will was doing a thriving business. Most of the land around this region was planted with corn to feed the animals, cattle, poultry, and pigs. Corn is also used to make syrup, oil, and food supplements.

I studied the map for a day and didn't know how to go. Steve went through the map with me. I wanted a route north towards Pennsylvania, New York State, Vermont, and then onto Maine.

"There is a beautiful route going north into Pennsylvania. You don't have to take the main highway. There is a parallel Highway 11 going in that direction. It won't be as busy. You can branch out later and take another route to where you wanna go."

"Are the roads flat along the way?"

"You are in a mountainous part of the country. It's full of ridges like the ones on the route when we picked you up in Culpeper. You might have to go a long way before getting a better route."

It was an experience being with Michael and Steve, two special people who decided, in the end, to take me to Delaware to catch a ferry to New Jersey. Negotiating those mountainous roads would have been the end of me. On our way, two accidents on the highway caused us delays of several hours. We changed our route and ended up in the Northwest of New Jersey. It was across from Philadelphia in a small town called Audubon. Michael's daughter Julia lives there with her husband and two children. It was pleasant to spend a couple of hours with them. They were both schoolteachers living a tranquil life in suburbia. As we left, we passed Cherry Hill, where Mohammed Ali once lived. The town was rich with magnificent houses, street cafés and pavements, just like in Europe.

Eventually, they dropped me at a motel. It took them seven hours to get back to their house. Michael and Steve must have been dead on their feet. I had offered to pay for them to stay the night in a motel, but they wanted to get back. I felt tired and redundant that day, stuck in numerous traffic jams, and sat in the car for long hours. They have two lovely dogs, one each, and they travelled with us.

Stuck in my motel room for two days. The rain lashed down. Everywhere looked bleak. The road outside was dangerous, with traffic speeding over puddles of water, jetting out streams onto the hard shoulder. There was nothing to see as though the grey clouds above had descended to the ground. It was like dense fog, reducing any visibility to fifty yards. I felt restless. I decided that whatever the weather was on the third day, I would be on the road. It rained in the morning. I was ready and made my way to Point Pleasant. It was a tough seventy-mile trek on a wet road surface drenched to the skin.

Chapter 26: On To New York

After 4,182 miles of trekking, I decided that this would be my final part of the journey by walking and bicycle. It was an emotional moment, but it hadn't all sunk in. The plan was to go to Maine and stay with friends from the Findhorn Circle. The journey hadn't ended; it had changed, this time by bus and train. I wrote on the blog, "I plan to keep writing, so please stay with me."

The original idea was to push on until Maine. While in the Shenandoah Valley with Michael and Steve, I pondered about ending my journey. The ridges near the Appalachian Mountains convinced me it would be hard to traverse the difficult, testing, undulating roads. We discussed an alternative route, hugging the coastline to Maine. Steve reassured me that keeping away from the major towns and cities still involved crossing some big towns and seven states. There wasn't any way to avoid countless ridges, and the distance of over eight hundred miles to my destination was close to a two-week trek. To take a wider arc to Maine was out of the question. The nearer we got to New Jersey, the heavier the traffic became. That was a crucial key to ending the journey. The traffic meant I couldn't cut through the cities and hug the coastline. It rained for two days, foul weather unless you were ducks. The sky didn't look like changing.

With nothing to do, I watched the changing sky to different shades of grey, from medium to dark to silver. The lightning was visible in the far distance, and a clapping of thunder would be overhead with a heavy downpour. Even when cleared, a heaviness hung with more to come. It was a bad time for holidaymakers, an awful time for motorists, and not great for a mad trekker on a bicycle with an orange trailer. In the motel near Cherry Hill, I became downhearted. I read, watched TV, wrote in my diary, and read more. I felt restless about losing contact with JJ due to the black spot. I became convinced I should end the journey, at least by bike/foot, once I reached Point Pleasant by sea.

After a ten-hour trek on a wet road, I arrived at Point Pleasant late. I made inquiries in several motels before finding one suitable for my budget. A young receptionist, Chelsea, helped and pointed me to an appropriate motel. As soon as I checked in, this overwhelming sensation came over me. Realising what I had been through on my trail brought numbness to all my senses. I recalled many months before and cruised from the eastern seaboard to Los Angeles. The thought after touchdown was that it was an impossible journey. The distance had seemed too big from the air. Anxiety had preoccupied me and all the people that I would let down. My first words were, "I can't do this trek; the distance is too vast." It took one thousand miles of trekking before I felt I might manage it. Before that, the thought of ending it lingered every hour and a day.

Those four thousand miles got the better of me in the motel lobby at Point Pleasant. The young woman at the desk tried to console me without knowing what was wrong. After doubts in California, I didn't allow myself the room to ponder on failure. I was too stubborn and determined even to contemplate not finishing.

In the evening, in the restaurant, a young woman, Jenifer, who waited on me, identified that I was not a local or American and became curious and asked me questions. London seemed much more interesting than Paris to everyone I met. In films in the fifties, the obsession was with Paris.

She asked, "Are you on a holiday trip to Point Pleasant?"

I gave her a brief account of the trek. She looked surprised. She took my order and walked away. The big restaurant was only a quarter full of only a couple of families sitting at the far end. It was a busy holiday area. The rain over the last two days must have shattered business everywhere. The background, with the moody music by Norah Jones, added to the ambience. As she walked away, her long, silky hair swayed to the rhythm from side to side with her tall, elegant frame. She could have been on a catwalk. She only had one other table to deal with and gave me all her attention. She wanted to know more about me, but I turned the conversation around and asked about her.

"I'm a second-year student at university doing literature." She was from New York and needed work to subsidise her studies.

"What do you want to do afterwards?"

"I haven't given it much thought. I can't project what the future will bring. For now, I want to finish my course first. I might travel a little and visit London."

She giggled at her suggestion. Her full lips concealed her teeth at first.

"Is marriage in your plan?"

She looked a little embarrassed by the question. She had a boyfriend for a couple of years, but it ended.

"We drifted. He had other ambitions."

She looked shy saying it.

"Was it upsetting?"

She paused for a while, assessing my intrusive question.

"Ye, not as much as I thought it would be. The university cushioned me. Friends there gave me support. It's been over a year, and my focus has changed. It helped a lot being involved in my studies."

She asked if I was married, and I said no. "Have you ever been hurt?"

That was a surprise, like a dose of castor oil on a Saturday morning or the first time in a dentist's chair. It was a fair question, on par with my probing. Perhaps she was searching for a comparison, an assessment of how others might cope. There was a sense that she was not over her breakup, though her mood did not show it. The ripple effect of such a happening goes deep into the memory cells. The past has a way of hurtling back and adhering to the present. The intensity of love can be brief, healing and forgetting long.

"Yes, I have been hurt, and I have hurt others too. In a long life, the passion of emotions can throw you off-balance if your feelings run deep. Logic and common sense go straight out of the window.

"We are all different, and everyone behaves according to their sensibilities. Sometimes, no one is to blame for the hurt. It happens, and feelings fade away from the complacency of everyday life. You wake with apathy for the person next to you. The love went AWOL, or something had vanished. The grieving and the hurt have to do with this loss. This trek was linked with such a loss."

"Do you still feel pained?"

"The trek helped me to find a cure. It's no longer raw like a flesh wound recently healed when pressed bears the residual pain. If she stood before me, I wouldn't know my reaction."

"It's how I feel. Sometimes, I think I have let it all go. I try not to think about it. But on some days, it comes back. I lock myself in my room,"

"Don't do that. Better to walk it off. Keep walking until you are out of the mood."

She laughed and said, "Just like you."

Later, when I asked for the bill – Jennifer went away and took a long time coming.

When she returned, she said, "It's on the house. It's a compliment from the chef and all of us."

I gave her a tip, the cost of the meal and the wine.

The next day, I said goodbye to my bike and trailer, for they had served me well. I donated them to a church that served meals in the area and provided a service to the needy of the community. "The bike and trailer will come in handy," someone had said. As I walked away to the train station, for the first time in months, I felt unattached and numb. To grieve for a couple of pieces of machinery seemed absurd. I couldn't help it, for they had been my companions, all that I possessed, my world. Even with my rucksack, I felt naked and light-headed, like a death had occurred.

Kim, working for the church, was helpful. She wrote on my blog, "I just wanted to let you know that your bike went to someone that day who had a real need. So happy to have met you. Learning more about you after the fact, I am sorry that there was not more of a celebration of your accomplishment when you came in. Glad to have met you."

Within an hour, I was on the train to New York. As the train moved from town to town and village to village, it surprised me to see what huge forests still filled the landscape. I had spent a long time walking and bicycling, taking the essence of everything around me and being part of it. The speed of the train changed my perspective of the land. The trees sped by the details became blurred. It was like an unfolding tableau of printed colourful pages passing on a conveyor belt with no end. There was no sound of animal life, no smell of the open air. Instead, the sounds were the jabbering of a congregation in a confined space. The background noise of the hum of the locomotive echoed as sen-surround. For a while, everything was alien. How quickly this change in me occurred. It filled me with the sensation of being a child again, travelling for the first time on a train, not knowing where I was going. A sense of being innocent and pure without complications and seeing the world as big outside for the first time.

There was a strong feeling spinning inside. Manhattan promised to be a surprise. I have seen many photos, documentaries, and films of the city and suspected that being there would excite me. The place immediately impacted me when I came out of the train station on 8th Street (or was it 42nd Street?). I was brought up in the city. One of the greatest on the planet, I love cities much more than the countryside. I had yearned for the buzz, the hustle, the bustle, the pollution, and the proximity of everything one would need. I had missed the sheer volume of the geometric abstract creation of concrete in architectural ventures. Manhattan impacted, overwhelmed me, and made me small with all the magnificence of its grandeur. The diversity of the human faces seemed to have converged on the city. There exists every human feature of the planet on that small island. How incredible that this island should be a small window into our big world.

There was little time for transit. The bus to Boston was leaving at five that afternoon. I arrived at the gate early to check on the tickets' availability. My luck was in, together with a man from Jamaica, well dressed in a dark grey suit.

The driver said, "I have two spare tickets for seats at three o'clock. Do you want them?"

We jumped at the chance. The Jamaican was heading to Canada and spent most of his time on the telephone conducting business in a low voice. I sat near Raphael, who was from Brazil, and we chatted. He was from São Paulo, holidaying on his own. His wife was seven months pregnant, and he said: "This would be my last chance to travel alone." He took advantage as his wife agreed for him to spread his wings for the last time before family life took over. Unlike his brothers and sisters, he said, "By twenty, I had left home and gone into the interior of Brazil near the Amazon River."

He worked there for three years on the effects of deforestation. When a new job came up, he rushed back to São Paulo. Initially, the work in the Amazon region suited him, but "I became isolated, so I took the first job I saw and got lucky." But he didn't elaborate on why he felt isolated. He now works for a prestigious company that pays him well. His English was fluent, and he also spoke Spanish. He planned to stay with his wife's cousin in Boston for a week before returning to Brazil. "Paris, London, and Madrid were enjoyable cities, but 'Barcelona' was the city I enjoyed most. I liked the atmosphere, the architecture of Gaudy, the cathedral, the street cafés, and the long promenade." He forgot about the soccer team, and I didn't push him.

The vibration of the bus sent most people into dreamland, Raphael included. In this silence, except for the background hum of the engine, the bus appeared overcrowded. Bags were scattered everywhere in the aisle and the overhead rack. It was claustrophobic, nauseating even. I closed my eyes to block out this annoyance. And pictured alone in an open space in the desert, mountains, or forest. Throughout these months, I screamed so loud that my echo could be heard tailing off three or four times. For days on end, I would drift into this great hush and feel liberated, unassailable.

When I woke up, the bus had reached the outskirts of Boston. It was early evening, and I wanted to get to Boothbay Harbor, Maine. I needed another bus to Portland and one more to Wiscasset. There, I would meet Robert Blakesley, my host. I enquired about staying in Boston for the night, and the woman at the information office said hotels in Boston were costly. A quick inquiry told me that a bus was leaving for Portland within thirty minutes. I booked a ticket, and the man at the counter said hotels were right opposite the bus station in Boothbay, and the price was reasonable. We left at a quarter past eight. I sat near Rosemary.

She was a charming person in her fifties, easy to get along with, confident, and unassuming. She had been a counsellor for disturbed children and became a lawyer in the same field. She had recently retired but was still involved in a certain capacity. Each other's life stories stimulated us, and the two-hour ride seemed to pass quickly. Her husband was due to pick her up at the station. He was waiting, and he introduced himself as Allan. They said they would give me a lift to the nearest motel, but first, I needed to find the bus schedule for the next day to Wiscasset. They waited, and when I returned, they said, "Why don't you stay with us tonight? We have a nice bed and some wine, and we can drop you off tomorrow." How could I refuse? Allan was a lawyer, too, in the fieldwork of company policies. While he opened a bottle of white wine, Rosemary prepared a substantial salad for the two of us. Their Alsatian dog took to me.

Rosemary said, "He has never taken to a stranger before."

It was late, and we all had had a long day. My room was grand, with a bed fit for an emperor. In the morning, Rex, the dog, shuffled around me, and Rosemary said, "He is protecting you against us." We all left early as they had to go to work, which gave me a chance to visit downtown Portland, and then they promised to drop me at the bus station at noon.

I had three hours to kill and knew nothing of Portland. The few hours gave me a small glimpse of the place. As its name suggested, it was a pleasant city by the sea, an old port. All the old warehouses were now converted into offices, cafés, and flats. People here differed from the rest of the US in their mannerisms, accents, and size as they looked slimmer and fitter. They had a broader interest in the form of their civic buildings. Their extensive library, art galleries, and the little shops which no longer exist in other parts of the US. And the street cafés and pavements just as in Europe.

Downtown was a mixture of old and new, well-organised and spruce-clean. Back in Yorkshire, England, my vegan friend Lynn Van Dyke wrote on my blog, "Portland has the highest number of vegans in the USA."

I sat in an outside café near a pristine square and sipped an espresso. A homeless man in rags, looking wretched, came to me. He couldn't have been more than forty but looked a lifetime older than his age. His hazel eyes were glassy, long matted salt and pepper hair sported a full beard like a weaver bird's nest that may support more life than it was meant to. His skin was ash grey, leathery, and wrinkled. He didn't speak; he lifted his hand with some effort not quite to his mouth, suggesting he wanted a cigarette. His hands were yellowish-brown with black tip fingernails. I said nothing, just hand signalled no cigarettes. He stood there and stared at me, motionless, lost in the calculation of thoughts circulating in the Hadron's collider of his brain. I tapped my cup of coffee to suggest if he wanted a drink, but there was no response. I asked him if he wanted a coffee. He only stared at me, a void look, like a statue. An anachronism of the landscape of downtown, the missing piece in one of Jack Vettriano's sleek canvases. The waiter came out to hush him away.

I said, "Ask him if he wants a sandwich."

"It's bad business seeing him hustling customers."

"He is no bother; ask him."

"He smells like a dead rat."

I hadn't noticed his stench; he was a few yards from me. I paid the bill and asked him to follow me. I had him walking behind me. He carried this putrid smell of a rotting corpse, lumbering. At any time, he could have fallen and spelt the end. I bought him a packet of cigarettes and put it in his hand. His palm was wrinkled, black, caked with dirt and sores between his fingers, alien forms eating at his skin and flesh. I moved away from the threshold of his odour as it involuntarily entered my nostrils. He looked at me with those glassy eyes, staring into emptiness, and said nothing.

"Smoke," I said, mimicking the act of smoking.

It then occurred to me that he didn't have matches. I bought him a lighter and left.

Back in the café on my second double espresso, I pondered how he got to sink so low. What disruption in his childhood put him on this collision course into adulthood? Could it have been a breakdown in his marriage or relationship? Maybe he was uneducated, and work would have been his only goal: salvation. When he couldn't find work, he became depressed. There were stories told to me on this trek during the recent Stock Market crash; unemployment rose to a high. Many lost their homes, jobs, or life savings without medical insurance coverage. Families were living in small caravans, on patches of land, and hunting possums, squirrels, or whatever they found in the woods to feed their families and survive. Josh, whom I met on the bus to Phoenix, Arizona, was returning to Kentucky because the work had dried up in California. He said he would hunt wild game for meat, and there would always be food on the table and a place to sleep at home. He was lucky because he had a room in his parents' house.

This man in Portland had fallen out of society's tribal mindset and was viewed as an outcast. Perhaps the pressures of responsibility for a job, home life, and what was expected of him proved too overwhelming. Perhaps he was like the Chinese student during the final university examination who screamed the loudest cries of desperation, saw everything as a blank on the exam papers, and broke down instantly. Pressure to achieve and the failure that goes with it can be a factor that sends one on a road of no return. There was a possibility he was a war veteran who, on the front line, survived and came home but lost the last battle to readjustment.

When asked why I took on such a daunting journey across America from coast to coast, the answer hadn't been easy. But I took it for granted that it was a continuity of the walk of Santiago de Compostela, and I was doing it for charities. There was another reason I hadn't been myself. My three-year relationship had broken down the same week of my mother's death, and all the plans to move to France went down. Perhaps I had been blind and hadn't seen the breakdown coming. It came as a sudden shock, just a telephone call that said, "I needed time to reconsider." I knew it was over; even her voice's vibration spelt it. Something broke inside me, and I felt touched by darkness. A void of such enormity descended in overwhelming pain that my belly and chest felt like they were about to implode.

Five months later, I was on the road in the desert of California, utterly unprepared for what was ahead of me. It's only now, through my state of hypersensitivity, after all the miles, that I realise; it was an attempt at a slow suicide. Who would have ventured into a desert and the Rockies from California, Arizona, New Mexico, and West Texas without looking and trying to measure what the landscape entailed? Death came sniffing too often. It is through luck that the journey remade me whole. It gave me a deeper understanding of where I had been and how to tap into the balance of my being.

The man near the café in Portland opposite the square perhaps started on the same footing as me. Perhaps he, too, travelled through a long voyage. We had the stars at night as our private gallery, the greater outdoors, and the elements as our blanket. Neither of us knew how it would all end. We happened from a different direction, that was all.

When it was time to leave, Rosemary and Allan came to pick me up at the place we had arranged down by the pier at the water's edge. They were on time, hugged me goodbye and bid me a safe voyage.

Rosemary said, "I read your blog briefly when I got to work this morning. It has been a pleasure and a privilege meeting you. Will you keep on writing?"

"Yes, and I shall mention you and the kindness you've offered me. That will stay with me."

As I waved to them at the bus station, I sensed that my luck was still holding.

Chapter 27: Moving on up to Maine

An hour later, Robert picked me up at the bus terminal. We drove to their beautiful home in Bayville by the sea in Maine. I stayed with Alina and Robert for five days, and they gave me five-star treatments, allowing me to put my feet up, relax, and enjoy the moment.

I knew that Alina and Robert would be an interesting couple. I sensed that in their emails long before I ended my journey. On this long trek, your sensitivity heightens, and each sentence, every word, and space between the lines hints at you and pierces your sensibilities from a distance.

At first, I had intended to go to Silvia further north in Camden, Maine. Silvia had been ill, and her situation at home was complicated. She thought it would be better if I stayed with Alina and Robert. Silvia and I exchanged many emails about travel writing with people who went on long journeys. When I arrived in Mississippi, the book, 'Tracks' by Robyn Davidson, a present from her, was waiting for me at Michael and Belinda's house. I needed the boost and wanted to get in the mindset/emotional centre of someone who had to embark on a long journey where all the resources of an entire being were called for to remain constant and focused. I was raw.

No matter how much one prepares, the journey can defeat all planning. It tests the preparation and constantly challenges willpower. At any moment, one could be tested, be it the terrain, the weather, a miscalculation, a burst tyre, or a threat by an animal or an individual. I learned of the dangers as I was going along. Davidson reaffirmed all my discoveries and gave me that extra reassurance to push on, knowing that I was on my path to this 'edge identity', to a deeper understanding of myself. Silvia also introduced me to other writers and sent me a reading list and sites that might interest me, always focusing on the inner/outer journey. She has inspired my writing, feeding me with many writers' various quotes and thoughts.

Robert took me to see Silvia twice. We drank wine, ate, talked, and touched on many subjects. It was very important for me to connect with her. I had never met Silvia, Robert, or Alina in person before. I knew it would be easy to connect with all of them, and I bonded with Silvia like we were friends for many decades.

It was with Alina and Robert as it was with Silvia. I felt relaxed at their home. When Robert picked me up at the bus station in Wiscasset, he gave me a warm hug. It was my birthday, the 5th of August, and so was the next day, the sixth. I am lucky to have two birthdays. (In the old colonial days in Mauritius, if one were born on the 6th like me, they would officially register you on the fifth. I never found out why). We celebrated with wine and food and long chats that evening. They treated me as a VIP with their hospitality, kindness, and exquisite room. Their two dogs, Jacques and Brendan, took to me.

Their garden was manicured beautifully by Alina. Robert told me he only cuts the grass. A huge variety of plants adorn the garden in a plethora of flowers.

Their beautiful house in Boothbay Harbour

The porch was L-shaped at the front and side of the house. It was furnished as an outside living room with flowers, glass hanging decanter feeders, and sugar water for hummingbirds. On the opposite side, hung bird feeders with sunflower seeds for goldfinches, chickadees, and many varieties of birds. Squirrels and chipmunks danced about in the garden. The view from the porch was tall pines, oaks in the foreground, and the sea as the backdrop for two descending minutes' walk away into Linekin Bay. We ate and drank, and if we were lucky, as we had been, we watched the full supermoon rise over the ocean in its beauty. It sent a zigzag luminous light along the rippling water.

On that first evening, Alina told me I would get a reflexology massage at eleven the following day for my birthday gift.

On the way to her surgery, Robert said, "It had been difficult for Alina to settle in the US after we moved here from Scotland. We met in the Findhorn community centre. She took a long time to find her feet – years. Her British qualifications were not valid, and she had to re-qualify. Now she owns the property where she works. She rents the rest of the building to three separate businesses. As you know, she loves gardening. Here, she grows organic vegetables," pointing to the ground where she works. Robert was American, and Alina was English.

Entering her workspace was like entering a meditative chamber. The music was relaxing, I sat in a reclining chair. At the bottom was a mini-jacuzzi for the feet, warming and cleansing them for a few minutes as part of the preparation. Afterwards, with my feet resting on a padded footstool, she began working my left foot first with lavender oil and foot cream. It was an exhilarating experience. She concentrated for half an hour on each foot and, when she had finished one, moved to the other; it seemed she was massaging both simultaneously. A transforming impact occurred, putting me into a meditative mood, and then an emotional outpouring came. It came out of nowhere and I did not understand why this should have happened.

I asked her, "Does this happen to other clients?"

"Quite often, a few feel embarrassed with their reaction. Others feel liberated and at ease. Some people don't know how to let go. They might have work-related stress or be affected by ailments. Many people come to me because they can't walk and have tried other forms of therapy that didn't work. What I do must work; otherwise, they wouldn't keep coming back for more."

I have done a reflexology course, but Alina was beyond anything I had ever experienced.

It was to be the start of my winding down. I knew that the endorphins were wearing out. I became wary that I would lose all the momentum, which kept me in a heightened state for months. Three days' rest was the maximum I would typically allow myself. (Mississippi was an exception – doctor's orders and to a lesser extent during the time on Jekyll Island when I reached the ocean in Georgia). It was a period that held me in a state of euphoria. There was an incident after finishing the Camino de Santiago, the winding down period had been dramatic – I sobbed like a child one night for no apparent reason. The Camino pilgrimage gave me a lifetime of bonding with others and mutual exchanges of experience. Somehow, people felt disarmed, and their long-held hang-ups evaporated into this elevated energy flow. On the Camino, Marie Josephe told me that she noticed how the French middle class befriended me and spoke openly, which was unusual. This journey from ocean to ocean and beyond has been different. It has been a lone and private affair, with no sharing of meals at the day's end and no bonding with anyone (apart from the people I met and lodged with and with JJ). No stories to tell or listen to and laugh at.

***

The little seaside village of Bayville, where I found myself, was too relaxing to maintain my 'on the road' momentum. We talked about the journey across America and that of the Camino, and Alina got hooked. We drank wine almost every evening. Alina cooked, and then I cooked a couple of times, Mauritian style, which they both liked and took second helpings. Alina was active and organised. On a typical daily routine, she would wake up at five, run or paddle her canoe, swim, and meditate by the sea. When she got back, she would get herself ready, groom for work, have breakfast, prepare her packed lunch, and get to work by nine. When she finished her day's work, the morning ritual was repeated, and if the wind were good, she would go sailing. It was the winding down period for her that helped her to relax. She plays the accordion and practices as much as she can, and does ballroom dancing once a week. Besides everything, she keeps a clean house and a terrific garden. She has a positive outlook on life, which keeps her young-looking and attractive. (Much later, she wrote to me and said she planned to do the Camino in the spring of the following year).

While Alina was at work, Robert and I talked a lot. We are both raconteurs; he would ask questions and read much of what I wrote on the blog, and I showed him some of my poems, too. He gave me a lot of encouraging feedback.

Robert & Alina in Maine my hosts.

Our conversation drifted to the people I met on the journey. I mentioned that I met JJ, and he wanted to know what she looked like. I showed him a photograph and he said, "She looks like an angel fallen from the sky." At that very moment, I received a text from JJ which said, "Your text messages muddled my brains yesterday. I couldn't think straight for an hour. You are timeless."

We talked about his past, from childhood to the present. He was an open person, calm and intelligent. He has been on a lifelong journey, searching and dealing with grief and regret, but this has led him to fundamental discoveries about himself and the immediate world around him.

Sometimes, it takes more than courage to change one's life. To take a leap of formidable defiance, go against the grain of all teachings and conditioning, and move on. Then, tap into an implicit memory of childhood innocence without knowing where that will lead. In doing so, people close to their hearts might feel hurt, leaving a burden of emptiness behind. The fallout could devastate for years. This Earth can be a magnet of incredible power. If it draws one forth and infiltrates the vital boundary of one being, then the universal energy and imagination become one, and the leap forward becomes effortless. Robert took such a leap, took a chance on life, and walked 'naked' as though he was reborn by reinventing himself. "You change it, or it will change you into a mask of yourself." He no longer wanted to wear the mask. Robert has written a book where he reveals all and it is told with such panache that it reads like a novel yet written in an easy form of blank verse. Each page is like a story, and every story is connected. The book is titled, 'Eveningtime, A Personal Journey' by Robert G. Blakesley.

We connected with little effort, and we would walk the dogs on the old tribal trails of the Abenaki, Wawenecks, Passamaquoddy, or Wabanaki Indians. We never found out which tribes lived in the area. The trails were in the forest, surrounded by the sea and the lakes around the area. Robert would take the dogs twice daily for long walks, part of his exercise to keep fit. He is getting on now, and his recent illness took it out of him, and it has taken him a long time to return to a good fitness level. I wrote about his illness on my blog. Still, he later commented, "One correction: I've had health ups and downs and issues, like prostate cancer and your diabetes, going along with reaching eighty-two, but not anything I would call an illness per se". He swims when he can if the water is not too fresh and goes sailing and canoeing. He likes reading and writing, and at that moment, he was in that space between finishing one book and finding the material for another.

He made peace with himself and his family after spending a few years in the Findhorn community in Scotland. This world is never enough as we all get a day older. If we are deep thinkers and prod for answers, our inner self will yearn for the next jigsaw piece to fit into our questioning. There will always be one blank space for us to question, more of whys.

After we had spent six good days together, he accompanied me to the bus station in Wiscasset, chatting, listening, laughing, eating, and drinking. I wished it could have been more. We all needed to get on with our own life's journeys. The bus was delayed for forty-five minutes, and we got talking to a young woman named Hannah, twenty-six of Ethiopian parentage, born in the USA. Robert told her of my trek across America while I was trying to buy an extension to my ticket at the cashier's window. She was going to Boston and on to New York like me. Robert suspected that we would sit beside each other, and he was right.

A single sunflower shadowed Robert from where he was standing. His face gleamed; Hannah's spark must have radiated him. He stood, waited, and waved at us with a big smile until the bus departed. The bus movements made me think of rebelling against the inevitable winding down, for New York was my destination, then back to London. Going back to where? It wouldn't be the same. There would never be a return. We can't return to where we've been. It is no longer there. I knew that. The movement is always forward. It is the way of the universe. At school, we were taught that everything was in perpetual motion. This idea of perpetual motion puts me back on an even keel. I was not going back; I was on a journey that would last the day. And when I wake up, it will continue until the next day, only to go on and on and finally to just go.

Chapter 28: Manhattan and on to London

On our way to Boston, Hannah and I chatted. She asked many questions. I switched on my tablet, and she looked at my blog and read a few articles. She paused after reading some and asked me why I had made this journey. It was clear before the journey had started that it was a continuation of the Camino de Santiago, but now that doesn't appear to be the real reason, just a part of it. I hadn't yet comprehended why I took the big plunge into this venture. That came later. I became hesitant with my answers because I had no clear vision of why. To switch the focus to her, I asked her why she was going to NY.

"I was born in Seattle and moved to NY with my boyfriend, who is a teacher. We both wanted to live in a more diverse community."

She now lives in Brooklyn and studies Community Relations at the university. She reminded me of Ama, a friend's daughter back in England. They could have been twin sisters. Later, I showed her photos of Ama on her Facebook. She looked shocked and repeated, "Oh my god, oh my god," as her eyes moistened as though she had seen a long-lost sister appearing like magic. The resemblance surprised her, her hairstyle, posture, features, and the elegance of her clothing.

Has she ever been out of the States?

"I spent a year in Cape Town, South Africa, working within a community relations organisation, helping to heal the rift which occurred during the long years of Apartheid."

She then told me of a horrific story during one demonstration in the immediate post-apartheid period.

"Two young American women working for the Community Relations (C.R) were dragged out of their car and killed. Later, they found the leaders of the demonstration killed them. They brought them to justice and were now serving prison sentences. But the healing process goes on, and the C. R Organisation brought the parents of those girls over and explained to them the context in which their daughters were killed. It took three years of effort for those parents to face the killers of their loved ones. The killers begged for forgiveness. The parents said they would never have been able to face those men without the C. R Organisation's help. They could close one door in the chapter of their girls' lives. Nelson Mandela wished to heal the nation through forgiveness rather than revenge. That was why I went there, to learn how it's done and to repeat the process here in the USA."

In Boston, we bought new tickets for New York with little time to spare. She purchased our tickets on her phone and refused to take my share of the cost. I insisted and gave her my fare. While I looked after our bags, she rushed and bought us a pizza each. On our way to NY, we chatted and drank some wine she had with her. She explained how to get to my hostel, Hosteling International USA – New York, in midtown Manhattan. We walked to the point where her boyfriend was meeting her, and we said goodbye. She said she would have liked to invite me to stay with them for a day or two, but the flat was too small.

I went to the subway and followed her directions, and I was in my room in the hostel by seven-thirty that evening. There were six of us in a room: two from England, two from the USA – Midwest and North California, and Marco from Italy, but lives in Barcelona. I had tried to book a hotel, and after three hours of trying on the previous day, I gave up. The prices were unaffordable, or the hotels were full. As it was, they charged $75 per night for the hostel. The dormitories were spacious and clean, with lockers. The building was huge; from the outside, it looked like a grand hotel. It had a very large garden with tables and chairs to relax and eat if you wished. There was a canteen, a dining/breakfast room, a computer room, and two substantial recreation rooms with pool tables. There was also a theatre room with a large screen for films and a kitchen in the basement with cooking facilities. Young people worldwide stayed there—a natural thoroughfare near Central Park and easy to go downtown.

Marco was the only one in the room when I arrived, and he had been out for the day and had a book full of tickets for his tourist trail. I didn't want that. I had only two days to spare, and besides, I prefer to tumble my way to discoveries rather than be part of the tourist herd. He was planning to see the lights on top of the Empire State Building, which he told me was one hundred and twenty-three stories high. I journeyed the whole day and wanted to be in a 'local' bar for the evening.

Later, on his way to his night-time adventure, we slipped into a bar and had a drink together, a lively bar. It was like being in England again. Walking along the road, I felt like I was in London.

Marco was twenty-six, a fine-looking man, the same height as me. He was in the second year of his PhD researching Biophysics – Photosynthesis in Photophosphorylation. He explained it to me, and I understood it then, but I had better not let it fall into fragments on these pages. He planned to see the Statue of Liberty the next day and on to other things. Monuments have never appealed to me. What interests me in any 'new city' are the way people go about doing their work, living their lives, the way they dress, and their mannerisms. I like to sit and watch the movement on the streets. My interests are to explore the city's hidden corners, the buildings' different shapes, and the volume and sheer mass of human ingenuity. In Manhattan, these buildings had a Gothic subliminal presence, overwhelming every space and corner.

I walked the day lost through the streets and allowed myself to be indoctrinated by the visual mass. I started in the Cathedral of St. John the Divine as it was near the hostel. Both Michael and Silvia had urged me to visit it. It had an exhibition on display by the Chinese artist Xu Bing suspended from the great height of the Cathedral. It is composed of two Phoenix, each weighing six tons and one hundred feet long, made from materials gathered in Beijing from the rubbish and debris of construction sites. In a way, they are fitting reminders of its symbolism of revival and renewal. The birds were made with great artistry and were full of texture and all shapes, sizes, and materials. The Phoenix symbolises rebirth and resurrection in most cultures. But in China, it didn't die and rise again but was immortal. Although these sculptures were monumental, they didn't take away the splendour of the cathedral. The monument was in the Gothic Revival of medieval European cathedrals. Its two wings were yet to be completed, even though the construction started in 1892. The cathedral didn't look like a cross from an elevated viewpoint.

I spent the rest of my day in the open spaces of Manhattan, dwarfed by the buildings. This is how I came to see Manhattan: people walking about in a city that had once belonged to 'giants.' The long walk took me to Times Square. Then, I walked back to my hostel in the late afternoon. I decided that two days were insufficient to visit such a place. I would scan the city and come back for a longer period another time. Perhaps I could spend more time in art galleries, museums, and other places in winter. When I returned to the hostel, I found that we had new visitors in the room: John, a Chinese fellow, and Allan from Aberdeen.

Allan didn't have a Scottish accent; he said his father was English and had lived in Alaska for ten years, but he didn't have an American twirl either. He looked young, around twenty-three years old. In the evening, Allan, Marco, and I went out for a meal and a drink at the Dead Poets bar on Amsterdam Avenue, heading towards downtown. I had my first two pints of Guinness since I arrived here. It didn't have the same flavour as in England or Ireland, and soon, we chatted with four young women celebrating a birthday.

Marco didn't return until two in the morning after his tourist excursion. We spent the day together the following day and walked Central Park. He took photos, and we had lunch in a posh restaurant in the park with live jazz music in the background. I said, "Aren't we two lucky people," he laughed. He was heading towards Washington to see more monuments that afternoon and flew back to Barcelona three days later. We travelled together on the subway, and I got off and headed to JFK airport late in the afternoon. My plane was not due until nine-thirty that evening but was delayed for two hours. Eventually, when it took off and in mid-air, I could see all the magnificent lights of New York, much better than the view from the Empire State Building Marco had described.

It was strange being back in London. I was no longer myself. While on the underground train from the airport, I missed being on the road. The continuity of not knowing what to expect at every turn, each day. Out of Chancery Lane station, I emerged into the city's brightness. It was near lunchtime, and the street cafés and shops were busy. Danny Burton greeted me with a beaming smile, busy at his fruit stall.

His friendliness with the people he served, his chatty personality and his affectionate smile exuded calm and typified the spirit of London life. Being near him for a few minutes reminded me of the familiarity of home.

"Where have you been? I ain't seen you for a long time," he asked.

The lunch hour queue of ten or more customers kept him on the go.

"I'll speak to you later when you are less busy."

Epilogue: The Enigma of Homecoming

In those months of self–imposed exile, I was able to understand my inner state of being. I had moved out of my comfort zone, out of myself, and looked for an extension. I discovered part of me that I did not know existed on the road. Fresh discoveries emerged every day for seven months, and I walked and pedalled into the unknown. Old conditioning and outdated ideas poured out of me, and new findings filtered in. My newness was jumbled up, and there was no order, pattern, or clear vision of what they were. My arrival in London, my place of familiarity, rather than settled me, added further to the extension of my unfamiliar self.

I adjusted to the daily change and now had to get used to a day-to-day routine. I was unsure whether I wanted to return to living in that order. It was comforting, safe, and travel through fluidly, a knowledgeable haven. But there was no edge to it, no untested everyday factor for 'breakfast' that would whet the appetite or give you indigestion. The adrenaline flow and the expectation of being 'free' was missing. My body was here, walking the streets of London, but my mind and emotions were still in mid-ocean or in a flashback state. The knowledge that it would be practically impossible to escape familiarity. Even on the road, it was a daily routine, but with a difference. It was that variation that was difficult to keep a hold of—the contrast of the day's unpredictability.

London was my domain, a beautiful city, and it was part of me. Somehow, during all my travels worldwide, only Manhattan matched up to it. I felt equally comfortable in either metropolis. After my arrival, being here was like swallowing the 'hair of the dog'. I decided to travel again and took a little break in unfamiliar surroundings. Within a week, I went off to Spain to walk, think and swim in the waters of Middle Earth. I knew it wouldn't change my feelings or alter my inner space. However, I aimed to put myself in a better frame of mind to decide how to push on to my next stage. I left London in a blaze of sunshine and felt spring in the air in the late August summer. I wanted to plunge myself into the September heat coming from the Sahara. I felt good without fully being myself.

Back in London two weeks later, I couldn't imagine a standstill. The following day, I visited my daughters in Scotland for a week. I booked a ticket to Italy while there and felt deflated when I returned. A couple of friends, Klaus Löbach and Vladimir Vdovic, and I had met on the Camino de Santiago three years before suggesting doing half the Camino in late November of that year. I couldn't wait to get back on track. The walk in the cold December brought clarity to my mind. I knew I would have to bite hard at something to put me back in the centre.

In the New Year, I locked myself in my small flat and wrestled between the walls for three months, pondering whether I had the energy to write about the journey. I started walking ten miles per day and, by May, flew to Spain again, putting pieces of writing together. In July, I escaped to Italy for six weeks and healed myself under the hot sun. When I returned in late August, I realised it had been a year since I ended the journey. Sea Ryder in

Mississippi also took a year to find her own space, her equilibrium. I came to understand that the journey was unending. I had begun on an odyssey, this time set between four walls through the imagination that may go on and then some more.

During that time of feeling unsettled, JJ and I kept in contact through emails. Then, by the end of April, the correspondence had faded out. When I returned from Italy at the end of August a year later, I received a one-line email – "Can you still see me." I looked for a photograph attachment, but there was none. Minutes later, I realised she didn't want our connection to end. In that instance, something gripped me, like when we first met. I didn't want to let her go, either. We set up Skype and spoke daily. Our feelings grew into love from afar. By February 2016, she came to London. I met her at Heathrow Airport. While looking for her upon arrival, she came from behind and touched me. As we embraced, it felt like we had always known each other. We spent a blissful fortnight together. We have become inseparable since she visited London a few times and met my family and friends.

She said, "You are my indigo man."

I asked what she meant. She said, "Since you are a humanist, you are gifted – creative, intelligent, and with a strong sense of mission."

She often says that we are from the same sun. I'll buy all that. It was an extraordinary encounter.

Like the wind, I have passed through, leaving no trails except on these pages and only bits as faded recollections. It will be remembered; two other encounters were astonishing. The first was while climbing the Rockies and meeting alien-like figures. The second time, it was on the frontier in Georgia on the road, in the middle of a forest. Suddenly, this figure appeared after a bend, looking like a scarecrow-like holy man. I had no answer at the time for these encounters.

I asked myself questions. Such as: How did I end up in this other world, so utterly alien? Were these figures from another planet? The concept of distance in light-years ruled out any possibility of that ever happening. Besides, why should these aliens be in human form? They were not threatening, but why did one keep flashing at me? Why did they let me go? I had read and seen documentaries where they say aliens abducted Americans. They had sworn to it. I didn't want to pursue that avenue. I am not a believer in anything extraterrestrial. Did I have a noetic experience? I realised that I must have entered a different dimension.

When I returned to London, I tried to look further into this. I firmly believed this must have been the product of chemical and electrical activity in my brain. The daily trek activated endorphins and Brain-derived neurotrophic factors (BDNF). These would not have had such a powerful effect on me. After researching, I found literature suggesting a similar experience can happen when taking DMT (Dimethyltryptamine). A powerful life-altering drug was as potent as LSD or Ayahuasca. It exists in plants, animals as well as in humans. It's what dreams are made of.

Photos of a talk I gave after returning to London.

After reading many dissertations on the effects of DMT, I understood that I had found the catalyst for those extraordinary experiences. They describe strange creatures, elves or dwarves, revolving quadrate vortices, and conversations with intelligent alien-type creatures. I had been transported into an alternate world through hallucination "produced through endogenously occurring DMT." Some of the articles considered a possible factor to be the cause of alien abduction experiences. I hope these won't be the last of my alien experiences. I would love to be above the treetops once again.

For seven months, I had an outdoor life, living an expansive existence. While writing this book, I was lodged between four walls for nearly three years. In both experiences, I felt liberated.